Photographs by Stephen Shames

Minority Studies:

A Selective Annotated Bibliography

PRISCILLA OAKS

G. K. HALL & CO. 70 LINCOLN STREET BOSTON MASS

Copyright © 1975 by Priscilla Oaks

Library of Congress Cataloging in Publication Data

Oaks, Priscilla.
    Minority studies.

    Includes index.
    1. Minorities--United States--Bibliography.
I. Title.
Z1361.E4O24 [E184.A1]   016.973'04   75-32551
ISBN 0-8161-1092-1

Photographs by Stephen Shames/Photon West
Copyright © 1972 Stephen Shames

This publication is printed on permanent/durable acid-free paper.
MANUFACTURED IN THE UNITED STATES OF AMERICA

To those good people,

my parents,

Ruth and George I. Cohen

The stranger within my gate
  He may be true or kind
  But he does not talk my talk--
  I cannot feel his mind.
I see the face and the eyes and the mouth,
  But not the soul behind.

The men of my own stock,
  They may do ill or well,
  But they tell the lies I am wonted to,
  They are used to the lies I tell;
And we do not need interpreters
  When we go to buy and sell.

                    --Rudyard Kipling

Contents

	Entries	Page
Acknowledgments		ix
Introduction		xi

I.   General Studies
    A. Bibliographical Works — 1-13 — 1
    B. Periodicals — 14-16 — 3
    C. General Cultural Studies — 17-60 — 3
    D. Racism — 61-131 — 11

II. Native Americans
    A. Bibliographical Works — 132-171 — 25
    B. Periodicals — 172-196 — 31
    C. History, Politics, Law and Government — 197-291 — 34
    D. Education — 292-302 — 51
    E. General Culture and Community Life — 303-437 — 53
    F. Literature by and about Native Americans — 438-610 — 74
    G. Arts and Crafts — 611-665 — 102

III. Spanish Americans
    A. General Spanish Americans — 666-670 — 113
    B. Mexican Americans
       1. Bibliographical Works — 671-699 — 114
       2. Periodicals — 700-704 — 119
       3. History, Geo-History (Exploration and Migration), Politics, Economics and Agricultural Labor — 705-797 — 119
       4. Education and Bi-Cultural Programs — 798-813 — 134
       5. General Culture and Community Life — 814-860 — 137
       6. Literature by and about Spanish Americans — 861-958 — 146
    C. Puerto Rican Americans
       1. Bibliographical and Reference Works — 959-966 — 160
       2. General Culture and Community Life — 967-1006 — 161

Contents

			Entries	Page
IV.		Afro-Americans		
	A.	Bibliographical Works	1007–1029	169
	B.	Periodicals	1030–1039	172
	C.	History and Politics	1040–1161	174
	D.	Education	1162–1170	191
	E.	General Culture and Community Life	1171–1212	193
	F.	Literature by and about Afro-Americans	1213–1477	198
V.		Asian Americans		
	A.	General Asian Americans		
		1. Bibliographical Works and Directories	1478–1499	233
		2. Periodicals	1500–1513	236
		3. General Culture and Community Life and United States Relations	1514–1536	238
	B.	Chinese Americans		
		1. History, Politics, Immigration, Racism, United States/China Relations	1537–1560	242
		2. General Culture and Community Life	1561–1580	247
		3. Literature by and about Chinese Americans	1581–1612	251
	C.	Japanese Americans		
		1. History, Immigration, Racism, Relocation and United States/Japanese Relationships	1613–1639	256
		2. General Culture and Community Life	1640–1654	261
		3. Literature by and about Japanese Americans	1655–1698	264
	D.	Hawaiian Americans		
		1. General History and Culture	1699–1713	271
	E.	Pilipino Americans		
		1. Bibliographical Works	1714–1717	273
		2. Periodicals	1718–1721	274
		3. History, Politics and Revolution	1722–1742	274
		4. General Culture and Community Life	1743–1753	277
		5. Literature by and about Pilipinos	1754–1789	278
	F.	Korean Americans	1790–1800	283
Author/Title Index				285

Acknowledgments

How can I thank everybody for their help with this bibliography?

A project like this uses the leg, eye, mouth, and brain energies of a lot of people. Checking and rechecking names, dates, and book titles, plus spanning through thousands of pages for annotation, takes a lot of time and concentration.

First, I would like to thank all the people who struggled to write the books we annotated. Their "chile was bad and their water was far away," but they kept on writing what they had to write, in order that their books could be defaced in libraries around the world, to paraphrase black author Ishmael Reed is irony, but also so worn copies of their works could be traded around by those who loved their truths and did not fear them.

Second, I'd like to thank all the publishers who printed those books. A very special thanks goes to the small presses. Working mostly on cooperative elbow grease and stardust, they have produced texts of beautiful design and inspiration on budgets that probably starved their cockroaches.

Institutions come next, those venerable sources of research libraries and funds. Thank you, Radcliffe Institute, where I was a Visiting Scholar and began this bibliography.

Thank you, Harvard University, for your various libraries, especially the Peabody Museum Library with its excellent cataloguing of Native American studies. And thank you, Shu Yan Chan, for being my research supervisor and also such able and willing researchers as Lewis Gannett, Phil McLellan, Toby Smith, and Jim Steeter.

Thank you, California State University, Fullerton (CSUF) where I teach, for your help with two Fullerton Foundation grants. And thank you, CSUF Library for allowing Jan Leach, Larry Martinez, Deja Camera, Diana Shames, and Penny Moffet, who did research and the tedious final title checkouts there. Thanks also go to

Acknowledgments

University of California, Santa Cruz students, Steve Wetch and Sarah Shames for coming down and giving their help and advice.

Thank you, University of New Mexico Library at Albuquerque, for your special Chicano Studies' collections, culled through for me by Suzanne Shames.

I spent many, many hours in the University of California, Los Angeles minority libraries. Above all, I am grateful to Barbara Al Biayti, who runs the American Indian Culture and Research Center Library so smoothly. Also thanks go to Roberto Cabello-Argandona, director of the Chicano Research Library. Thanks also, Professor Ramon Paredes, for spot-checking titles for me. At the Asian-American Center Library, I was helped by Sue Houchins, Penny Chan, and especially by Lowell K. Y. Chun-Hoon, Paul Hernandez, and Casimiro Tolentino, who shared his impossible-to-find Pilipino resources with me. Thanks, Cas.

Third World books, often the best ones, don't always turn up on academic library shelves. Thank you, Mayme Clayton, proprietor of the Third World Ethnic Bookstore, for drinking coffee with me while we talked about Black literature and history as I browsed. And thanks again to all you good folks at the Amerasian Bookstore, for your advice and tea. Both these bookstores, located in Los Angeles, are among the best sources available for minority books.

In keeping with the style of minority books, this bibliography reflects its subject matter with illustrations; in this case, with the fine photographs by Stephen Shames. Thank you, Stephen.

Everywhere I travelled the past year or two, I was constantly looking, culling, and asking about books for this bibliography. To all those people I met on my way, a more grateful and hearty thanks for their warm response and good advice.

Finally, may I express indebtedness to my friendly-family and family-friends, who tempted me away from the typewriter and performed such labors of love as re-alphabetizing tipped over card-files. They all mean so much to me. And, for sure, this book would not have been possible without them.

Introduction

One of the handicaps of the twentieth
century is that we still have the vaguest
and most biased notions..of what makes the
United States a nation of Americans...

-- Ruth Bendict

This is a selective working minority studies bibliography, but...
Who is Imamu Amiri Baraka?
Who is Black Elk?
Where are Alurista and Frank Chin?

In attempting to answer the above questions for the general
reader, students, teachers, browsers, and would-be experts, it
has been necessary to be not overly selective but inclusive,
broad and narrow in scope, practical and high-flying. Included
are the very best books ever written in American minority studies
and some, just plain notoriously bad.

First of all, a bibliography about Native Americans, Spanish
Americans, Afro-Americans, and Asian Americans as this one is,
means that the emphasis is always primarily on people. And when
the truth pertains to human beings, it is always paradoxical and
a mess of contradictions.

So you will find here, a selective working bibliography, full
of basic books with which to start reading about any given topic,
and a few for deeper reading. The focus has also been on books
that are easy to locate in public libraries and on paperbacks
that are cheapest to buy. But also included are potboilers like
Dr. Fu Manchu, racist by any standard, and some books so hard to
find that they must be special ordered from the Library of
Congress or looked at in the special collections of university
libraries.

Introduction

The area of ethnic or minority cultures, or Third World studies*, as it is also called, is only about ten years old at most American educational institutions. A lot of what minority people have to say or what needs to be said has not yet been published, or has been neglected until it is out of print, although some old falling-apart book might have the crucial word on the subject. None of it has been thoroughly studied. So, where there is a gap, certain understandings can be gained by reading a book that says the opposite of the truth. Wallace Irwin's interpretation of Japanese Americans can help you grasp your own feelings or put together a concept you might not realize any other way.

This brings up a second point. It is the general nature of comprehensive bibliographies to aim for objectivity and have no philosophical basis. But selection, involving inclusion and exclusion, always connotes a value system. This bibliography is critical, and is highly selective.

The original concept of this bibliography was to explore the plurality of the American experience as shown by the similar yet different life-styles of the minority cultures as they found their distinctive ways of survival in and out of American history. This problem of survival is organic to the entire American experience, but for minorities, it is centered on racism. Many thousands died for no other reason than the undemocratic idea that some people are inferior to others, different from the "right" ones, perhaps not human at all.

The viewpoint of this bibliography is given clearly by emphasizing "Racism" in the first section. Racism has been called "Manifest Destiny" in the past, and is often termed "Progress" today. It is part of the deepest ethos of the United States and always a part of the life experiences of ethnic people and thus by inversion, everyone's experience. It comes in both institutionalized and personal forms and both types are annotated in this important first section.

The other four sections of the bibliography were to follow the patterning of the reading materials very different in emphasis for

---

* The term "Third World" is a political expression now being applied to wider cultural areas. It originally referred to all those peoples colonized by the First and Second Worlds, or America, sometimes spelled with a "k" in this context, and Russia. It assumes imperialism and oppression. It also assumes that the colonial peoples are people of color. Since colonialism can take place within a country as well as outside of its borders, Third World is gaining increasing acceptance as a synonym for minorities in the United States.

Introduction

each ethnic group and treated differently by the majority group. For example, it is impossible to find books on the Black experience under "Anthropology." They are always listed under "Sociology" in academia. Native Americans are to be found in "Anthropology" catalogues.

This is possibly because nineteenth century concepts are with us yet. Indians were supposed to vanish--if not die out, at least disappear on their Museums, oops, Reservations, so nobody would have to see or think about them other than to observe the quaint customs and artifacts of the aborigines. Blacks similarly were to stay out of the middle class adult world where they became "social" problems when they did not.

Originally, the sectioning of this bibliography tried to mediate concepts such as these and there were many topic headings, reflecting as much as possible the emphasis of each separate group. What is religion to Native Americans is not necessarily a form of Black religious experience and this bibliography tried to categorize according to the ethos of each group. As many publications as possible by ethnic writers were included, even if many were not considered authorities. Similarly, critical comments by Third World experts were included in the annotations. Great emphasis was put on "Autobiography" as a particularly expressive form of primary material. Separate sections were given for Anglo writers of literature about each minority group.

However...
So be it...
DANGEROUS...
Antidote One...

Antidote Two. Enjoy. As reflections of each individual culture, many of the minority books, especially those printed by the small ethnic presses, are very handsome in design and illustration. They bring to their publications long traditions of combining the beautiful and useful.

Antidote Three. Don't stop short with yourself and draw no conclusions. The presentation of all the new minority studies will take many years and cause much controversy. A lot of it is beginning to appear in short articles in minority magazines as well as in established academic publications. Since there was no room in this bibliography to include such articles, essays, dissertations and theses, use this book as a starting point. And, whatever your topic, don't overlook the literature sections, particularly the autobiographies. Use well, also, the sections on community newspapers and magazines.

Introduction

Antidote Four. Accept the ancient philosopher's statement that the nature of men is identical, but what divides them is their customs and look around you with open mind... For....

Brothers, Sisters
understand this:

you are in passage--
wherever you go...

--Lawson F. Inada

I. GENERAL STUDIES

A. Bibliographical Works

1   BENGELSDORF, WINNIE. Ethnic Studies in Higher Education:
      State of the Art and Bibliography. Washington, D. C.:
      American Association of State Colleges and Universities,
      1972. 13p.
        Afro-American, American Indian, Mexican American,
      Puerto Rican and White ethnic, as well as Asian American
      studies in higher education arranged by ethnic group,
      alphabetically by author and by topics.

2   CALIFORNIA State Library Quarterly. Bibliography of Cultural
      Differences. Sacramento: California State Library.
        Annotated brief reviews by ethnic groupings and topics
      such as "Housing," or "Psychology."

3   CASELLI, RON, comp. The Minority Experience: A Basic Bib-
      liography of American Ethnic Studies. Santa Rosa,
      California: Sonoma County Supt. of Schools, 1970. 61p.
        Emphasis on sociology, economics, and psychiatry.
      Listings of 950 books and periodicals dated between 1940
      and 1969. Primarily for teachers and students. Blacks,
      Mexican Americans, and Native Americans constitute the
      minorities. Also included are motion pictures and film
      strips.

4   KEATING, CHARLOTTE MATTHEW. Building Bridges of Under-
      standing Between Cultures. Tucson, Arizona: Palo Verde
      Publishing Company, 1971. 233p.
        Annotated headings of materials for primary through
      high school grades. Listings under subject matter and
      education-levels.

5   LOS ANGELES Superintendent of Schools Office. Portraits:
      The Literature of Minorities. Los Angeles, 1970. 70p.
        Annotated bibliography for junior and senior high
      school reading. Contains literature, folktales, essays,

1

Minority Studies: An Annotated Bibliography

GENERAL STUDIES

(LOS ANGELES Superintendent...)
speeches, etc., by American Indians, Chicanos, Blacks, and
Asian Americans.

6   MENDES, RICHARD H. P. Bibliography on Community Organization.
     Washington, D. C.: President's Committee on Juvenile
     Delinquency and Youth Crime, June, 1965. 98p.
        Theory and practice of community organizations. Special
     section devoted to citizen participation in voluntary
     democratic associations.

7   POTTS, ALFRED M., comp. Knowing and Educating the Disad-
     vantaged: An Annotated Bibliography. Alamosa, Colorado:
     Center for Cultural Studies, Adams State College 1965.
     460p.
        ERIC annotated bibliography planned for those needing
     help in working out projects for migratory farm workers.
     A large compendium of information about Puerto Ricans,
     Blacks, Spanish Americans, and Indians and includes book
     titles as well as audio-visual materials.

8   SANTA BARBARA County Board of Education. The Emerging
     Minorities in America: A Resource Guide for Teachers.
     Santa Barbara, California: Clio Press, 1972. 256p.
        Source book primarily of biographical information about
     Afro-Americans, Asian Americans (Japanese, Chinese,
     Filipino), Indian Americans, and Mexican Americans. Each
     section has a brief historical introduction and a re-
     sources bibliography listing books and other aids for
     teachers, and books for children. Historical Appendix of
     names included at the end.

9   SCHERMERHORN, RICHARD A., ed. Psychiatric Index for Inter-
     disciplinary Research: A Guide to the Literature 1950-
     1961. Washington, D. C.: U. S. Department of Health,
     Education and Welfare, Vocational Rehab. Adm. Div. of
     Research Grants and Demonstrations, 1964. 1249p.

10 U. S. CABINET Committee on Opportunity for the Spanish
     Speaking. Directory of Spanish Speaking Community Organ-
     izations in the United States. Washington, D. C.: U. S.
     Govt. Printing Office, July 1970. 224p.
        The address, date established, and type of organization
     are listed in this large directory, sub-divided by states.

11 U. S. DEPARTMENT of Justice. Directory of Organizations
     Serving Minority Communities. Washington, D. C.: U. S.
     Govt. Printing Office, 1971. 88p.

Minority Studies: An Annotated Bibliography

(U. S. DEPARTMENT...)
Directory arranged by state and sub-divided by type of organization or group. Lists names and addresses of public and private organizations, colleges, newspapers, and media serving American Indians, Blacks, Spanish-Speaking peoples, Asian Americans, and women.

12   U. S. NATIONAL Institute of Mental Health. Bibliography on Racism. Rockville, Maryland: Government Publication HF 20.2417 R11, 1972. v.p.
By Center for Minority Group Mental Health Programs.

13   WEED, PERRY L. Ethnicity and American Group Life, A Bibliography. New York: National Project on Ethnic America, The American Jewish Committee, 1972. 21p. 50¢.
Non-annotated introduction to the field of ethnic studies. Covers history, sociology, religion, etc.

B. Periodicals

14   INTERNATIONAL Migration Review. Staten Island, New York: Center for Migration Studies.
Publishes an annual: "The Puerto Rican experience on the U. S. Mainland."

15   THE JOURNAL of Ethnic Studies. College of Ethnic Studies, Western Washington State College. Bellingham, Washington.
Interdisciplinary journal founded in 1973. Includes articles, book reviews, and creative writing.

16   THE RACE Relations Reporter. Nashville, Tennessee: Race Relations Information Center.
This may now be out of production.

C. General Cultural Studies

17   AUERBACH, F. L. Immigration Laws of the United States. Indianapolis, Indiana: Bobbs-Merrill, 1961. 584p.
Well researched compendium of immigration laws. Reprint of 1955 edition.

BANKS, CAROLYN. See 29.

18   BANKS, JAMES A. Teaching Ethnic Studies. Washington, D. C.: National Council for Social Studies, 1973. 297p.

Minority Studies: An Annotated Bibliography

GENERAL STUDIES

19   BARRON, MILTON L., ed. <u>Minorities in a Changing World</u>. New York: Alfred A. Knopf, 1967. 481p.
        Collection of sociology essays on minorities in a worldwide struggle. But also includes sections on Mexican Americans and Puerto Ricans in America.

20   BAYLEY, DAVID H. and HAROLD MENDELSOHN. <u>Minorities and the Police; Confrontation in America</u>. New York: The Free Press, 1971. 209p.
        Disturbances in Denver, Colorado, described with national implications. Bibliography. Reprint of 1968 edition.

21.   BERG, IVAR E., assisted by SHERRY GORELICK. <u>Education and Jobs: The Great Training Robbery</u>. Boston: Beacon Press, 1971. 200p.
        Economic aspects that result from educational inequalities in the United States. Employee morale and labor turnover also point to specific disparities between various ethnic groups. Reprint of 1970 edition.

22   BLAUNER, ROBERT, TROY DUSTER, JACK FORBES, ISAO FUJIMOTO and OCTAVIO ROMANO. <u>The Third World Within</u>. Belmont, California: Wadsworth Publication Company, 1973.

BRADSHAW, BARBARA. <u>See</u> 25.

23   COLEMAN, JAMES S. and others. <u>Equality of Educational Opportunity</u>. Washington, D. C.: U. S. Department of Health, Education, and Welfare, Office of Education, 1966. 737p.
        Publication by the National Center for Educational Statistics. Covers such subjects as Black education, segregated education, and the role of the National Center. There is also a development of some of the ideas of the earlier Coleman Report.

DUSTER, TROY. <u>See</u> 22.

24.   ENLOE, CYNTHIA HOLDEN. <u>Ethnic Conflict and Political Development</u>. Boston: Little, Brown and Company, 1973. 282p.
        Reprint of 1972 edition.

25   FADERMAN, LILLIAN and BARBARA BRADSHAW. <u>Speaking for Ourselves</u>, revised edition. Glenview, Illinois: Scott, Foresman and Company, 1974. 640p.
        Excellent collection of ethnic groups as well as Third World groups and can easily be used as a class textbook. Reprint of 1969 edition.

26 FORBES, JACK D. The Education of the Culturally Different:
A Multi-Cultural Approach. Washington, D. C.: U. S.
Government Printing Office, 1969. 64p.
Personal statement calling for a reevaluation and re-
definition of the role of the school. Calls for a multi-
cultural approach to education. Revision of 1968 edition.

FORBES, JACK D. See 22.

27 No Entry.

28 FRAZIER, THOMAS R., comp. The Underside of American History;
Other Readings 2 vols. New York: Harcourt, Brace, Jovanovich, 1971. 351, 348p.
Volume 1 deals with articles about America to 1877;
volume 2 takes up the period after 1865. Has selections
by Nancy Lurie on Indians, Winthrop D. Jordan on Blacks,
Roger Daniels on Orientals, etc. A good compendium of
articles. Bibliographies.

29 FREEDMAN, MORRIS and CAROLYN BANKS, eds. American Mix; The
Minority Experience in America. Philadelphia: J. B.
Lippincott, 1972. 453p.
Anthology of literature about minorities and the prob-
lems they have to deal with such as immigration, assimila-
tion and stereotyping.

FUJIMOTO, ISAO. See 22.

30 GLASRUD, BRUCE A. and ALAN M. SMITH. Promises to Keep: A
Portrayal of Nonwhites in the United States. Chicago:
Rand McNally, 1972. 398p.
Representative historical literature from all nonwhite
groups that have developed America. Six chronological
groupings. Many deal with minority intergroup relationships. Bibliography.

GORELICK, SHERRY. See 21.

31 HALL, EDWARD TWITCHELL. The Silent Language. Greenwich,
Connecticut: Fawcett Publications, 1969. 192p.
Originally written for the education of American military personnel in Asia who needed to learn how to communi-
cate with and understand other peoples. The silent language is essentially body language, all the non-verbal ways
in which people tell each other how they are feeling and
thinking. Reprint of 1959 edition.

Minority Studies: An Annotated Bibliography

GENERAL STUDIES

32 HAMBERG, JILL. Where It's At. Ann Arbor, Michigan: Radical
    Education Project, P. O. Box 625.
        Guide to community action with projects for organizing
    a community. Gives ways to find underground, ethnic, and
    grass roots sources of information.

33 HANDLIN, OSCAR. The Newcomers: Negroes and Puerto Ricans
    in a Changing Metropolis. Garden City, New York: Double-
    day and Company, 1962 2nd edition. 171p.
        Well-documented study that was part of the New York
    Metropolitan Regional Study project. Compares Blacks and
    Puerto Ricans to other immigrants, such as the Irish and
    the Jews. Discusses the historical background of New
    York City, and immigrant patterns of adjustment and forms
    of social action. Bibliography and notes. Reprint of 1959
    edition.

34 HASLAM, GERALD W. Forgotten Pages of American Literature.
    Boston: Houghton Mifflin, 1970. 398p.
        Anthology of ethnic American literature divided into
    four major sections: Indian, Asian, Latino, and Afro-
    American. The Afro-American section is particularly good
    and has selections from Baldwin, Malcolm X, Cleaver and
    others.

35 HEATH, G. LOUIS. Red, Brown, and Black Demands for Better
    Education. Philadelphia: Westminster Press 1972. 216p.
        Modern study of the cultural mis-education of minority
    groups in America. Ethnic Studies programs at Southern
    Illinois and Berkeley are analyzed. The Chimera of open
    admissions as well as "de facto" segregation in the cities
    probed.

36 HEIZER, ROBERT FLEMING. The Other Californias: Prejudice
    and Discrimination Under Spain, Mexico and the United
    States to 1920. Berkeley: University of California Press
    1971. 278p.

37 HERZOG, STEPHEN J., comp. Minority Group Politics; A Reader.
    New York: Holt, Rinehart, and Winston, 1971. 358p.
        Blacks, Chicanos, and American Indians and their politi-
    cal problems are presented in documents and excerpts from
    tracts, poems, and writings along with related legal mater-
    ials. The two main sections are titled: "Areas of Con-
    flict" and "Methods of Change."

38 HORGAN, PAUL. The Heroic Triad: Backgrounds of our three
    Southwestern cultures. New York: World Publishing, 1971.

6

(HORGAN, PAUL)
   256p.
      Three sections on the Indians, Latins, and Anglo-Ameri-
   cans of the Southwest depict the backgrounds and mutual
   influences of these these three Southwestern cultures. A
   history written with a lyrical quality. Bibliography.
   Reprint of 1954 edition.

HORNER, VIVIAN M. See 41.

39   HOWARD, JOHN R. Awakening Minorities - American Indians,
     Mexican Americans, Puerto Ricans. Chicago: Trans-action
     Books, Aldine Publishing, 1972. 189p.
        Collection of essays from the "Trans-action" magazine
     showing some of the tensions and conflicts between these
     various groups and White American society. Articles from
     Indian school dropouts to the Puerto Rican Independence
     Movement.

40   JACOBS, PAUL and SAUL LANDAU with EVA PELL. To Serve the
     Devil: Vol. 1: Natives and Slaves: A Documentary Anal-
     ysis of America's Racial History and Why It Has Been
     Hidden. New York: Vintage Books, 1971. 360p.
        Twenty-two Indian documents included along with a
     lengthy historical essay-introduction. The other sections
     are concerned with Blacks and Chicanos. Bibliography.

41   JOHN, VERA P. and VIVIAN M. HORNER. Early Childhood Bilingual
     Education. New York: Modern Language Association, 1971.
     187p.
        Well-documented study of Puerto Ricans and Chicanos.
     Bibliography.

42   KANE, MICHAEL B. Minorities in Textbooks; A Study of Their
     Treatment in Social Studies Texts. Chicago: Quadrangle
     Books in cooperation with the Anti-Defamation League of the
     B'nai B'rith, 1970. 148p.
        45 social studies texts examined for balance, concrete-
     ness, validity, inclusiveness, comprehensibility, unity,
     and realism.

43   LABOV, WILLIAM and others. A Study of the Non-Standard Eng-
     lish of Negro and Puerto Rican Speakers in New York City.
     New York: Columbia University Press, 1968. 2 vols.
        Study of dialects under the auspices of the U. S. Edu-
     cational Resources Information Center.

GENERAL STUDIES

LANDAU, SAUL. <u>See</u> 40.

44 LOWENFELS, WALTER, ed. <u>The Writing on the Wall</u>: 108 Ameri-
    <u>can Poems of Protest</u>. Garden City, New York: Doubleday
    and Company, 1969. 189p.
        Everybody's protest poetry from Walt Whitman to Lenore
    Kandel.

45 _____ . <u>From the Belly of the Shark: A New Anthology of</u>
    <u>Native Americans</u>. New York: Vintage Books, 1973.

        Chicano, Eskimo, Hawaiian, American Indian, U. S. A.
    Puerto Rican, and related Black and White poetry are all
    included in this interesting anthology. Brief introduc-
    tions by ethnic authorities and biographical notes on the
    poets at the end. Most of the poetry is contemporary.

46 McLEAN, ROBERT. <u>Old Spain in New America: Issued by the</u>
    <u>Council of Women for Home Missions</u>. New York: Association
    Press, 1916. 161p.
        Interdenominational home mission study course on how to
    work with peoples living in the mainland Southwest, Cuba,
    and Puerto Rico. Will give any reader some basic insights
    into the attitudes of the period towards those brothers
    and sisters who must be "raised up."

47 MAJOR, MABEL, REBECCA W. SMITH and T. M. PEARCE. <u>Southwest</u>
    <u>Heritage, A Literary History</u>. Albuquerque: University of
    New Mexico Press, 1973. 199p.
        Bibliographies and discursive guides to Southwestern
    materials. Reprint of 1938 edition.

MENDELSOHN, HAROLD. <u>See</u> 20.

48 NATIONAL Urban Coalition. <u>Minority Business Opportunities</u>:
    <u>A Manual on Opportunities for Small and Minority Group</u>
    <u>Businessmen and Professionals in HUD Programs</u>. Washington,
    D. C.: Office of the Assistant Secretary for Equal Op-
    portunity, 1970. 398p.

49 NATIONAL Council for the Social Studies. <u>Teaching Ethnic</u>
    <u>Studies; Concepts and Strategies</u>. Washington, D. C.:
    National Council for the Social Studies, 1973. 297p.
        How to teach cultural pluralism: Afro-American, Black,
    Chicano, American Indian, Puerto Rican, and White ethnic
    experiences.

8

MINORITY STUDIES: AN ANNOTATED BIBLIOGRAPHY

General Cultural Studies

50   NEWMAN, KATHARINE D., comp. <u>The American Equation: Literature in a Multi-Ethnic Culture</u>. Boston: Allyn and Bacon, 1970. 380p.
The basic American equation insists that everyone is equal but not alike. A distinguished selection of writings probes this statement and also shows the multi-ethnic influence present in American literature.

51   _____., ed. <u>Ethnic-American Short Stories</u>. New York: Washington Square Press, 1975.
Pre-publication announcement of a well-edited collection of short stories written by American Indian authors, Blacks, etc.

PEARCE, T. M. See 47.

PELL, EVA. See 40.

52   REED, ISHMAEL, ed. <u>19 Necromancers From Now</u>. Garden City, New York: Doubleday and Company, 1970. 369p.
Anthology of Third World writings, prose, poetry, and drama, which includes many experimental writers and which ought to give any reader an excellent introduction into the excitement of ethnic writings and some insight into what it is all about.

53   REGHABY, HEYDAR, ed. <u>Philosophy of the Third World</u>. Berkeley, California: Lewis Publishing, 1974. 180p.
Anthology of papers given several years ago at a Third World conference at Deganawidah-Quetzalcoatl University. Includes materials on art, literature, philosophy, and politics by Jack Forbes, Priscilla Shames (a/k/a/ Oaks), and Jorge Acevado, among others.

ROMANO, OCTAVIO. See 22.

54   SEWARD, GEORGENE, ed. <u>Clinical Studies in Culture Conflict</u>. New York: The Ronald Press, 1958. 598p.
Group of Psychiatrists write articles about culture-personality dynamics. Include color and conflict for Blacks, the Spanish legacy as it affects the "Americanization" of Chicanos, Puerto Ricans, and Filipinos, Asian American cultural dilemmas, and displaced Europeans.

SMITH, ALAN M. See 30.

SMITH, REBECCA W. See 47.

9

Minority Studies: An Annotated Bibliography

GENERAL STUDIES

55 SPICER, EDWARD and RAYMOND H. THOMPSON, eds. Plural Society
    in the Southwest. New York: Interbook, Incorporated,
    1972. 367p.
        Articles from a symposium of historians, anthropologists,
    and sociologists who are concerned with both the racial and
    religious Southwestern cultural groups: Indians, Mexicans,
    Catholics, Mormons, etc. Bibliography.

    THOMPSON, RAYMOND H. See 55.

56 TURNER, MARY, ed. We, Too, Belong: An Anthology About Minori-
    ties in America. New York: Dell Publishing, 1969. 219p.
        Good anthology for high school use, divided into two
    sections: Patterns, and Lifting Shadows. Includes selec-
    tions by Jack London, Chief Joseph, Harry Golden, and
    Countee Cullen, all pretty tame stuff, though.

56a U. S. BUREAU of the Census, Population Division, "Projections
    of the Population of the U. S. by Age, Sex, and Color to
    1990 with Extensions of Population by Age and Sex to 2015."
        Current Population Reports, Series P-25, estimates No.
    381, December 18, 1967, Washington, D. C., Supt. of Docu-
    ments.

57 VLAHOS, OLIVIA. New World Beginnings: Indian Cultures in the
    Americas. New York: Viking Press, 1970. 320p.
        North and South American cultures and societies as they
    existed before Europeans discovered the New World. Repre-
    sentative groups are discussed such as the Ojibwa of North
    America and the Siriono of South America. Bibliography.

58 WEISMAN, JOHN. Guerilla Theater: Scenarios for Revolution.
    Garden City, New York: Anchor Press, 1973. 201p.
        Selection from American street theater. Includes acts
    and descriptions of both West and East Coast players as
    well as the Motown Theater Concept. Among those listed are
    El Teatro Campesino, The San Francisco Mime Troupe, and the
    Soul and Latin Theater.

59 WEISS, KAREL, ed. Under the Mask: An Anthology About Prej-
    udice in America. New York: Dell Publishing Company,
    1974. 320p.
        Sections include: "Between Two Worlds," "Removal,"
    "Ghettos of the Mind," and "Resisting." Includes a wide
    variety of well-chosen short selections.

60 WHITAKER, BEN, ed. THE FOURTH World: Victims of Group Oppres-
    sion: Eight Reports From the Field Work of the Minority

10

(WHITAKER, BEN)
   Rights Group. New York: Schocken Books, 1973. 342p.
      Reprint of 1972 edition.

60a WRIGHT, KATHLEEN. The Other Americans; Minorities in American
      History. Greenwich, Connecticut. Fawcett Publications
      Company, 1969. 256p.
         Recounts the many-faceted contributions of America's
      minority groups to the creation of our cultural heritage
      and the development of America. The ideals and aspirations
      of the Declaration of Independence and the Constitution are
      contrasted to the reality encountered by many of America's
      minorities.

D. Racism

61 ABRAHAM, HENRY JULIAN. Freedom and the Court; Civil Rights
      and Liberties in the United States. New York: Oxford Uni-
      versity Press, 1972. 397p.
         Civil Rights and the U. S. Supreme Court decisions.
      Bibliography. Revision of 1968 edition.

62 ADORNO, T. W. ELSE FRENKEL-BRUNSWIK, DANIEL J. LEVINSON, and
      R. NEVITT SANFORD. The Authoritarian Personality. New
      York: W. W. Norton and Company, 1969. 990p.
         An examination of the nature and definition of prejudice
      in terms of high and low ethnocentrism, and democratic ver-
      sus authoritarian personalities. Theories illustrated with
      copious case studies, statistics, and interviews in an at-
      tempt to discover the nature of anti-Semitism. Bibliog-
      raphy. These hypotheses have recently been challenged as
      the sole or central basis of prejudice. Reprint of 1950
      edition.

ALLEN, ANNE. See 121.

63 ALLPORT, GORDON W. The Nature of Prejudice. Cambridge, Massa-
      chusetts: Addison-Wesley Publishing Company, 1954. 537p.
         Psychological interpretation of a socio-cultural phenom-
      enon. Maintains that we are living in the Stone Age of hu-
      man interrelationships. We prejudge, separate human groups,
      and categorize differences to create stereotypes. Goes
      through the various theories of prejudice and shows how it
      can be learned, what its dynamics are in terms of "scape-
      goating," and what the character structure of the prejudice
      personality consists of. A final section deals with re-
      ducing group tensions.
         Considered a basic text and a fine introduction into the
      field. Reading references.

11

Minority Studies: An Annotated Bibliography

GENERAL STUDIES

64   ANDERSON, DAVID D. and ROBERT L. WRIGHT, eds. <u>The Dark and Tangled Path: Race in America</u>. Boston: Houghton Mifflin Company, 1971. 444p.
     Chronological series of documents that includes excerpts from Bret Harte, Newsweek, and Abraham Lincoln. Introductions with each section.

65   BAKER, RAY STANNARD. <u>Following the Color Line</u>. New York: Harper and Row, 1964. 311p.
     Study of race relationships in the United States with emphasis on Negro history.

66   BARZUN, JACQUES. <u>Race: A Study in Superstition</u>, Revised. New York: Harper and Row, 1965. 263p.
     "We" and "They" make up superstitions and then institutionalize them. A fascinating study of the development of this theory via the Nordic European myth, how it became theorized, how it was revealed through the arts, and how race concepts create wars. An Appendix gives the most commonplace excerpts on race-thinking. Bibliographic footnotes. Reprint of 1937 edition. A book worth reading.

67   BERRY, BREWTON. <u>Race and Ethnic Relations</u>. Boston: Houghton, Mifflin and Company, 1965. 435p.
     Sociology text that covers points of view, such as apologist, assimilationist, pluralist, race concepts, techniques of dominance, strategies, and realism. Reprint of 1951 edition.

68   BETTELHEIM, BRUNO and MORRIS JANOWITZ. <u>Social Change and Prejudice, Dynamics of Prejudice</u>. New York: Free Press of Glencoe, 1964. 337p.
     Important book that goes into the psychological reasons for prejudice using much evidence from Nazi Concentration Camps. Includes also: <u>Dynamics of Prejudice</u> (1950), the earlier book, here re-evaluated.

69   BINSTOCK, ROBERT H. and KATHERINE ELY, eds. <u>The Politics of the Powerless</u>. Cambridge, Massachusetts: Winthrop Publications, 1971. 340p.
     Collection about the struggles of powerless groups to better the conditions of their lives in American society.

70   BLALOCK, HUBERT M., JR. <u>Toward a Theory of Minority-Group Relations</u>. New York: John Wiley and Sons, 1967. 227p.
     Minority group relationships seen as power struggles between the dominant group and minority group.

71 BLAUNER, ROBERT. <u>Racism Oppression in America</u>. New York:
    Harper and Row, 1972. 309p.
        Solid book of essays divided into three sections: the
    theory of racism, racism and culture, and case studies of
    institutional racism. Introduction for each section. De-
    velops the theory of internal colonialism in the United
    States and distinguishes therein the distinctions between
    Afro-American, other Third World peoples, and European im-
    migrants in their American experiences.

72 BOAS, FRANZ. <u>Race, Language and Culture</u>. New York: The Free
    Press, 1966. 647p.
        Selected essays covering a period of 1887-1939. "Race"
    is defined physiologically, language is discussed in terms
    of classification, and culture goes into ethnology and
    folklore. Reprint of 1940 edition.

73 _____. <u>Race and Democratic Society</u>. New York: Biblo and
    Tannon, 1969. 219p.
        Series of papers on America and racism which Boas began
    to edit and did not completely rework before his death.
    Reprint of 1945 edition.

74 BOYD, W. C. <u>Genetics and the Races of Man; An Introduction to
    Modern Physical Anthropology</u>. Boston: Little, Brown and
    Company, 1950. 453p.
        Excellent study of the demographic breakdown of races
    throughout the world. Genetic descriptions that are compre-
    hensible to the general reader. Uses maps and charts to
    show relationships between skin color and climate, blood
    types and geographic locations. Bibliography.

75 BROWN, FRANCIS JAMES and JOSEPH SLABEY ROUCEK, eds. <u>One
    America, The History, Contributions and Present Problems of
    Our Racial and National Minorities</u>. Englewood Cliffs, New
    Jersey: Prentice-Hall, 1952. 764p.
        Gives the history, accomplishments, and present problems
    of our racial and national minorities. A selected bibliog-
    raphy for each group. Originally published in 1937 as <u>Our
    Racial and National Minorities</u>. Reprint of 1945 edition.

    BURROWS, DAVID J. <u>See</u> 97.
    CAMPBELL, DONALD T. <u>See</u> 98.

76 COX, ARCHIBALD, MARK DEWOLFE HOWE and J. R. WIGGINS. <u>Civil
    Rights, The Constitution, and The Courts</u>. Cambridge,
    Massachusetts: Harvard University Press, 1967. 76p.
        Lectures given at the Massachusetts Historical Society.
    They touch on such subjects as Black civil rights, the

Minority Studies: An Annotated Bibliography

GENERAL STUDIES

(COX, ARCHIBALD...)
government's resistance to civil rights, and the relationship between crime and the press. Bibliographic footnotes.

77   COX, OLIVER CROMWELL. Caste, Class and Race: A Study in Social Dynamics. New York: Monthly Review Press, 1959. 624p.
What makes people dislike people they have never seen, is the question asked and answered in this study of modern racism. An international approach which includes Caste and Hinduism, European Facism, and an analysis of the literature about "class." Bibliography. Reprint of 1948 edition.

78   DANIELS, ROGER and HARRY H. L. KITANO. American Racism: Exploration of the Nature of Prejudice. Englewood Cliffs, New Jersey: Prentice-Hall, 1970. 155p.
Explores the cause and results of prejudice using California as the un-melting pot of racism in this country. Includes California Indian problems and the relocation of the West Coast Japanese during World War II.

79   DE TOCQUEVILLE, ALEXIS. Democracy in America. New York: Alfred A. Knopf, 1948, 2 vols. 434, 401p.
One of the most famous books about America ever written. Still important today for anyone desiring an understanding of nineteenth-century concepts and their influence on our times. Of special significance is Chapter XVIII, "The Present and Probable Future Condition of the Three Races that Inhabit the Territory of the United States." Gives clear readings of the popular opinions of the time about Blacks and Indians. Reprint of 1835 edition.

80   DINNERSTEIN, LEONARD and FREDERIC COPLE JAHER, eds. The Aliens: A History of Ethnic Minorities in America. New York: Appleton-Century-Crofts, 1970. 347p.
Selections from colonial times to the present with a selected bibliography for each section. Ethnic minorities classified as all groups of non-English speaking origin: Scots, Irish, German, Negroes, Orientals, Indians, and Jews.

DISCH, ROBERT. See 119.
ELLIS, WILLIAM RUSSELL, JR. See 110.
ELY, KATHERINE. See 69.

81   FELDSTEIN, STANLEY, ed. The Poisoned Tongue: A Documentary History of American Racism and Prejudice. New York: William Morrow and Company, 1972. 330p.
Anthology of prejudice tracts, from colonial times through the 1960s. Emphasis mainly on Black oppression. There are sections, however, on Indian, Oriental, and Jewish racism.

82   FRANKLIN, JOHN HOPE, ed. Color and Race. Boston: Beacon
Press, 1969. 391p.
      Book-print of a Daedalus magazine special issue. Dis-
cusses race in Africa, Asia, North America, etc. Reprint
of 1968 edition.

FRENKEL-BRUNSWIK, ELSE. See 62.

83   GLAZER, NATHAN and DANIEL P. MOYNIHAN. Beyond The Melting Pot.
Cambridge, Massachusetts: M.I.T. Press, 1970. 363p.
      Culture, economic life, and relations to both the new
and old country of Irish, Italians, Jews, Blacks, and
Puerto Ricans. Reprint of 1964 edition.

84   GLOCK, CHARLES Y. and ELLEN SIEGELMAN, eds. Prejudice U. S. A.
New York: Praeger, 1969. 196p.
      Partly based on the proceedings of a symposium held at
University of California, Berkeley in March, 1968. A special section is devoted to minorities. Bibliographical
references.

85   GORDON, MILTON. Assimilation in American Life: The Role of
Race, Religion, and National Origins. New York: Oxford
University Press, 1967. 276p.
      Subculture, melting pot, and cultural pluralism are dis-
cussed, but emphasis is on assimilation as a solution to intergroup problems. Bibliography. Reprint of 1964 edition.

86   GOSSETT, THOMAS F. Race: The History Of An Idea In America.
New York: Schocken Books, 1968. 510p.
      Excellent all-around book on the development of racism in
this country from colonial times to the present day. Chapters on the Indian and Blacks, American imperialism, and the
battle against prejudice. Bibliographical notes. Reprint
of 1963 edition.

87   GRANT, MADISON. The Passing Of The Great Race: Or, The Racial
Basis of European History, 4th revised edition. New York:
Charles Scribner's Sons, 1923. 476p.
      One of this country's great racists takes a look at Euro-
pean history and extolls the Anglo-Saxons as the ideal man.
Reprint of 1918 edition.

88   HANDLIN, OSCAR. Race and Nationality in American Life. Garden
City, New York: Doubleday and Company, 1957. 226p.
      Analysis of minorities and their treatment in modern
America in terms of psychological and sociological inter-
pretations. Feels that racism decreased after 1930. Reprint of 1950 edition.

15

GENERAL STUDIES

HERMANDEZ, DELUVINA. See 121.

89   HIGHAM, JOHN. Strangers In the Land; Patterns of American
        Nativism, 1860-1925. Corrected and revised with new Pre-
        face. New York: Atheneum, 1963. 431p.
           Probing of the ethnocentric basis of American Anglo-Saxon
        nativism and its fear of immigrants, especially Catholics.
        Starting after the Civil War and describing the homefront
        efforts during World War I, shows the development of early
        twentieth-century Anglo-Saxon racial attitudes. Also demon-
        strates the decreasing overt racism of American intelli-
        gentsia during the '20s. Examples of the Ku Klux Klan and
        anti-Bolshevism movements are given. Excellent notes. Re-
        print of 1955 edition.

HOWE, MARK DEWOLFE. See 76.

90   JACOBS, PAUL and SAUL LANDAU. To Serve The Devil, Vols. I and
        II. New York: Random House, 1971.
           Documentary history of racism in the United States. The
        first volume deals with the Indian and Black experience,
        the second documents conquest of the Hawaiians and Puerto
        Ricans, and oppression of Japanese and Chinese immigrants.
        Bibliographies.

JAHER, FREDERIC COPLE. See 80.

91   JALEE, PIERRE. The Pillage of the Third World. New York:
        Monthly Review Press, 1968. 115p.
           Delineates and unfolds the major themes of imperialism
        and the non-technological (underdeveloped) world. Transla-
        tion from the French; international in scope. Bibliography.

JANOWITZ, MORRIS. See 68.

92   JONES, JAMES M. Prejudice and Racism. Reading, Massachusetts:
        Addison-Wesley, 1972. 196p.
           Socio-historical approach to race relations in America.
        Stresses the need for a cultural revolution, specifically
        an end to the concepts of White supremacy, individuality
        without social responsibility, competition and conflict
        without support of the basic goal of the value of human
        life. Bibliography.

93   KAHN, SI. How People Get Power; Organizing Oppressed Communi-
        ties For Action. New York: McGraw Hill, 1970. 128p.
           Book for organizers with examples drawn from the rural
        South. A problem-solving type book to help poor people
        (Whites, Blacks, Indians, students, women, older people,

(KAHN, SI)
   etc.) work together better. Includes chapters on develop-
   ing leadership, power tactics, and self-help strategies.
   Bibliography.

94   KANE, MICHAEL B. Minorities in Textbooks; A Study of Their
     Treatment in Social Studies Texts. Chicago: Quadrangle
     Books, in cooperation with the Anti-Defamation League
     of B'nai B'rith, 1970. 148p.
        Good study of the social conditioning processes that in-
     fluence students in secondary education. Bibliography.

KEESING'S RESEARCH REPORT. See 111.
KITANO, HARRY H. L. See 78.

95   KNOWLES, L. L. and K. PREWITT. Institutional Racism in
     America. Englewood Cliffs, New Jersey: Prentice-Hall,
     1970. 180p.
        Study of racial discrimination in business, government,
     law, schools, and churches. Reprint of 1969 edition.

96   KOVEL, JOEL. White Racism: A Psychohistory. New York:
     Pantheon Books, 1970. 300p.
        Psychological aspects of racial discrimination treated
     historically. Bibliography.

LANDAU, SAUL. See 90.

97. LAPIDES, FREDERICK R. and DAVID J. BURROWS, eds. Racism:
     A Casebook. New York: Thomas Y. Crowell, 1971. 305p.
        Essays and fiction which define, examine, trace, and
     evaluate racism.

98   LEVINE, ROBERT A. and DONALD T. CAMPBELL. Ethnocentrism:
     Theories of Conflict, Ethnic Attitudes and Group Behav-
     iour. New York: John Wiley and Sons, 1971. 310p.
        Interdisciplinary text giving theories from anthropol-
     ogy, sociology, political science, psychology, and psy-
     choanalysis on the reasons for intergroup hostilities and
     war.

LEVINSON, DANIEL J. See 62.

99   LEVI-STRAUSS, CLAUDE. Race and History. Paris: UNESCO,
     1968. 47p.

GENERAL STUDIES

(LEVI-STRAUSS, CLAUDE)
Short pamphlet touching on the diversity of cultures, ethnocentric attitudes, primitive cultures, and the problem of cross-currents in cultures.

100 McWILLIAMS, CAREY. Brothers Under The Skin. Boston: Little, Brown, 1964. 364p.
Most minority groups are examined in this book, including: Negroes, American Indians, Puerto Ricans, Jews, Chinese, and Japanese. The author feels the problem is national and the federal government has a responsibility to correct it. McWilliams' books are still authorities on their topics. His moral indictment of racism is always upheld by the factual information he has obtained and uses. Reprint of 1942 edition.

101 MACK, RAYMOND. Race, Class and Power. New York: American Book Company, 1968. 468p.
Mack, who has written or compiled a number of books on prejudice and racism, makes political and economic connections between color, caste, and control. Bibliography. Reprint of 1963 edition.

102 MARDEN, CHARLES F. and GLADYS MEYER. Minorities in American Society, 3rd edition. New York: American Book Company, 1968. 486p.
Comprehensive textbook about all American minority groups. Good definitions and discussion topics plus suggested readings at the end of each chapter.

103 MEMMI, ALBERT. The Colonizer and The Colonized. New York: Boston: Beacon Press, 1967. 153p.
Analyzes the motivations and aims of the colonizer and the reactions of the colonized. Not many concrete examples, but a sensitive analysis of the injurious effects of the erosion of traditional institutions. A good primer book on colonialism. Reprint of 1965 edition.

MEYER, GLADYS. See 102.

104 MONTAGU, ASHLEY. The Concept Of Race. New York: Free Press of Glencoe, 1964. 270p.
Barriers that keep men apart-physiologically, geographically, and socially. Montague is a prime authority in this field. Bibliography.

105 _____, ed. Man and Aggression. New York: Oxford University Press, 1968. 178p.

18

(MONTAGU, ASHLEY)
Fourteen experts offer a critique to the Hobbesian view of man with its conception of man's inborn "aggressive drive." Not only are the now-popular forms of neo-Social Darwinism analyzed, but several hypotheses about man's "instinctual" nature are proposed. Warns against the acceptance of masks of theories which actually distort the actual behaviors of nature.

106   _____. Man's Most Dangerous Myth: The Fallacy of Race. New York: Columbia University Press, 1945. 304p.
Contemporary scientific information about race, and race theory. A primary book to read in this field.

107   _____. Statement On Race. New York: Henry Shuman, 1951. 172p.
UNESCO statement on race, enlarged and annotated.

MOYNIHAN, DANIEL P. See 83.

108   MUROKAWA, MINAKO, comp. Minority Responses: Comparative Views and Reactions To Subordination. New York: Random House, 1970. 376p.
Collection of addresses, essays, etc., by representatives of various minority groups. Subordination and White supremacy given the depth treatment. Bibliography.

109   NASH, GARY B. and RICHARD WEISS. The Great Fear: Race in the Mind of America. New York: Holt, Rinehart and Winston, 1970. 214p.
Historical study of the paranoia that makes up the American mind, Anglos and minorities alike.

110   ORLEANS, PETER and WILLIAM RUSSELL ELLIS, JR., Race, Change, and Urban Society. Beverly Hills, California: Sage Publications, 1971. 640p.
Problems and prospects faced by minorities in urban society are considered in twenty articles. Bibliography of the literature on race and cities.

PREWITT, K. See 95.

111   RACE Relations in the USA 1954-1968: Keesing's Research. New York: Charles Scribner's Sons, 1970. 280p.
The Keesing Contemporary Archives is a documentary service that has compiled in clear and highly readable form the development of Black/White relationships in the past two decades. Details the social groupings, such as Black

GENERAL STUDIES

(RACE RELATIONS...)
Muslims, and the KKK, and the governmental and political
activities for and against Civil Rights. Ends with the
death of Martin Luther King.

112   REPORT OF the National Advisory Commission on Civil Disorders.
New York: Bantam Books, 1968. 609p.
Also called the Kerner Report and is the result of President Johnson's response to the riots and civil disturbances,
such as the Watts Riots, that took place in the mid-60s.
The Commission was appointed in 1967 and was criticized by
street people and others for the conservative makeup of the
group. This made the final report even more compelling.
If we have a national conspiracy, it is that of the "haves"
indifference to the "have nots." We are a nation divided
into two groups, one living in the ghetto and without ac-
cess to the goods and privileges of those outside. A comparison of White immigrants and Blacks in terms of their
American experiences is used as evidence of discrimination.

113   RICHARDSON, KEN and DAVID SPEARS, eds. Race and Intelligence:
The Fallacies Behind the Race IQ Controversy. Baltimore,
Maryland: Penguin Books, 1972. 205p.
The nature-nurture controversy that has recently been
renewed, is reexamined to prove that every racial group has
its quota of brain power (or lack of it). Examples from
the Japanese, Chinese, Anglos, and Blacks in California.

114   ROSE, ARNOLD M. and CAROLINE B. ROSE, eds. Minority Problems;
A Textbook of Readings in Intergroup Relations. 2nd edi-
tion. New York: Harper and Row, 1965. 438p.
Classic series of articles on a variety of minority
problems, including such groups as women, Catholics, and
Italians. Bibliography.

ROSE, CAROLINE B. See 114.

115   ROSE, PETER I. They and We: Racial and Ethnic Relations in
the United States. New York: Random House, 1974. 256 p.
Updating and rewriting of the final sections to bring it
past Civil Rights Movement and backlash of the 60s into the
ethnic resurgence period of the 70s. A good annotated
bibliography of about 150 books. Reprint of 1962 edition.

116   ROUSSEAU, JEAN JACQUES. A Discourse Upon The Origin of
Equality Among Men and Foundation of the Inequality Among
Mankind. London: R. and J. Dodsley, 1761. 260p.
Important document in the history of democratic thought.
Discusses the most fundamental questions and issues involved

(ROUSSEAU, JEAN JACQUES)
    with natural law and human equality. Reprint of 1755
    edition.

117 RUCHAMES, LOUIS, ed. Racial Thought In America: A Documentary
     History. Amherst: University of Massachusetts Press,
     1969.
        From the Puritans to Abraham Lincoln, both official and
     unofficial, this history documents American racial thought.
     Bibliography.

SANFORD, R. NEVITT. See 62.

118 SCHERMERHORN, R. A. These Our People: Minorities in American
     Culture. Boston: D. C. Heath, 1949. 635p.
        Analysis of the minority groups with the largest popula-
     tion base. Also concerned with minority patterns of ad-
     justment to various minority programs, prejudice, and other
     problems.

119 SCHWARTZ, BARRY N. and ROBERT DISCH, eds. White Racism: Its
     History, Pathology and Practice. New York: Dell, 1970.
     622p.
        Jam-packed with evidence about the pathological nature
     of white society that breeds racism in the white psyche.
     Articles and literary excerpts used plus government reports
     and statements by international authorities. The fine in-
     troduction is well worth reading for itself alone. It gives
     a history of racism in the United States in succinct terms.

SEIGELMAN, ELLEN. See 84.

120 SIMPSON, GEORGE E. and MILTON YINGER. Racial and Cultural
     Minorities; An Analysis of Prejudice and Discrimination,
     3rd edition. New York: Harper and Row, 1965. 582p.
        Gives good definitions of prejudice and discrimination.
     Emphasis on social interaction between groups in America
     and racism seen as a social problem. Standard college text
     and a good one for detailed general reading. Reprint of
     1958 edition. Bibliography.

SLABEY, JOSEPH. See 75.

121 SMITH, ARTHUR L., DELUVINA HERMANDEZ and ANNE ALLEN. How to
     Talk With People of Other Races, Ethnic Groups and Cultures.
     Los Angeles: Trans-Ethnic Education/Communication Founda-
     tion, 1971. 36p.
        First of a series of monographs articulating the prob-
     lems of intercultural communication and some methods to
     help people live better together.

GENERAL STUDIES

122   SNYDER, LOUIS L., ed. The Idea of Racism. Princeton, New
        Jersey: Van Nos Reinhold, 1962. 192p.
          Meaning and history of racism in the United States.
        Snyder feels that the term "racism" is being replaced by
        the biological category of "ethnic group." Bibliography.

      SPEARS, DAVID. See 113.

123   STEINFIELD, MELVIN, comp. Cracks In The Melting Pot: Racism
        and Discrimination in American History. Beverly Hills:
        Glencoe Press, 1973. 370p.
          Racism in the world and in the United States. Stein-
        field uses material on the Anti-Indian wars, the treatment
        of Chicanos after the Mexican War, the anti-immigration
        policies, and various discriminations. Ends with a section
        on the future of racism. Bibliography.

124   STOCKING, GEORGE W., JR. Race, Culture, and Evolution:
        Essays In The History of Anthropology. New York: The Free
        Press, 1968. 380p.
          Fascinating though difficult book for the general reader.
        Deals with the nineteenth-century concept that civilization
        was related directly to certain races and their distinguish-
        ing heritages and that the twentieth century saw the testing
        and breakdown of this concept. After essays on methodology
        and the development of American anthropology, also analyzes
        patterns of racial thought in line with the work of Franz
        Boas. Copious annotated footnotes.

125   STODDARD, LOTHROP. Revolt Against Civilization: The Menace
        of the Under Man. New York: Charles Scribner's Sons,
        1922. 274p.
          The title speaks for itself in this book by a famous
        racist of the early twentieth century. Others of that era
        include Henry Osborn, Clinton Stoddard Burr, and Charles
        Winthrop Gould, who wrote: America, A Family Matter (1920).

126   STODDARD, THEODORE LOTHROP. Rising Tide of Color Against
        World Supremacy. New York: Charles Scribner's Sons, 1920.
        320p.
          A challenging analysis of "white and colored relations"
        in which the author describes that dangers to the white
        race of the rising tide of yellow, brown, black, and red
        races, and sees this as the crisis of the age. Formulates
        a solution which would segregate the races by continents.
        An influential book much quoted by racists during the
        1920s.

127　STONEQUIST, EVERETT V.　The Marginal Man; A Study in Personal-
　　ity and Culture.　New York:　Russell and Russell, 1961.
　　228p.
　　　　Sociological study of those living in an alien culture
　　and the need to identify with some group:　ethnic, racial,
　　religious.　Many interviews with students show the problems
　　in behavior that can rise from the lack of identity that
　　can come from a cultural or even a personality split.　Re-
　　print of 1937 edition.

128　U. S. COMMISSION ON CIVIL RIGHTS:　A Report on Equal Oppor-
　　tunity in State and Local Government.　For All The People,
　　By All The People.　Washington, D. C.:　U. S. Government
　　Printing Office, 1969.　277p.
　　　　Investigation of whether minorities received fair treat-
　　ment in federal, state, and local government jobs.　Con-
　　cludes that ethnic peoples do not have equal opportunity.

129　VAN DEN BERGHE, PIERRE L.　Race and Racism:　A Comparative
　　Perspective.　New York:　John Wiley and Sons, 1967.　169p.
　　　　Standard short text on race relations as a field of
　　study.　Traces the development of assimilationist theories
　　and other sociological attitudes toward intercultural be-
　　haviour and then gives the history of racism from the nine-
　　teenth century and Social Darwinism through the 1920s and
　　on into the cultural relativism of the 1930s and the de-
　　velopment of anti-racism.　Comparative study going into
　　racial problems in Mexico, Brazil, the United States, and
　　South Africa.　Bibliography.

130　VAN DER ZANDEN, JAMES WILFRID.　American Minority Relations.
　　New York:　Ronald Press, 1972.　494p.
　　　　Classic college text explores the nature of minority
　　relationships in America.　Sections include:　sources of
　　racism, intergroup relations within America, minority re-
　　actions to dominance, and social change.　Bibliography.
　　Reprint of 1963 edition.

131　WEINBERG, ALBERT K.　Manifest Destiny:　A Study of Nationalist
　　Expansionism in American History.　Chicago:　Quadrangle
　　Books, 1963.　559p.
　　　　Important classic study, details the overt push westward
　　of the U. S. government.　Gives the philosophical rational-

GENERAL STUDIES

(WEINBERG, ALBERT K.)

izations and American social attitudes that gave permission for such a policy. Bibliographic notes. Reprint of 1935 edition.

WEISS, RICHARD. See 109.
WIGGINS, J. R. See 76.
WRIGHT, ROBERT L. See 64.
YINGER, MILTON. See 120.

II. NATIVE AMERICANS

A. Bibliographical Works

132 AMERICAN Indian Education: A Selected Bibliography (With Eric
Abstracts) Eric/Cress Supplement No. 3. Las Cruces, New
Mexico: Eric/Cress, March 1973. 437p.
An enormous annotated compendium which requires a com-
puter mentality to enjoy. Listings are by Accession number
with a subject index in alphabetical order. Dates from
1969 through summer of 1972. Descriptors are topical.

133 AMERICAN Indian Historical Society. Index to Literature on
the American Indian. San Francisco: The Indian Historian
Press, 1970-
Annually published source book includes sixty-three subject areas and a total of 275 periodicals in the 1970
edition.

134 AMERICAN Indians: An Annotated Bibliography of Selected
Library Resources. Minneapolis: University of Minnesota,
Library Services, Institute for American Indians, 1970.
Listings evaluated by representatives from Indian groups
as to their effectiveness as teaching materials about Indians. Includes books, teaching materials, such as maps and
charts, Indian newspapers and periodicals, audio-visual
materials, and a speakers bureau.

135 AMERICAN Indian Media Directory 1974. Washington, D. C.:
American Indian Press Association.
An annual directory.

136 BARROW, MARK V., JERRY D. NISWANDER and ROBERT FORTUINE.
Health and Disease of American Indians North of Mexico: A
Bibliography, 1800-1969. Gainesville: University of
Florida Press, 1972. 147p.
The contents of this non-annotated bibliography are by
topics under the general headings: general, studies of
healthy individuals, Indian health and disease - general
and unspecified, health programs for Indians, infectious

NATIVE AMERICANS

(BARROW, NISWANDER, FORTUINE...)
 agents and diseases, neoplasms, mental health and psychiatric disorders, pregnancy, childbirth, and gynecological
 conditions, congenital malformations, plus lots of diseases.
 Author, Subject and Tribe Index.

137　BERCAW, LOUISE O., ANNIE M. HANNAY and NELLIE G. LARSON, comps.
 Corn in the Development of the Civilization of the Americas: A Selected and Annotated Bibliography. New York:
 Burt Franklin, 1971. 195p.
　Excellent annotation including both ancient and modern
 entries with many government pamphlets and monographs
 listed.

BOLLING, PATRICIA. See 146.

138　BONNERJEA, BIREN. General Index, Annual Reports of the Bureau
 of American Ethnology, Vols. 1-48, 1879-1931. Washington,
 D. C.: U. S. Bureau of American Ethnology Annual Report,
 48th, 1930/31.
　See later reports under: Smithsonian Institute, No. 163.

139　BRIGHAM Young University. Bibliography of Nonprint Instruc-
 tional Materials on the American Indian. Provo, Utah:
 Brigham Young University Priting Service, 1972. 221p.
　A bibliography of audio-visual materials accumulated by
 Brigham Young University; includes 16mm and 8mm film loops,
 filmstrips, 35mm slides, overhead transparencies, study
 prints, maps, charts, recordings, and multimedia kits.

BROWN, ELLA. See 148, 149.
BRUGGE, DAVID M. See 142.
CAMP, CHARLES L. See 170.

140　CEREMONIAL Indian Book Service Order Catalog. Gallup, New
 Mexico.
　An annotated catalog of books arranged in an informal
 geographical order. Includes Central and South America as
 well as North America. Difficult to use because of lack of
 alphabetical order, but a good general bibliography of
 current books in print that can be ordered by mail.

141　CORRELL, J. LEE, EDITHA L. WATSON, and DAVID M. BRUGGE.
 Navajo Bibliography, Revised Edition 2 vols. Window Rock,
 Arizona: Research Section, The Navajo Tribe, 1969.
　All references to the Navajo in books, magazines, pam-
 phlets, and some educational films are listed. Two indexes
 -- alphabetical and by subject.

142   _____. Supplement No. 1 to the 1969 Navajo Bibliography with Subject Index. Research Report No. 2. Window Rock, Arizona: Research Section. The Navajo Tribe, 1973. 122p.
    A listing of the most current holdings.

143   DAVIS, D. M. Bibliography of Resources on the American Indian for Students and Teachers in the Elementary Schools. Minneapolis: Library Services Department, Board of Education for Public Schools, 1967.

144   DAWDY, DORIS OSTRANDER, comp. Annotated Bibliography of American Indian Painting. New York: Museum of the American Indian. 1968. 27p.
    A twenty-seven page listing of art works concerning the Indian. Part of a series for the Museum of the American Indian, New York.

FORTUINE, ROBERT. See 136.

145   FREEMAN, JOHN F., comp. and MURPHEY SMITH, ed. A Guide to Manuscripts Relating to the American Indian in the Library of the American Philosophical Society. Philadelphia: American Philosophical Society, 1966. 491p.
    Over 50,000 items classified; first, by titles, then by Indian dialect, and thirdly, by geography.

HANNAY, ANNIE M. See 137.

146   HARDING, ANNE DINSDALE and PATRICIA BOLLING, comps. Bibliography of Articles and Papers on North American Indian Art. New York: Kraus Reprint Company: 1969. 365p.
    Lists many works done in connection with the United States government's Indian Arts and Crafts Board. Indexes articles by content, by craft, and by tribe. A good reference to pre-Depression art literature about American Indians.

147   HARGRETT, LESTER. A Bibliography of the Constitutions and Laws of the American Indians. Cambridge, Massachusetts: Harvard University Press, 1947. 124p.
    Excellent sourcebook listing the formal policy measures and laws adopted by the U. S. Government, towards the American Indians. Over 225 printed constitutions, tribal statutes, resolutions, and other legal papers described along with biographical and some historical materials.

148   HARKINS, ARTHUR M., I. KARON SHERARTS, ELLA BROWN, and RICHARD G. WOODS, comps. A Bibliography of Urban Indians in the

NATIVE AMERICANS

(HARKINS, SHERARTS, BROWN, WOODS...)
United States. Minneapolis: University of Minnesota.
Training Center for Community Programs and Office of Community Programs, Center for Urban and Regional Affairs,
July, 1971.
    Books, articles, and films listed alphabetically by
author. Emphasis is heavy on sociology topics.

149   HARKINS, ARTHUR M., I. KARON SHERARTS, ELLA BROWN and RICHARD
       G. WOODS, comps. Modern Native Americans: A Selective
       Bibliography. Minneapolis: University of Minnesota,
       Training Center for Community Programs, 1971. 131p.
           An ERIC report, a large unannotated bibliography with
       names in alphabetical order. Includes books and articles
       from 1927 through 1970. No topical selection.

150   HAYWOOD, CHARLES. A Bibliography of North American Folklore
       and Folksong 2nd revised edition. New York: Dover,
       1961, 2 vols.
           Songs, legends, speech, customs, etc., with reference to
       250 tribes. Very comprehensive. Includes biographies and
       history. Also an indexing of serial publications.

151   HIRSCHFELDER, ARLENE B., comp. American Indian and Eskimo
       Authors, A Comprehensive Bibliography. New York: Association on American Indian Affairs, 1973. 99p.
           The most complete bibliography of Native American
       authors in existence, an enlargement of an earlier edition
       (1970). Also includes a list of Indian periodicals.

152   HUEBNER, JOSEPH A. American Indian Index. Chicago; Joseph
       A. Huebner, 1953.
           A compendium of books and articles about Indians issued
       in mimeographed bulletin form. The series has now been
       taken over by Russell L. Knor.

       ICOLARI, DANIEL. See 155.

153   IRVINE, KEITH, general ed. Encyclopedia of Indians of the
       Americas. St. Clair Shores, Michigan: Scholarly Press,
       1974. 20 vols.
           A twenty-volume reference series with articles by Indian
       scholars and other experts.

154   JOURNAL of American Folklore. Analytical Index, vols. 1-70;
       1888-1957. Philadelphia: American Folklore Society, 1958.
           Many entries on American Indians in the various sections.

155 KLEIN, BERNARD and DANIEL ICOLARI, ed. Reference Encyclopedia
of the American Indian. New York: B. Klein Company,
1967. 536p.
Both a dictionary and an encyclopedia with emphasis on
the social sciences. Listings also of Indian museums,
libraries with Indian collections, and extant Indian
reservations.

KNOR, RUSSELL L. See 152.
LARSON, NELLIE G. See 137.

156 LYNAS, LOTHIAN. Medicinal and Food Plants of the North
American Indians, A Bibliography. New York: Library of
the New York Botanical Garden, 1972. 21p.
Can be ordered for $1.25.

157 MARKEN, JACK W. The Indians and Eskimos of North America: A
Bibliography of Books in Print Through 1972. Vermillion:
University of South Dakota Press, 1973. 100p.

158 MARQUIS, ARNOLD. A Guide to America's Indians, Ceremonials,
Reservations, and Museums. Norman: University of Oklahoma
Press, 1974.

159 MURDOCK, GEORGE PETER. Ethnographic Bibliography of North
America, third edition. New Haven: Yale University Press,
Human Relations Area Files, 1960. 168p.
Lists books and articles by tribal or cultural area.
Regularly revised and up-dated.

160 NEWBERRY Library. Dictionary Catalog of the Edward A. Ayer
Collection of Americana and American Indians, The Newberry
Library. Boston: G. K. Hall and Company, 1961. 16v.
8062p. Supp. 1, 1970, 3v, 2017p.
Great collection contains over 90,000 books on North and
South America. Includes accounts concerned chronologically
with prehistory to date.

NISWANDER, JERRY D. See 136.

161 OSBORN, LYNN R. A Bibliography of North American Indian
Speech and Spoken Language. Washington, D. C.: ERIC
Reports, 1968. 54p.
600 items published between 1810 and 1967.

NATIVE AMERICANS

162   PRICE, JOHN A. U. S. and Canadian Indian Periodicals.
       Minneapolis: University of Minnesota, Training Center
       for Community Programs, 1971. 21 leaves.
           A listing of over 50 periodicals with mailing addresses.

       SHERARTS, I. KARON. See 148, 149.
       SMITH, MURPHEY. See 145.

163   SMITHSONIAN Institute. Index of the Bureau of American
       Ethnology, Bulletin 1-100. Washington, D. C.: Smithsonian
       Institution Publication, 1963.

164   SNODGRASS, MARJORIE P. Economic Development of American
       Indians and Eskimos 1930 through 1967, A Bibliography.
       Washington, D. C.: U. S. Department of the Interior,
       Bibliography Series, 1968. 263p. (Departmental Library.
       Bibliography series no. 10).
           Annotated bibliography contains mostly U. S. Senate and
       Bureau of Indian Affairs documents plus various scientific
       articles.

165   STOUTENBURGH. JOHN L., JR. Dictionary of the American Indian.
       New York: Philosophical Library, 1960. 459p.
           General definitions for words such as "wampum" and
       "canoe" with identifications of famous Indians.

166   ULLOM, JUDITH C., comp. Folklore of the North American
       Indians. Washington D. C.: Library of Congress,
       1969. 127p.
           A well-annotated bibliography of folklore categorized
       by cultural areas. The first section is devoted to general
       background and has a section on the primitive folktale.
       Illustrations are excellent. Special sections listing
       folklore for children. Highly recommended as a basic
       collection.

167   U. S. Bureau of Indian Affairs. Library. Biographical and
       Historical Index of American Indians and Persons Involved
       in Indian Affairs. Boston: G. K. Hall, 1966, 8v. 4853p.
           An index developed out of the materials in the BIA
       Library, which have finally been consolidated and located
       in the Department of the Interior.

168   University of Nebraska Press. Bison Books. Lincoln:
       University of Nebraska Press.
           A college press which makes a specialty of featuring
       well-researched and documented books about the Plains
       Indians.

169   UNIVERSITY of Oklahoma Press. The Civilization of the
       American Indian Series. Norman: University of Oklahoma
       Press.
              Series includes reprints and writings commissioned by
       the Press. All are of high quality and of historical and
       cultural interest. Catalog on request.

170   WAGNER, HENRY R. The Plains and the Rockies: A Bibliography
       of Original Narratives of Travel and Adventure, revised by
       Charles L. Camp. Columbus, Ohio: Long's College Book
       Company, 1953. 299p.
              A sample of the types of materials that must be investi-
       gated when looking for materials about Native Americans.
       These narratives, written by white travelers, traders, and
       trappers, include many Indian experiences. Reprint of
       1937 Edition

       WATSON, EDITHA L. See 142.
       WOODS, RICHARD G. See 148, 149.

171   YALE University Press. Western Americana Series. New Haven:
       Yale University Press.
              Another famous press which features Indian materials.

                              B.   Periodicals

172   ABC: Americans Before Columbus. 201 Hermosa NE, Albuquerque,
       New Mexico 87108.
              The publication of the National Indian Youth Council.
       Monthly.

173   AKWESASNE Notes. Mohawk Nation via Rooseveltown, New York
       13683. 8 times a year.
              A national newspaper which has no fixed rate of sub-
       scription and is run by mostly volunteer staff. News is
       clipped from other Indian newspapers all over the country
       and included along with special articles, book reviews, and
       editorials. Also includes articles of international import
       about Los Indios. Centerfold is usually a fine poster
       picture. Support it if you can!

174   ALCHERINGA: Ethnopoetics. 600 West 163 Street, New York,
       New York 10032. Published twice a year.
              A magazine that began in 1971, edited by a poet and an
       anthropologist. Reflects a new approach to Indian studies.
       and other cultural studies emphasizing the oral and picto-
       rial traditions. Alcheringa sometimes comes with records,

NATIVE AMERICANS

(ALCHERINGA: Ethnopoetics)
   often with drawings that reflect a response to the words,
   very freely translated and interpreted.

175 THE American Indian. American Indian Council, Inc., 3053 16th
   Street, San Francisco, California. Published monthly.
      An Indian journal emphasizing current national problems.
   Will be sent on request.

176 AMERICAN Indian Law Review. College of Law, 630 Parrington
   Oval, Norman, Oklahoma 73069.
      A new periodical put together by the American Indian Law
   Students Association at the University of Oklahoma. First
   issue contains articles on Blue Lake, alcoholism and law,
   and hunting and fishing rights, among others, as well as
   book reviews.

177 THE Amerindian (American Indian Review). 1263 W. Pratt Blvd.,
   Chicago, Illinois 60626. A bimonthly newspaper of national
   scope. Book reviews.

178 BULLETIN of the Bureau of American Ethnology, Washington,
   D. C.: Smithsonian Institute.
      Many articles on Indian research.

179 DINÉ Baa-Hani. P.O. Box #527, Fort Defiance, Navajo Nation
   86504.
      A lively little newspaper that is politically oriented
   in its news coverage and very much less conservative than
   the Navajo Times in its editorial policy.

180 EARLY American. 708 Mills Avenue, Modesto, California 95350.
   Published every two months.
      A variety of items are included in this newsletter such
   as meetings of Indian groups, editorials, and book reviews.
   But the main emphasis is on education.

181 INDIAN Affairs. Association of American Indian ffairs. 432
   Park Avenue, South, New York, New York 10016.
      Current news of national interest put out by a non-Indi-
   an group dedicating to promoting Indian arts, crafts, and
   culture.

182 INDIAN Education. NIEA Publication. 3036 University Avenue,
   Minneapolis, Minnesota 55414.

183 THE INDIAN Historian. American Indian Historical Society,
   1451 Masonic Avenue, San Francisco, California 94117.

(THE INDIAN...)
Published quarterly. 1967.
Emphasis in this scholarly magazine is on history from a Native American viewpoint. Excellent short bibliographies and book reviews.

184 INDIAN Law Reporter. 1035 30th Street, N. W., Washington, D. C. 20007.
A new monthly journal published by the American Indian Lawyer Training Program.

185 INDIGENA: News From Indian America. P.O. Box 4073, Berkeley, California 94704. Published quarterly.
Indigena, the Spanish word for Native American, is another new newspaper. Concerned with the Western Hemisphere and publishes news from both North and South America.

186 JOURNAL Of American Indian Education. College of Education, Arizona State University, Tempe, Arizona 85281.

187 MANY Smokes: National Indian Magazine. P.O. Box 5895, Reno, Nevada 89503. Published monthly.
A chatty journal of national Indian news. Also contains articles and book reviews.

188 THE Navajo Times. P.O. Box 428, Window Rock, Arizona 86515. Published weekly.
One of the largest Indian newspapers.

189 THE NCAI Sentinel. National Congress of American Indians, 1346 Connecticut Avenue, N.W., Room 1019, Washington, D. C., 20036. Published quarterly.
News with a political bent. Emphasis on news of interactions between the federal government and the Indian tribes.

190 REPORTS ON Indian Legislation. Friends Committee on National Legislation, Washington, D. C.
A compilation of federal cases concerning Indian affairs.

191 ROSEBUD Sioux Herald. Box 65, Rosebud, South Dakota 57570. Published weekly.
Owned by The Rosebud Sioux Tribe, newspaper also includes a student newspaper, The Woyakapi.

192 SMOKE Signals. Indian Arts and Crafts Board. U. S. Department of the Interior, Washington, D. C. 20240

NATIVE AMERICANS

(SMOKE Signals)
   A magazine that was put out by the Board which concerned
itself with Indian artists and craftsmen, museum news,
special events, recent publications, etc. Distributed free
upon written request, as long as the out-of-print supply
lasts.

193   THE WARPATH. P.O. Box 26149, San Francisco, California 94126.
   Publication of the United Native Americans, Incorporated.
Tells about Red Power activities in America and Canada.

194   TRIBAL News. 636 North St. Andrews Place, Los Angles, California 90004.
   A new monthly newspaper that began publication in
August, 1974. Scope is national; emphasis in the first
issue was on Los Angeles activities.

195   WASSAJA: A National Newspaper of Indian America. The American Indian Historical Society, 1451 Masonic Avenue, San
Francisco, California 94117. Published monthly.
   Started in January, 1973 to provide national coverage
of pertinent information on issues involving the American
Indian today, especially U.S./Indian relationships. Book
reviews and editorials, as well as long feature articles.

196   THE WEEWISH Tree, 1971. A Magazine of Indian America for
   Young People. The American Indian Historical Society,
1451 Masonic Avenue, San Francisco, California 94117.
   A handsome and delightful magazine that grownups ought
to subscribe to for their children so that they can read
it themselves. Published six times during the school year.
"Weewish," in case you haven't read Cahuilla (Southern
California) lately, means acorn food.

         C. History, Politics, Law and Government

ABERLE, SOPHIA D. See 209.
ADAMS, GEORGE R. See 262.

197   AMERICAN Friends Service Committee. Uncommon Controversy:
   Fishing Rights of the Muchleshoot, Puyallup, and Nisqually
Indians. Seattle: University of Washington Press,
1970. 200p.
   The Indians' side of the conflict over fishing rights
in Puget Sound. Documents the changing perspective towards
treaty rights by courts, administrators, and the public
during the past century. Bibliography.

198   ANDRIST, RALPH K. The Long Death: The Last Days of the
      Plains Indians. New York: Collier Books, 1969. 371p.
          A classic of the last struggles between the Plains Indi-
      ans and the United States military. Bibliography. Re-
      print of 1964 edition.

199   ATHEARN, ROBERT G. William Tecumseh Sherman and the Settle-
      ment of the West. Norman: University of Oklahoma Press,
      1956. 371p.
          A detailed history of General Sherman's activities from
      1865 to 1883, when he was successively in command of the
      Military Division of the Missouri (most of the Great Plains
      and the Rocky Mountain areas) and General of the Army under
      President Grant. These were the years of some of the most
      bloody confrontations with the Plains Indians. Reprint
      of 1949 edition.

200   BAILEY, L. R. Indian Slave Trade in the Southwest. New York:
      Tower Publications, 1967. 236p.
          A detailed study of an often-overlooked aspect of Ameri-
      can Indian history. Slaves were not a widespread part of
      southwest life, but were used when expedient.

201   BANCROFT, HUBERT HOWE. "The Native Races" (note: Pacific
      Coast) in Works. San Francisco: A. L. Bancroft and Com-
      pany, 5 vols., 1882-1886.
          I always like to include dear old Bancroft because he
      was the historian whose writings reflected those attitudes
      of the intelligentsia who influenced the illiterati in
      their racial views.

202   BARROWS, WILLIAM. The Indian's Side of the Indian Question.
      Freeport, New York: Books for Libraries Press, 1972. 206p.
          Barrows addresses himself to the question: Did American
      Christianity do its best to preserve the lives and cultures
      of the American Indian? Reprint of 1887 edition.

203   BEADLE, JOHN HANSON. The Undeveloped West: Or Five Years in
      the Territories. New York: Arno Press, 1973. 823p.
          Description of travel through the Far West from 1860 to
      1897. This reprint has all the original illustrations and
      type. Reprint of 1873 work.

204   BEAL, MERRILL D. "I Will Fight No More Forever": Chief
      Joseph and the Nez Perce War. New York: Ballantine
      Books, 1971. 357p.

NATIVE AMERICANS

(BEAL, MERRILL D.)
A searching history of the Nez Perce War and the Nez Perce Indians who struggled to hold their Northwest lands in the 1870s. Bibliography. Reprint of 1963 edition.

205   BOURKE, JOHN G. On the Border With Crook. Lincoln: University of Nebraska Press, 1971. 491p.
The account of a staff member of General George Crook who subjugated many of the Plains and Southwest Indian tribes. Reprint of the 1891 classic of American history.

206   BOYCE, GEORGE A. When Navajos Had Too Many Sheep: The 1940's. San Francisco: Indian Historical Press, 1973. 284p.
The Director of Navajos Schools in the 1970s describes the crisis that came to The People when the federal government ordered a stock reduction program. Statistics.

207   BRANDON, WILLIAM. The American Heritage Book of Indians. New York: Dell Publishing Company, 1966. 425p.
A basic historical account of North American Indians, beginning with ancient Mexican cultures and then focusing on the United States during the conflict between the Indian and White civilizations. Bibliography. Reprint of 1961 edition.

208   _____. The Last Americans. New York: McGraw Hill, 1974. 553p.
A rewrite of Brandon's Heritage book to include recent archeological data and current studies of North American Indian life and culture. A section of original Indian poetry is included. Bibliography.

209   BROPHY, WILLIAM A. and SOPHIE D. ABERLE, comps. The Indian: America's Unfinished Business: Report of the Commission on the Rights, Liberties, and Responsibilities of the American Indian. Norman: University of Oklahoma Press, 1969/1966. 236p.
Prime emphasis in this excellent and comprehensive book is on the legal relationships and policies of the U. S. government with the Indians. Reprint of 1966 edition.

210   BROWN, DEE. Bury My Heart at Wounded Knee: An Indian History of the American West. New York: Holt, Rinehart and Winston, 1970. 487p.
Nineteen episodes reconstructed out of the oral tradition to form a history of the conquest of the American West as the victims saw it happen and in terms of their

(BROWN, DEE)
feelings about it. This book became a best seller when
published and is considered a work of good scholarship.

211   BURNETTE, ROBERT and JOHN KOSTER. The Road to Wounded Knee
(The Passionate Life, Death and Rebirth of the American
Indian). New York: Bantam Books, 1974. 332p.
Wassaja, in reviewing this book (July, 1974) describes
it as giving the historical background of Wounded Knee,
from the U. S. Cavalry massacre in the nineteenth century
to the 1973 defiance by AIM and other Indians. The internal problems of the Lakota Sioux and other local tribal
groups also receive attention from Burnette, who is tribal
chairman of the Rosebud Sioux.

212   BURT, JESSE and ROBERT B. FERGUSON. Indians of the Southeast:
Then and Now. Nashville, Tennessee: Abingdon Press,
1973. 304p.
A history of the Southeastern Indian tribes: Choctaws,
Chickasaws, Cherokee, Creek, Seminole, Lumbee, Catawba,
Tuscarora, and Coushatta. Photographs, painting repro-
ductions also. Bibliography.

213   CAHN, EDGAR S. ed. Our Brother's Keeper: The Indian in
White America. New York: World Publishing Company,
1972. 193p.
This publication by the Citizens' Advocate Center with
Indian guidance surveys the current socio-economic situation of the modern, White-educated Indian and sensitively
portrays his relationship with the U. S. government, particularly the Bureau of Indian Affairs. Bibliographical
references. Reprint of the 1970 edition.

CASAS, BARTOLOMÉ DE LAS. See 237.

214   CASAS, BARTOLOMÉ DE LAS. History of the Indies. New York:
Harper and Row, 1971. 302p.
A translation and abridgement of the original history
and description of the Spaniards in America from 1492 to
about 1520 by the noted monk and defender of the Indians.
The account is highly critical of contemporary injustices.
The editing by Andreé Collard helps clarify the historical
biases in which Casas was steeped. There has been a recent
revivial of interest in this missionary priest and humanist
whose writings were controversial in Spain and in the States
and used by the British to blacken the reputation of the
Spanish in the New World in order to justify their own con-
quests of Spanish holdings.

NATIVE AMERICANS

215   CHEROKEE Executive Committee. The Constitution and Laws of
       the Cherokee Nation: 1839-51. Tahlequah, Oklahoma:
       Cherokee Executive Committee, 1973. 349p.
           The constitution and tribal laws created by the Cherokee
       Nation after their forced removal to Oklahoma by the United
       States Government.

       CHIEF JOSEPH. See 204.

216   COHEN, FELIX SOLOMON. Handbook of the Federal Indian Law.
       Albuquerque: University of New Mexico Press, 1971. 662p.
           Felix Cohen was an important defender of Indian rights
       for many decades. This book was extensively revised and
       "corrected" by the federal government in 1958. The new
       edition restores the correct and extensive data on Indian-
       Federal relationships. A key book on Indian law. Bibliog-
       raphy. Reprint of 1942 edition.

217   _____. The Legal Conscience; Selected Papers...Edited by Lucy
       Kramer Cohen. Amdon, Connecticut: Archon Books,
       1970. 505p.
           A compilation of the best essays of a man dedicated to
       the fight for American Indian rights. Reprint of 1960
       edition.

       COHEN, LUCY KRAMER. See 217.
       COLLARD, ANDREE. See 214.

218   COLLIER, JOHN. Indians of the Americas: The Long Hope.
       New York: New American Library, 1947. 326p.
           A record of the American Indian from the Paleolithic
       Age to the late 40s by the man who served as U. S. Com-
       missioner of Indian Affairs under Franklin Delano Roosevelt
       and was responsible for creating "the New Deal for Indians"
       during his administration.

219   _____. On the Gleaming Way: Navajos, Eastern Pueblos, Zunis,
       Hopis, Apaches, and Their Land; and Their Meanings to the
       World. Denver: Sage Books, 1962. 163p.
           An introductory book on the various tribes of the title.
       Illustrated with photographs. Reprint of 1949 edition.

       COPELAND, ALAN. See 239.

220   THE COUNCIL on Interracial Books for Children, comp. and ed.
       Chronicles of American Indian Protest. Greenwich, Connect-
       icut: Fawcett Publications, 1971. 376p.

(THE COUNCIL...)
Compilation of historical sources on the treatment of American Indians with commentaries.

221　CROOK, GEORGE. Crook's Resume of Operations Against the Apache Indians, 1882 to 1886. London: Johnson-Taunton Military Press, 1971. 28p.
An interesting document giving a fair sample of the American military mind and how it looked at Indians. Reprint of 1886 edition.

222　DEBO, ANGIE. And Still the Waters Run: The Betrayal of the Five Civilized Tribes. Princeton: Princeton University Press, 1972. 417p.
Traces the history of the Cherokee, Choctaw, Chickasaw, Creeks, and Seminoles from the nineteenth century to the present. Focuses on the tribal experiences in Oklahoma. Bibliography. Reprint of 1940 edition.

223　_____. A History of the Indians of the United States. Norman: University of Oklahoma Press, 1970. 386p.
A general history that emphasizes Indian/White relationships. Begins with the first White explorers and examines present United States policies. Bibliography.

224　DELORIA, VINE, JR. Behind the Trail of Broken Treaties, An Indian Declaration of Independence. New York: Delacorte Press, 1974.
The legal status and laws concerning the North American Indians.

225　_____. Custer Died For Your Sins, An Indian Manifesto. New York: Macmillan, 1969. 279p.
One of the leading national figures of the Red Power movement discusses the White/Indian situation today with much ironic humor and gives the background for the current situation.

226　_____. Of Utmost Good Faith: The Case of the American Indian Against the Federal Government of the United States. New York: Bantam Books, 1971. 402p.
An excellent source book and collection of documents chronicling the history of American Indian - U. S. Government relations and the shortcomings and unfulfilled promises, treaties and agreements.

227　_____. We Talk, You Listen: New Tribes, New Turf. New York: MacMillan, 1970. 227p.

NATIVE AMERICANS

(DELORIA, VINE, JR.)
Diagnoses the central problems of modern American life -
racial conflict, genocide, imperialism, capitalism, etc. --
and notes that in this rapidly changing and disintegrating
society the culture which has emerged as the most stable
and sensible model is that of the Indian. Argues that the
varied "tribal" elements of modern America must unite
through the creation of a common experience and mythology.

228   ELLIS, RICHARD N., ed. The Western American Indian: Case
Studies in Tribal History. Lincoln: University of Nebraska Press, 1972. 203p.
Fourteen case studies by Indian historians and anthropologists, concerning war and peace in the Southwest and
West from the Walla Walla Council of 1855 to the termina-
tion bills of the 1950s. Recommended Readings.

229   EMBREE, EDWIN R. Indians of the Americas. New York: Macmillan, 1970. 268p.
A general survey of the Indians of both continents with
focus on North America. Rejects the concept of Indian
assimilation. Selected annotated bibliography. Reprint
of 1939 edition.

230   ERDOES, RICHARD. The Sun Dance People: The Plains Indians,
Their Past and Present. New York: Vintage, 1972. 218p.
This is an interesting book because it groups Native
Americans by region rather than tribe. It makes for dif-
fusion, in no way clarified by the many excellent pictures
that go along with Erdoes' history.

231   FEDERAL FIELD Committee for Development Planning in Alaska.
Alaska Natives & the Land. Washington, D. C.: U. S.
Government Printing Office, Federal Field Committee for
Development Planning in Alaska, Anchorage, Alaska, October
1968. 565p.
Deals with the inhabitants, culture, land and ethnic
relationships, natural resources, economic development,
and the issue of the land. Full of maps, pictures, and
factual information. Many statistics and a bibliography.

FELTSKOG, E. N. See 263.
FERGUSON, ROBERT B. See 212.

232   FEY, HAROLD E. and D'ARCY McNICKLE. Indians and Other Americans: Two Ways of Life Meet. New York: Harper and Row,
1970. 274p.

(FEY and McNICKLE...)
An assessment of the past history of U. S./Indian relations, the various policies and acts, and how they affected
both Indian and White societies. Reprint of 1959 edition.

233 FINERTY, JOHN F. War-Path and Bivouac, Or the Conquest of the
Sioux. Norman: University of Oklahoma Press, 1962. 356p.
A personal narrative account of the Sioux campaigns
during the wars of 1876-81. The author was a correspondent
for the Chicago Times covering the battlefront.

234 FORBES, JACK D., ed. The Indian in America's Past. Englewood Cliffs, New Jersey: Prentice-Hall, 1964. 181p.
A selection of documents relevant to Indian/White relationships with explanatory materials.

235 _____. Native Americans of California and Nevada. Healdsburg, California: Naturegraph Publications, 1969. 197p.
An Indian scholar gives a historical interpretation of
Indian problems in California and Nevada. However, in the
opinion of some students at UCLA, this book tends to avoid
much of the crucial material surrounding land and water
rights: "The history an Indian can use."

236 FOREMAN, GRANT. The Five Civilized Tribes. Norman: University of Oklahoma Press, 1934. 455p.
The history of the Choctaws, Chickasaws, Creeks, Seminoles, and Cherokees as they were pushed westward during
the nineteenth centry.

237 FRIEDE, JUAN and BENJAMIN KEEN, eds. Bartolomé de Las Casas
in History: Toward an Understanding of the Man and His
Work. Dekalb: Northern Illinois University Press,
1971. 632p.
This biography of Las Casas also includes study of his
work as a Colonial Reformer and of the conflicts he encountered; both political and religous. This mission
priest was, both in Europe, and the Americas, acclaimed
for his "evangelical charity." His teachings of the unity
of mankind, the principle of self-determination, and the
right of men to satisfy their elementary material and cultural needs were very striking and needed, then and now.
Bibliographic notes.

238 GILBREATH, LARRY KENT. Red Capitali$m: An Analysis of the
Navajo Economy. Norman: University of Oklahoma Press,
1973. 157p.

NATIVE AMERICANS

(GILBREATH, LARRY KENT)
A study of the Navajo business community as an island of poverty in a sea of American plenty. Legal and political problems, educational limitations and recommendations are also included. Bibliography. The Indian Historian (Vol. 6:3) criticizes this book for its limited scope and narrow research. It is not an analysis of the Navajo economy for its does not say much about agribusiness nor the sheep industry.

239   GORDON, SUZANNE. Black Mesa: The Angel of Death. New York: John Day Company, 1973. 113p.
Discusses the strip mining of the sacred Navajo mountain, Black Mesa, and the ecological, political, cultural, and other problems created. Excellent photographs by Alan Copeland.

240   GRINNELL, GEORGE B. The Fighting Cheyennes. Norman: University of Oklahoma Press, 1971. 453p.
Classic depiction of the Cheyenne Indian Wars. Bibliography. Reprint of 1915 edition.

241   HAGAN, WILLIAM T. American Indians. Chicago: University of Chicago Press, 1966. 190p.
A short history giving the basic facts of Indian/White struggles on the continent. Suggested reading list. Reprint of 1961 edition.

242   _____. Indian Police and Judges; Experiments in Acculturation and Control. New Haven: Yale University Press, 1966. 194p.
A general history of the Indians' plight divided into the Colonial period, the friends and foes era between the American and British during 1776 to 1816, the removal of the Indians from their lands onto reservations in the early nineteenth century, the wars of the mid-1880s, and finally a section of the duress of acculturation with the effects of the New Deal philosophy. Bibliography.

243   HERTZBERG, HAZEL W. The Search for an American Indian Identity: Modern Pan-Indian Movements. Syracuse: Syracuse University Press, 1971. 362p.
Primarily chronicles the extent of Pan-Indianism as it has developed in this country in the form of various reform movements, cults, and organizations, such as the society of American Indians (1911). Deals with various aspects of Pan-Indianism in other sections on reform, religious, and fraternal Pan-Indianism. Bibliographic essay.

(HERTZBERG, HAZEL W.)
The review in The Indian Historian (Vol. 4:2), while criticizing some of Ms. Hertzberg's research, commends her for her topic.

244 HORSMAN, REGINALD. Expansion and American Indian Policy.
East Lansing: Michigan State Unviersity Press, 1967. 209p.
Deals with U. S. Government relations with North American Indians from 1789-1869, including specific events displaying the treatment of the Native Americans. Bibliography.

245 HOYT, OLGA. American Indians Today. New York: Abelard-Schuman, 1972. 190p.
A summary account of modern Indian tribal life today written up in journalistic style.

246 JACKSON, HELEN HUNT. A Century of Dishonor; A Sketch of the United States Government's Dealings with Some of the Indian Tribes. New Edition Enlarged by the Addition of the Report of the Needs of the Mission Indians of California. New York: Harper and Row, 1963. 342p.
Reissue of a famous crusading book that produced public outrage about the plight of the American Indian but not much action. President Theodore Roosevelt condemned Ms. Jackson for being a meddler in governmental affairs. Reprint of 1881 edition.

247 JOSEPHY, ALVIN M., JR., ed. Red Power: The American Indians' Fight for Freedom. New York: American Heritage Press, 1971. 259p.
An optimistic documentary history of the emergence in the 60s of an American Indian militant movement. The 26 selections range from movement manifestoes to excerpts from congressional committee reports. A general introduction and prefaces to each of the selections is provided.

248 KAPPLER, CHARLES, J. Laws and Treaties, 5 volumes.
Interland Publications, 1972.
A comprehensive compilation of Indian treaties beginning with the Delaware Treaty of 1778. This series of texts is commonly known as the Kappler Report and was originally put out by the U. S. Government. Akwesasne Notes comments that the long delay in republishing these important volumes indicates the low aspect with which the Indian treaties were held. Reprint of 1904 edition.

NATIVE AMERICANS

KEEN, BENJAMIN. See 237.

249 KELLY, LAWRENCE C. The Navajo Indians and Federal Indian
     Policy, 1900-1935. Tucson: University of Arizona Press,
     1970. 221p.
        A study of the Navajo Indian and government relation-
     ships on the reservation and in general. Also a complete
     bibliography. Reprint of 1968 edition.

KOSTER, JOHN. See 211.

250 LA FARGE, OLIVER. A Pictorial History of the American Indian.
     New York: Crown Publishers, Incorporated, 1956. 272p.
        A generalized book for the lay reader put together by an
     authority.

251 LEWIS, MERIWETHER. History of the Expedition Under the Com-
     mand of Captains Lewis and Clark to the Sources of the
     Missouri, Thence Across the Rocky Mountains and Down the
     River Columbia to the Pacific Ocean, Performed During the
     Years 1804-5-6 by Order of the Government of the United
     States, 3 vols. New York: AMS Press, 1973.
        A complete reprint of the Biddle edition of 1814 to
     which all the members of the expedition contributed, with
     an account of the Louisiana Purchase by John Bach McMaster,
     and notes on the route.

LLOYD, HERBERT M. See 258.
McMASTER, JOHN BACH. See 251.
McNICKLE, D'ARCY. See 232.

252 McNICKLE, D'ARCY. Native American Tribalism: Indian Survi-
     vals and Renewals. New York: Oxford University Press,
     1973. 190p.
        Tries to define: Who are the Indians and how have they
     retained their identity. Recommended for quick general
     reading.

253 MAGUSSON, MAGNUS and HERMANN PALSSON, trans. The Vinland
     Sagas: The Norse Discovery of America, Graenlendiga Saga
     and Elri's Saga. Baltimore: Penguin Books, 1970. 123p.
        The first recorded encounters of Europeans with the
     "skraalings" or "wretched ones"--Indians--is given in these
     ninth and tenth-century Scandinavian sagas. Christopher
     Columbus is presumed to have studied these chronicles be-
     fore his own journeys. Bibliography. Reprint of 1965
     edition.

Minority Studies: An Annotated Bibliography

254   MARX, HERBERT L., comp. The American Indian: A Rising Ethnic
      Force. New York: H. W. Wilson Comapny, 1973. 188p.
         Government relations with the North American Indians
      since 1934. Bibliography.

255   MATHEWS, JOHN JOSEPH. The Osages, Children of the Middle
      Waters. Norman: University of Oklahoma Press, 1961. 826p.
         Everything you ever wanted to know about the Osage tribe.
      Mathews is Osage, English and French. Extensive
      bibliography.

256   MEINIG, D. W. Southwest: Three Peoples in Geographical
      Change 1600-1970. New York: Oxford University Press,
      1971. 151p.
         A short historical and geographical study of the inter-
      action between peoples and the land in the Southwest.
      Especially interesting perspectives gives on the Spanish/
      Indian involvement. Bibliography.

257   MEYER, WILLIAM. Native Americans: The New Indian Resistance.
      New York: International Publishers, 1971. 95p.
         A summary of the current background and development of
      the struggles for Indian rights being undertaken by vari-
      ous present-day American Indian groups and organizations.
      Bibliography.

258   MORGAN, LEWIS H. League of the Ho-De'-No-Sau-Nee or Iroquois,
      2 vols. Edited and annotated by Herbert M. Lloyd. New
      York: Burt Franklin, 1901. 338, 332p.
         Reprint of a famous study of the Iroquois made in 1851,
      replete with fine engravings.

259   NAMMACK, GEORGIANNE C. Fraud, Politics, and the Dispossession
      of the Indians. Norman: University of Oklahoma Press,
      1969. 128p.
         Covers the conflicts, politics, and rivalries between
      the Iroquois and the British overland control from 1664
      to the outbreak of the American Revolution. Scholarly
      historical study. Bibliography.

260   NASH, GARY. Red, White, and Black. Englewood Cliffs, New
      Jersey: Prentice-Hall, 1974. 350p.
         This history of early America does not begin with the
      Pilgrims nor Columbus but with the native North Americans.
      Views the Europeanization of the New World as only one
      crucial stage in the evolution of colonial society.

NATIVE AMERICANS

261   NAVAJO Treaty. Flagstaff: Northland Press.
       Complete text of treaty between the Navajos and the
       United States Government. Includes the confrontation be-
       tween Navajo Chief Barboncito and General William Sherman
       at the treaty signing.

262   NICHOLS, ROGER L. and GEORGE R. ADAMS, eds. The American
       Indian: Past and Present. Waltham, Massachusetts: Xerox
       College Publishing, 1971. 295p.
       A chronological collection of essays, which attempts to
       provide information and exposure to various aspects of
       American Indian history, within the context of the history
       of the U. S. Good selection for general topical reading.

       PALSSON, HERMANN. See 253.

263   PARKMAN, FRANCIS. The Oregon Trail: Sketches of Prairie and
       Rocky Mountain Life, edited by E. N. Feltskog. Madison:
       University of Wisconsin Press, 1969. 758p.
       This book and others by this famous nineteenth century
       historian are important because his attitudes towards In-
       dians (not positive) had wide influence on his opinions of
       Americans. A facsimile of the 1892 edition with illustra-
       tions by Frederic Remington.

264   PRICE, MONROE E. Law and the American Indian: Readings,
       Notes and Cases. Indianapolis: Bobbs-Merrill Company,
       1973. 807p.
       A complement to Felix Cohen's book on Indian law. Takes
       up the power of the states, concepts of property, land ten-
       ure and use, and tribal governments.

265   PRIEST, LORING B. Uncle Sam's Stepchildren: The Reformation
       of the U. S. Indian Policy, 1865-1887. New York: Octagon
       Books, 1972. 310p.
       Governmental relations with and treatment of Indians
       of North America are extensively analyzed in this difficult
       period of U. S. Government-Indian relations. Bibliograph-
       ical references. Reprint of 1942 edition.

266   PRUCHA, FRANCIS PAUL. American Indian Policy in the Formative
       Years: The Indian Trade and Intercourse Acts, 1790-1834.
       Cambridge: Harvard University Press, 1962. 303p. Bibliog-
       raphy.
       Analyzes U. S. Government relation with the Indians from
       1789-1869. Traces the early Colonial and Indian policy
       through the formation of an Indian department, the con-
       fining of the Indians to specified lands, along with gov-
       ernmental regulation of the Indian fur trade.

46

267   ROOSEVELT, THEODORE. <u>Winning of the West.</u> London and New
York: G. P. Putnam's Sons, 1889-1896. 4 v.
    A lively historical account of the opening up and "civ-
ilizing" of the Mississippi Valley, Ohio Valley, Louisiana,
Old Northwest, Kentucky, and Tennessee. The various areas
are analyzed chronologically in the order in which the
White man came to them. Roosevelt's writings are must
reading for anyone who asks: But how did it happen? How
could they kill so many Indians?

268   SANDOZ, MARI. <u>The Battle of Little Bighorn.</u> Philadelphia:
J. B. Lippincott Company, 1966. 191p.
    One of the best accounts of Custer's demolition. In-
cludes a comparatively good description of the Indian
point of view, especially in showing their attitudes towards Custer.

269   _____. <u>Cheyenne Autumn.</u> London: Eyre and Spottiwoode,
1946. 283p.
    An epic about 278 northern Cheyenne who left their
reservation in 1878 to return to their ancestral homelands,
pursued by 10,000 U. S. troops. Biographical accounts of
the Cheyenne chiefs, Dull Knife and Little Wolf, also
included.

270   SAUER, CARL ORWIN. <u>Sixteenth Century North America: The
Land and The People as Seen by the Europeans.</u> Berkeley:
University of California Press, 1971. 319p.
    Draws on contemporary accounts to provide a view of the
Indians and the land of North America as they were before
repeated contacts and settlement. Bibliography.

271   SAUM, LEWIS O. <u>The Fur Trader and the Indian.</u> Seattle:
University of Washington Press, 1954. 324p.
    One of the finest books out on early nineteenth century
American history; well documented and well written. Tells
about the relationships between the Indians and the early
settlers, trappers, and traders. Shows how the concepts
of savagery and civilization developed from these racial
contacts. A fine analysis of the image of the Indian as
an idea. Notes and bibliography.

272   SCHUSKY, E. <u>The Right to be Indian.</u> San Francisco: The
Indian Historian Press, 1970. 67p.
    A good booklet outlining and discussing the special
nature of civil rights as they apply to Native Americans.

NATIVE AMERICANS

273 SENUNGETUK, JOSEPH E. Give or Take a Century: An Eskimo Chronicle. San Francisco: The Indian Historian Press, 1971. 206p.
   Perhaps the first full-length book in English ever written and published by an Eskimo author. Includes an appendix that contains a chronology of Alaskan native history, plus leading Eskimos, and their organizations.

274 SHEEHAN, BERNARD W. Seeds of Extinction: Jeffersonian Philanthropy and the American Indian. New York: Norton, 1974. 301p.
   Sheehan's thesis is that during the early national period there was a broad philanthropic consensus among American leaders and reformers on how to deal with Indians. The goal was to lead them from "savagery" to "civilization" and finally to incorporate them into American society. This program failed because of its various delusions, and led directly to Indian Removal. Published for the Early American History and Culture, Williamsburg, Pennsylvania.

SHERMAN, WILLIAM TECUMSEH. See 199.

275 SORKIN, ALAN L. American Indians and Federal Aid. Washington, D. C.: Brookings Institution, 1971. 231p.
   Analysis of government program-- "...most reservations remain 'open-air slums' to which many Indians return after a losing battle with urban life."

276 SPECK, GORDON. Breeds and Half Breeds: Our Vagabond Heroes of the American Frontier. New York: Clarkson N. Potter, Incorporated, 1969. 361p.
   These are frontier stories of historical interest about the voyagers and mountain men who helped open us this country.

277 SPICER, EDWARD H. Cycles of Conquest. Tucson: University of Arizona Press, 1962. 609p.
   Covers the cycles of Manifest Destiny from 1533 and the arrival of the Spaniards to 1960. Bibliography.

278 STEINER, STAN. The New Indians. New York: Dell Publishing Company, 1968. 348p.
   The Indians like this book because it shows them as proud and resourceful people. Discusses the Indian activists in their relationships to themselves and the Anglos. A good survey of the Contemporary Indian and the development of Red Power. Good selected bibliography.

279 TEBBEL, JOHN. The Compact History of the Indian Wars. New
     York: Hawthorn Books, 1966. 334p.
        Covers the entire history of U. S. vs. the Indians
     beginning with the Spanish in Florida and ending with the
     Battle of Wounded Knee against the Sioux in 1890.

280 TRADERS ON the Navajo Reservation: A Report on the Economic
     Bondage of the Navajo People. Window Rock, Arizona:
     Southwestern Indian Development, Incorporated, 1968. 43p.
        A short study of the trading post system on the Eastern
     and central portions of the Navajo Reservation. The field
     work was conducted by eight Navajo students and includes
     several business policy suggestions by them.

281 TURNER, KATHERINE C. Red Men Calling on the Great White
     Father. Norman: University of Oklahoma Press, 1951. 235p.
        Narrative accounts of the pilgrimage of many Indian
     tribal leaders to Washington, D. C., and the meetings they
     held with U. S. governmental leaders and the executive
     branch in an attempt to change the Indian policies of the
     U. S. over the course of the 19th and 20th centuries.

282 TYLER, S. LYMAN. Indian Affairs, A Study of the Changes in
     Policy of the U. S. Toward Indians. Provo, Utah:
     Brigham Young University, 1964. 199p.
        Written in 1958, this book documents the change in the
     attitude of the U. S. government towards the Indians. In
     terms of negotiating status, the Indians were supposed to
     have a bilateral equality as partners. After the 1870s,
     the official policy changed to overt unilateralism. There
     is some evidence that the same attitude currently exists.
     Bibliography.

283 UNDERHILL, RUTH M. Red Man's America: A History of the
     Indians in the United States. Chicago: University of
     Chicago Press, 1971. 395p.
        A general narrative history of the Indians who live in
     the United States. Bibliography. Reprint of 1953 edition.

284 U. S. BUREAU of Indian Affairs. Annual Report. Washington,
     D. C.: U. S. Government Printing Office.
        Related publications include: general publications,
     laws relating to Indian affairs, and statistics concerning
     Indian education.

285 UTLEY, ROBERT M. The Last Days of the Sioux Nation. New
     Haven: Yale University Press, 1963. 314p.

NATIVE AMERICANS

(UTLEY, ROBERT M.)
The defeat of the Sioux and their inability to adjust to the restrictions of Reservation life or the White culture outside. Bibliography.

286   VAN EVERY, DALE. Disinherited: The Lost Birthright of the American Indian. New York: Avon, 1970. 279p.
A chronicle history of the U. S. Government's dispersal of the Indian nations of the Southwest in the nineteenth century. Bibliography. Reprint of 1966 edition.

287   VOGEL, VIRGIL, J., ed. This Country Was Ours: A Documentary History of the American Indian. New York: Harper and Row, 1972. 473p.
Original documents with short introductions. Bibliography.

288   WALLACE, ANTHONY F. C. The Death and Rebirth of the Seneca. New York: Vintage Books, 1972. 384p.
The history of the Seneca Indians and the biography of their prophet, Handsome Lake, who, acting on his visions, tried to revitalize his tribe. Bibliography. Reprint of 1969 edition.

289   WASHBURN, WILCOMB E., ed. The Indian and the White Man. Garden City, New York: Doubleday & Company, 1964. 480p.
A collection of documents dealing with many aspects of American Indian/white man relations over the course of U. S. History. Bibliography.

290   _____. Red Man's Land/White Man's Law: A Study of the Past and Present Status of the American Indian. New York: Charles Scribner's Sons, 1971. 280p.
An important study of the contemporary legal status of the American Indian. Bibliography.

291   WELLMAN, PAUL I. The Indian Wars of the West. Garden City, New York: Doubleday, 1956. 484p.
An account of the various Indian campaigns and battles in the last half of the nineteenth century, written in narrative accounts and chronologically arranged. Volume two, A Death in the Desert (1934, reprinted 1965), emphasizes Geronimo and the Apaches. Reprint of 1947 edition.

D. Education

292 AMERICAN INDIAN Historical Society. Textbooks and the American Indian. San Francisco: The Indian Historical Press, 1970. 269p.
    School texts, especially in California, are analyzed for their presentation of the Indian in history and sociology. Most range from biased to racist.

293 BAERREIS, DAVID A., ed. The Indian in Modern America. Madison: Wisconsin State Historical Society, 1956. 70p.
    A symposium on governmental relations with the Indian, particularly as it pertains to education.

294 BERRY, BREWTON. The Education of the American Indians, A Survey of the Literature. Washington, D. C.: U. S. Government Printing Office, 1969. 121p.
    A reprint of the report made by a special governmental subcommittee on Indian education. The best survey of the literature on Indian education to date. Bibliography.

295 CONFERENCE on California Indian Education. Report of the First All-Indian Statewide Conference on California Indian Education. Modesto, California: California Indian Education Association, 1967.
    A conference by the California tribes to survey how Indians are educated in California. Recommendations could benefit other Third World groups.

296 FARMER, GEORGE L. Education: The Dilemma of the Indian-American. Los Angles: School of Education, University of Southern California, 1969. 96p.
    One of a series on the education of minority peoples being published by the University of Southern California. Discusses besides education, Indian culture, housing, employment, and religion. Maps, tables and bibliography.

297 FUCHS, ESTELLE and ROBERT J. HAVINGHURST. To Live on This Earth: American Indian Education. New York: Doubleday, 1972. 390p.
    Broad and detailed survey of Indian education: a sociological review at both federal and state levels. Attention is given to Indian/White relationships, Native American communities, cultural conflicts, language problems, and the effect of public opinion.

HAVINGHURST, ROBERT J. See 297.

NATIVE AMERICANS

298   HENRY, JEANNETTE. The American Indian in American History.
      San Francisco: The Indian Historian Press, 1970. Indian
      Handbook Series #1.
          A survey of American history textbooks, mainly at the
      grade and high school level and an analysis of their ac-
      curacy in presenting Native Americans. Most books are
      judged to be prejudicial in their treatment of Indians.
      Recommendations for improvement.

299   NATIONAL ADVISORY Council on Indian Education. First Annual
      Report to the Congress of the United States, 2 vols. Wash-
      ington, D. C.: National Advisory Council on Indian Ed-
      ucation, 1974. 49, 569p.
          Self-determination through education is the slogan used
      in the introduction to this lengthy and detailed report.
      Part One details the recommendations for management, edu-
      cation personnel, and proper language development of Indian
      children plus recommendations for the BIA and a bicenten-
      nial educational goal. Part Two comments on two other fed-
      eral reports, which are included: Indian Education: A
      National Tragedy-A National Challenge (Senate Report, 1969)
      and Between Two Milestones (1972). General conclusions:
      federal Indian education is a dismal and scandalous
      failure.

300   ROESSEL, RUTH, ed. Navajo Studies at Navajo Community
      College. Many Farms, Arizona: Navajo Community College
      Press, 1971.
          An excellent example of recent publications designed
      for and by Navajos; the booklet deals with the Navajos
      Studies Program and provides a wide range of information
      on Navajo history and present day culture from a Navajo
      point of view.

301   SMITH, SUSAN and MARGARET WALKER. Federal Funding of Indian
      Education: A Bureaucratic Enigma. Washington, D. C.:
      Bureau of Social Science Research, 1973. 142p.
          A good study of the red tape, pun intended, that takes
      place when appropriations come up for Indian education.

302   THOMPSON, HILDEGARD. Education for Cross-Cultural Enrichment.
      Washington, D. C.: U. S. Department of the Interior,
      Bureau of Indian Affairs, 1964. 309p.
          Series of articles chosen from Indian Education 1952-
      1964 concerns Indian education from 1944-51. Divided by
      categories such as: administration, local and national
      levels; law and the Indians; Indian children in public
      schools; methods in high school; art, music, recreation;

(THOMPSON, HILDEGARD)
 language; health; job placement; and the goals and aims of
the educational branch of the Bureau in light of the find-
ings of these studies.

WALKER, MARGARET. See 301.

E. General Culture and Community Life
(Anthropology, Archaeology, Cooking, Folk-Tales, Linguistics,
Medicine, Music and Songs, Mythology, Philosophy,
Psychology, Religion and Sociology)

ALBERT, ETHEL M. See 429.

303 ALEXANDER, HARTLEY BURR. North American Mythology. New York:
Cooper Square Publishers, 1964. 325p.
 Each chapter gives a summary of the culture of the area
covered plus the myths. Reprint of 1916 edition.

304 _____. The World's Rim; Great Mysteries of the North American
Indians. Lincoln: University of Nebraska Press, 1967. 259p.
 This eminent philosopher, poet, and anthropologist has
analyzed some of the religious and philosophical significance of such Indian ceremonies as: use of the Peace pipe,
the Sun Dance, rites at death, the sweat-bath, and many
others. Bibliography. Reprint of 1953 edition.

305 ALLEN, T. D. Navahos have Five Fingers. Norman: University
of Oklahoma Press, 1970. 245p.
 The joint authors, Don and Terry Allen, spent much time
with the Navaho. Though they are not anthropologists in
the formal sense, they convey a deep understanding and sym-
pathy for the Diné. Reprint of 1963 edition.

306 AMERICAN INDIAN Historical Society. Indian Voices: The First
Convocation of American Indian Scholars. San Francisco:
The Indian Historical Press, 1970. 390p.
 Publication of the papers and proceedings of this first
meeting at Princeton University. Among the topics covered
were: philosophy, education, history, Native American arts,
tribal governments, land development, and psychology.

ANDERSON, JEAN. See 365.

307 APPLEGATE, FRANK G. Indian Stories From the Pueblos.
Glorieta, New Mexico: Rio Grande Press, 1971. 178p.
 Pueblo religious beliefs, several legends with some il-
lustrations, are narrated. Ancestral eagles, snakes and

NATIVE AMERICANS

(APPLEGATE, FRANK G.)
priests, and the symbol of Holy water, are all used in this
collection of legends. Illustrated. Reprint of 1929 edition.

308 BAHR, HOWARD M., A. CHADWICK, and ROBERT DAY. Native Americans
Today: Sociological Perspectives. New York: Harper and
Row, 1972. 547p.
The urban Indian seen as a neo-Indian. Pan Indianism
also discussed.

309 BALLARD, LOUIS WAYNE. Koshare, An American Indian Ballet.
n.p.: Harkess Ballet Company, 1966.
Ballard is a Quapaw-Cherokee composer. Besides this
ballet, he has composed The Gods Will Hear, an oral cantata
for soloists, mixed chorus, piano, and percussion using
Native American themes, and "Ritmo Indian" a woodwind
quintet using Indian rhythms.

310 BANDELIER, ADOLF F. The Delight Makers. New York: Harcourt,
Brace, Jovanovich, Incorporated, 1971. 490p.
A fine, even though old, ethnological and archaeological
study of the Pueblo Indians of New Mexico. The author spent
eight years with various tribes and devotes the majority of
his attention to the Tehuas and the Queres. Reprint of
1890 edition.

311 BENEDICT, RUTH F. Zuni Mythology. New York: Columbia University Press, 1935, 2 vols. 342, 345p.
A source book of Zuni tales including abstracts of common stories and a concordance of Pueblo folk materials.

312 BERRY, BREWTON. Almost White. New York: Macmillan, 1963.
212p.
The story of a contemporary group of people who are the
product of mixed marriages, and who live almost as outcasts
on the edge of the majority culture. The first few chapters
deal with the Indian and his status in Anglo society. Then
come varying viewpoints as both Whites and Blacks look at
these "different" people. The last chapters present the
life styles and problems these Indians have to deal with.
Extensive bibliography.

BLACK ELK. See 317.

313 BOAS, FRANZ. Introduction to Handbook of American Indian
Languages. Edited by Preston Holder. Lincoln: University
of Nebraska Press, 1966. 221p.
This introduction is the first half of a book on language
which is shared with J. W. Powell. Boas discusses race and

(BOAS, FRANZ)
language, environment and language in an attempt to formulate some idea of what the characteristics of language are. Essay breaks new linguistic ground. Reprint of 1911 edition.

314 _____. Kwakiutl Tales, New Series. New York: Columbia University Press, 1935-43, 2 vols. 387p. Columbia University Contributions to Anthropology, 26.
A sample of the texts collected by anthropologist Boas. Bibliography.

315 _____. Race, Language and Culture. New York: Macmillian, 1940. 640p.
A collection of anthropologist Boas' essays written at the turn of the century and later, concerning folklore and myth. Bibliographic footnotes.

316 BRINTON, DANIEL G. The Lenape and Their Legends; With the Complete Text and Symbols of the Walam Olum, A New Translation, and an Inquiry Into Its Authenticity. Philadelphia: D. G. Binton, 1885. 262p.
A fascinating document which includes pictographs, text, and translation on each page. The Walum Olum or Red Bundle, tells the story of the Algonquin migration over many centuries. Archaeologists feel that this document contains evidence of the crossing of the Bering Strait. This relatively unnoticed story was translated in 1943, but the new version is not as poetic.

317 BROWN, JOSEPH EPES, ed. The Sacred Pipe: Black Elk's Account of the Seven Rites of The Oglala Sioux. Baltimore: Penguin Books, 1971. 144p.
Black Elk recounts the ancient and sacred rites of the Sioux. Reprint of 1953 edition.

318 BROWN, VINSON. Voices of Earth and Sky, The Vision Life of the Native American and Their Culture Heroes. Harrisburg, Pennsylvania: Stackpole Books, 1974. 224p.

319 BRYDE, JOHN F. Modern Indian Psychology. Vermillion: Institute of Indian Studies, University of South Dakota, 1971. 414p.
A textbook for Indian children to help them cope with the non-Indian world. The author takes Indian values and applies them to non-Indian surroundings.

320 BUNZEL, RUTH LEAH. Zuni Texts. New York: AMS Press, 1974. 285p.
Reprint of work by a leading American anthropologist.

NATIVE AMERICANS

321 CALLOWAY, SYDNEY M. Grandfather Stories of the Navahos.
Chinle, Arizona: Navaho Curriculum Center, Rough Rock
Demonstration School, 1968. 77p.
One of the publications prepared by the Navajo educators
for Navajo classroom use.

322 CAMPBELL, JOSEPH. Where the Two Came to Their Father, A
Navaho War Ceremonial. Told by Jeff King, recorded by Maud
Oakes, commentary by Joseph Campbell. Princeton: New
Jersey: Princeton University Press, Bolligen Series I,
1969. 55p.
A beautiful book and the 17 serigraph prints that come
with the text can be framed as they are large (12" x 17")
and of satisfying color and design.

323 CASWELL, HELEN R. Shadows From the Singing House; Eskimo
Folk Tales. Rutland, Vermont: C. E. Tuttle Company,
1968. 108p.
A good selection of tales especially for children.
Lists primary source material in the bibliography. Illus-
trations are by an Eskimo artist, Robert Mayokuk.

CHADWICK, A. See 308.
CHANIMUN. See Gillham, 349.

324 CHEE, HOSTEEN CLAH, told to Frank J. Newcomb. Navajo Bird
Tales. Wheaton, Illinois: Theosophical Publishing House,
1970. 125p.
A compendium of sixteen tales related by a very famous
medicine man as if to a shepherd boy and his friends.
Well-illustrated by Na-Ton-Sa-Ka of the Navajo Ceremonial
Arts Museum, Santa Fe.

325 CLARK, ELLA E. Indian Legends From the Northern Rockies.
Norman: University of Oklahoma Press, 1966. 350p.
Stories from 12 tribes of Idaho, Montana and Wyoming--
myths, legends, personal narratives, historical traditions.
Bibliography.

326 CLARK, LA VERNE HARRELL. They Sang for Horses: The Impact
of the Horse On Navajo and Apache Folklore. Tucson: University of Arizona Press, 1966. 225p.
A fascinating study of how the Indians incorporated the
horse into their religion and myth. Bibliography.

327 COFFIN, TRISTAM P., ed. Indian Tales of North America: An
Anthology for the Adult Reader. Philadelphia: American
Folklore Society, 1961. 157p.

(COFFIN, TRISTAM P.)
A collection of representative tales with introductions plus a discussion of Indian folktales as stories. Bibliography and an index to Indian materials in the Journal of American Folklore.

328 CORNPLANTER, JESSE J. Legends of the Longhouse. Port Washington, New York: Ira J. Friedman, Incorporated, 1963 [1936]. 216p.
Senecan folktales.

329 COSTO, RUPERT. Contributions and Achievements of the American Indian. San Francisco: The Indian Historian Press, 1973.
Details the achievements of the North and South American civilizations in their contributions to art, religion, philosophy, medicine, agriculture, and oral tradition.

330 CURTIS, NATALIE, ed. The Indians' Book: An Offering By the American Indians of Indian Lore, Musical and Narrative, to Form a Record of the Songs and Legends of Their Race. New York: Dover Publications, Incorporated, 1969. 30p.
Traditional songs recorded by Curtis personally from 18 Indian tribes. Each song has an introduction and an English translation of the words. Reprint of 1907 edition.

DAY, ROBERT. See 308.
DEETZ, JAMES J. F. See 395.

331 DELORIA, ELLA CARA. Dakota Texts. New York: G. E. Stechert and Company, 1932. 279p.
Sioux transcriptions and the author's translation from tales she gathered herself in North and South Dakota.

332 DELORIA, VINE, JR. God is Red. New York: Grosset and Dunlap, 1973. 376p.
Series of essays by a national Indian leader written with forebearance and humor. Considered and contrasted are European religion and concepts of time and space, and tribal religions and their attitudes towards now, then, and the land. Deloria suggests that Indian religious beliefs be looked at by contemporary peoples in order to shift from a blind and destructive world view to a more mature look at the universe than that presently held by Westerners, i.e.. Christians. He ends by asking for a sane redemption of the lands and religion used as a force for harmonious unity of lands and peoples. Notes and Appendices.

333 DOBIE, J. FRANK. The Voice of the Coyote. Lincoln: University of Nebraska Press, 1970. 386p.

NATIVE AMERICANS

(DOBIE, J. FRANK)
The natural history and mythology of the coyote, or Señor Coyote, Don Coyote, Brother Coyote, Huehuecoyotl, or Old Coyote, as the Aztecs called him. Entails thirty years of research and experience with both the real animal and the mythic Indian trickster-hero. Notes and credits amount to a decisive bibliography. Reprint of 1961 edition.

334   DOCKSTADER, FREDERICK J. The Kachina and the White Man: The Influences of the White Man On the Hopi Indian Kachina Cult. Bloomfield Hills, Michigan: Cranbrook Institute of Science, Bulletin No. 35, 1954. 185p.
The origins and development of Hopi and Zuni rituals and the changes brought by the White culture described. Short history of the Hopi.

335   DOZIER, EDWARD P. The Pueblo Indians of North America. New York: Holt, Rinehart & Winston, 1970. 224p.
A classic history and cultural interpretation of the Pueblos written by a well-known cultural anthropologist, himself from the Santa Clara Pueblo. The Pueblos today and yesterday are discussed as well as traditional Pueblo society and culture. Notes, tables, and bibliography.

336   DRIVER, HAROLD E. Indians of North America, Second edition, revised. Chicago: University of Chicago Press, 1969. 632p.
A widely encompassing anthropological approach to the civilization of the North American Indians, a standard resource text. Chapter headings include: Language, Subsistence patterns, Art, Government, Education, and Religion. Also Indian/White Relations in the United States and Indian Culture Change. 45 maps and an extensive bibliography. Reprint of 1961 edition.

337   DUTTON, BERTHA P. Indians of the American Southwest. New York: Prentice-Hall, November, 1974.

338   EASTMAN, CHARLES ALEXANDER. Red Hunters and the Animal People. New York: Harper and Brothers, 1904. 248p.
Hunter and warrior tales and Sioux legends about animals are described.

339   EGGAN, FREDERICK RUSSELL. The American Indian; Perspectives for the Study of Social Change. Chicago: Aldine Publishing Company, 1966. 193p.
Lectures covering such sociological subjects as the Cheyenne concept of ecology, its relationship to society,

(EGGAN, FREDERICK RUSSELL)
and the pressured acculturation of the Choctaws. Bibliography.

340   ERIKSON, ERIK H. Childhood and Society, second edition, revised and enlarged. New York: W. W. Norton, 1963. 445p.
       Part Two is an examination of childhood in two Indian tribes: the Sioux and the Yurok. Shows how childhood training forms the cultural outlook of adult peoples. Revision of the 1950 edition, now considered classic.

341   FARB, PETER. Man's Rise to Civilization as Shown by the Indians of North America From the Primeval Times to the Coming of the Industrial State. New York: E. P. Dutton and Comapny, 1968. 332p.
       A study of North American Indians by a cultural anthropologist interested in demonstrating the evolution of human development in terms of social change and environmental adaptation. Deals with acculturalation and adaptation and ends with a plea for the preservation of primitive cultures. Notes, sources, and bibliography. An informative book. This has received praise in academic reviews, but many Indians do not like this book.

342   FELDMANN, SUSAN, ed. The Storytelling Stone: Myths and Tales of the American Indians. New York: Dell, 1971. 271p.
       Myths and tales for the general reader using such themes as the origin of the earth and man, the theft of fire, and flood.

343   FENTON, WILLIAM N. American Indian and White Relations to 1830. New York: Russell & Russell, 1957. 138p.
       Essay attempts to combine two traditional White approaches to the study of Indian life: that of the humanistic historian, and that of the anthropologist or ethnologist. Seeks a view of the Indian both in terms of White culture and in terms of his own culture. Large bibliography appended to the essay is provided to back up the perspective developed.

344   FERGUSSON, ERNA. Dancing Gods: Indian Ceremonials of New Mexico and Arizona. Albuquerque: University of New Mexico Press, 1966. 286p.
       A personalized account of the tribal religious ceremonies of the Pueblo peoples, the Navajos, the Zunis, and the Apaches. Reprint of 1931 edition.

NATIVE AMERICANS

FISCHER, ANTHONY D. See 395.

345 FLETCHER, ALICE CUNNINGHAM. Indian Games and Dances with
Native Songs, Arranged From American Indian Ceremonials
and Sports. Boston: C. C. Birchard and Company,
1915. 137p.
These are games especially for boys and girls.

346 FORBES, JACK D. Apache, Navajo, Spaniard. Norman: University of Oklahoma Press, 1960. 304p.
The interrelationships of the three cultural groups when
they had to live with one another and the adjustments they
had to make in order to do so. Part of The Civilization of
the American Indian series, v. 115.

347 FREDERICK, CALVIN J. Suicide, Homicide, and Alcoholism Among
American Indians: Guidelines for Help. Washington, D. C.:
U. S. Government Printing Office, 1973. 36p.
Brief study prepared by the National Institute of Mental
Health, Center for Studies of Crime and Delinquency.

348 GEARING, FREDERICK O. The Face of the Fox. Chicago: Aldine
Publishing Company, 1970. 158p.
Traces the changes in viewpoint of a young anthropologist living with the Fox Indians. A particularly important book for newcomers to ethnic studies.

349 GILLHAM, CHARLES E. Beyond the Clapping Mountains; Eskimo
Stories from Alaska. New York: Mcmillan, 1943. 134p.
Thirteen stories simplified for children but authentic
and engaging in style. Illustrations by the Eskimo artist,
Chanimun.

350 GLASS, PAUL. Songs and Stories of the North American Indians,
With Rhythm Indications for Drum Accompaniment. New York:
Grosset and Dunlap, 1968. 61p.
Pawnee, Sioux, Pagago, Yuma, and Mandan drum music.

351 GRIFFIS, JOSEPH K. (TAHAN). Indian Story Circle Stories.
Burlington, Vermont: Free Press Printing Company,
1928. 138p.
Tales from storytellers of the Kiowa, Cherokee, Choctax,
and Malecite tribes.

352 GRINNELL, GEORGE BIRD. By Cheyenne Campfires. Lincoln:
University of Nebraska Press, 1971. [1926] 305p.
The folktales of the Cheyenne as told to a noted anthro-
pologist during his residence during the winter months

(GRINNELL, GEORGE BIRD)
with the Cheyenne. Includes stories of heroes, their wars, and their relationship with supernatural powers.

GUIE, HEISTER D. See 387.

353 HAINES, FRANCIS. The Buffalo. New York: Crowell, 1970. 242p.
The natural domain of the American buffalo and this animal's relationship to the American Indians are traced. The great slaughter and near extinction of this once powerful species are depicted with many good illustrations. Bibliography.

354 HALE, HORATIO EMMONS. The Iroquois Book of Rites. New York: AMS Press, 1969. 222p.
Iroquois, Mohawk, and Onondaga texts. 1883 reprint of what was originally No. 2 of the Library of Aboriginal American Literature.

355 HANKE, LEWIS. Aristotle and the American Indian: A Study in Race Prejudice in the Modern World. Bloomington: Indiana University Press, 1970. 164p.
An enlightening study of the Spanish conquest of the "New World" and the resulting racial prejudice and genocide perpetrated upon Native Americans. Bibliographic notes. Reprint of 1959 edition.

356 HARVARD UNIVERSITY. Peabody Museum of American Archaeology and Ethnology. Papers. Cambridge, Massachusetts: Peabody Museum, 1888–
Excellent series of articles and studies, with much work devoted to the American Indians from art to dress styles, to religious artifacts. Bibliography.

357 HEIZER, ROBERT FLEMING and M. A. WHIPPLE, comps. The California Indians: A Source Book. Berkeley: University of California Press, 1971. 619p.
A good source book of articles in various categories such as history and ethnography. Reference bibliography. Reprint of 1951 edition.

358 HODGE, FREDERICK WEBB, ed. Handbook of Indians North of Mexico. New York: Greenwood Press, 1969. 2 vols.
Although "dated" this handbook is cherished as neither handy nor a book, but rather a compendium of exhaustive details about Indian tribes, their folklore, history, art, customs, and their famous. Approved by the American

NATIVE AMERICANS

(HODGE, FREDERICK WEBB)
Indian Historical Society because of its accuracy and
references to primary source material. There is a bibliography in volume 2. Reprint of 1907 edition.

HOLDER, PRESTON. See 313, 402.

359   HUNT, WOLF R. The Dancing Horses of Acoma, and Other Acoma
Indian Stories. Cleveland: World Publishing Company,
1963. 163p.
An Acoma storyteller's accounts of heroes, animals, and
supernatural powers. Primarily for children.

360   IGAUER, EDITH. The New People; The Eskimo's Journey Into
Our Times. New York: Doubleday and Company, 1966. 205p.
Discusses the Eskimo's efforts to exist in his own
culture while trying to adapt to the White world.

IRVING, MARY B. See 405.

361   JORGENSEN, JOSEPH G. The Sun Dance Religion: Power for the
Powerless. Chicago: University of Chicago Press,
1972. 360p.
A political and economic analysis of the Sun Dance and
the effect it plays on the Utes and Shoshones' sense of
hope and power. Many references and tables and a
bibliography.

362   JOSEPHY, ALVIN M., JR. The Indian Heritage of America. New
York: Alfred A. Knopf, 1968. 384p.
Archeology, ethnology, and history are woven together
in this compendium about Indian tribes of both North and
South America from prehistory to the present. Bibliography.

KILPATRICK, ANNA GRITTS. See 363.

363   KILPATRICK, JACK FREDERICK and ANNA GRITTS KILPATRICK, eds.
Friends of Thunder, Folktales of the Oklahoma Cherokees.
Dallas: Southern Methodist University Press, 1964. 197p.
A collection of stories taken down by the Kilpatricks
from members of their own tribe.

364   _____. Run Toward the Nightland: Magic of the Oklahoma
Cherokees. Dallas: Southern Methodist University Press,
1967. 197p.
A volume of medicine and magic formulas with musical
notation and verse translation by the Kilpatricks.

365   KIMBALL, YEFFE and JEAN ANDERSON. The Art of American Indian
Cooking. Garden City, New York: Doubleday and Company,

62

(KIMBALL, YEFFE and JEAN ANDERSON)
1965. 215p.
Recipes for easy cooking of such delicacies as salmon chowder, sunflower seed soup, and fresh corn puffs, plus many of the usual standards of Indian cooking.

KING, JEFF. See 322.

366   KLUCKHOHN, CLYDE and DOROTHEA LEIGHTON. The Navaho, revised edition. New York: Natural History Library. Garden City, New York: Natural History Library, 1962. 355p.
History economics, religion, and social structure are discussed in this comprehensive study by two famous anthropologists. A quick comparison of Navaho and English is given to show the differing thought processes which created each language and are necessary to understand them. Bibliography. Reprint of 1942 edition.

367   _____. The Navaho Door, revised edition. Cambridge: The Harvard University Press, 1973.
An introduction to daily Navaho life and custom. First edition in 1944.

368   KLUCKHOHN, CLYDE. Navaho Witchcraft. Boston: Beacon Press, 1967. 254p.
Describes witchcraft and magic and analyzes the Navaho rites related to them. Bibliography. Reprint of 1944 edition.

KLUCKHOHN, LUCY WALES. See 436.

369   KROEBER, ALFRED LOUIS. Handbook of the Indians of California. Berkeley: California Book Company, 1967. 995p.
A facsimile of a U. S. Bureau of American Ethnology Bulletin and is put here as an example of the Bureau's and the anthropologist's work. Maps and charts. Reprint of 1925 edition.

370   KROEBER, THEODORA. The Inland Whale. Bloomington: Indiana University Press, 1959. 205p.
A charming collection of California Indian tales.

KUNITZ, STEPHEN J. See 377.

371   LA BARRE, WESTON. The Peyote Cult, enlarged edition. New York: Schocken Books, 1969. 260p.
A study on the ethnology of peyotism. Discusses the Native American Church and other peyote churches. Also covers the botanical, physiological, and psychological aspects of peyote. Reprint of 1959 edition.

NATIVE AMERICANS

372 LASKI, VERA. Seeking Life. Philadephia: American Folklore
        Society, 1958. 176p.
            Insights into Pueblo religion, culture, and philosophy
        given through a presentation of the Rain god Ceremony at
        San Juan Pueblo and a description of the making of a medi-
        cine man. Bibliography.

373 LAVINE, SIGMUND A. The Games the Indians Played. New York:
        Dodd, Mead and Company, 1974. 93p.
            Discusses the games played by the North and Central
        American Indians such as lacrosse, cat's cradle, dice
        games, and horse racing.

374 LEACOCK, ELEANOR BURKE and NANCY O. LURIE, eds. North Ameri-
        can Indians in Historical Perspective. New York: Random
        House, 1971. 498p.
            An excellent selection of articles by experts in con-
        temporary American Indian sociology, history, and anthro-
        pology. Bibliography. Highly recommended.

375 LEIGHTON, ALEXANDER H. and DOROTHEA LEIGHTON. The Navaho
        Door. Cambridge: Harvard University Press, 1944.
            Administrative and medical policies of the United States
        government and the results of these among the Navaho
        peoples with good discussions of the effect of the govern-
        ment's attempts at socialization and acculturation. Offi-
        cial policy during the 1940s. Bibliography.

     LEIGHTON, DOROTHEA. See 366, 367.

376 LEVINE, STUART and NANCY O. LURIE, eds. The American Indian
        Today, revised edition. Baltimore: Pelican Books,
        1970. 352p.
            A collection of essays by Indian and White anthropolo-
        gists who examine the problems confronting the contempor-
        ary American Indian. Very highly recommended.

377 LEVY, JERROLD E. and STEPHEN J. KUNITZ. Indian Drinking:
        Navajo Practices and Anglo-American Theories. New York:
        John Wiley and Sons, 1974. 257p.
            Alcoholism seen as a deviance. Included are personal
        stories of involvement with alcohol. Bibliography.

378 LIGHTHALL, J. I. The Indian Folk Medicine Guide. New York:
        Popular Library, 1972. 158p.
            A famous Indian medicine man here describes nearly 100
        organic remedies from roots, flowers, barks, leaves, and
        herbs. Reprint of 1883 edition.

379   LINK, MARGARET S.   The Pollen Path; A Collection of Navajo
         Myths Retold.   Stanford, California: Stanford University
         Press, 1956.   205p.
            Stories taken from religious ceremonials and chantways
         and tribal storytellers.   Some of the material is a re-
         working of the primary sources recorded by Washington
         Matthews.

380   LOWIE, ROBERT H.   Indians of the Plains.   New York: Natural
         History Press, 1963.   358p.
            An organized study of the Plains Indian culture.
         Reprint of 1955 edition.

      LURIE, NANCY O.   See 374, 376.
      McLEAN, ROBERT E.   See 414.

381   MARRIOTT, ALICE and CAROL K. RACHLIN.   American Indian
         Mythology.   New York: New American Library, 1972.   211p.
            More than twenty major American Indian tribes are re-
         presented in this anthology of myths and legends.   Bibliog-
         raphy.   Reprint of 1968 edition.

382   MARRIOTT, ALICE.   Saynday's People: The Kiowa Indians and
         The Stories They Told.   Lincoln: University of Nebraska
         Press, 1967.   226p.
            Divided into two sections: the first is a collection
         of myths and stories dealing with the Creator, Saynday;
         the second section describes the life and culture of the
         Plains Indians.   Drawn from the experiences of the author
         with the Kiowa Indians of Southwestern Oklahoma and at-
         tempts an overall picture of the Indians of the Great
         Plains.

      MASSON, MARCELLE.   See 422.

383   MATHEWS, JOHN JOSEPH.   Wah'Ko N-Tah: The Osage and the
         White Man's Road.   Norman: University of Oklahoma Press,
         1969.   359p.
            This is Mathews' most famous book.   Wah'Kon-Tah means
         great mystery, something not understood, the great god
         spirit that is in the sun, wind, and all living things.
         This is the recreated story of Major Laban J. Miles who
         came to the Osages in 1878 as their agent and who died
         there in 1931.   Mathews draws on his notes and other
         records.   Reprint of 1932 edition.

NATIVE AMERICANS

384   MATHEWS, WASHINGTON, collector. <u>Navaho Legends</u>. New York:
       Kraus Reprint Company, 1969.
           Mathews collected much Navaho material and is consid-
       ered the leading anthropologist of his time in this area.
       Reprint of 1897 edition.

       MAYOKUK, ROBERT. <u>See</u> 323.

385   MEAD, MARGARET. <u>The Changing Culture of an Indian Tribe</u>, with
       a new introduction by the author. New York: Capricorn
       Books, 1966. 313p.
           Claims that the impact of a modern culture upon a Plains
       Indian tribe leads to conditions of disequilibrium. Case
       studies of 25 delinquent Indian women. Worth reading to
       see how viewpoint has changed since the thirties. Consid-
       ered to have a White bias. Reprint of 1932 edition.

386   MOONEY, JAMES. <u>The Ghost-Dance Religion and the Sioux Out-
       break of 1890</u>. Chicago: University of Chicago Press,
       1970. 359p.
           A classic investigation of the millenial cult conducted
       by the author for the Bureau of American Ethnology. Des-
       criptive of many aspects of the phenomenon and carefully
       written.

387   MOURNING DOVE. <u>Coyote Stories</u>, edited by Heister D. Guie.
       Caldwell, Idaho: Caxton Printers, 1933. 228p.
           Grandfather stories about Coyote, that trickster, told
       informally and colorfully.

388   MURPHEY, EDITH VAN ALLEN. <u>Indian Uses of Native Plants.</u>
       Fort Bragg, California: Mendocino County Historical
       Society, 1959. 72p.
           A survey of native plants and how they were used for
       medicines, dyes, tanning, and other purposes.
       Bibliography.

389   NEQUATEWA, EDMUND. <u>Truth of A Hopi: Stories Relating to
       The Origin, Myths, and Clan Histories of The Hopi</u>. Flag-
       staff: Northland Press, 1973. 136p.
           Clan histories and myths retold. Bibliography. Reprint
       of 1936 edition.

390   NETTL, BRUNO. <u>North American Indian Musical Styles</u>. Phila-
       delphia: American Folklore Society, 1954. 51p.
           Memoirs of the American Folklore Society, Volume 45.
       A serious study of American Indian music. Bibliography.

NEWCOMB, FRANK J. See 324.

391 NIETHAMER, CAROLYN. American Indian Food and Lore: 150
Authentic Recipes. New York: Macmillian, 1974. 191p.
Indian foods of the Southwest and the ethnobotany of
the area. Wassaja (August, 1974) claims not all the recipes are authentic and several involving acorns and piñon
nuts do not give the proper preparations before using so
that they can be dangerous to eat or poisonous.

OAKES, MAUD. See 322.

392 ORTIZ, ALFONSO, ed. New Perspectives on the Pueblos. Albuquerque: University of New Mexico Press, 1972. 340p.
A Native American anthropologist has collected articles
that deal with a wide range of topics such as ethnohistory
and ethnomusicology. Bibliography.

393 _____. The Tewa World. Chicago: University of Chicago
Press, 1969. 197p.
A noted Indian anthropologist writes about his heritage.
Bibliography.

394 OSWALT, WENDELL H. This Land Was Theirs: A Study of the
North American Indian. New York: J. Wiley and Sons,
1966. 560p.
Ten tribes are studied, each selected to represent a
geographical region of the United States and Alaska.
Bibliography.

395 OWEN, ROBERT C., JAMES J. F. DEETZ, ANTHONY D. FISCHER, comps.
The North American Indians, A Source-Book. New York:
Macmillan, 1967. 752p.
Besides articles, contains a bibliography of films on
Native Americans.

396 OWL, MS. SAMSON. Catawba Texts, edited by Frank G. Speck.
New York: Columbia University Press, Columbia University
Contributions to Anthropology, XXIV, 1934.
Both Catawba and English translations presented in this
series of stories by Ms. Owl and others.

397 PARKER, ARTHUR CASWELL. The History of the Seneca Indians.
Port Washington, New York: I. J. Friedman, 1967. 162p.
Parker was a famous Senecan anthropologist. Most of
his writings are now being reprinted. Reprint of 1926
edition.

NATIVE AMERICANS

398   PARKER, ARTHUR CASWELL. <u>Seneca Myths and Folk Tales</u>.
       Buffalo: Buffalo Historical Society, 1923. Buffalo His-
       torical Society Publications, Vol. 27. 465p.
          Collection of the mythic and folktales of his people.
       Parker was an anthropologist who lived both in the tribal
       and academic worlds.

399   PARSONS, ELSIE CLEWS, ed. <u>American Indian Life</u>. Lincoln:
       University of Nebraska Press, 1967. 419p.
          An anthropological folklore anthology with a variety of
       articles by leading scholars. Sections cover tribes from
       the Eskimo to the Mexican. Notes and bibliography. Re-
       print of 1922 edition.

400   PHINNEY, ARCHIE. <u>Nez Perce Texts</u>. New York: Columbia Uni-
       versity Press, Columbia University Contributions to Anthro-
       pology, XXV, 1934. 497p.
          Nez Perce and English texts of Mr. Phinney's collection
       of tales told by his mother, Wayilatpu.

401   PIETROFORTE, ALFRED. <u>Songs of the Yokuts and Paiutes</u>.
       Healdsburg, California: Naturegraph Press, 1965, 64p.
          Songs gathered through tape-recorded interviews in the
       field, attempt to provide an introduction to the methods
       and substance of the music of the California Indian. A
       tape of the songs can be obtained from the publisher.

402   POWELL, J. W. <u>Indian Linguistic Families of America North of
       Mexico</u>. Edited by Preston Holder. Lincoln: University
       of Nebraska Press, 1966. 83-221ps.
          American Indian language is divided into linguistic
       stocks or families and compared. The second part of a book
       shared with Franz Boas on language. Reprint of 1891
       edition.

403   PROCTOR, EDNA DEAN. <u>The Song of the Ancient People</u>. Boston
       and New York: Houghton & Mifflin and Company, 1893. 69p.
          Artistic book about Pueblo Indians with eleven aquatints
       by Julian Scott.

       RACHLIN, CAROL. <u>See</u> 381.

404   RADIN, PAUL. <u>The Trickster; A Study in American Indian
       Mythology</u>. New York: Bell Publications Company,
       1965. 211p.
          Good study of the religion and mythology of the Winne-
       bago Indians. Reprint of 1956 edition.

405 ROBBINS, MAURICE and MARY B. IRVING. The Amateur Archaeol-
    ogist's Handbook. New York: Thomas Y. Crowell Company,
    1973. 288p.
        Shows how to survey a site, acquire maps, digging,
    dating artifacts, and restoring the finds. A site at New
    Bedford, Massachusetts is used as a case study. Practical
    guide to archaelogical methods. Bibliography. Reprint
    of 1965 edition.

406 ROE, FRANK GILBERT. The Indian and the Horse. Norman:
    University of Oklahoma Press, 1968. 434p.
        A rather artistic and sensitive narrative concerning
    the relationship of the Indian and his horse. Involves
    the acquisition of the horse, Indian cultivation and
    breeding, as well as various uses of the horse. Inter-
    laced with some of the more famous Indian-horse paintings.
    Reprint of 1955 edition.

407 ROESSEL, ROBERT A., JR. Coyote Stories of the Navaho People.
    Rough Rock, Arizona: Navaho Curriculum Center, 1968. 141p.
        Designed and published primarily for use by Navaho chil-
    dren. This collection of tales is excellent and includes
    charming illustrations.

408 ROESSEL, RUTH, comp. Papers on Navajo Culture and Life.
    Tsaile Lake, Arizona: Navajo Community College Press,
    1970. 193p.
        A variety of articles which include the autobiography
    of a Navajo weaver, the hogan, Indian power and Indian
    unity, and teaching and education.

409 SANDOZ, MARI. These Were the Sioux. New York: Hastings
    House, 1961. 118p.
        Traces the processes of development of a boy and girl
    in traditional Sioux culture from birth to manhood and
    womanhood; relies on personal experience of growing up
    with Sioux.

410 SCHOOLCRAFT, HENRY R. Indian Legends from Algic Researches
    (The Myth of Hiawatha, Oneota, The Red Race in America and
    Historical and Statistical Information Respecting the Indi-
    an Tribes of the United States). Edited by Mentor L.
    Williams. East Lansing: Michigan State University Press,
    1956. 322p.
        A compilation of three volumes of Schoolcraft's writings
    from 1839 to 1856. Publication records are given at the
    end of each story. Schoolcraft has had much influence not
    only on writers (Longfellow) but also on anthropologists.

NATIVE AMERICANS

SCOTT, JULIAN. See 403.

411   SETON, ERNEST THOMPSON AND JULIA M. SETON. The Gospels of
        the Redman: A Way of Life. Brooklyn, New York: Theo.
        Gaus' Sons Incorporated, 1966. 108p.
            An attempt to present the basic tenets and unwritten
        faith and beliefs of Indian thought in a short, simplified
        form. Reprint of 1963 edition.

SETON, JULIA M. See 411.

412   SIMPSON, GEORGE E. and MILTON YINGER, eds. The American
        Indian and American Life. Millwood, New York: Kraus
        Reprint Company, 1973. 226p.
            A compendium of anthropological articles on Indian
        culture, Indian integration, and tribal relationships with
        the Federal government. Emphasizes the place of Indians in
        American life. They are particularly concerned with the
        government's constantly changing attitude towards the Indi-
        ans. Reprint of 1957 edition.

413   SMITHSONIAN Institution. Annual Report. Washington, D. C.:
        U. S. Government Printing Office, 1853--.
            Reports contain many materials about Native Americans.
        Among other government documents, try also: U. S. Board
        of Indian Commissioners Annual Report (1869--) U. S. Bureau
        of American Ethnology Annual Report (1879/80) to 1900/31.

SPECK, FRANK G. See 396.

414   SQUIRES, JOHN L. and MC LEAN, ROBERT E. American Indian
        Dances: Steps, Rhythms, Costumes and Interpretation.
        New York: Ronald Press, 1965. 132p.
            Many illustrations accompany the descriptions of North
        American Indian dance costumes.

415   STARKLOFF, CARL F. People of the Center: American Indian
        Religion and Christianity. New York: Seabury Press, 1974.

416   STEIGER, BRAD. Medicine Power: The American Indian's Revival
        of His Spiritual Heritage and Its Relevance for Modern
        Man. Garden City, New York: Doubleday and Company,
        1974. 226p.
            Suggests that the psycho-religious systems of the var-
        ious tribes were centuries ahead of the White man's psy-
        chology and medicine. Explores what past and present In-
        dian mystics and prophets say about man's future. Also
        included are surveys of herbal medicine, consciousness

(STEIGER, BRAD)
altering drugs, rituals designed to enhance psychic powers, and the role of prophecy. A fascinating analysis of the Amerindian religion in light of current parapsychological research.

417 STONE, ERIC. Medicine Among the American Indians. New York: Hafner Publishing Company, 1962. 139p. Bibliography.

418 STORM, HYEMEYOHSTS. Seven Arrows. New York: Harper and Row, 1972. 371p.
A mystic book explaining the Great Balancing Harmony of the Total Universe, the Breath of Wisdom, and Universal Understanding in terms of Cheyenne traditions. Interspersed with reproductions of fine old photographs and colored Cheyenne Shields.
The Indian Historian (Vol. 5:2), however, attacks this book for being a fraud, and Wassaja (August, 1974) reports that Cheyenne traditionalists have denounced the book and doubted that the author is Cheyenne as he claimed to be.

419 SWANTON, JOHN REED. The Indians of the Southeastern United States. Grosse Pointe, Michigan: Scholarly Press, 1969. 943p.
Ethnological study of the Southeastern Indians by a leading scientist. Includes a description of the geography of the area and the Indian population. The greater part of the work is devoted to a discussion and description of the tribes, their language, food, horticulture, housing, clothing, ornamentation, and their arts. Perhaps the best part of the work includes the last few chapters on social and ceremonial life. Reprint of 1946 edition.

TAHAN. See 351.

420 TERRELL, JOHN UPTON. The Navajos: The Past and Present of a Great People. New York: Harper & Row, 1970. 310p.
A combination historical and anthropological study that presents a factual picture of the Navajo Indians, past and present. Select bibliography.

421 THOMPSON, STITH, comp. Tales of the North American Indians. Bloomington: Indiana University Press, 1966. 386p.
Still one of the better collections. Annotated and with a good bibliography. Reprint of 1929 edition.

NATIVE AMERICANS

422   TOWENDOLLY, GRANT. <u>A Bag of Bones.</u> Healdsburg, California: Naturegraph Publishers, n. d. Edited by Marcelle Masson. 130p.
     The legends and myths of a tribe of Northern California Indians.

423   TRAVELLER BIRD. <u>The Path to Snowbird Mountain.</u> New York: Farrar, Straus and Giroux, 1972. 87p.
     Legends of Eastern Cherokees about Snowbird Mountain of North Carolina, remembered from their telling during old reunions.

424   UNDERHILL, RUTH M. <u>Red Man's Religion.</u> Chicago: University of Chicago Press, 1965. 301p.
     A survey of the religious customs and rituals of various tribes and the importance of religion in their lives.

425   VAUDRIN, BILL. <u>Tanaina Tales From Alaska.</u> Norman: University of Oklahoma Press, 1969. 133p.
     A collection of grandfather tales from Alaska, as told by a Chippewa.

426   VELARDE, PABLITA. <u>Old Father, The Story Teller.</u> Globe, Arizona: Dale Stuart King, 1960. 66p.
     Family stories retold by a Pueblo Indian artist from Santa Clara.

427   VIZENOR, GERALD, ed. <u>Anishinabe Adisokan.</u> <u>Tales of the People</u>. Minneapolis: Nodin Press, 1970. 149p.
     A collection of folktales originally published before the turn of the 20th century in <u>Progress</u>, a weekly newspaper of the White Earth Reservation. Composed of tales of the Woodland people, or the Anishinabe. A good primary sampler.

428   VOGEL, VIRGIL J. <u>American Indian Medicine</u>. Norman: University of Oklahoma Press, 1970. 583p.
     Shows the effect of Indian medicinal practices on White civilization. A thorough and provocative book. Bibliography.

429   VOGT, EVON Z. and ALBERT, ETHEL M., eds. <u>People of Rimrock: A Study of Values in Five Cultures</u>. New York: Atheneum. 1970. 342p.
     A comprehensive report on the Rimrock region of New Mexico and the interrelationship of the various cultures and values found there, especially that of the Zuni and

(VOGT, EVON Z. and ALBERT, ETHEL M.)
Navaho Indians versus the European-introduced people.
Bibliography.

430   WADDELL, JACK O. and WATSON, MICHAEL, eds. The American
      Indian in Urban Society. Boston: Little, Brown and Com-
      pany, 1971 414p.
          A collection of essays by nine anthropologists and one
      Native American in an attempt to discover and analyze the
      role and problems facing the American Indian in an urban-
      izing America and within the urban city itself.

431   WATERS, FRANK. Masked Gods: Navaho and Pueblo Ceremonialism.
      Chicago: Swallow Press, 1950. 438p.
          An account of the significance of ceremonialism. Inter-
      prets the mythic and symbolic meanings of the rituals and
      delves into the values of Southwest religion and the Pueblo
      philosophy of life.

WATSON, MICHAEL. See 430.
WAYILATPU. See 400.

432   WEBB, GEORGE. A Pima Remembers. Tucson: University of
      Arizona Press, 1965. 126p.
          Pima stories as recorded by a young Pima who was upset
      that so few of his generation could remember their oral
      inheritance. Reprint of 1959 edition.

433   WELTFISH, GENE. The Lost Universe. The Way of Life of the
      Pawnee. New York: Ballantine Books, 1971. 617p.
          A reconstruction of the Pawnee Indians culture and life
      style as it existed in the late 1860s. A thorough and
      extensive attempt to present a whole and entirely differ-
      ent world that has been lost to history. Reprint of 1965
      edition.

WHIPPLE, M. A. See 357.
WILLIAMS, MENTOR. See 410.

434   WILSON, EDMUND. Apologies to the Iroquois. New York: Vin-
      tage Books, 1966. 310p.
          Reprint of Wilson's articles which originally appeared
      in the New Yorker magazine. Tells about the politics and
      culture of the Iroquois Nation-- the Senecas, the Tuscar-
      oras, etc. Also includes "The Mohawks in High Steel" by
      Joseph Mitchell. A very well-written book.

NATIVE AMERICANS

435   WISE, JENNINGS C. The Red Man in the New World Drama, revised
      and updated. New York: Macmillan, 1971. G23p.
      Discusses the interrelationships of Indians and Whites
      in religion and politics, a complicated mix, in both the
      19th and 20th centuries.

436   WISSLER, CLARK. Indians of the United States: Four Centuries
      of Their History and Culture, revised by Lucy Wales Kluck-
      hohn. Garden City, New York: Doubleday and Company,
      1965. 336p.
      A comprehensive and basic textbook summarizing the cul-
      tural life of the various tribes. The book is divided into
      three parts: Prehistoric, Great Indian families, Indian
      life in general. Bibliography. Reprint of 1940 edition.

      YINGER, MILTON. See 412.

437   ZUNI PEOPLE. The Zunis: Self-Portrayals. Albuquerque:
      University of New Mexico Press, 1972. 245p.
      Forty-six stories of myth, prophecy, and history from
      the oral literature of the Zuni Indians of New Mexico.
      Represents only a fraction of the Zuni literature.

      F.   Literature by and about Native Americans
(Anthologies, Autobiography, Biography, Captivity Narratives, Drama,
   Literary Criticism and History, Oratory, Poetry and Prose)

      ALLEN, HENRY. See 497.

438   ALLEN, HERVEY. The Forest and the Fort. New York: Dell
      Books, 1943. 447p.
      Novel about the American frontier and the Indians.
      Gripping, lusting story, good for the study of American
      pioneer and Indian stereotypes.

      ALLEN, T. D. See 547.

439   ALLEN, TERRY. The Whispering Wind: Poetry by Young Ameri-
      can Indians. New York: Doubleday and Company, 1972. 128p.
      Biographical sketches of each author given with each
      individual collection of poems.

440   ALWORTH, E. PAUL. Will Rogers. New York: Twayne Publishers,
      1974. 236p.
      Rogers, who was part American Indian, was always proud
      of his heritage. For, as he said, when you folks came over,
      my folks met the boat. This is a study of the famous
      comic's newspaper columns, published in the twenties and
      thirties.

441   AMERICAN INDIAN Historical Society. The American Indian
      Reader. San Francisco: The Indian Historian Press,
      1971-   . 5 vols.
           To date there are five volumes in this series which sur-
      vey the following areas: anthropology, education, litera-
      ture; the poets and storytellers, and history; current
      affairs. Recognized authorities in these various fields
      form the bulk of the selections. Bibliographies.

442   ANDREWS, RALPH W. Indian Leaders Who Helped Shape America,
      1600-1900. Seattle: Superior Publishing 1971. 184p.
           Illustrations and a bibliography.

443   ARMER, LAURA ADAMS. Southwest. London: Longmans, Green
      and Company, 1935. 224p.
           The autobiography of a well-known writer of children's
      Indian stories.

444   ARMSTRONG, VIRGINIA IRVING, comp. I Have Spoken; American
      History Through the Voices of the Indians. Chicago:
      Sage Books, 1971. 206p.
           A collection of oratory from the 17th through the 20th
      centuries. Emphasis placed on speeches focusing on Indi-
      an/white relationships, especially treaty negotiations. A
      few letters and other writings also included.

445   ARNOLD, ELLIOT. Blood Brother. New York: Duell, Sloan and
      Pearce, 1947. 558p.
           A fictitious history of Cochise, chief of the Chirica-
      hua Apaches, and his efforts to save his people from
      extinction.

446   ASTROV, MARGOT, ed. American Indian Prose and Poetry: An
      Anthology. New York: Capricorn Books, 1962. 366p.
           One of the first, and still one of the best of the col-
      lections of American Indian prose and poetry. Divided by
      geographical regions. Notes. Reprint of 1946 edition.

447   AUSTIN, MARY. American Rhythm: Studies and Reexpressions of
      Amerindian Songs. New York: Cooper Square Publishers,
      1970. 174p.
           Mary Austin devoted her life to the Southwest experi-
      ence and to American Indian culture. This book contains
      the interesting theory that American writing by Anglos as
      well as by Indians has been strongly influenced by the
      continental land rhythmns. Reprint of 1930 edition.

NATIVE AMERICANS

448   AUSTIN, MARY. <u>The Arrow Maker: A Drama in Three Acts</u>, Rev.
      ed. New York: AMS Press, 1969. 168p.
         The original 1911 play was about an Indian hero, and
      struck the hearts of playgoers in America and Europe in
      the early twentieth century as representing the noble
      savage at his best.

449   BABCOCK, CLARENCE MERTON, comp. <u>Walk Quietly the Beautiful</u>
      <u>Trail: Lyrics and Legends of the American Indian</u>. Kansas
      City, Missouri: Hallmark, 1973. 61p.
         Translations of Indian Poetry.

450   BAIRD, W. DAVID. <u>Peter Pitchlynn: Chief of the Choctaws</u>.
      Norman: University of Oklahoma Press, 1972. 238p.
         The mixed-blood son of a White interpreter, Peter Pitch-
      lynn assumed an important role in tribal affairs. He did
      much speculative buying of Kansas properties, but spent
      most of his time working in Washington, D. C.
      Bibliography.

451   BARNES, NELLIE. <u>American Indian Love Lyrics and Other Verse</u>;
      <u>From the Songs of the North American Indians</u>. New York:
      MacMillan, 1925. 190p.

      BARRETT, STEVEN M. <u>See</u> 501.
      BASS, ALTHEA. <u>See</u> 590.

452   BEDFORD, DENTON R. <u>Tsali</u>. San Francisco: The Indian His-
      torian Press, 1972. 252p.
         A true story written down by a Minsee Indian. It is
      about an unsung, religiously devout Cherokee hero who
      is finally shot on orders of the White military. Well-
      illustrated.

453   BELTING, NATALIA MAREE. <u>Our Fathers Had Powerful Songs</u>.
      New York: Dutton, 1974.
         Poems from various American Indian Tribes celebrating
      the creation and life of man.

454   _____, comp. <u>Whirlwind is a Ghost Dancing</u>. New York:
      Dutton, 1974. 30p.
         A collection of poems translated from Iroquois, Micmac,
      Shoshoni, and other Indian tribes.

455   BENNETT, KAY. <u>Kaibah: Recollections of a Navajo Girlhood</u>.
      Los Angeles: Westernlore Press, 1964. 253p.
         Navajo life during the 1930s.

456   BERGER, THOMAS. Little Big Man. New York: Dial Press,
      1964.
          Tells of a 111-year-old man's recollections of the Indi-
      an wars, his growing up as a captive of the Cheyenne, his
      recapture by the settlers, and his heroism on both sides
      of the battles. Very funny. Ultimate hero is the old
      Indian Chief, Old Lodge Skins.

457   BERRIGAN, TED. The Sonnets. New York: "C" Press, 1964.
      Unpaged.
          Poems by a Choctaw Irishman.

458   BIERHORST, JOHN. Four Masterworks of American Indian Liter-
      ature. New York: Farrar, Straus and Giroux, 1974. 371p.
          A translated collection. Includes: "Quetzalcoatl,"
      "The Ritual of Condolence," and "The Night Chant" of the
      Navajos among the listings. Bibliography.

459   _____, ed. In the Trail of the Wind: American Indian Poems
      and Ritual Orations. New York: Farrar, Straus and Giroux,
      1971. 201p.
          American Indian poetry under various general topics such
      as war, home, deer, and death. A good introduction to
      the oral tradition. Sources and explanatory notes.

      BLACK ELK. See 553.

460   BLACK HAWK. Black Hawk: An Autobiography, edited by Donald
      Jackson. Urbana: University of Illinois Press,
      1964. 177p.
          The Sauk chief's version of his battles with other
      tribes and with the U. S. Cavalry. Reprint of 1833
      edition.

461   BORLAND, HAL GLEN. When the Legends Die. Philadelphia:
      Lippincott, 1963. 288p.
          The story of a broncobuster who was brought up in tra-
      ditional Indian ways in the Colorado wilderness and who
      tried to make it in the White world.

462   BRANDON, WILLIAM, ed. The Magic World: American Indian
      Songs and Poems. New York: William Morrow and Company,
      1971. 145p.
          Songs and poems in lyric translation from all of North
      America. A fine book with which to start reading Indian
      poetry.

NATIVE AMERICANS

BRANT, CHARLES S. See 606.

463 BRINTON, DANIEL GARRISON. Aboriginal American Authors and
     Their Productions; Especially Those in the Native Language;
     A Chapter in the History of Literature. Philadelphia:
     1883, printed privately by author. 63p.
        Brinton, a well-known anthropologist of the turn of the
     century, translated and collected American Indian
     literatures.

BUFFALO BILL. See 560.

464 BUSCH, NIVEN. Duel in the Sun. New York: Bantam Books,
     1968. 207p.
        A popular novel about a wild, half-breed girl suggesting
     certain White stereotypes about Indian women as well as
     demonstrating the relationship of the Indians living near
     the Rio Grande river with their land and river. Reprint
     of 1966 edition.

CALLAWAY, SYDNEY M. See 517.

465 CAMPBELL, MARIA. Half-Breed. New York: Saturday Review
     Press, 1973. 157p.
        This is the story of Cheechum, Ms. Campbell's great
     grandmother, a Cree Indian who lived with the family when
     Maria was little and who became her role model for bravery
     and endurance.

466 CAPOTE, TRUMAN. In Cold Blood. New York: New American
     Library, 1965. 384p.
        Capote writes the true story of a Kansas family's
     murder by two young men, one part-Indian. The capture,
     trial, and execution of the killers brings out many in-
     herent prejudices against Indians.

467 CAPPS, BENJAMIN. A Woman of the People. Greenwich, Connect-
     icut: Fawcett Publication, Incorporated, 1968. 224p.
        In this popular novel, Helen Morrison is captured by
     the Comanches and adopted into the tribe, marries Burning
     Hand and finally is forced to come to terms with her desire
     to escape and return to White society and her love for her
     adopted people. Reprint of 1966 edition.

468 CARLSON, VADA F. Cochise: Chief of the Chiricahuas. Irving-
     ton-on-Hudson, New York: Harvey House, 1973. 174p.
        A biography of the Apache chief and distinguished
     warrior. Bibliography.

469 CASH, JOSEPH T. and HERBERT T. HOOVER, eds. To Be An Indian:
     An Oral History. New York: Holt, Rinehart and Winston,
     1971. 239p.
        This book reflects a new trend in the publishing and
     teaching business. It uses the oral tradition to bring
     you together with people where they happen to be. The
     interviews take pictures and transcribe their tapes so you
     are there with everybody, listening to their talk and
     seeing them in the middle of what they do. Consists of
     pictures and interviews with over fifty Native Americans
     (mainly from the South Dakota area) with focus on the
     following topics: Things that guide the people, reserva-
     tion life, depression, war, a revival of self-government,
     and today and tomorrow.

470 CATHER, WILLA. The Professor's House. New York: Alfred A.
     Knopf, 1925. 283p.
        Remarkable for its symbolic use of Southwest Indian
     materials. The professor's house, its isolation and the
     disintegration of a family are contrasted with Blue Mesa
     in the second section of the book called "Tom Outland's
     Story."

     CHALMERS, HARVEY. See 551.
     CHIEF JOSEPH. See 514.

471 CHONA, MARIA. Autobiography of a Papago Woman, edited by
     Ruth Underhill. Kraus Reproductions, 1969.
        The story of a Papago of Arizona as told to a famous
     American anthropologist. Reprint of 1936 edition.

472 CLARK, ANN NOLAN. Journey to the People. New York: Viking
     Press, 1969. 128p.
        A teacher of Indian children and a fine writer of chil-
     dren's books about Native Americans records her experiences.

     COCHISE. See 468.

473 COHEN, LEONARD. Beautiful Losers. New York: Viking Press,
     1966. 243p.
        A surreal novel about three surreal people, one of them
     the persona of Catherine Tekakwitha, an Iroquois girl who
     is up for sainthood as the first North American saint.
     Catherine, or Katerina, was a real historic personage and
     it is interesting to see what she symbolizes in the novel
     and what is happening to create an American folk figure
     out of her.

NATIVE AMERICANS

474   COOPER, JAMES FENIMORE. The Last of the Mohicans. Boston:
       Houghton, Mifflin, 1958. 372p.
              One of many editions of this classic example of racism
       in literature. Cooper is supposed to have set up the
       sterotypes of the "good" and "bad" Indians of American
       literature. The dialogue is stilted, but it's still a good
       adventure story and reflects all the social attitudes of
       the early nineteenth century. Noteworthy in this novel
       is the presence of Hawk Eye or Leatherstocking, an arche-
       typal character and hero of four other Cooper tales. Re-
       print of 1826 edition.

475   CORLE, EDWIN. Fig Tree John. New York: Liveright,
       1971. 310p.
              A fine novel about an Apache who migrates to the Salton
       Sea. Describes how he tries to bring up his son in the old
       ways and how his son becomes Americanized. Reprint of 1935
       edition.

476   CRASHING THUNDER. Crashing Thunder: The Autobiography of a
       Winnebago. Paul Radin, editor. New York: Dover Publica-
       tions, 1963. 91p.
              Sam Blowsnake told this tale about himself and Radin
       translated and wrote it down. It details his early life,
       the tribal ceremonies and customs, religious attitudes,
       and his tribe's relationship with the Whites. An impor-
       tant book because it was told at a time when the Winnebago
       culture was disintegrating but still not assimilated into
       the American dream. Reprint of 1920 edition.

       CRAZY HORSE. See 581.

477   CRONYN, GEORGE W., ed. American Indian Poetry: An Anthology
       of Songs and Chants. New York: Liveright, 1962. 360p.
              Translations of songs and chants, sectioned geograph-
       ically. The Indian Historian (Vol 4:1) feels this book
       leaves much to be desired but is valuable historically as
       a demonstration of Indian poetry as seen by a non-Indian.
       Reprint of 1918 edition.

478   COUTOSKI, VICTOR. Broken Treaties. New York: New Reviews
       Press, 1973. 85p.
              Poems. Distributed by Serendipity Books, 1790 Shattuck
       Avenue, Berkeley, California 94707.

479   CROOK, GEORGE. General George Crook, His Autobiography,
       edited by Martin E. Schmitt. Norman: University of Okla-
       homa Press, 1960. 326p.

(CROOK, GEORGE)
Tells of the famous general's life and his own account
of his campaigns against the Plains and Western Indians.
Reprint of 1946 edition.

480   CROW-WING. Memoirs. Menasha, Wisconsin: American Anthropological Society, 1925. 123p.
See also their publication American Anthropologist,
1888--. A Pueblo Indian journal of 1920-1921 that con-
centrated on Hopi Indian social life and customs.

481   CUERO, DELPHINA. The Autobiography of Delphina Cuero: A
Diegueño Indian. Florence C. Shipek, editor. Los Angeles:
Dawson's Book Shop, 1968. 67p.
The story of a traditional Indian woman's life in a
California tribal community.

482   CUSHMAN, DAN. Stay Away, Joe. New York: Bantam Books,
1968.
A modern stereotype of the lady-killing, broncobusting
Indian veteran who rides back to the reservation. Very
interesting depiction of the Indian hero. Reprint of 1953
edition.

483   CUSTER, ELIZABETH B. "Boots and Saddles" or, Life in Dakota
with General Custer. Norman: University of Oklahoma
Press, 1961. 312p.
The defense of General Custer and his reputation, as
written by his widow. Reprint of 1885 edition.

CUSTER, GEORGE ARMSTRONG. See 483.

484   CUSTER, GEORGE ARMSTRONG. My Life on the Plains. Edited by
Milo Milton Quaife. Lincoln: University of Nebraska
Press, 1971. 626p.
The text is taken directly from the magazine Galaxy's
series of articles of January 1872-October, 1874. Custer
is either a great hero or a heel, depending on which evidence the reader accepts. The current view of historians
is that he was not a great general. See the fictional
depiction of him as vain and foolish in Thomas Berger's
Little Big Man. Reprint of 1952 edition.

485   DAVES, FRANCIS M. Cherokee Woman. Boston: Brandon Press,
1973. 444p.
Focus on the Cherokee Removal of 1838.

NATIVE AMERICANS

486 DAVID, JAY, ed. The American Indian: The First Victim. New
York: William Morrow and Company, 1972. 192p.
Twenty-six selections of narrative, autobiography,
fiction, and poetry, almost all written by American Indians.

487 DAVIS, BRITTON. The Truth About Geronimo. New Haven: Yale
University Press, 1926. 253p. First Edition, 1929.
A recent biography of the Apache chief. Bibliography.

488 DAY, A. GROVE, ed. The Sky Clears: Poetry of the American
Indians. Lincoln: University of Nebraska Press,
1971. 204p.
Poetry of over forty American Indian tribes, arranged
geographically, in English translations along with excellent
discussions of the nature of such poetry. A fine bibliography. Reprint of 1951 edition.

489 DE ANGULO, JAIME. Indian Tales. New York: Hill and Wang,
1965. 246p.
A charming collection of Pit River folklore, illustrated
and fictionally reinterpreted by the author who lived with
the Pit Indians in California for many, many years.

DENETSOSIE. See 517.
DEZBA. See 572.

490 DICKSON, LOVAT. Half-Breed, The Story of Grey Owl. London:
Peter Davie's, 1939. 345p.
The autobiography of Wa-Sho-Quon-Asin, 1888-1938.

491 DIXON, JOSEPH KOSSUTH. The Vanishing Race, The Last Great
Indian Council: A Record in Picture and Story of the Last
Great Indian Council. Glorieta, New Mexico: Rio Grande
Press, 1973. 231p.
Eminent Indian chiefs from nearly every Indian reservation, in the United States, together with the story of
their lives, as told by themselves--their speeches and
folklore tales, their solemn farewell and the Indians'
story of the Custer fight. Originally published in Philadelphia by the National American Indian Memorial Association Press which should give some idea of the hold the
stereotype "vanishing American" had at that time. Reprint
of 1913 edition.

DODGE, ROBERT K. See 538.
DRINNON, RICHARD. See 515.
DYK, WALTER. See 529.

492   EASTLAKE, WILLIAM.   3 By Eastlake: The Early Fiction:
      Portrait of an Artist with 26 Horses, Go in Beauty, the
      Bronc People. New York: Simon and Schuster, 1970. 745p.
         A trilogy of good popular novels about the Indians of
      New Mexico, tourists, white traders, and the landscape.
      Reprint of 1955 edition.

493   EASTMAN, CHARLES ALEXANDER (OHIYESO) Indian Boyhood. New
      York: Dover Publications, 1971. 247p.
         The first of three in a series of autobiographical
      accounts of Ohiyesa, a Santee Sioux and well-known scholar.
      Written between 1900-1915, they describe a period fifty
      years earlier. Ohiyesa was raised in the old ways, and
      then became educated in European ways; this first volume
      recounts his first fifteen years, describing religious
      practice, medicine work, and training for the hunt. The
      other books in the series are: The Soul of the Indian,
      and Old Indian Days. The former emphasizes Dakota reli-
      gious beliefs and the latter fictionalizes the daily life
      of the Sioux. Dover has reprinted all these books from
      the original plates and with the original illustrations.
      They are fine period pieces, both in book style and in
      Eastman's treatment of himself and his people as "pagan"
      and hence picturesque. Reprint of 1902 edition.

      ERDOES, RICHARD. See 528.

494   FAIRCHILD, HOXIE NEALE. The Noble Savage; A Study in Roman-
      tic Naturalism. New York: Columbia University Press,
      1928. 535p.
         A most interesting study of the development of an intel-
      lectual idea. Bibliography.

      FEIKEMA, FEIKE. See 540.

495   FERGUSSON, HARVEY. Followers of the Sun: A Trilogy of the
      Santa Fe Trail: Wolf Song, In Those Days, and the Blood
      of the Conquerors. New York: Alfred A. Knopf, 1936.
      756p.
         Three short novels about the freedom and spirit of the
      Indian, and the encroachment and "civilizing" of the West
      by the White man. The writer was a man of pioneering indi-
      viduality and of a great love of nature and of natural man.

496   FIEDLER, LESLIE A. The Return of the Vanishing American.
      New York: Stein and Day, 1968. 192p.

NATIVE AMERICANS

(FIEDLER, LESLIE A.)
   A literary critic develops his own theory of the literary myth of the Indian as a "literary anthropologist."
Discusses the New Western, which pokes fun at the old, and
the American dream which is the West, which is a peculiar
form of madness. Takes up the novels of the 1960s and
relates them to captivity narratives and the drug culture.

497   FISHER, CLAY. (Henry Allen). Nino. New York: Pocket Books,
      1962. 178p.
         The story of the Apache Army Scout who became one of the
      most hunted fugitives in the Southwest. The Apache Kid
      was a legend within his own lifetime. Reprint of 1961
      edition.

498   FISHER, VARDIS. Pemmican. New York: Pocket Books, 1965.
      341p.
         Novel about the Hudson Bay territory in 1815 and the
      conflict between the fur traders and the Indians. Action-
      packed, full of battles. Reprint of 1956 edition.

FORD, CHELLAN STEARNS. See 559.

499   FOREMAN, GRANT. Sequoyah. Norman: University of Oklahoma
      Press, 1970. 85p.
         A biography of the chief who created the Cherokee
      alphabet. Reprint of 1938 edition.

FRIAR, NATASHA. See 500.

500   FRIAR, RALPH and NATASHA FRIAR. The Only Good Indian: The
      Hollywood Gospel. New York: Drama Book Specialists, 1972.
      330p.
         A highly entertaining and revealing study of how the
      popular media, particularly film, have contributed to
      America's racism.

GALANTIÈRE, LEWIS. See 569.
GERONIMO. See 487.

501   GERONIMO. Geronimo: His Own Story, edited by Steven M.
      Barrett. New York: E. P. Dutton, 1970. 190p.
         An autobiography dictated by the Apache chief while
      imprisoned at Fort Sill. Reprint of 1906 edition.

502   GILDNER, GARY. Digging for Indians. Pittsburgh, Pennsylvania:
      University of Pittsburgh Press, 1970. 67p.
         Poems.

503   GILLMOR, FRANCES. Traders to the Navajo. Albuquerque: University of New Mexico Press, 1952. 265p.
The frontier and pioneer life of the Southwest told in terms of the lives of the Wetherills of Kayenta. Bibliography. Reprint of 1934 edition.

504   GREENE, A. C. The Last Captive. Austin: Encino Press, 1972. 161p.
The life of Herman Lehmann, who as a boy was taken by the Indians and adopted by them; his career as a warrior with the Apache and Comanche tribes; his subsequent restoration to his family and the difficulties and fusions faced in adjusting his savage training to a civilized society; his experiences carrying him from the time of the scalping knife to the very threshold of our atomic age, together with verifying accounts by members of his family and others who shared some of those extraordinary and historical events.

505   GREGG, ELINOR D. The Indians and the Nurse. Norman: University of Oklahoma Press, 1965. 173p.
The personal recollections of a nurse who served both the Sioux and the Navajos. She became the first supervisor of nurses in the Indian Service of the U. S.

GREY OWL (WA-SHO-QUON-ASIN). See 490.

506   GRIDLEY, MARION E. American Indian Women. New York: Hawthorn Books, 1974. 178p.
Includes old-timers such as Pocahantas and Sacajawia and contemporaries such as the ballerina Maria Tallchief.

507   _____. Contemporary American Indian Leaders. New York: Dodd, Mead, 1972. 201p.
26 famous contemporary American Indians written up in biographical essays. Includes Hank Adams, Vine DeLoria, Jr., LaDonna Harris, Peter MacDonald, N. Scott Momaday, and Louis Ballard.

508   _____, ed. Indians of Today, 4th edition. n.p.: Indian Council Fire Publication, 1971. 494p.
A Whos' Who of Indian leaders in business, the arts, science, and other fields. Each biography comes with a picture.

509   GRIFFIS, JOSEPH K. (CHIEF TAHAN). Tahan: Out of Savagery Into Civilization. New York: George H. Doran Company, 1915. 263p.

NATIVE AMERICANS

(GRIFFIS, JOSEPH K.)
The life of an Osage who was a warrior, medicine man and Salvation Army Captain. Note title: a comment on attitudes during the early twentieth century.

510 HALSELL, GRACE. Bessie Yellowhair. New York: Morrow, 1973. 213p.
Autobiography of a Navajo woman.

511 HANNUM, ALBERTA. Paint the Wind. New York: Ballantine Books, 1972.
Sequel to Hannum's Spin A Silver Dollar. Begins during World War II, when Beatien, or Jimmy Toddy (now big Marine shirt) meets up with the Lippincotts again and returns during peacetime to the Reservation. His painting continues and he has a romance with Elizabeth before going off to school. Reprint of 1958 edition.

512 _____. Spin A Silver Dollar; The Story of a Desert Trading Post. New York: Ballantine Books, 1972. 148p.
A fictionalized biography of childhood of the Navajo artist, Beatien Yazz (Little No Shirt) and his relationship with the Lippincotts who ran the trading post at Wide Ruins, Arizona. The traders also encouraged a revival of weaving crafts using natural dyes. Reprint of 1946 edition.

513 HARSHA, WILLIAM JUSTIN. Ploughed Under; The Story of an Indian Chief, Told by Himself. New York: Fords, Howard and Hulbert, 1881. 268p.
An interesting nineteenth-century fictional biography. Documents the systematic plundering of Indian Removal.

HOOVER, HERBERT T. See 469.

514 HOWARD, HELEN ADDISON and [DAN L. McGRATH]. Saga of Chief Joseph. Caldwell, Idaho: Caxton Printers, 1965. 395p.
A thorough biography of the Nez Perce chief.

515 HUNTER, JOHN DUNN. Memoirs of Captivity Among the Indians of North America. Edited by Richard Drinnon. New York: Schocken Books, 1973. 252p.
The author was captured by Indians in infancy and assimilated easily into the Kansa and Osage tribes. Valuable for its descriptions of Indian customs and interesting as a nineteenth-century attack on White prejudices. An edited version of the original work which appeared in 1823-4. Bibliography.

516   IRVING, WASHINGTON. The Adventures of Captain Bonneville,
U. S. A. in the Rocky Mountains and the Far West Digested
From His Journal, edited and an introduction by Edgeley W.
Todd. Norman: University of Oklahoma Press, 1961. 424p.
    Story of Captain Bonneville, a trader, explorer, and
observer of Indian life. Irving was one of the first
American men of letters. The combination of adventurer
and writer of such high esteem makes a good book. Amply
illustrated. Appendices and bibliography.

ISHI. See 524.
JACKSON, DONALD. See 460.

517   JOHNSON, BRODERICK H., ed., SYDNEY M. CALLAWAY and others.
Denetsosie. Rough Rock, Arizona: Board of Education.
Rough Rock Demonstration School (and) Navajo Curriculum
Center, 1969. 51p.
    A biography about a Navajo leader and medicine man
written primarily for children. However, such a biography
is so rarely written about a twentieth century contemporary leader that is is well worth looking into by all.

518   JONES, HETTIE, comp. The Trees Stand Shining. New York:
Dial Press, 1971. 32p.
    Thirty-two poems from the oral tradition of 15 North
American Indian tribes.

519   JONES, LOUIS THOMAS, ed. Aboriginal Indian Oratory; The
Tradition of Eloquence Among Indians of the United States.
Los Angeles: Southwest Museum, 1965. 136p.
    Quotations and segments of speeches by prominent Indian
leaders from Tecumseh to Houston B. Teehee.

520   JOSEPHY, ALVIN M., JR. The Patriot Chiefs; A Chronicle of
American Indian Resistance. New York: Viking Press,
1969. 364p.
    Gives the biographies of Hiawatha, King Philip, Pope,
Pontiac, Tecumseh, Osceola, Black Horse, Crazy Horse, and
Chief Joseph. Originally called "A Chronicle of American
Indian Leadership." Bibliography. Reprint of 1958
edition.

521   KEISER, ALBERT. The Indian in American Literature. New York:
Octagon Press, 1970. 312p.
    A descriptive analysis of the character of the Indian
in the writings of various American authors, particularly
in the nineteenth century. Bibliography. Reprint of 1933
edition.

NATIVE AMERICANS

KILPATRICK, ANNA GRITTS. See 522.

522 KILPATRICK, JACK FREDERICK and ANNA GRITTS KILPATRICK, eds.
Walk in Your Soul: Love Incantations of the Oklahoma
Cherokees. Dallas: Southern Methodist University Press,
1965. 164p.
The translations of these love charms and magic incantations are accompanied by explanations and background
material.

KLAH, HOSTEEN. See 556.

523 KOPIT, ARTHUR. Indians. New York: Hill and Wang, 1969.
94p.
Drama tells of Buffalo Bill's nightmare when he relives
his life in an attempt to see where he went wrong. The
conquest of the West is acted out in the center ring of
Buffalo Bill's Wild West Show. Originally produced in
England.

524 KROEBER, THEODORA. Ishi in Two Worlds: A Biography of the
Last Wild Indian in North America. Berkeley: University
of California Press, 1971. 255p.
A very moving story about the last Indian in California
who came to live at the U. C. Berkeley campus museum. He
had no place else to go (until he died of TB). Ms.
Kroeber, as fine an anthropologist as her husband, gives
a background of the California Indian tribes and their
persecution and annihilation by settlers. Bibliography.
Reprint of 1961 edition.

525 LA FARGE, OLIVER. Laughing Boy. Boston: Houghton, Mifflin
and Company, 1929. 302p.
This book, a Pulitzer Prize winner, created the first
twentieth-century Indian hero in American fiction. Laughing Boy's discovery of his skill as an artist and his love
affair and marriage to Slim Girl are written about with
beauty and understanding. Several paperback editions.

526 LAFFERTY, R. A. Okla Hannali. Garden City, New York:
Doubleday and Company, 1972. 221p.
A story about Hannali Innominee presented in a mock epic
style. Hannali is a Choctaw, born in 1800 or thereabouts.
His life and loves and adventures told. His death finishes
the book.

527   LA FLESCHE, FRANCIS. The Middle Five: Indian Schoolboys
      of the Omaha Tribe. Madison: University of Wisconsin
      Press, 1963. 152p.
          A well-known Indian anthropologist writes about his
      life at the Presbyterian Mission School in Nebraska during
      the 1860s. Reprint of 1900 edition.

LA FLESCHE, SUSETTE. See 608.

528   LAME DEER (JOHN FIRE) and RICHARD ERDOES. Lame Deer Seeker
      of Visions: The Life of a Sioux Medicine Man. New York:
      Simon and Schuster, 1972. 288p.
          Tahca Ushte has a gift for story telling and can go
      from the sublime to the ridiculous so fast that you find
      yourself awed and laughing almost at the same time. Lame
      Deer is a profoundly religious person and a rascal all
      rolled up in one human medicine bundle.

529   LEFT, HANDED. Son of Old Man Hat: A Navajo Autobiography.
      As told to Walter Dyk. Lincoln: University of Nebraska
      Press, 1967. 378p.
          A unique and lively autobiography of an old man remem-
      bering his youth and free ways. Reprint of 1938 edition.

LEHMANN, HERMAN. See 504.

530   LEWIS, ANNA. Chief Pushmataha: American Patriot. New York:
      Exposition Press, Incorporated, 1961. 104p.
          The moving story of the Choctaw's struggle for survival
      led by their great chief during the early nineteenth
      century.

531   LEWIS, RICHARD. I Breathe A New Song; Poems of the Eskimo.
      New York: Simon and Schuster, 1971. 128p.

532   LIBERTY, MARGOT and JOHN STANDS IN TIMBER. Fights with the
      Shoshone, 1855-1870: A Northern Cheyenne Indian Narrative.
      Missoula: Montana State University Press, Occasional
      Papers #2, February 1961.
          John Stands in Timber is the Cheyenne tribal historian.
      He narrates, in prose epic form, three Cheyenne battles.

LIBERTY, MARGOT. See 589.

533   LIMBAUGH, RONALD H., comp. Cheyenne and Sioux: The Reminis-
      cences of Four Indians and a White Soldier. Stockton,
      California: Pacific Center for Western Historical Studies,
      University of the Pacific, 1973. 79p.

NATIVE AMERICANS

(LIMBAUGH, RONALD H.)
Iron Teeth, a Cheyenne old woman, a Cheyenne old man, James Tangled Yellow Hair, a Cheyenne scout, Jules Chaudel, a White soldier with the Cheyenne scouts, and Oscar Good Shot, a Sioux farmer are included in this historical account.

LINDERMAN, FRANK B. See 567.

534   LONE-DOG, LOUISE. Strange Journey: The Vision Quest of a Psychic Indian Woman. Healdsburg, California: Naturegraph Company, 1964.
A Mohawk-Delaware woman tells her life story and describes her visions and their import.

535   LONGFELLOW, HENRY WADSWORTH. The Song of Hiawatha. New York: Bounty Book, 1968. 248p.
Manabozho, the Algonquin, revisited in this American classic that romanticized Indian America for thousands of readers in the United States and Europe and still does. Enforces the noble savage myth. Reprint of 1855 edition.

536   LOTT, MILTON. Dance Back the Buffalo. New York: Pocket Books, 1968. 325p.
Historical novel about the Sioux and how many of these Indians fell prey to the prophecies of an Indian "Messiah." Reprint of 1958 edition.

537   LOWRY, ANNIE. Karnee: A Paiute Narrative, edited by Lalla Scott. Reno: University of Nevada Press, 1966. 149p.
The autobiography of a Paiute woman who is half-white and who tries to live in two worlds. Paiute customs are well described.

LURIE, NANCY OESTRICH. See 552.

538   McCULLOUGH, JOSEPH B. and ROBERT K. DODGE, eds. Voices From Wah'Kon-Tah: Contemporary Poetry of Native Americans. New York: International Publishers, 1974. 144p.
Brief biographies of each poet accompany the works.

McGINNIS, DUANE, See 558.

539   McNICHOLS, CHARLES LONGSTRATH. Crazy Weather. Lincoln: University of Nebraska Press, 1967. 195p.

(McNICHOLS, CHARLES LONGSTRATH)
A novel about the coming of age of a White boy and his best friend who is a Mohave. How each seeks his own culture for his adult identity. Reprint of 1944 edition.

540   MANFRED, FREDERICK (FEIKE FEIKEMA). Conquering Horse. New York: New American Library, 1965. 275p.
No Name is a Yankton Sioux and this is the story of his coming to his vision and his maturity as warrior and chief. Interspersed with this main theme is No Name's romance with Leaf and his capture of the great white horse. Reprint of 1959 edition.

MARIA. See 542.

541   MARQUIS, THOMAS BAILEY. Wooden Leg: A Warrior Who Fought Custer. Lincoln: University of Nebraska Press, 1962. 384p.
A Cheyenne fighter tells about the Battle of Little Big Horn as he saw it.

542   MARRIOTT, ALICE. Maria: The Potter of San Ildefonso. Norman: University of Oklahoma Press, 1963. 294p.
A popular account of a famous Indian potter, a Pueblo woman who revived and developed the famous black pottery of her tribe, creating a new source of livelihood for many there.

543   MATHEWS, JOHN JOSEPH. Talking to the Moon. Chicago: University of Chicago Press, 1945. 243p.
Mathews comes back to his Osage homeland and builds a sandstone house where he watches the seasons pass and writes a series of autobiographical essays on nature and the world of men.

544   MILTON, JOHN R., ed. The American Indian Speaks. Vermillion: University of South Dakota Press, 1969. 194p.
The best anthology to date of contemporary Indian writing. Includes short stories, articles, and poetry, none of it in translation, plus art work.

545   _____, ed. Conversations with Frank Waters. Chicago: Sage Books, 1971. 90p.
Milton and Fred Manfred, among others, talk back and forth with the philosopher and writer of classic books about the Southwest. Conversations cover a variety of topics and much autobiography.

NATIVE AMERICANS

546   MILTON, JOHN R., ed. Four Indian Poets. Vermillion: University of South Dakota Press, 1974. 67p.
      The poetry of John Barsness, Paula Gunn Allen, L. Haycock, and Jeff Saunders are presented. Wassaja (July, 1974) singles out the poetry of Barsness for special praise.

547   MITCHELL, EMERSON BLACKHORSE and T. D. ALLEN. Miracle Hill: The Story of a Navaho Boy. Norman: University of Oklahoma Press, 1967. 230p.
      The autobiography of a fine creative writer.

548   MOMADAY, N. SCOTT. House Made of Dawn. New York: New American Library, 1969. 191p.
      This novel about Abel, a young Indian caught between the White and Red worlds. Momaday sets his story in the Southwest and shows the interweaving of the Catholic-Spanish, Anglo, and Indian cultures there.

549   ____. The Way to Rainy Mountain. Albuquerque: University of New Mexico Press, 1969. 119p.
      A mixture of autobiography, history, and tribal myth, beautifully illustrated by Momaday's father. Details the author's pilgrimage back to the home of his people. Each short piece is divided into three sections: the personal response, the historic account, and the mythic evaluation of the same experience, or place.

550   MOMADAY, NATACHEE SCOTT. American Indian Authors. Boston: Houghton Mifflin Company, 1972. 151p.
      An anthology that begins with a speech of Chief Joseph and Indian legends, and jumps to contemporary writers such as Grey Cohoe and Littlebird.

551   MONTURE, ETHEL BRANT and HARVEY CHALMERS. Joseph Brant, Mohawk. West Lansing: Michigan State University Press, 1955. 364p.
      A biography of the Mohawk chief written by a descendant.

552   MOUNTAIN WOLF WOMAN. Mountain Wolf Woman, Sister of Crashing Thunder: Autobiography of a Winnebago Indian, edited by Nancy Oestreich Lurie. Ann Arbor: University of Michigan Press, 1966. 142p.
      An old woman tells about her early life in Nebraska and Wisconsin. Reprint of 1961 edition.

      NABAKOV, PETER. See 597.

553   NEIHARDT, JOHN G. <u>Black Elk Speaks</u>: Being the Life Story of
      a Holy Man of the Oglala Sioux. Lincoln: University of
      Nebraska Press, 1961. 280p.
             The best-selling life story of Black Elk. A good intro-
      duction to American Indian life and philosophy. Highly
      readable; gives many insights into the life change that
      Native Americans had to undergo when they became wards of
      the U. S. Government. Tells how Black Elk became a Sioux
      Medicine Man who had his first vision when he was nine years
      old and who tried to become a leader to his people during
      their time of troubles. Gives an account of the 1890
      massacre at Wounded Knee. Reprint of 1932 edition.

554   _____. <u>A Cycle of the West.</u> Lincoln: University of Nebraska
      Press, 1967. 110p.
             Poetry deals with the tragic defeat of the Plains Indi-
      ans. Includes: "The Song of Three Friends," "The Song of
      Hugh Glass," "The Song of Jed Smith," "The Song of the
      Indians Wars," and "The Song of the Messiah." Reprint of
      1953 edition.

555   _____. <u>When the Tree Flowered: The Fictional Autobiography</u>
      <u>of Eagle Voice, A Sioux Indian.</u> Lincoln: University of
      Nebraska Press, 1970. 248p.
             A fictional narrative-autobiography of a Sioux Indian.
      Neihardt has been called the Longfellow of the West. Re-
      print of 1951 edition.

556   NEWCOMB, FRANC JOHNSON. <u>Hosteen Klah: Navaho Medicine Man</u>
      <u>and Sand Painter.</u> Norman: University of Oklahoma Press,
      1964. 227p.
             Biography of a famous Navaho medicine man and weaver.
      Klah was responsible for the translation of many of the
      Navaho chants and legends. Gives the history of the family
      covering a period of about 200 years and their experiences
      with other tribes, the Spaniards, and the Americans.
      Bibliography.

557   NEWLAND, SAM and JACK STEWART. <u>Two Paiute Autobiographies</u>,
      as told to Julian Haynes Steward. Berkeley: University
      of California Press, 1934.
             Two old men recount their memories about the coming
      of the White man in the middle of the last century.

558   NIATUM, DUANE. <u>After the Death of an Elder Klallam, and</u>
      <u>Other Poems.</u> Phoenix: The Baleen Press, 1970. 52p.
             Duane Niatum, or Duane McGinnis, as he is sometimes
      anthologized, is one of the new young Indian poets who

NATIVE AMERICANS

(NIATUM, DUANE)
write in English. See also his second book of poems:
Ascending Red Cedar Moon (1973).

559 NOWELL, CHARLES JAMES. Smoke From Their Fires: The Life of
a Kwakiutl Chief. Edited by Chellan S. Ford. Hamden,
Connecticut: Archon Books, 1968. 248p.
Nowell's autobiography and the culture of his people.
Reprint of 1941 edition.

560 O'CONNOR, RICHARD. Buffalo Bill: The Noblest Whiteskin.
New York: Putnam, 1973. 320p.
Account of the many careers of William Cody, with an
aim to provide perspective on the legend. No new material
Bibliography.

OHIYESA. See 493.

561 OLD MEXICAN. Old Mexican, A Navajo Autobiography. New York:
Viking Fund Publications in Anthropology, November 8, 1974.
218p.
Old Mexican's life story from 1871 to 1919.

562 OSKISON, JOHN MILTON. Tecumseh and His Times: The Story
of a Great Indian. New York: G. P. Putnam's Sons, 1938.
244p.
An Indian writer does an interesting biography of the
Great Shawnee chief.

563 OWEN, GUY. The White Stallion and Other Poems. Winston-
Salem, North Carolina: John F. Blair, 1969. 67p.

564 PARKER, ARTHUR CASWELL. Red Jacket: Last of the Senecas.
New York: McGraw Hill, 1952. 228p.
A famous Senecan anthropologist describes the conflicts
between the White settlers and his tribe in the autobiography of its famous fighter chief of the nineteenth
century.

565 PAYTIAMO, JAMES. Flaming Arrow's People. New York: Duffield
and Green, 1932. 157p.
A personal narrative which describes the life and customs of the Acoma.

566 PEARCE, ROY HARVEY. Savagism and Civilization: A Study of
the Indian and the American Mind. Baltimore: The John
Hopkins Press, 1965. 260p.

(PEARCE, ROY HARVEY)
   Deals with the concept of Indianism as a creation of
the Anglo imagination and a polar concept to contrast with
his high ideals about his civilization. Illustrations
from American literature. Bibliography. Reprint of 1953
edition.

PEEK, WALTER. See 580.
PITCHLYN, PETER. See 450.

567 PLENTY-COUPS. Plenty-Coups, Chief of the Crows, edited by
   Frank B. Linderman. Lincoln: University of Nebraska
   Press, 1970. 324p.
      After forty years of association with the Crow people,
   Linderman has tried to take down the life story of his old
   friend, who was born in 1848 and lived through the passing
   of the buffalo and the defeat of his tribe by the Pecunies.
   Reprint of 1930 edition.

568 POKAGON, SIMON. Queen of the Woods. Hartford, Mich.:
   C. H. Engle, 1901. 220p.
      Biography of Chief Potawatoni. Reprint of 1899 edition.

569 PONCINS, GONTRAN DE MONTAIGNE in collaboration with LEWIS
   GALANTIERE. Kabloona: The White Man. New York: Bantam,
   1971. 339p.
      The Eskimo Indians and the Arctic regions. The author
   changes his writing and thinking patterns through the
   course of the book (and his travels) from that of the
   European mentality to one more aligned with Eskimo feelings
   and sentiments. Reprint of 1941 edition.

570 PRATT, THEODORE. Seminole: A Drama of the Florida Indian.
   Gainesville: University of Florida Press, 1953. 171p.
      Narrator and actors.

PUSHMATAHA. See 530.

571 QOYAWAYMA, POLINGAYSI (Elizabeth Q. White). No Turning Back;
   A True Account of a Hopi Indian Girl's Struggle to Bridge
   the Gap Between the World of Her People and the World of
   the White Man, as told to Vada F. Carlson. Albuquerque:
   University of New Mexico Press, 1964. 180p.
      The story of a little girl forced into an Anglo educa-
   tion who succeeds thereafter in making the transition into
   the White world to lead a Hopi-Christian life.

QUAIFE, MILO MILTON. See 484.
RADIN, PAUL. See 476.
RED JACKET. See 564.

NATIVE AMERICANS

572 REICHARD, GLADYS AMANDA. Dezba, Woman of the Desert. Glorietta, New Mexico: Rio Grande Press, 1971. 161p.
The life of a Navajo woman. Includes Navajo social
customs and a description of daily life. Reprint of 1939
edition.

573 _____. Spider Woman; A Story of Navajo Weavers and Chanters.
Santa Fe: Rio Grande Press, 1968. 287p.
Anthropologist Reichard went to live with the Navajos
in the 1930s. This is her account. Goes into excellent
details about the Navajo textile industry. Reprint of
1934 edition.

574 RICHTER, CONRAD. A Country of Strangers. New York: Alfred
A. Knopf, 1966. 169p.
Another captivity-based tale. Deals with a White girl
who is happy with her Indian husband and child but is
forced back into the White world. Finally, with her husband and son dead, she escapes with True Son to find her
Indian world again.

575 ROESSEL, RUTH. Navajo Stories of the Long Walk Period.
Tsaile, Arizona: Navajo Community College Press, 1973.
272p.
A very important study of taped narrations of Navajos
who could remember the Navajo massacre in Canyon del
Muerto. Investigation was to see who was to blame for the
Long Walk to Fort Sumner in the 1860s.

576 ROGERS, JOHN. Red World and White: Memories of a Chippewa
Boyhood. Norman: University of Oklahoma Press, 1974.
153p.
Autobiography of a chief. Bibliography. Reprint of
1953 edition.

ROGERS, WILL. See 440.

577 ROSEN, KENNETH, ed. The Man to Send Rain Clouds: Contemporary Stories by American Indians. New York: Viking Press,
1973. 178p.
Some fine short stories and tone poems: Included are:
Leslie Silko, Joseph Little, Anne Lee Walters, Aaron Scott
Yava, Opal Lee Popkes, Larry Littlebird, Simon Ortiz,
and R. C. Gorman. Illustrated.

578 ROTHENBERG, JEROME, ed. Shaking the Pumpkin: Traditional
Poetry of the Indian North Americas. Garden City, New
York: Doubleday and Company, 1972. 475p.

(ROTHENBERG, JEROME)
   A wide selection of Indian poetry including the complete
text of a "sacred-clown" fertility drama of the Pueblo Indians; picture poems from the Cuna and Chippewa; Nathaniel
Tarn's version of a major section of the never-before-
translated pre-Conquest Mayan play, "Rabinal Achi" and many
others. This book has been criticized for its interpretive
translations, i.e., the policy of recreating the mood and
meaning of the poem rather than the literal meaning of
each word.

SAH-GAN-DE-OH. See 609.

579   SANCHEZ, THOMAS. Rabbit Boss. New York: Ballantine Books,
      1974. 532p.
         A historic novel about 4 generations of a Washo Indian
      family. Includes the Donner Pass disaster when the Whites
      became cannibals. This has become a cult book on the West
      Coast among college students.

580   SANDERS, THOMAS EDWARD and WALTER W. PEEK, eds. Literature of
      the American Indian. New York: Glencoe Press, 1972. 534p.
         Songs, legends, history, stories from the fireside, ora-
      tory and poems are all included in this anthology. Highly
      praised by Akwesasne Notes.

581   SANDOZ, MARI. Crazy Horse: The Strange Man of the Oglalas,
      A Biography. New York: Alfred A. Knopf, 1942. 428p.
         Crazy Horse, a "glorious warrior" as Mari Sandoz puts
      it, was one of the chiefs who defeated Custer at Little
      Big Horn.

SCHMITT, MARTIN E. See 479.

582   SCHULTZ, JAMES WILLARD. My Life as an Indian. New York:
      Duell, Sloan and Pearce, 1957. 151p.
         The story of a squaw man who lived with the Blackfoot
      Indians. Reprint of 1907 edition.

583   _____. Why Gone Those Times? Eugene Lee Silliman, ed.
      Norman: University of Oklahoma Press, 1974. 271p.
         Autobiographical tales of the Blackfoot Indian.

SCOTT, LALLA. See 537.

584   SEKAQUAPTEWA, HELEN. Me and Mine: The Life Story of Helen
      Sekaquaptewa, with the assistance of Louise Udall. Tucson,
      Arizona: University of Arizona Press, 1969. 262p.

NATIVE AMERICANS

(SEKAQUAPTEWA, HELEN)
A personal account of a Hopi woman who adapts from her own traditional Hopi ways to those of modern American society.

SEQUOYAH. See 499.

585 SEWID, JAMES. Guests Never Leave Hungry: The Autobiography of James Sewid, A Kwakiutal Indian, edited by James P. Spradley. New Haven: Yale University Press, 1969. 310p.
The life of a chief of a Northwestern tribe.

586 SHAW, ANNA MOORE. A Pima Past. Tucson: University of Arizona Press, 1974. 262p.
A description of Pima life and ways in an autobiographical account.

SHIPEK, FLORENCE C. See 481.
SILLIMAN, EUGENE LEE. See 583.
SIMMONS, LEO W. See 591.
SITTING BULL. See 599.
SPRADLEY, JAMES P. See 585.

587 STANDING BEAR, LUTHER. My Indian Boyhood. Boston: Houghton Mifflin Company, 1931. 189p.
White school, marriage and life on the Sioux reservation and the struggles to relate the two.

588 _____. Land of the Spotted Eagle. Boston: Houghton, Mifflin Company, 1933. 259p.
The chief describes his family and his life as a Sioux.

589 STANDS IN TIMBER, JOHN. Cheyenne Memories, A Folk History, as told to Margot Liberty and Robert M. Utley. New Haven: Yale University Press, 1967. 330p.
An informative and delightful autobiography.

STEINER, STAN. See 610.
STEWARD, JULIAN HAYNES. See 557.
STEWART, JACK. See 557.

590 SWEEZY, CARL. The Arapaho Way: A Memoir of an Indian Boyhood, as told to Althea Bass. New York: Clarkson N. Potter, Incorporated, 1966. 80p.
The Arapaho way of life shown in words and drawings.

TAHAN. See 509.

591 TALAYESVA, DON C. Sun Chief: The Autobiography of a Hopi
Indian. Edited by Leo W. Simmons. New Haven: Yale Uni-
versity Press, 1969. 460p.
Life in Oraibi on Third Mesa and school in Arizona and
California. Includes Sun Chief's mystic call to lead his
people. Reprint of 1942 edition.

TECUMSEH. See 562.

592 TEDLOCK, DENNIS, trans. and ed. Finding the Center: Narrative Poetry of the Zuni Indians. New York: Dial Press,
1972. 298p.
A collection and translation of spoken prose and poetry
of the Zuni Indians, one of the Pueblo groups in Western
New Mexico, obtained by observing and recording them as
they were performed or recounted to the translator.

593 THATCHER, B. B. Indian Biography. Glorietta, New Mexico:
Rio Grande Press, 1973. 2 vol. 324, 320p.
Excellent source book on Eastern American Indians as
they were seen by others in the early nineteenth century.
Reprint of a 1832 classic historical account of Indian
orators, warriors, statesmen.

594 THRAPP, DAN L. Victorio and the Mimbres Apaches. Norman:
University of Oklahoma Press, 1974. 393p.
Well-told biography of the Apache guerilla fighter.
Photos and bibliography.

595 TIBBLES, THOMAS HENRY. Buckskin and Blanket Days: Memoirs
of a Friend of the Indians. Garden City, New York:
Doubleday, 1957. 336p.
The autobiographical account of a White activist on
behalf of the Indians, particularly the Ponca Tribe.
Tibbles, besides having been a Squaw Man and Indian sup-
porter, also ran as a vice-presidential nominee for the
People's Party. Reprint of 1905 edition.

TODD, EDGELEY W. See 516.
TSALI. See 452.

596 TURNER, FREDERICK W. III, ed. The Portable North American
Indian Reader. New York: Viking Press, 1973. 628p.
Literature by and about the American Indian: myths,
tales, poetry, oratory, and autobiography. White writers
such as Diaz and Parkman and contemporary Indian authors

NATIVE AMERICANS

(TURNER, FREDERICK W. III)
such as Luther Standing Bear, N. Scott Momaday, Vine
Deloria, Jr., Thomas Berger, and Gary Snyder are all included. Bibliography.

597   TWO LEGGINGS. Two Leggings: The Making of a Crow Warrior.
Edited by Peter Nabakov. New York: Thomas Y. Crowell,
1967. 226p.
    A nineteenth-century Crow warrior tells about his daily
life.

UDALL, LOUISE. See 584.
UNDERHILL, RUTH. See 471.
UTLEY, ROBERT M. See 589.

598   VAN DER BEETS, RICHARD, ed. Held Captive by Indians: Selected Narratives --1642-1836. Knoxville: University
of Tennessee Press, 1973. 374p.
    Accounts of Indian massacres and captivities comprised
America's first literature of catharsis. Here are eighteen
narratives which depict a chronological sampling of cap-
tivities in the seventeenth, eighteenth and nineteenth
centuries, and illustrate their cultural, historical, and
ethnological significance. Since captives often had the
most intimate and lengthy relations with Indians, many of
their recorded observations give some of the most accurate
explanations of hunting, warring, customs and manners, religion, and council procedures. Commentary on such tribes
as the Mohawks, Hurons, Maliseets, Penobscots, Cherokees,
Shawnees, and Comanches.

599   VESTAL, STANLEY. Sitting Bull: Champion of the Sioux: A
Biography. Norman: University of Oklahoma Press, 1972.
352p.
    The most thoroughly researched biography of this great
chief who was so well respected by Indians and White men.
Many photographs as well as Sitting Bull's own hieroglyphic
autobiography are included. Reprint of 1932 edition.

VICTORIO. See 594.

600   VIZENOR, GERALD ROBERT. Seventeen Chirps. Minneapolis:
Nodin Press, 1964. Unpaged.
    Poems by a contemporary Chippewa poet.

601   WALTRIP, LELA and RUFUS WALTRIP. Indian Women. New York:
David McKay, 1964. 169p.

(WALTRIP, LELA and RUFUS WALTRIP)
Sketches the biographies of 13 Indian women who lived from 1535 to the present. All but three are relatively unknown to the public. Written in simple and direct style.

WALTRIP, RUFUS. See 601.
WA-SHO-QUON-ASIN (Grey Owl). See 490.

602 WATERS, FRANK. The Man Who Killed the Deer. Chicago: Sage Books, 1972. 311p.
The story of Martiniano who comes back to his tribe after a White education and tries to readjust to this life. His love story with Flowers Playing is beautifully told. A classic about Pueblo life. Reprint of 1942 edition.

603 WATERS, FRANK. Pumpkin Seed Point. Chicago: Sage Books, 1969. 175p.
An autobiographical account of the author's three year experience living with the Hopi Indians in Arizona. Good insights into Hopi life.

604 WELCH, JAMES. Riding the Earthboy 40: Poems by James Welch. New York: World Publishing Company, 1971. 54p.
Probably the first complete book of poems published by a contemporary Indian poet writing in English. A fine collection.

THE WETHERILLS OF KAYENTA. See 503.

605 WHITE, E. E. Experiences of a Special Indian Agent. Norman: University of Oklahoma Press, 1965. 340p.
Personal recollections of the author who was a special field agent for the Indian Service from 1885 to 1890. Reprint of 1893 edition.

WHITE, ELIZABETH Q. See 571.

606 WHITEWOLF, JIM. Jim Whitewolf: The Life of a Kiowa Apache Indian, edited by Charles S. Brant. New York: Dover Publications, 1969. 144p.
An excellent autobiography of a Kiowa Apache who was born and lived during the second half of the nineteenth century, and who saw the disintegration of his tribe's culture and tells how it personally affected him. The influence of the White culture is vividly portrayed. A cultural and historical background is provided by the editor in his introduction.

NATIVE AMERICANS

607   WILDER, ROBERT. Bright Feather. New York: G. P. Putnam's
      Sons, 1948. 408p.
            Historical novel about the bloody 1830s Florida Seminole
      War.

608   WILSON, DOROTHY CLARKE. Bright Eyes: The Story of Susette
      La Flesche, An Omaha Indian. New York: McGraw Hill, 1974.
      396p.
            A biography of a remarkable woman which is also a his-
      torical romance in its depiction of nineteenth-century
      America. The destruction of the Omaha tribe is told as
      well as the life of a woman of great fortitude and skill
      who lived in both the White and Indian worlds and fought
      for her people.

609   WINNIE, LUCILLE. Sah-Gan-De-Oh, The Chief's Daughter. New
      York: Vantage Press, 1968. 190p.
            The autobiography of a Senecan woman who grew up on the
      reservations and then had to adapt to White society.

610   WITT, SHIRLEY HILL and STAN STEINER, eds. The Way: An An-
      thology of American Indian Literature. New York: Vintage
      Books, 1972. 261p.
            A large number of authors represented by short stories
      and poems under such major headings as: songs of the
      People; the new Indians; the laws of life: tribal and
      legal; the ritual of death; and the prophecies of the
      future.

      WOODEN LEG. See 541.
      YAZZ, BEATIEN. See 512.
      YELLOWHAIR, BESSIE. See 510.

                          G.   Arts and Crafts

611   ADAIR, JOHN. The Navajo and Pueblo Silversmiths. Norman:
      University of Oklahoma Press, 1946. 220p.
            A well-illustrated history of the development of silver-
      smithing in the Southwest among the Pueblo and Navajo
      tribes. Reprint of 1944 edition.

      ADAIR, JOHN. See also 663.

612   AMSDEN, CHARLES A. Navajo Weaving: Its Technique and Its
      History. Chicago: Rio Grande Press, Incorporated, 1964.
      261p.

(AMSDEN, CHARLES A.)
Traces the development of the Navajo textile and fabric industries as well as chronicling the diversity of fabric patterns. Bibliography. Reprint of 1949 edition.

613 ANDREWS, RALPH. Curtis' Western Indians. Seattle, Washington: Superior Publishing Company, 1962. 176p.
Takes the best and most representative from the twenty-volume edition originally published in 1907. Edward Curtis travelled the West on a stipend from J. P. Morgan in order to record the vanishing American before he had disappeared.

614 APPLETON, LEROY H. American Indian Design and Decoration. New York: Dover Publications, 1971. 277p.
A study of nature symbolism and its religious significance in American Indian crafts such as pottery, fabrics, masks, and work tools. Images of the sun, moon, mountains, forests, rivers and lakes are depicted and explained. Bibliography. Reprint of 1950 edition.

615 ART IN America. 60:4. (July–August, 1972).
Entire issue on American Indians.

616 BAD HEART BULL, AMOS. A Pictographic History of the Oglala Sioux. Helen Blish, editor. Lincoln: University of Nebraska Press, 1967. 530p.
Drawings of Sioux people that were made by Bad Heart Bull between 1890 and 1913. Bibliography.

BAHNIMPTEWA, CLIFF. See 664.

617 BEDINGER, MARGERY. Indian Silver: Navajo and Pueblo Jewelers. Albuquerque: University of New Mexico Press, 1973. 264p.
A definitive account of the working of metals by Southwest Indians, from their first acquisition from the Spanish to the sophisticated silvercraft of the present-day Navajos and Pueblos. Illustrated with 155 photographs and drawings, 9 in color. Discusses the origins of the basic forms and decorative designs: conchas, crosses, najas, pomegranates. The effects of tourism, commercialization, and imitation on the original forms are well-detailed.

618 BELOUS, RUSSELL and ROBERT A. WEINSTEIN. Will Soule, Indian Photographer at Fort Sill, Oklahoma, 1869–74. Los Angeles: The Ward Ritchie Press, 1972. 120p.

NATIVE AMERICANS

(BELOUS, RUSSELL and ROBERT A. WEINSTEIN)
A collection of eighty photographs of Indian chiefs and warriors taken by one of the old-time great photographers. Reprint of 1969 edition.

BLISH, HELEN. See 616.

619 BRODY, J. J. Indian Painters and White Patrons. Albuquerque: University of New Mexico Press, 1971. 238p.
The cross-cultural influences that make Indian painting a combination of art and social history. Maintains that until 1962, Indian painting was a passive response to White paternalism and not truly a native expression. Bibliography.

CARPENTER, EDMUND. See 624.

620 CATLIN, GEORGE. Episodes From Life Among the Indians, and Last Rambles. With 152 Scenes and Portraits, by the Artist. Norman: University of Oklahoma Press, 1959. 357p.
A reprint of one of Catlin's most beautiful books of pictures and text.

621 ____. Illustrations of Manners, Customs, and Conditions of the North American Indians. 2 vols. New York, 1857-66. 1841.
Catlin was one of our finest artists and his paintings and sketches of the Indians are beautiful as well as authentic. Includes 360 engravings from the author's original paintings. Well worth reading.

622 COHOE, WILLIAM. A Cheyenne Sketchbook. Norman: University of Oklahoma Press, 1964. 96p.
Commentary of E. Adamson Hoebel and Karen Daniels Petersen. Sketches of free plains life, riding and hunting, tribal ceremonies, and prison. Cohoe was at Fort Marion, Florida in 1875.

623 COLLIER, DONALD. Indian Art of the Americas. Chicago: National History Museum, 1959. 64p.
Covers the Indian arts of both continents in a comprehensive approach. Bibliography.

624 COLLINS, HENRY B., FREDERICA DE LAGUNA, EDMUND CARPENTER and PETER STONE. The Far North: 2000 Years of American Eskimo and Indian Art. Washington, D. C.: National Gallery of Art, 1973. 289p.

(COLLINS, HENRY B., FREDERICA DE LAGUNA, EDMUND CARPENTER and PETER STONE)
A handsome catalogue of the National Gallery's exhibit with articles on the art written by the above editors.

625   COLTON, HAROLD S. Hopi Kachina Dolls; With a Key to Their Identification. Revised edition. Albuquerque: University of New Mexico Press, 1970. 156p.
The most complete book about the hand-carved Kachinas. Full of illustrations. The standard book for collectors. Kachinas are representations of spirits and are sacred to the Hopis. Bibliography. Reprint of 1949 edition.

626   COVARRUBIAS, MIGUEL. The Eagle, The Jaguar, and The Serpent; Indian Art of the Americas. North America: Alaska, Canada, The United States. New York: Knopf, 1954. 314p.

A handsome book by an artist himself; it is full of drawings and reproductions, many of them in color. Bibliography.

CURTIS, EDWARD. See 613.

627   CURTIS, EDWARD S. Portraits From North American Indian Life. New York: Promontory Press, 1972. 176p.
One of the greatest chroniclers of the North American Indian, Curtis documented all aspects of a culture which was being inexorably destroyed. Through photography, he retains much of the spirit and simple beauty of the Indian peoples. The tone of his work has a sobriety and richness, rarely found in photography.

DE BRY, THEODORE. See 644.
DE LAGUNA, FREDERICA. See 624.
D'HARNONCOURT, RENÉ. See 629.

628   DOCKSTADER, FREDERICK J. Indian Art in America: The Arts and Crafts of the North American Indian. Greenwich, Connecticut: New York Graphic Society, 1966. 223p.
A comprehensive survey of Indian art as well as a beautiful book to look at in itself. Over 250 illustrations with a bibliography. Reprint of 1961 edition.

629   DOUGLAS, FREDERIC H. and RENÉ D'HARNONCOURT. Indian Art of the United States. New York: Museum of Modern Art, 1948. 219p.
An excellent collection with a clear introduction. Over 200 illustrations and a bibliography.

Minority Studies: An Annotated Bibliography

NATIVE AMERICANS

630   DUNN, DOROTHY. American Indian Painting of the Southwest and Plains Areas. Albuquerque: University of New Mexico, 1968. 429p.
      A thorough treatment of the Indian art of the Western United States. Relationships between art and culture stressed. Bibliography.

631   EWERS, JOHN C. Artists of the Old West. Garden City, New York: Doubleday, 1965. 240p.
      Illustrated text about the White artists who travelled across the Western frontier and depicted the Indian cultures. Included are Remington, Bodner, Catlin and Charles Bird Kina.

632   FEDER, NORMAN. American Indian Art. New York: Harry N. Abrams, n. d.
      This is a large, expensive and beautifully constructed book based on museum collections of "postcontact" Indian art, i.e. those beadworks and constructs made after European immigration began. There is a premise here in the book that Indian culture is destined to become assimilated into the larger Anglo culture and that Indian art, thus, will disappear.

633   FOLSOM, FRANKLIN. America's Ancient Treasures: Guide to Archeological Sites and Museums. New York: Rand, McNally, 1971. 202p.
      Brings together information on the prehistoric sites North of Mexico open to the public, and the museum collections featuring prehistoric exhibits. Bibliography.

634   FRINK, MAURICE. Photographer on An Army Mule. Norman: University of Oklahoma Press, 1965. 151p.
      Another chronicler of the Indians who went out to photograph a vanishing race that wouldn't vanish. Bibliography.

635   GILPIN, LAURA. The Enduring Navaho. Austin: University of Texas Press, 1971. [1968]. 263p.
      A beautiful book of photographs and narrative about the Navaho world in terms of landscape and people. Laura Gilpin, who still lives in Santa Fe, knows her country, her Navajos, and her camera all equally well. Bibliography.

636   HARVEY, BYRON. Ritual in Pueblo Art: Hopi Life in Hopi Painting. New York: Museum of the American Indian, Heye Foundation, 1970. 81p.
      Contributions from the Museum of the American Indian Heye Foundation Vol. XXIV. Paintings by five Hopi artists

106

(HARVEY, BYRON III)
   depicting contemporary Hopi life cycle, ritual, etc., including economic life and ceremonials involving clowning
   and curing. Each of the 185 reproductions is analyzed.
   Bibliography.

HEIZER, ROBERT F. See 642.
HOEBEL, E. ADAMSON. See 622.

637   HOWLING WOLF. Howling Wolf: A Cheyenne Warrior's Graphic
      Interpretation of His People. Palo Alto: American West
      Publishing Company, 1968. 63p.
         Text by Karen Daniels Peterson. Sketches done from
      1875 to 1878 when Howling Wolf was a prisoner at Fort
      Marion, Florida. A beautiful book to look at and read.
      Contains also a fine introduction by John C. Ewers: "The
      History and Development of an American Art Form."

HOWLING WOLF. See 665.

638   HUNT, W. BEN. The Complete How-To Book of Indiancraft.
      New York: MacMillan Publishing Company, 1973. 187p.
         Scoutcraft book includes saddle, teepee, clothing,
      crafts. It shows how to make rather fake and poor quality
      pseudo-Indian crafts. An example of the "Let's be Indian"
      type of books. Reprint of 1942 edition.

639   HYDE, PHILIP and STEPHEN C. JETT. Navajo Wildlands. New York:
      Sierra Club/Ballantine, 1969. 159p.
         Collection of magnificent photographs in black and white
      and color by the Sierra Club. Interspersed with quotations
      from White and Navajo literature.

640   INVERARITY, ROBERT B. Art of the Northwest Coast Indians.
      Berkeley: University of California Press, 1971. 243p.
         An art critic and anthropologist has put together a
      beautiful book with an informative introduction and plenty
      of art plates. Bibliography. Reprint of 1950 edition.

JETT, STEPHEN C. See 639.

641   KING, CHARLES BIRD. The Redwood Library Collection of North
      American Indian Portraits. New York: Parke-Bernet
      Galleries, Incorporated, 1970. 49p.
         A fine catalog prepared by the famous auction gallery,
      of the paintings of Charles Bird King who tried to create
      a National Indian Portrait Gallery in the early nineteenth

NATIVE AMERICANS

(KING, CHARLES BIRD)
century. The Gallery, with works mostly by King, was part of the Smithsonian Institution until most of it was destroyed by fire in 1865.

642   KROEBER, THEODORA and ROBERT F. HEIZER. <u>Almost Ancestors: The First Californians.</u> New York: Sierra/Ballantine, 1968. 168p.
    A compilation of over 100 Indian portraits from old plates. A fine brief text of explanation and quotation accompanies the pictures.

643   LAMB, FRANK W. <u>Indian Baskets of North America.</u> Riverside, California: Riverside Museum Press, 1972. 155p.
    Also includes a list of basket-making tribes of North America. Illustrated.

LE MOYNE, JACQUES. <u>See</u> 644.

644   LORANT, STEFAN, ed. <u>The New World: The First Pictures of America.</u> Made by John White and Jacques Le Moyne and engraved by Theodore De Bry. New York: Duell, Sloan and Pearce, 1946. 292p.
    Excellent study of the first illustrations and impressions of the American Indians. To study just the ways the Indians were depicted by the Europeans can be a very vivid lesson in understanding early White attitudes towards the "savages."

645   McCRACKEN, HAROLD. <u>The Frederic Remington Book: A Pictorial History of the West.</u> Garden City, New York: Doubleday, 1966. 284p.
    Reproductions of paintings, drawings, and bronzes by one of the great American illustrators, famous for his portraits of Indians. Explanatory text and index of pictures with mention of where a complete Remington bibliography can be found.

646   McLUHAN, T. C. <u>Touch the Earth: A Self-Portrait of Indian Existence.</u> New York: Pocket Books, 1972. 185p.
    The text consists of quotations from oratory and records, the pictures are taken from the plates of Edward S. Curtis. A beautiful book of text and pictures. Text is also contemporary. Reprint of 1971 edition.

MAHOOD, RUTH I. <u>See</u> 660.

647   MALLERY, GARRICK. Picture-Writing of the American Indians,
          2 vols. New York: Dover Publications, 1972. 822p.
          Full of drawings and pictures, plus old-style type and
       book design, makes the reading a pleasurable experience.
       Colonel Mallory put this together for the Smithsonian, so
       it is learned and treats many communication forms such as
       knotted cords, notched or marked stocks, wampum, mnemonic
       pictures, winter count calendars, charms, and pictographs.
       Bibliography. Reprint of 1893 edition.

       MILLER, ALFRED JACOB. See 652.

648   MILLER, MARJORIE. Indian Arts and Crafts: A Complete "How To"
          Guide to Southwestern Indian Crafts. Los Angeles: Nash,
          1972. 118p.
          A how-to and where-to-buy book.

649   MINOR, MARZ N. The American Indian Craft Book. New York:
          Popular Library, 1972. 416p.
          The how-to guide to Indian recipes, hair styles, cloth-
       ing ornaments, jewelry, games. You can even learn to make
       your own teepee. Well-illustrated.

650   PENDLETON, MARY. Navajo and Hopi Weaving Techniques. New
          York: Macmillan, 1974.
          Reprint of 1973 edition.

       PETERSON, KAREN DANIELS. See 622, 637.

651   PRATSON, FREDERICK JOHN. Land of the Four Directions. Green-
          wich, Connecticut: Chatham Press, 1970. 131p.
          Photographic essay of Maine Indians.

       REMINGTON, FREDERIC. See 645.

652   ROSS, MARVIN C., ed. The West of Alfred Jacob Miller, re-
          vised and enlarged edition. Norman: University of Okla-
          homa Press, 1968.
          The Indian pictures of a famous nineteenth-century
       artist.

653   SCHOLDER, FRITZ. Scholder/Indian. Flagstaff, Arizona: North-
          land Press, 1972. 115p.
          A catalog of the paintings of a leading member of the
       Santa Fe School of contemporary American Indian art.
       Bibliography.

NATIVE AMERICANS

654 SNODGRASS, JEANNE O. American Indian Painters: A Biographical Dictionary. New York: Museum of the American Indian, Heye Foundation, 1968. 269p.
A biographical directory of over one thousand Native
American artists compiled by the Indian art curator of the
Philbrook Art Center. Tribal index. Public museum holdings and private collections also indexed. Bibliography.

SOULE, WILL. See 618.
STONE, PETER. See 624.

655 TAFT, ROBERT. Artists and Illustrators of the Old West,
1850-1900. New York: Scribners, 1953. 400p.
A survey of the pictures and illustrations of the Western U. S. during the period 1850 to 1900, and the men who
made them.

656 TANNER, CLARA LEE. Southwest Indian Craft Arts. Tucson:
University of Arizona Press, 1968. 206p.
Includes descriptions and copious illustrations of
baskets, textiles, silver, jewelry, Kachinas, pottery,
carvings, musical instruments, and glass bead work.
Bibliography.

657 _____. Southwest Indian Painting: A Changing Art, second
edition. Tucson: University of Arizona Press, 1973.
477p.
Begins with the old roots of Indian art and goes on to
the new directions of an emerging art that combines European techniques and materials, and old traditions. Discusses the Rio Grande Pueblos, the Hopi, Zuni, Navajo, and
Apache. Many Illustrations. Bibliography. Reprint of
1957 edition.

658 UNITED STATES Arts and Crafts Board. Contemporary Indian
Artists: Montana, Wyoming, Idaho. Rapid City, South
Dakota: Tipi Shop, 1972. 80p.
From graphic realism to impressionistic concepts, Indian
contemporary artists cannot be stereotyped. This book
represents works of major twentieth-century artists with
slight biographical details.

659 VILLASEÑOR, DAVID. Tapestries in Sand: The Spirit of Indian
Sandpainting. Healdsburg, California: Naturegraph Publishing Co., 1966. 112p.
An illustrated explanation of the Navajo art of sandpainting by a well-known artist and lecturer.

660 VROMAN, ADAM CLARK. Photographer of the South West. Los Angeles: Ward Ritchie Press, 1961. 127p. Edited by Ruth I. Mahood.
A selection from the work of a famous turn-of-the-century photographer who took many photographs of Indian life, especially in the Pueblo country.

WEINSTEIN, ROBERT A. See 618.
WHITE, JOHN. See 644.

661 WHITE, MARY. How To Do Bead Work. New York: Dover Publications, 1972. 142p.
Patterns, operations, selection of materials. Reprint of 1904 edition.

662 WHITEFORD, ANDREW HUNTER. North American Indian Arts. New York: Golden Press, 1970. 160p.
Analyzes the art and industries of the modern American Indians.

663 WORTH, SOL and ADAIR, JOHN. Through Navajo Eyes. An Exploration in Film Communication and Anthropology. Bloomington: Indiana University Press, 1972. 286p.
A fascinating and original book documenting a unique experiment conducted at the Navajo reservation in the Southwest, where members of the tribe were trained in the use of motion picture equipment and technique, and asked to make film statements of their culture and themselves. Bibliography.

664 WRIGHT, BARTON. Kachinas: A Hopi Artist's Documentary. Flagstaff, Arizona: Northland Press, 1973. 262p.
The beautiful paintings of Cliff Bahnimptewa, which depict a variety of Kachinas, are individually explained.

665 ZO-TIM. 1877: Plains Indian Sketchbooks of Zo-Tim and Howling Wolf. Flagstaff, Arizona: Northland Press, 1969.
A collection of 59 sketches made when the two Cheyenne artists were held captive at Fort Marion, Florida.

III. SPANISH AMERICANS

A. General Spanish Americans

666 ALFORD, HAROLD J. The Proud Peoples: The Heritage and Cul-
     ture of Spanish-Speaking Peoples in the United States.
     New York: McKay, 1972. 325p.
        Discusses the development of all the Spanish-American
     cultures in the United States. Sometimes spotty in dis-
     cussing Puerto Ricans and Cubans but solid on the history
     of Mexican immigration. Bibliography.

     ARCINIEGA, TOMAS A. See 669.

667 BURMA, JOHN H. Spanish Speaking Groups in the United States.
     Durham, North Carolina: Duke University Press, 1954. 214p.
        Mexican Americans, Filipinos and Puerto Ricans are
     among those discussed in this sociological study of their
     problems. Bibliography.

668 CALIFORNIANS OF Spanish Surname: Population, Education, Em-
     ployment, Income. San Francisco: California State Depart-
     ment of Industrial Relations, Division of Fair Employment
     Practices, 1964. 54p.
        The State of California has many reports on specific
     subjects such as: Public school surveys, Mexicans in Cal-
     ifornia, agricultural resources and labor. Statistics.

669 DE LA GARZA, RUDOLPH O., Z. ANTHONY KRUSZEWSKI and TOMÁS A.
     ARCINIEGA, comps. Chicanos and Native Americans. Engle-
     wood Cliffs, New Jersey: Prentice-Hall, Incorporated, 1973.
     203p.
        Includes some rewritten papers presented at the Work-
     shop on Southwest Ethnic Groups: Sociopolitical Environ-
     ment and Education, held in El Paso in 1972. Its emphasis
     is upon political attitudes held by Chicanos and Native
     Americans and outside response.

113

SPANISH AMERICANS

670   HEMOS TRABAJADO Bien. A Report On the First National Confer-
      ence of Puerto Ricans, Mexican Americans and Educators on
      the Special Educational Needs of Puerto Rican Youth.
      New York: Aspira Press, 1968.

      KRUSZEWSKI, Z. ANTHONY. See 669.

                    B. Mexican Americans

                    1. Bibliographical Works

671   ALTUS, DAVID M. Mexican American Education, A Selected Bib-
      liography Supplement No. 1. Las Cruces, New Mexico: ERIC/
      Cress Publications, 1971. n.p.
           A computerized, annotated bibliography which contains
      abstracts of articles written between June, 1969 and De-
      cember, 1970 in Research in Education (RIE). Section II
      consists of abstracts of articles written between January,
      1969 and June, 1970 in the Current Index to Journals in
      Education (CIJE). This supplements a previous ERIC/Cress
      bibliography of 150 RIE citations.

672   BARRIOS, ERNIE and OTHERS. Bibliografia de Aztlán: An
      Annotated Chicano Bibliography. San Diego: Centro de
      Estudios Chicanos, California State University, San Diego,
      1971. 157p.
           An annotated and topical bibliography compiled by the
      center. Materials are listed in terms of relevance as
      source materials for specific Chicano studies courses in-
      cluding higher education programs. Topical listings in-
      clude: Contemporary Chicano history, Education, Health
      Research Materials, History of Mexico, Literature, Philos-
      ophy, and Chicano Journals.

673   BURGER, HENRY G. Ethno-Pedagogy: A Manual in Cultural
      Sensitivity, with Techniques for Improving Cross-Cultural
      Teaching to Fit Ethnic Patterns, 2nd edition. Albuquerque:
      Southwestern Cooperative Educational Laboratory, 1968.
      318p.
           Attempts to present the basic information that inter-
      ethnic classroom teachers need. Socio-cultural relations
      within the classroom and cross cultural adaptations are
      discussed. A theory of the development of educational
      anthropology as applied to cultures found in the United
      States is presented in this practical manual. Bibliography.

      CABELLO-ARGANDONA, ROBERTO. See 677.

674   CALIFORNIA STATE College, Sacramento. Chicano Bibliography, Selected Materials on Americans of Mexican Descent. Sacramento, California: Sacramento State College, 1970. 124p.
      Divided by subject including the call numbers. Not annotated but with over one thousand entries.

675   CASTILLO, GUADALUPE and HERMINIO RIOS. Toward A True Chicano Bibliography: Mexican-American Newspapers: 1848-1942. El Grito III (Summer, 1970). 17-24p.
      193 Mexican-American newspapers listed by states.

676   CLARK Y MORENO, JOSEPH A. A Bibliography of Bibliographies Relating to Mexican-American Studies. El Grito III (Summer, 1970). 25-31p.
      A variety of general bibliographies listed from general history to folklore to general ethnic problems in Southern California.

677   DURÁN, PATRICIA HERRERA and ROBERTO CABELLO-ARGANDOÑA, comps. The Chicana: A Preliminary Bibliographic Study. Los Angeles: Chicano Research Library, Chicano Studies Center, University of California, Los Angeles, 1974.
      273-entry brochure which grew out of a UCLA course on the Chicana. Included are books, documents and papers, articles, theses and dissertations, films, and newspapers. Indexed.

678   FRESNO STATE Library. Afro- and Mexican-Americans: Books and Other Materials in the Library Relative to the History, Culture and Problems of Afro-Americans and Mexican-Americans. Fresno: Fresno State Library, 1969.
      A rich and wide-ranging index into literature on the history, culture, and problems of Americans of African and Mexican descent. Books, graduate theses, government publications and periodicals are included. Represents holdings as of January, 1969, as well as materials on order.

679   GOMEZ-Q., JUAN, comp. Selected Materials on the Chicano. Los Angeles: University of California, Los Angeles, Mexican-American Cultural Center, 1970. 14p.
      A brief but excellent bibliography which includes listings for history and literature, law, folklore, statistics, and films.

680   GROPP, ARTHUR E. A Bibliography of Latin American Bibliographies--Supplement. Metuchen, New Jersey: Scarecrow Press, Inc., 1971. 277p.
      A continuation of the original bibliography published in 1968 which is an updating of Cecil Knight Jones's

SPANISH AMERICANS

(GROPP, ARTHUR E.)
Bibliography of Latin American Bibliographies (1942).
Arranged by subject and then by country in both Spanish
and English.

681 GUZMAN, RALPH. Mexican-American Study Project Revised Bibliography with bibliographical essay by Ralph Guzman.
Advance Report No. 3. Los Angeles, California: Division
of Research, Graduate School of Business, University of
California, 1967. 99p.
    Extensive listing of books, journal articles and bibliog-
raphies as well as doctoral and master's dissertations and
other unpublished materials.

682 HEATHMAN, JAMES E. and CECILIA J. MARTINEZ. Mexican American
Education: A Selected Bibliography. Las Cruces: ERIC,
Clearing House on Rural Education and Small Schools, New
Mexico State University, 1969. 56p.
    Especially strong on bilingualism. Contains teacher
guides and program evaluations. Subject index.

683 HILTON, RONALD, ed. Handbook of Hispanic Source Materials and
Research Organizations in the U. S., Second edition.
Stanford: Stanford University Press, 1956. 448p.
    Includes Spanish, Portuguese as well as the more usual
listings. Divides its sections by state collections and
locality as well as by topic, such as humanities, fine arts,
social sciences.

684 HISPANIC SOCIETY of America. Catalog of the Library, 10 vols.
Boston: G. K. Hall and Company, 1962. First Supplement,
1970.
    A listing of the Society's library of over 100,000 vol-
umes from 1700 to date. Spain, Portugal and colonial Hispanic America are included. Emphasis on the culture of
each group.

685 HUERTA, JORGE A. A Bibliography of Chicano and Mexican
Dance, Drama, and Music. Oxnard, California: Colegio
Quetzalcoatl, 1972. 59p.
    Listings from pre-Columbian times to present. Books,
journals, and records.

686 JOHNSON, JOHN J., ed. The Mexican-American. A Selected and
Annotated Bibliography. Palo Alto: Stanford University
Center for Latin American Studies, 1969. 139p.
    274 annotated titles, gleaned from the social sciences.

687   JORDAN, LOIS B. Mexican Americans: Resources to Build Cul-
      tural Understanding. Littleton, Colorado: Libraries Un-
      limited, Inc., 1973. 265p.
         An annotated bibliography of over 1000 entries dealing
      with printed materials, audiovisual materials, maps and
      other media. Topics covered are: Mexican history, Mexican
      Americans in the United States, the arts, literature,
      biography, fiction, and general references. In separate
      appendices are listed distinguished Mexican-American per-
      sonalities, organizations, periodicals and newspapers.
      Intended especially for high school and college students.

MARTINEZ, CECILIA J. See 682.

688   MEIER, MATT S. A Bibliography for Chicano History. San
      Francisco: R. and E. Research Associates, 1972. 96p.
         Arranged by chronological periods, a bibliography of
      books, periodicals, dissertations, and theses. Subdivi-
      sion by topics.

689   MEIER, MATT S. and FELICIANO RIVERA. A Selective Bibliography
      for the Study of Mexican American History. San Francisco:
      R. and E. Research Associates, 1972. 79p.
         Collection of historic materials. Reprint of 1971
      edition.

690   NAVARRO, ELISEO. The Chicano Community; A Selected Bibliog-
      raphy for Use in Social Work Education. New York: Council
      of Social Work Education, 1971. 57p.
         Annotated and coded by subject matter, emphasizes his-
      tory as well as the social sciences, and includes materials
      on the land grant situation, Chicano education, and labor
      unions.

691   NOGALES, LUIS G., ed. The Mexican American, A Selected and
      Annotated Bibliography, 2nd edition, revised and enlarged.
      Stanford: Stanford University Press, 1971. 162p.
         A critically annotated bibliography utilizing books and
      articles on a variety of sociological, historical, psycho-
      logical, etc., topics. Four hundred and forty-four works
      examined and evaluated.

PUTNAM, HOWARD. See 693.

RIOS, HERMINIO. See 675.

692   RIVERA, FELICIANO. Mexican American Sourcebook with Study
      Guideline. Menlo Park, California: Educational Consulting
      Associates, 1970. 196p.

SPANISH AMERICANS

(RIVERA, FELICIANO)
   A study guideline and selected bibliography of materials
   for use in primary and secondary education. Also special
   sections on the Missions of California, pictures of outstanding Mexican Americans, as well as text and background
   of the Guadalupe Hidalgo Treaty.

RIVERA, FELICIANO. See also 689.

693   SANCHEZ, GEORGE ISADORE and HOWARD PUTNAM. Materials Related
      to the Education of Spanish-Speaking People in the U. S.:
      An Annotated Bibliography. Westport, Connecticut: Green-
      wood Press, 1971. 76p.
         Books, articles, monographs, bulletins, dissertations,
      etc., included in this compendium. Also lists courses of
      study. Reprint of 1959 edition.

694   SCHRAMKO, LINDA FOWLER. Chicano Bibliography, Selected
      Materials on Americans of Mexican Descent. Sacramento,:
      Sacramento State College Library, Bibliographic Series No.
      1, 1970. 124p.
         Arranged by subject matter, lists the library's holdings
      through spring, 1969. Includes books, articles, govern-
      ment publications, periodicals, and ERIC items.

695   STANFORD UNIVERSITY Center for Latin-American Studies. The
      Mexican American - A Selected and Annotated Bibliography.
      Stanford: Stanford University, 1969. 139p.
         Stronger emphasis on social science selections than the
      humanities. Does not cover government documents, confer-
      ence proceedings, or unpublished dissertations.

696   U. S. CABINET Committee on Opportunity for the Spanish Speak-
      ing. The Spanish Speaking in the United States: A Guide
      to Materials. Washington, D. C.: U. S. Government Print-
      ing Office, 1971. 175p.
         1,300 items about Mexican Americans, Puerto Ricans, and
      Cubans with emphasis on politics, education, and institu-
      tions. Lists books, articles, audiovisual materials,
      Spanish-speaking radio and TV stations, and unpublished
      materials.

697   U. S. DEPARTMENT of Commerce. Bureau of Census. Population
      Characteristics: Persons of Spanish Origin in the United
      States. Washington, D. C.: U. S. Government Printing
      Office, 1971. 88p.
         The 1969 census; includes geography, age, education,
      job status, etc.

698 U. S. INTER-AGENCY Committee on Mexican American Affairs. The Mexican American, A New Focus on Opportunity: A Guide to Materials Relating to Persons of Mexican Heritage in the United States. Washington, D. C.: U. S. Government Printing Office, March, 1969. 186p.
Divided into categories according to media type: books, reports, hearings, etc., magazines, dissertations and manuscripts, bibliographies, and audiovisual.

699 UNIVERSITY OF Texas Library. Catalog of the Latin American Collection. Boston: G. K. Hall and Company, 1969, 31 v. 22,854p. First Supplement, 1971. Second Supplement, 1973.
Lists over 160,000 books from the fifteenth century to date. Also contains entries for manuscripts, pamphlets, and periodicals, newspapers and microfilm. Author, title and subject index.

2. Periodicals

700 ATISBOS: Journal of Chicano Research. Scheduled for publication in 1974 at Stanford University, Palo Alto, California.

701 AZTLÁN: Chicano Journal of the Social Sciences and the Arts. Mexican American Cultural Center. University of California, Los Angeles. Los Angeles, California 90024.
An academic journal which contains articles on Chicano sociology and the arts.

702 CHICANO Law Review. Chicano Law Student Association, School of Law: University of California at Los Angeles. Los Angeles, California 90024.
Volume 1, number 1 appeared in the Summer of 1972.

703 CON SAFOS. A Chicano literary and sociological magazine concerned with life in the Barrios, 1968. P. O. Box 31004, Los Angeles.

704 EL GRITO: A Journal of Contemporary Mexican American Thought. Quinto Sol Publications, P. O. Box 9275, Berkeley, California 94709.
Excellent magazine, full of very well-researched articles and art reproductions. Quinto Sol is also establishing itself as a leading publisher of Chicano written literature.

3. History, Geo-History (Exploration and Migration), Politics, Economics and Agricultural Labor

705 ACUÑA, RUDY. The Story of the Mexican Americans: The Men and the Land. New York: American Book Company, 1969. 140p.
A standard history of the Mexican Americans in the United States, the hardships they had to overcome and the

SPANISH AMERICANS

(ACUÑA, RUDOLFO)
successes and achievements won. Good for high school
students. Contains biographical data on prominent Mexican
Americans.

706 ALLEN, STEVE. The Ground is Our Table. Garden City, New
York: Doubleday, 1966. 141p.
Agricultural laborers, migrant labor, and Mexicans in
the U. S.

707 BAKER, BONNIE LEA, RICHARD A. WALD, and RITA ZAMORA. Econom-
ic Aspects of Mexican and Mexican-American Urban Households.
San Jose, California: Institute for Business and Economic
Research, San Jose State College, 1971. 150p.
Written in both English and Spanish.

708 BALLIS, GEORGE. Basta! La Historia de Nuestra Lucha:
Enough! The Tale of Our Struggle. Delano, California:
Farm Worker Press, 1966. 72p.
Text from the Plan of Delano. Chiefly illustrations.

709 BANCROFT, HUBERT HOWE. History of Arizona and New Mexico,
1530-1888. Albuquerque: Horn and Wallace, 1962. 829p.
A facsimile of the 1889 edition published coincidentally
with the 50th anniversary of New Mexico and Arizona state-
hood. According to W. A. Morris in the Quarterly of the
Oregon Historical Society, v. 4, p. 311-333, this work
was written by H. L. Oak. Published in 1888 as v. 12 of
Bancroft's History of the Pacific States of North America
under the title Arizona and New Mexico. Bibliography.

710 BANDELIER, ADOLPH F. A. The Gilded Man and El Dorado.
Chicago: Rio Grande Press, 1962. 302p.
Reprint of the 1873 history about New Mexico from the
Spanish occupation to the Mexican American war.

711 BANNON, JOHN FRANCIS. The Spanish Borderlands Frontier,
1513-1821. New York: Holt, Rinehart and Winston, 1970.
308p.
The frontier seen by an Anglo historian as a socializing
process. Summarizes Southwest historical literature and
explains the three "corridors" of Spanish exploration and
expansion leading to California, Arizona, New Mexico, and
Texas.

712 BARTLETT, JOHN RUSSELL. Personal Narrative of Explorations
and Incidents in Texas, New Mexico, California, and Chihua-
hua Connected with the United States and Mexican Boundary

(BARTLETT, JOHN RUSSELL)
   Commission During the Years 1850, '51, '52, and '53.
   Chicago: Rio Grande Press, 1965. 2 vols. 624p.
      A classic account of exploration reproduced with all
   of the original's copious and beautiful engravings. Con-
   tains important descriptions and characterizations of
   Mexicans in the region. Reprint of 1854 edition.

713   BAYITCH, S. A. and JOSÉ LUIS SIQUEIROS. Conflict of Laws:
      Mexico and the United States; A Bilateral Study. Coral
      Gables, Florida: University of Miami Press, 1968. 296p.

714   BECK, WARREN A. and DAVID A. WILLIAMS. California: A History
      of the Golden State. Garden City, New York: Doubleday,
      1972. 552p.
         Current Mexican American history included in the story
      of the great state's development.

715   BECK, WARREN A. New Mexico: A History of Four Centuries.
      Norman: University of Oklahoma Press, 1962. 363p.
         The land and its meaning to the various peoples on it:
      The Indians, the Spanish, the Anglo, the Mexican immigrant.
      Extensive bibliography.

716   BLAWIS, PATRICIA BELL. Tijerina and the Land Grants: Mexi-
      can Americans in Struggle for Their Heritage. New York:
      International Publishers, 1971. 191p.
         The history of the original land grants and the devel-
      opment of the 1960s land grant movement in Northern New
      Mexico. The details are given of the Alanza Federal de
      Pueblos Libre of Reies Lopez Tijerina and his courthouse
      battle.

717   BOGARDUS, EMORY S. The Mexican in the United States. New
      York: Arno Press, 1970. 126p.
         A book still valuable. Describes the kinds of immi-
      grants to the United States, their communal and camp life.
      Goes into economics, legislation, and repatriation prob-
      lems. Bibliography. Reprint of 1934 edition.

718   BOLTON, HERBERT EUGENE. Anza's California Expeditions. New
      York: Russell and Russell, 1966. 5 vols.
         The account of the explorer's travels in the 18th cen-
      tury, in a time before Lewis and Clark, when Anza opened
      up the road from Sonora to Monterrey and led a colony
      from Mexico to settle in the new lands. Reprint of 1930
      edition.

SPANISH AMERICANS

719   BOLTON, HERBERT EUGENE. The Spanish Borderlands; A Chronicle
      of Old Florida and the Southwest. New Haven: Yale Univer-
      sity Press, 1921. 320p.
          A classic description and history of the areas, explored
      by De Vaca, De Soto, Coronado, Cabrillo, and Vizcaino
      among others. Bibliography.

720   _____. Spanish Exploration in the Southwest, 1542-1706. New
      York: Barnes and Noble, 1967. 487p.
          Documents of the discovery of the Southwest, such as
      excerpts from Cabrillo's diary, with excellent introductions
      by the famous historian.

721   BUSTAMENTE, CHARLES J. and PATRICIA L. The Mexican-American
      and the United States. Mountain View, California: Patty-
      Lar Publications, 1969. 60p.
          This brief history crams in a lot of information in-
      cluding the Spanish conquest, Mexican American war, World
      War II. Also topical coverage such as labor, poverty, dis-
      crimination in employment and education, the Community
      Services Organization, and the grape strike at Delano.
      Brief biographies of leaders.

      BUSTAMENTE, PATRICIA L. See 721.

722   CARRANZA, ELIU. Pensamientos on Los Chicanos. Berkeley:
      California Book Company, Ltd., 1969. 29p.
          Informal essays concerning the Mexican-American as
      distinguished from the Chicano, the Chicano, the New Hu-
      manism, and new forms of education, ending with a plea for
      unification.

723   CASAS, BARTOLOMÉ DE LAS. Historia de Las Indias. Madrid:
      M. Aguilar, 1927. 3 vols.
          One of the oldest histories of the discovery and explora-
      tion of America and the establishment of the Spanish
      colonies. Translated by the British and used to establish
      the "Black Legend" of Spanish cruelty in the New World.
      Reprint of 1561 edition.

724   CASTAÑEDA, CARLOS E. The Mexican Side of the Texan Revolution
      (1836) by the Chief Mexican Participants. Austin: Graphic
      Ideas Incorporated, 1970. 402p.
          A selection of documents, such as diaries and accounts,
      from Mexicans who participated in the war. Includes Santa
      Ana. Reprint of 1928 edition.

725   THE CHICANO. Berkeley: University of California Press, The
      Pacific Historical Review, Vol. XLII:3. (August, 1973).
      441p.
          Special issue of the Pacific Historical Review worth
      ordering for Arthur M. Corwin's controversial assessment
      of Mexican American history. A descriptive bibliographic
      essay of the current materials available.

726   CLINE, HOWARD. The United States and Mexico, revised and en-
      larged. New York: Atheneum, 1969. 484p.
          A history of modern Mexico with a review of its past
      heritages. Main emphasis is on twentieth-century political
      and economic developments. An excellent bibliographical
      essay. Reprint of 1953 edition.

727   CLISSOLD, STEPHEN. The Seven Cities of Cibola. New York:
      C. Potter, Incorporated, 1961. 191p.
          Tales of the Spanish 15th- and 16th-century explorers
      and their quests for gold and the fountain of youth.
      Bibliography.

728   COLES, ROBERT. Uprooted Children: The Early Life of Migrant
      Farm Workers. Pittsburgh: University of Pittsburgh Press,
      1970. 142p.
          Captures the physical, psychological, and emotional
      hardships of the migrant law workers and is especially
      sensitive to the lives of the children of these workers
      who must go out into the fields so young.

729   CRAIG, RICHARD B. The Bracero Program; Interest Groups and
      Foreign Policy. Austin: University of Texas Press, 1971.
      233p.
          A history of agricultural labor concerning the braceros.
      Bibliography.

730   CUELLAR, ALFREDO B. and JOAN MOORE. Mexican Americans. Engle-
      wood Cliffs, New Jersey: Prentice-Hall, 1970. Various
      paging.
          The social, economic, educational, and occupational
      disparities of the Mexican-Americans, particularly those
      of the Southwest. A well-documented historical study.

731   DAY, MARK. Forty Acres: César Chávez and the Farm Workers.
      New York: Praeger, 1971. 222p.
          Traces the struggle of the United Farm Workers from the
      first days in Delano. Includes an introduction by César
      Chávez. Probes the efforts and frustrations of the Church.

SPANISH AMERICANS

(DAY, MARK)
The moving story of James Coswell among others brings forth
many of the feelings and attitudes of the Farm Workers
movement. Bibliography.

732   DELGADO, ABELARDO. The Chicano Movement: Some Not Too Objective Observations. Denver: Totinem Press, 1971. 40p.
Prepared by the Colorado Migrant Council, a history of
the Chicano movement, both locally and nationally. Includes the methodology at Aztlán, scope of the movement,
and its participation in politics, education, economic
institutions, drug addiction, the draft, and the rural and
urban Chicano cultural revolution.

733   _____. Chicano; Twenty Five Pieces of a Chicano Mind. Santa
Barbara: La Causa, Incorporated, 1971. 36p.
One of the leading Brown Power people tells it as he
sees it.

734   DE VOTO, BERNARD. The Year of Decision, 1846. Boston:
Houghton Mifflin, 1943. 538p.
The history of the Mexican American War against a background of United States history from 1815 to 1861. Some
bibliography.

735   DUNNE, JOHN GREGORY. Delano, The Story of the California
Grape Strike. New York: Farrar, Straus, and Giroux, 1967.
176p.
An account of César Chávez, the Union, the Chicanos,
the Filipinos, and the Grape Strike.

736   ELDER, DAVID PAUL. The Old Spanish Missions of California;
An Historical and Descriptive Sketch. San Francisco: P.
Elder and Company, 1913. 89p.
Well-illustrated.

737   FAULK, ODIE B. Land of Many Frontiers: A History of the
American Southwest. New York: Oxford University Press,
1968. 358p.
Begins in 1519 and traces the Spanish explorers, the
occupation of the Southwest by the Anglo, the conquest of
the Indian and the present state politics of the area, all
particularly well. Bibliography.

738   FERGUSSON, ERNA. New Mexico - A Pageant of Three Peoples.
New York: Knopf, 1966. 408p.
Spanish Colonial history. The accounts of the nineteenth
century are especially well-done. Reprint of 1951 edition.

739 FERGUSSON, HARVEY. Rio Grande. New York: Alfred A. Knopf,
1933. 296p.
Describes the life and feelings of the Pueblo farmers,
their past, and the encroaching of the White explorers and
then the missionaries to the Rio Grande area. Good
photographs. Bibliography.

740 FERNANDEZ-FLOREZ, DARIO. The Spanish Heritage in the United
States, 3rd Corrected and Enlarged Edition. Madrid: Publications Espanolas, 1971. 376p.
Usable handbook collecting various documents, pieces of
history, and miscellaneous information concerning the Spanish involvement in North America. Spanish influence on
Native American art in the United States is ably treated.

741 FOGEL, WALTER A. Mexican Americans in Southwest Labor Markets.
Los Angeles: Mexican-American Study Project, Advanced Report No. 10, Division of Research, Graduate School of
Business Administration, University of California, Los Angeles, 1967. 222p.
An inquiry into a variety of aspects of the Mexican-
American labor market experience. The study does not claim
to be comprehensive and analytically exhaustive, since
resource limitations were restrictive. Instead, the analysis focuses on specific problems such as: regional com-
parisons of the market status of Mexican Americans in the
Southwest, temporal changes in market status, generational
differences, and migration. Bibliographical notes.

742 FORBES, JACK D. Aztecas Del Norte: The Chicanos of Aztlán.
Greenwich, Connecticut: Fawcett Publications, Incorporated,
1973. 336p.
Forbes, a Native American, sees the Chicano movement
as an Indian movement within the confines of Aztlán, a
geographical area that knows no national boundaries, but
which is simply called "the Southwest." Grouping all the
peoples together, he calls them Anishinabes, and in his
Introduction discusses the Mexican approach to United States
history. This book is not a political history, but a collection of historical documents, statements, and poetry,
with brief introductions.

743 FUSCO, PAUL and GEORGE D. HORWITZ. La Causa: The California
Grape Strike. New York: Collier Books, 1970. 158p.
A photographic and written essay on the strike.

744 GALARZA, ERNESTO. Merchants of Labor: The Mexican Bracero
Story: An Account of the Managed Migration of Mexican

SPANISH AMERICANS

(GALARZA, ERNESTO)
Farm Workers in California, 1942-1960. Santa Barbara,
California: McNally and Loftin, 1964. 284p.
A general discussion of the bracero and his history in
the United States from 1880 onward. Goes into the details
of the structural control system used by labor management
to manipulate bracero work pools and discusses also future
perspectives.

745 GALARZA, ERNESTO, HERMAN GALLEGOS, and JULIAN SAMORA. Mexican-Americans in the Southwest. Santa Barbara: McNalley
and Loftin, 1969. 90p.
A study of Mexican Americans in the Southwest area
during the 1960s. Statistics on population, immigration,
employment, and political involvement.

746 GALARZA, ERNESTO. Spiders in the House and Workers in the
Field. Notre Dame, Indiana: University of Notre Dame
Press, 1970. 306p.
An account of the DiGiorgio Fruit Corporation and its
workers. Bibliogrpahy.

747 _____. Strangers in Our Fields. Washington, D. C.: U. S.
Section, Joint U. S.-Mexico Trade Commission, 1956, 80p.
Based on a report regarding compliance with the con-
tractual, legal, and civil rights of Mexican agricultural
contract labor in the U. S. made possible through a grant-
in-aid from the Fund for the Republic, Washington, D. C.

GALLEGOS, HERMAN. See 745.

748 GAMIO, MANUEL. Mexican Immigration to the United States: A
Study of Human Migration and Adjustment. New York:
Arno Press, 1971. 262p.
A sociological study of the travels and assimilation
of the Mexican immigrant after he crosses the border into
the United States. A companion book to The Mexican
Immigrant: His Life Story.... Bibliography and appendices.
Reprint of 1930 edition. See also 898 and 899.

749 GARDNER, RICHARD. Grito! Reies Tijerina and the New Mexican
Land Grant War of 1967. Indianapolis: Bobbs-Merrill
Company, 1970. 292p.
In June, 1967, the courthouse at Rio Arribo in the
village of Tierra Amarilla, New Mexico was taken over by
Chicanos. Gardner has done much research for this book,
using taped interviews to come to an understanding of the

(GARDNER, RICHARD)
   meaning of the event to Chicanos. A good insightful piece
   of historical-sociological writing.

750   GILPIN, LAURA. The Rio Grande, River of Destiny; An Inter-
       pretation of The River, The Land, and The People. New
       York: Duell, Sloan, and Pearce, 1949. 243p.
          Essentially a book of photography, or art, or history,
       however you regard Laura Gilpin's work. Bibliography.

751   GOMEZ, DAVID. Some Chicanos: Strangers in Our Own Land.
       Boston: Beacon Press, 1973. 204p.
          The Chicano movement as seen by a priest activist who
       has been involved in it.

752   GONZALEZ, NANCIE L. The Spanish-Americans of New Mexico:
       A Heritage of Pride. Albuquerque: University of New
       Mexico Press, 1969. 246p.
          The history of the Hispanos of New Mexico from the
       nineteenth century to date of publication, plus a study of
       them as a class in comparison, also, with other Mexican
       American groups elsewhere. Developed out of a UCLA re-
       search project. Bibliography.

753   GREBLER, LEO, JOAN MOORE and RALPH GUZMAN. The Mexican-
       American People, The Nation's Second Largest Minority.
       New York: Free Press, 1970. 777p.
          An important study of Mexican Americans in their rela-
       tionship to the Anglo-American society. Cultural values,
       religion, economic and social conditions, politics, and
       assimilation surveyed with much data. A review in El Grito
       (IV:4, Summer 1971) equated this sociological study in
       value to Myrdal's An American Dilemma. The critic, how-
       ever, does not like the narrowness of considering Chicano
       life in terms of "The Chicano Problem" and the conclusion
       that socio-cultural assimilation is the solution for any
       achievement of economic mobility.

754   GREBLER, LEO. Mexican Immigration to the United States: The
       Record and Its Implications. Los Angeles: Mexican-Ameri-
       can Study Project Advance Report No. Division of Research,
       Graduate School of Business Administration, University of
       California, 1966. 106p.
          A solid compendium of materials on Mexican immigration.
       Includes statistics and analysis as well as a comparison
       of the pattern of border crossing as compared to European
       immigration.

MEXICAN AMERICANS

755   GUTIERREZ, JOSE ANGEL. El Politico: The Mexican American
       Elected Official. El Paso, Texas: Mictla Publication
       Books, 1972.

       GUZMAN, RALPH. See 753.

756   HADDOX, JOHN HERBERT. Los Chicanos: An Awakening People.
       El Paso: University of Texas Press, 1970. 44p. South-
       western Studies Monograph No. 28.
          Probes the problem of White educational institutions
       instilling a sense of inferiority into the Mexican American
       student. Good illustrations accompany the text.

757   HAMMOND, GEORGE P. The Treaty of Guadalupe Hidalgo, 1848.
       Berkeley: Friends of the Bancroft Library, 1949.
          A reproduction of the historic treaty between the United
       States and Mexico with an introduction and notes.

758   HANKE, LEWIS. The First Social Experiments in America, A
       Study in the Development of Spanish Indian Policy in the
       Sixteenth Century. Cambridge: Harvard University Press,
       1935. 99p.
          Investigates the treatment of the Indians by analyzing
       the administration and corruption of the Spanish colonies.

759   HEINS, MARJORIE. Strictly Ghetto Property: The Story of Los
       Siete de La Raza. Berkeley: Ramparts Press, 1972. 324p.
          The story of the trial of The Seven (Los Siete) in San
       Francisco. The seven men were picked up after the killing
       of a policeman. They were acquitted but subjected to
       police brutality and racism before the trial and harassment
       afterwards. Discusses the ghetto experience, the Brown
       Movement, and the Black Panther Party.

760   HORGAN, PAUL. Conquistadors of North American History.
       London: Macmillan Company, 1963. 303p.
          A chronological account of the Spanish explorers and
       their adventures on the continent.

761   _____. Great River: The Rio Grande in North American His-
       tory, 2 vols. New York: Minerva Press, 1968. 1020p.
          See especially Volume 1, Indians and Spain for Horgan's
       treatment of early history. These two volumes are infor-
       mative as well as poetic to read. Reprint of 1954 edition.

762   _____. The Heroic Triad: Essays in the Social Energies of
       Three Southwestern Cultures. New York: Holt, Rinehart
       and Winston, 1970. 256p.

(HORGAN, PAUL)
> The interweaving of the Indian, Latin, and Anglo-American cultures in the Rio Grande region. Bibliography. Reprint of 1954 edition.

HORWITZ, GEORGE D. <u>See</u> 743.

763   JENKINSON, MICHAEL. <u>Tijerina.</u> Albuquerque, Paisano Press, 1968. 103p.
> A journalistic history of the June, 1967 land grant conflict.

764   KNBC. <u>Mexican-American Heritage</u>, Volume 1. n.p.: KNBC, 1971.
> Ten programs in the form of TV scripts reproduced as they appeared on NBC in July 1971: Aztlán, Myths of the Southwest; the Mexican-American War Period; Conflict and Resistance - the Myth of Docility; Spiders in the House; the War Years; Economic Repression of the Chicano; Mexican-Americans and Education--Quo Vadis, America?; Barrio Life and Cultural Democracy; Stereotypes in the Mass Media.

765   LANGE, DOROTHEA and PAUL TAYLOR. <u>An American Exodus: A Record of Human Erosion in the Thirties</u>. New Haven: Yale University Press, 1969. 145p.
> A short account of migratory workers, their family life and their present situation. Pictures.

LEONARD, IRVING A. <u>See</u> 786.

766   McWILLIAMS, CAREY. <u>Factories in the Field; The Story of Migratory Farm Labor in California</u>. Boston: Little, Brown and Company, 1939. 334p.
> A famous history of migratory farm workers which at the time of its publication caused a Senate investigation. Bibliography.

767   _____. <u>Ill Fares the Land; Migrants and Migratory Labor in the United States</u>. New York: Barnes and Noble, 1972. 419p.
> A historic description of the process of land migration and the labor exodus westward in the United States.

MARSHALL, GRACE. <u>See</u> 770.

768   MARTINEZ, JOHN. <u>Mexican Emigration to the United States, 1910-1930</u>. San Francisco: R. and E. Research Associates, 1971. 100p.
> A probing study of the various motivations of the emigrants. The Mexican Revolution, the Selective Service Act

SPANISH AMERICANS

(MARTINEZ, JOHN)
of 1917, and the post war need for labor in the United
States all affected this substantial migratory movement.
The efforts to control emigration by Mexican American Labor as well as the policies of both the Mexican and U. S.
governments are treated. Bibliography.

769 MEIER, MATT S. and FELICIANO RIVERA. The Chicanos: A History
of Mexican Americans. New York: Hill and Wang, 1972. 302p.
Indian, Mexican, Spanish, and Anglo have confronted one
another and intermixed from earliest explorations to the
present. This book traces the Mexican migration northward
and the efforts made to preserve their culture. Good sections also included on current farm labor problems and
political activism.

770 MITTELBACH, FRANK G. and GRACE MARSHALL. The Burden of
Poverty. Los Angeles: A Mexican American Study Project,
Advance Report No. 5. Division of Research, Graduate
School of Business Administration, University of California,
Los Angeles, 1966. 65p.
Deals with the Chicano in the Southwest and the economic
conditions under which he exists. Bibliography.

MITTELBACH, FRANK G. See also 771.

771 MOORE, JOAN W. and FRANK G. MITTELBACH. Residential Segre-
gation in the Urban Southwest; A Comparative Study. Los
Angeles: Mexican American Study Project Advance Report
No. 5, Division of Research, Graduate School of Business,
University of California, Los Angeles, 1966.
Another in the series of studies that examined the
various sociological situations of the Mexican American
in the 1960s. Examines 35 cities for the degree of segre-
gation to be found.

MOORE, JOAN. See 730, 753.

772 MOORE, TRUMAN E. The Slaves We Rent. New York: Random
House, 1965. 171p.
A sociological history of the migratory labor forces in
this country including Blacks as well as braceros. A
bibliography and list of organizations who can give information on migrants.

773 MOQUIN, WAYNE, ed. with CHARLES VAN DOREN. A Documentary
History of the Mexican Americans. New York: Praeger
Publishers, 1971. 399p.

Mexican Americans

(MOQUIN, WAYNE with CHARLES VAN DOREN)
Sixty-five documents from the year 1536 to the present
touching on the Spanish conquest, the settlement of the
Southwest, the Anglo conquest, Mexican laborers, and current writings on Chicano society and politics. Bibliography: a few selected readings.

774 MORALES, ARMANDO. Ando Sangrado (I Am Bleeding); A Study of
Mexican American Police Conflict. La Puente, California:
Perspective Publications, 1972. 143p.

775 MURPHY, JAMES M. The Spanish Legal Heritage in Arizona.
Tucson, Arizona: Pioneers' Historical Society, 1966.
46p. (Arizona History Series #1).
Details the common law and Roman law pertaining to
Arizona. Bibliography.

776 NABOKOV, PETER. Tijerina and the Courthouse Raid. Albuquerque: University of New Mexico, 1970. 285p.
Considered one of the best accounts of the June, 1967
land grant activities.

777 NATIONAL ADVISORY Committee on Farm Labor. Farm Labor Organizing, 1905-1967; A Brief History. New York: National
Advisory Committee on Farm Labor, 1967. 40p.
A brief historical survey of the unionization of farm
laborers.

778 NATIONAL DIRECTORY of Spanish Surname Elected Officials.
Los Angeles: Aztlán Publications, 1974.

779 NAVA, JULIAN. Mexican Americans: A Brief Look at Their
History. New York: Anti-Defamation League of B'nai
B'rith, 1970. 56p.
A short introductory history for the general reader.
Includes attempts at defining who and what a Mexican
American is, historical distortions, and the future for
Chicanos. Also a brief annotated guide to further reading.

780 _____. Mexican Americans; Past, Present, and Future. New
York: American Book Company, 1969. 120p.
A well-illustrated text, good for classroom use as it
contains review and analysis questions at the end of each
chapter. Emphasis on culture and history.

781 _____, ed. ¡Viva La Raza! Readings on Mexican Americans.
New York: Van Nostrad Reinhold Company, 1973. 169p.

SPANISH AMERICANS

(NAVA, JULIAN)
The development of the Chicano movement seen through documents. Sometimes Nava presents two readings about topics such as land tenure and labor exploitation.

782 NELSON, EUGENE. Huelga, The First Hundred Days of the Great Delano Grape Strike. Delano, California: Farm Workers Press, 1966. 122p.
A day-by-day account of the events, people, and issues involved in this historically noteworthy strike.

783 NEWMAN, PATTY. ¡Do It Up Brown! San Diego, California: Viewpoint Books, 1971. 392p.
A popularized version of the current Chicano political scene. More than half the book is devoted to biographies of Tijerina, Gonzales, and Chávez. Descriptions of the various Mexican American movements included.

784 NORTH, DAVID S. The Border Crossers: People Who Live in Mexico and Work In the United States. Washington, D. C.: TransCentury Corporation, 1970. 319p.
Excellent survey of the border crossing laborers, immigration policies, and commuting problems. Some analysis of the life style, consuming practices, and personal attitudes of the border crossing Mexican laborers.

785 PERRIGO, LYNN I. Texas and Our Spanish Southwest, revised edition. New York: Holt, Reinhart and Winston, 1971. 469p.
One of the few regional histories that tells adequately the role of the varied Spanish-speaking peoples in the development of the area. Bibliography. Reprint of 1960 edition.

786 PICÓN-SALAS, MARIANO. A Cultural History of Spanish America, From Conquest to Independence, translated by Irving A. Leonard. Berkeley: University of California Press, 1971. 192p.
An analysis of the European spiritual and intellectual concepts that underwent a change in migrating to the New World. Baroque learning and eighteenth-century Jesuit Hispanic humanism are discussed. A good background book.

787 RENDÓN, ARMANDO B. Chicano Manifesto. New York: Macmillan, 1971. 337p.
An outspoken account of the development of the Chicano movement in the United States. Rendón discusses the problems and aspirations of the Brown Power movement, ending

(RENDÓN, ARMANDO B.)
with the East Los Angeles confrontation with law and order in 1970.

RIVERA, FELICIANO. See 769.

788   RUIZ, RAMÓN EDUARDO, ed. The Mexican War--Was It Manifest Destiny? New York: Holt, Rinehart and Winston, 1963. 118p.
The selections attempt to show both viewpoints on the Mexican and American war. Bibliography.

789   SAMORA, JULIAN. Los Mojados: The Wetback Story. Notre Dame: University of Notre Dame Press, 1971. 205p.
An in-depth examination of the illegal mass movement of people from Mexico into the United States. The author ably shows the feelings and motivations for both the immigration of the Mexicans and for the reactionary tendencies among U. S. citizens.

SAMORA, JULIAN. See 745.

790   SÁNCHEZ, GEORGE ISIDORE. Forgotten People: A Study of New Mexicans. Albuquerque: University of New Mexico Press, 1967. 98p.
A fascinating book about the Hispanos, descendants of the first White settlers in the Taos area of Northern New Mexico. Sánchez shows that the Spanish, Mexicans, and Anglos have all ignored these people who have a variety of educational, economic, and cultural problems. Reprint of 1940 edition.

791   SERVIN, MANUEL PATRICIO, ed. The Mexican-Americans: An Awakening Minority. Beverly Hills, California: Glencoe Press, 1970. 235p.
A selection of historical articles, well-selected, arranged in chronological order. There is a gap between 1848 and 1900, however. Bibliography.

SIQUEIROS, JOSE LUIS. See 713.

792   STEINER, STAN. La Raza: The Mexican Americans. New York: Harper and Row, 1969. 418p.
A journalistic treatment of recent Chicano politics and cultural background with historical perspectives. A fine overall account of the Tijerina land grant struggle, and the Chávez grape strike as well as a good description of

SPANISH AMERICANS

(STEINER, STAN)
the past Los Angeles barrio. Includes extensive lists of source materials and a bibliography of barrio newspapers.

793 TAYLOR, PAUL S. An American-Mexican Frontier: Nueces County, Texas. New York: Russell & Russell, 1971. 337p.
A study in racism and violence, dealing with a small geographical area that has wide application to Anglo-Chicano problems in general. Raymund Parades says that Taylor was a real trailblazer and that his works on Mexican labor are fascinating because they reveal so much about Anglo attitudes towards Mexicans. Reprint of 1934 edition.

794 _____. Mexican Labor in the United States. New York: Arno Press and The New York Times, 1970.
A ten-part compendium of research on early Mexican immigrant labor. Reprint of 1928-1934 editions.

TAYLOR, PAUL. See 765.
VAN DOREN, CHARLES. See 773.
WALD, RICHARD A. See 707.

795 WEBB, WALTER PRESCOTT. The Great Plains. New York: Ginn and Company, 1931. 525p.
A classic history which includes the exploration of the Spanish, and the Mexican expansion North during the nineteenth century.

796 _____. The Story of the Texas Rangers. Austin: Encino Press, 1971.
Details the slaughtering of Mexicans and Americans at every turn. Reprint of 1956 edition.

797 WEBER, DAVID. Foreigners in Their Native Land: Historical Roots of the Mexican American. Albuquerque: University of New Mexico Press, 1973. 288p.
Essays and selections focusing on land and immigration conflicts until just before the great immigration pushes of the twentieth century. Bibliography.

WILLIAMS, DAVID A. See 714.
ZAMORA, RITA. See 707.

4. Education and Bi-Cultural Programs

798 ALTMAN, ROBERT A. and PATRICIA O. SNYDER, eds. The Minority Student on Campus: Expectations and Possibilities. Berkeley, California and Boulder, Colorado: Center for Research and Development in Higher Education, University of California, Berkeley and Western Interstate Commission

(ALTMAN, ROBERT A. and PATRICIA O. SNYDER)
for Higher Education, 1970. 219p.
Papers presented at the 12th College and University
Self-Study Institute at the University of California,
Berkeley, in 1970. Covers: overview of the situation, research and student perspectives on campus, power and pri-
orities, and non-curricular and curricular programs.

799 AMERICAN COUNCIL on Education, Committee on the Study of
Teaching Materials in Intergroup Relations. Intergroup
Relations in Teaching Materials; A Survey and Appraisal.
Washington, D. C.: American Council on Education, 1960.
231p.
One of a series of Work in Progress that includes also
Elementary Curriculum in Intergroup Relations; Case Studies
in Instruction (1950).

800 ANDERSON, THEODORE and MILDRED BOYER. Bilingual Schooling
in the United States, 2 vols. Austin: Southwest
Educational Development Laboratory, 1970. 292, 327p.
The history of bilingual programs in the United States
and elsewhere with recommendations, curriculum planning
suggestions, and descriptions of current programs. Bibliography. Appendices.

801 BEALS, RALPH LEON and NORMAN HUMPHREY. No Frontier to Learning; The Mexican Student in the United States. Minneapolis: University of Minnesota Press, 1957. 148p.
Interviews at UCLA in the 1950s used to discuss the
acculturation of Mexican college students in the United
States.

BOYER, MILDRED. See 800.

802 BRUSSELL, CHARLES B., ed. Disadvantaged Mexican American
Children and Early Educational Experience. Austin: Southwest Educational Development Laboratory, 1968. 105p.
Report by the Southwest Educational Development Laboratory. Bibliography.

803 CARTER, THOMAS P. Mexican Americans in School: A History
of Educational Neglect. New York: College Entrance Examination Board, 1970. 235p.
An overview of the problems, influences, failures, and
special educational programs for Mexican Americans. Includes personal interviews with educators, a review of
educational literature, and a bibliography.

SPANISH AMERICANS

804 CASKEY, OWEN L., ed. Guidance Needs of Mexican American Youth. Proceedings of the First Invitational Conference (November 10, 1967, Lubbock, Texas). Austin, Texas: Southwest Educational Development Laboratory, 1967. 87p.
    Papers concerned with the education and guidance of the Mexican American student.

805 CHICANO COORDINATING Council on Higher Education. El Plan de Santa Barbara. Oakland: La Causa Publications, 1969. 155p.
    A Chicano plan for higher education including analyses and positions by the Chicano Coordinating Council on Higher Education. Bibliography.

806 FORBES, JACK D. Mexican-American: A Handbook for Educators. Berkeley, California: Far West Laboratory for Educational Research and Development, 1967. 34p.
    Some practical approaches to Mexican American education.

    HERNANDEZ, WILLIAM J. See 808.
    HORNER, VIVIAN M. See 807.
    HUMPHREY, NORMAN. See 801.

807 JOHN, VERA and VIVIAN M. HORNER, co-directors. Early Childhood Bilingual Education Project. New York: Modern Language Association, 1971. 187p.
    Two noted educators put down the results of their research. Bibliography.

808 JOHNSON, HENRY SIOUX and WILLIAM J. HERNANDEZ. Educating the Mexican American. Valley Forge: Judson Press, 1970. 384p.
    Study in education devotes major sections to guidance, curriculum, bi-lingual education and the role of educational institutions.

809 MANUEL, HERSCHEL THURMAN. Spanish-Speaking Children of the Southwest: Their Education and the Public Welfare. Austin: University of Texas Press, 1970. 222p.
    A basic educational study on the education of Mexican American children in the Southwest, especially Texas. This reprint gives background analysis of the culture and occcupational characteristics of the children in U. S. public schools. Educator Julian Nava calls this the best study to date of the educational problems of Mexican American children. Notes and bibliography. Reprint of 1965 edition.

810   NATIONAL CONFERENCE on Educational Opportunities for Mexican
      Americans, Austin, Texas, 1968. Proceedings. Austin:
      Southwest Educational Development Laboratory, 1968. 130p.
         Includes many helpful aids to teaching Mexican Americans,
      presented in a very informal way.

811   NATIONAL EDUCATION Association of the United States. Depart-
      ment of Rural Education. The Invisible Minority; Report of
      the NEA-Tucson Survey on the Teaching of Spanish to the
      Spanish-Speaking. Washington, D. C.: NEA-DRE, 1966. 39p.
         Problems in bilingualism and the teaching of Spanish in
      the schools.

812   NATIONAL EDUCATIONAL Task Force della Raza. Annual Report:
      1971. Los Angeles: University of California, Los Angeles.
      56p.
         Shows the leadership taken by educators of Mexican Amer-
      ican descent to develop programs for the Mexican American
      youth of the Los Angeles community.

SNYDER, PATRICIA. See 798.

813   TOWARD QUALITY Education for Mexican Americans Report VI:
      Mexican American Education Study. Washington, D. C.:
      U. S. Commission on Civil Rights, February, 1974. 98p.
         Text includes student assignment practices, teacher edu-
      cation, and counseling analysis, with many statistics, con-
      clusions, and recommendations. Bibliography.

5. General Culture and Community Life
(Anthropology, Art, Ballads, Cooking, Folk-Dramas
and Tales, Law, Linguistics, Medicine, Music,
Philosophy, Religion and Sociology)

814   BARKER, GEORGE C. Pachuco: An American-Spanish Argot and Its
      Social Function in Tucson, Arizona. Tucson: University of
      Arizona Press, 1958. 46p.
         One of the most important studies of the Pachuco or
      "Pocho" dialect, a mixture of Spanish and English.

815   BOATRIGHT, MODY C., ed. Mexican Border Ballads and Other Lore.
      Dallas: Southern Methodist University Press, 1967. (Pub-
      lications of the Texas Folklore Society, No. 21, 1946.)
      143p.
         The Proceedings of the Texas Folklore Society from
      1943-46, including ballads and tales by W. M. Hudson, J. F.
      Dobie, H. Martin, J. M. Brewer, R. T. Clark, and A. F. Muir.
      Includes unaccompanied melodies with words and bibliograph-
      ical references.

BOATRIGHT, MODY. See also 825.

SPANISH AMERICANS

816   BURMA, JOHN H., ed. Mexican-Americans in the United States:
      A Reader. Cambridge, Massachusetts: Schenkman Publica-
      tions, 1970. 487p.
          A standard series of essays with sociological emphasis
      arranged by topics such as: prejudice, education, econom-
      ics, acculturation, etc. Bibliography.

817   CAMPA, ARTHUR LEON, ed. Los Comanches, A New Mexican Folk
      Drama. Albuquerque: Bulletin, University of New Mexico,
      Language Series, VII, Number 1 (April 1, 1942).
          One of the few poetic dramas from early American his-
      tory; deserves wider recognition in anthologies. Translated
      from the original Spanish by Gilbert Espinosa. The drama
      enacts the epic battle between the Spanish and the Comanches
      with the subsequent defeat of the Indians in 1774. This
      play was often put on in small towns at Christmas time,
      when the Comanches were depicted as kidnapping the Christ
      child.

818   _____. Treasure of the Sangre de Cristos: Tales and Tradi-
      tions of the Spanish Southwest. Norman: University of
      Oklahoma Press, 1963. 223p.
          Tales and traditions of the Spanish Southwest by a
      leading folklorist in this field. Campa has also done
      studies on Spanish religious folk theatre (1934), Spanish
      folk poetry (1946), and Spanish folk songs (1933, 1940).
      Bibliography.

819   CASTANADA, CARLOS. Journey to Ixtlan: The Lessons of Don
      Juan. New York: Simon and Schuster, 1972. 315p.
          The third book in the series about Don Juan, the brujo,
      though another book is supposed to be on its way. In this
      novel, Castenada, the disciple, learns to assume responsi-
      bility for much of his participation in "power" without
      helpers such as "the little smoke." Further development
      of the concept of the warrior also and the meaning of
      stopping the world.

820   _____. A Separate Reality: Further Conversations with Don
      Juan. New York: Simon and Schuster, 1971. 317p.
          A continuation of The Teachings of Don Juan: A Yaqui
      Way of Knowledge, this goes deeper into the nature of
      reality in terms of "looking" and "seeing" or perceiving
      the true meaning of everything. Delightful to read,
      whether you can accept all the physical phenomena in the
      book or not.

821   ____. The Teachings of Don Juan: A Yaqui Way of Knowledge.
      Berkeley: University of California Press, 1968. 196p.
        Takes the reader through a five-year apprenticeship with
      a Yaqui Man of Knowledge. A non-ordinary level of reality
      is revealed through Mescalito and Don Juan. Glimpses the
      Ancient Wisdom of the Mexican as still voiced by the
      "brujos" or "diableros" (witch doctors).

822 CLARK, MARGARET. Health in the Mexican American Culture.
      Berkeley: University of California Press, 1959. 253p.
        A study of Sal si Puedes, an unincorporated community
      on the Eastern edge of San Jose. Based on Clark's thesis
      that medicos study Chicano culture before giving services
      to the Mexican American community and that modern medicine
      and folk medicine should both be used.

823 DICKEY, ROLAND F. New Mexico Village Arts. Albuquerque:
      University of New Mexico Press, 1949. 266p.
        Does an excellent job of covering the history and devel-
      opment of New Mexican folk arts and in the process pro-
      vides an ethnic and political history of the state of New
      Mexico.

824 DOBIE, J. FRANK. Puro Mexicano. Austin: Texas Folklore
      Society, 1935. 261p.
        Folklore and songs, Mexican border tales, as well as
      migration songs and wise sayings. See: Songs of the
      Mexican migration. Also includes Rancho sayings of the
      border by H. D. Wesley.

825 DOBIE, J. FRANK, MODY BOATRIGHT, and HARRY RANSOM. Texan
      Stomping Grounds. Austin: Texas Folklore Society, 1941.
      162p.
        Sketches of post-war life in Eastern Texas, descriptions
      of early recreation and games, a reminiscence of ranching
      life in the West. Also includes the 1940 and 1941 pro-
      ceedings of the Texas folklore society.

826 DOBIE, J. FRANK. Tongues of the Monte. Garden City, New
      York: Doubleday, 1935. 301p.
        A good collection of Mexican folk beliefs containing
      many ghost and supernatural stories.

827   ____. A Vaquero of the Brush Country, Partly from the Rem-
      iniscences of John Young. Boston: Little, Brown, 1959.
      302p.

SPANISH AMERICANS

(DOBIE, J. FRANK)
An early study of frontier and pioneer life in Texas. Good background material for an introduction to the Anglo setting and attitudes of the Southwest. Bibliography. Reprint of 1929 edition.

828 ESPINEL, LUISA. Canciones de Mi Padre: Spanish Folksongs From Southern Arizona. Tucson: University of Arizona Press, 1946. 56p.
Excellent little book that captures the flavor of the Spanish folk songs of Arizona as well as the distinctively Mexican folk music of the area.

829 ESPINOSA, JOSÉ EDMUNDO. Saints in the Valleys: Christian Sacred Images in the History, Life and Folk Art of Spanish New Mexico. Albuquerque: University of New Mexico Press, 1967. 122p.
Illustrated book traces the art of Spanish New Mexico from the early sixteenth century through the nineteenth century.

830 FERGUSSON, ERNA. Mexican Cookbook. Albuquerque: University of New Mexico Press, 1967. 128p.
A famous writer about the Southwest gives you her collection of old Mexican recipes adapted for her own use. Reprint of 1934 edition.

831 FORBES, HARRIET REBECCA. Mission Tales in the Days of the Dons. Freeport, New York: Books for Libraries Press, 1970. 343p.
13 stories about the Spaniards, Mexicans, Indians, and Californians before the conquest by the Americans.

832 GARCIA, GEORGE J., ed. Selected Reading Materials on the Mexican and Spanish American. Denver, Colorado: Commission on Community Relations, City and County of Denver, Colorado, 1969. 103p.
Articles of history, culture, inter-cultural relations, and attitude and status of the Chicano, written by Mexican Americans. Bibliography.

833 GRIFFITH, BEATRICE WINSTON. American Me. Boston: Houghton-Mifflin Company, 1948. 341p.
A sociological description of barrio life done in terms of pseudo-fictional stories about Chicanos.

834 HALLENBECK, CLEVE and JUANITA H. WILLIAMS. Legends of the
Spanish Southwest. Ann Arbor, Michigan: Gryphon Books,
1971. 342p.
Tales out of the past romantic haze. Bibliography.
Reprint of 1938 edition.

HAUG, MARSHA J. See 860.

835 HELLER, CELIA STOPNICKA. Mexican American Youth: Forgotten
Youth at the Crossroads. New York: Random House, 1966.
113p.
Often-mentioned book about the conflicts and expectations
of the Chicanos in Los Angeles. Criticized in El Grito
(fall 1968) as basically negative towards Mexican Americans.

836 _____. New Converts to the American Dream? Mobility Aspirations of Young Mexican-Americans. New Haven: College and
University Press, 1971. 287p.
A sociological investigation attempting to discover if
Mexican American youth are pursuing the "American Dream"
by analyzing their educational and occupational skills
and goals. Research material came mostly from Los Angeles
youth in surveys during 1957-58 and 1965.

837 HELM, JUNE, ed. Spanish-Speaking People in the United States:
Proceedings of the 1968 Annual Spring Meeting of the American Ethnological Society. Seattle: University of Washington Press, 1968. 215p.
A group of thirteen papers which include such topics as:
Anthropological research, assimilation, quantitative analysis
of urban experiences, and the Anglo side of acculturation.

838 HENDERSON, ALICE. Brothers of Light; The Penitentes of the
Southwest. Chicago: Rio Grande Press, 1962. 126p.
A personalized, eye-witness account of penitente ceremonies plus a brief history of the group. Reprint of 1937
edition.

839 HERNANDEZ, DELUVINA. Mexican American Challenge to a Sacred
Cow. Los Angeles: Mexican American Cultural Center,
University of California, Los Angeles, 1970. 60p.
The sacred cow attacked is the stereotyping of Mexican
Americans by social scientists. A critique of social
science practices and research on Mexican-Americans in gen-
eral, and an attack on two UCLA sociology studies on Mexi-
can American academic achievements, in particular.

Minority Studies: An Annotated Bibliography

SPANISH AMERICANS

840 HERNANDEZ, LUIS F. A Forgotten American: A Resource Unit for
     Teachers on the Mexican-American. New York: Anti-Defama-
     tion League of B'nai B'rith, 1969. 56p.
          The sociology of the Mexican-American community is pre-
     sented here as a background for teachers. Guidelines for
     teaching Chicano children are given as well as a bibliog-
     raphy of extra readings.

841 HORKA-FOLLICK and LORAYNE ANN. Los Hermanos Penitentes; A
     Vestige of Medievalism in Southwestern United States.
     Los Angeles: Westernlore Press, 1969. 226p.
          A thorough account of the penitentes of New Mexico,
     their political and religious structure, their relation-
     ship with Anglos and Roman Catholics, and their part in
     the culture of their local villages. Also includes a
     history of penance cults and a chapter on penitene art.
     Bibliography.

842 KIEV, ARI. Curanderismo: Mexican American Folk Psychiatry.
     New York: Free Press, 1968. 207p.
          A study of the combination of medicine and belief which
     is used by healers on their patients. The curandero in the
     United States must deal with the stresses of patients
     caught between two cultures. A very interesting presenta-
     tion of the Mexican and American value systems.
     Bibliography.

843 McWILLIAMS, CAREY. North From Mexico: The Spanish-Speaking
     People of the United States. Westport, Connecticut:
     Greenwood Press, 1968. 324p.
          A classic as well as a pioneer in socio-history. Tells
     of the northern migration of peoples from Mexico and the
     effect of such a migration in the United States. Ends with
     World War II. Still influential. Chapter notes. Reprint
     of 1949 edition.

844 MADSEN, WILLIAM. Mexican-Americans of South Texas. New York:
     Holt, Rinehart and Winston, 1964. 112p.
          One of a series of case studies in cultural anthropolo-
     gy, based on field studies made from 1957 to 1961 in South
     Texas. Emphasis on the stresses involved in acculturation.
     Chapter headings are topical: La Raza, the family, re-
     ligion, sickness, health, education, etc. Conclusions and
     characterizations of the Mexican American have been widely
     challenged by Chicano scholars.

845 MILLER, ELAINE K. Mexican Folk Narrative From the Los Ange-
     les Area. Austin: University of Texas Press for the

(MILLER, ELAINE K.)
   American Folklore Society, 1973. 388p.
      A book worth learning Spanish for, since it is another
   example of the new trend in revisionist Third World
   scholarship: you go out and get the material - the
   stories, poems, myths, legends -- from the people themselves. You interpret according to your intellectual
   discipline, but you let the facts remain directly as they
   have been given to you. Folk stories about devils,
   buried treasures, animals, etc., in Spanish, with a summary in English. Introduction and explanations in English
   as well as a number of worthwhile appendices plus a bibliography. Included also is a glossary of Los Angeles
   Spanish.

846   MOUSTAFA, A. TAHER and GERTRUD WEISS. Health Status and
      Practices of Mexican Americans. Los Angeles: Mexican-
      American Study Project Advance Report No. 11, Division of
      Research, Graduate School of Business, University of Cali-
      fornia, Los Angeles, 1968. 52p.
         Disease, mental illness, death and health statistics,
      attitudes, and the treatment of Mexican Americans are sur-
      veyed here with a conclusion about the limited amount of
      such information available.

847   PAREDES, AMÉRICO. Folktales of Mexico. Chicago: University
      of Chicago Press. 1970. 282p.
         Worth reading for its implications about Chicano
      folklore.

848   _____. "With His Pistol In His Hand": A Border Ballad and
      Its Hero. Austin: University of Texas Press, 1971.
      262p.
         A classic folklore study of the life of Gregorio Cortez
      and how his history became legend and song. Reprint of
      1958 edition.

PAREDES, AMERICO. See also: 859

849   PAZ, OCTAVIO. The Labyrinth of Solitude: Life and Thought
      in Mexico. Translated by Lysander Kemp. New York:
      Grove Press, 1961. 212p.
         An important book in which Paz interprets the masks of
      the Mexican as they reveal his character. He also com-
      pares the philosophical-religious values of the United
      States and her neighbor. Reprint of 1950 edition.

SPANISH AMERICANS

850   PITT, LEONARD. The Decline of the Californios: A Social
        History of the Spanish-Speaking Californians, 1846-1890.
        Berkeley: University of California Press, 1966. 324p.
           The history of the leading colonial Californio families
        and how they lost their power, cultural superiority, and
        land. Bibliography.

      RANSOM, HARRY. See 825.

851   ROBE, STANLEY LINN. Index of Mexican Folktales. Berkeley:
        University of California Press, 1973. 276p. Folklore
        Studies: 26.
           Deceptive by title as it includes tales from not only
        Mexico, but Central America and Hispanic United States,
        the area around New Mexico and Arizona. Classification by
        the Aarne/Thompson method.

852   ROWEN, HELEN. The Mexican American. Washington, D. C.:
        U. S. Commission on Civil Rights, 1968. 70p.
           A survey of the Chicano communities today and the areas
        of concern which are: civil rights, education, employment,
        public policies and agencies, and identity.

853   RUBEL, ARTHUR J. Across the Tracks: Mexican-Americans in a
        Texas City. Austin: University of Texas Press, 1966.
        266p.
           Patterns of behaviour in a small city that is Anglo and
        Chicano. Using his own anthropological field materials,
        Rubel presents both the public and private relationships of
        Mexican-Americans in their own and in the Anglo community.
        Since this study was financed by the Hogg Foundation for
        Mental Health, special attention is given to communal
        health services and folk beliefs about illness.

854   SAMORA, JULIAN, ed. La Raza: Forgotten Americans. Notre
        Dame, Indiana: Notre Dame University Press, 1966. 218p.
           A collection of articles by Anglos and Mexican Americans
        touching on a variety of sociological topics including:
        demography, middle class values, the church, and discrimi-
        nation. Bibliographies with each section plus a concluding
        article on research areas that need exploring.

855   SAUNDERS, LYLE. Cultural Differences and Medical Care: The
        Spanish Speaking People of the Southwest. New York: The
        Russell Sage Foundation, 1954. 317p.
           The sociology of Spanish Americans in the Southwest is
        examined in terms of the welfare problems arising from
        cultural differences, which tend to show the Spanish

(SAUNDERS, LYLE)
    Americans as passive and apolitical. Includes an appendix
    of demographic characteristics.

856 SHALKOP, ROBERT L. Wooden Saints: The Santos of New Mexico.
    Feldafing: Buchein Verlag, 1967. 63p.
        An excellent text of the folk art of New Mexico when it
    was a remote outpost of Spain. A brief historical sketch
    preceeds the discussion of the art itself. The colored
    plates have explanatory notes.

857 SIMMEN, EDWARD, ed. Pain and Promise: The Chicano Today.
    New York: New American Library, 1972. 348p.
        Thirty-two essays about the socio-cultural condition of
    the Chicano divided into sections on identity, Brown Power,
    employment and discrimination problems, education, etc. A
    good bibliographic essay on La Raza by Robert L. Haro is
    included as a supplement at the end.

858 STODDARD, ELLWYN R. Mexican Americans. New York: Random
    House, 1973. 269p.
        This socio-history traces the formation of the Mexican
    American culture in terms of race, religion, and family,
    notes the shaping forces of language and education, and
    then illustrates the upward mobility of Chicanos and Chi-
    cano politics in America. Bibliography and charts. Re-
    print of 1970 edition.

859 TINKER, EDWARD L. Corridos and Calaveras. Notes and trans-
    lation by Américo Paredes. Austin: University of Texas
    Press, 1961. 58p.
        Song styles are the Mexican equivalent of troubador
    ballads and Caribbean calypsos all rolled into one.

860 WAGNER, NATHANIEL and MARSHA J. HAUG. Chicanos: Social and
    Psychological Perspectives. St. Louis: C. V. Mosby Co.,
    1971.
        Scholarly writings on the nature and effects of pre-
    judice, with some application to Chicanos. Main topics
    are perceptions and attitudes in and toward the Chicano
    Community.

WEISS, GERTRUD. See 846.
WILLIAMS, JUANITA H. See 834.

MINORITY STUDIES: AN ANNOTATED BIBLIOGRAPHY

SPANISH AMERICANS

6. Literature by and about Spanish Americans
(Anthologies, Autobiography, Biography, Drama, Literary Criticism
and History, Poetry and Prose)

861 ACOSTA, ADALBERTO JOEL. Chicanos Can Make It. New York:
Vantage Press, 1971. 340p.
The autobiography of a Mexican boy who immigrated due to
the Revolution of 1910 and travelled "up the ladder" from
Miami to California.

862 ACOSTA, OSCAR ZETA. The Autobiography of a Brown Buffalo.
San Francisco: Straight Arrow Books, 1972. 199p.
The odyssey of a big Chicano who manages to go through
law school and become an Oakland, California welfare lawyer
and a Chicano activist.

863 _____. The Revolt of The Cockroach People. San Francisco:
Straight Arrow Books, 1973. 258p.
barrio dweller's life in Los Angeles as lived by a
lawyer for militant Chicanos and demonstrators during the
1960s. This account is written in a highly readable racy
style.

864 ANAYA, RUDOLFO A. Bless Me, Ultima. Berkeley: Quinto Sol
Publications, 1972. 248p.
Ultima is an old woman, a curandera, who comes to live
with Antonio, the narrator, and his family in New Mexico,
during World War II. The episodic chapters of life, death,
and violence detail the growing up of a sensitive boy to
his religious and cultural heritage and to the meaning of
existence as taught him by Ultima. A fine and moving book.
The novel won the second Annual Premio Quinto Sol national
Chicano award for literature.

865 ANDERSON, MAXWELL. Night Over Taos. New York: S. French,
Ltd., 1932. 200p.
The Taos Rebellion of 1847 and the fall of Pablo
Montoya depicted in a poetic drama that shows conflict be-
tween two civilizations not only in public terms but in the
betrayal within Montoya's own family.

866 ANDERSON-IMBERT, ENRIQUE. Spanish-American Literature: A
History, vol. I, 1492-1910. vol. II, 1910-1963, translated
by John V. Falconieri. Detroit: Wayne State University
Press, 1969. 2nd edition revised and updated by Elaine
Malley. 761p.
A compendium of the writers of North and South America
catalogued in chronological fashion. Bibliographies are
broken down by genres as well as countries. Author index.
Reprint of 1963 edition.

867   ANDREW, MYRTLE. Red Chile. Santa Fe: Rydal Press, 1941. 175p.
       Novel about the Mexican Americans of New Mexico.

868   ARNOLD, ELLIOTT. The Time of The Gringo. New York: Alfred A. Knopf, Inc., 1953. 612p.
       A historical novel concerning the rise to power of Manuel Armijo, who became governor of New Mexico in the 1830s when the state was under Mexican rule. General Kearny and Indians also appear.

BACA, ELFEGO. See 883.

869   BARRIO, RAYMOND. The Plum Plum Pickers. Sunnyvale, California: Ventura Press, 1969. 201p.
       The Gutierrez family are migrant fruit pickers in the prune orchards of Santa Clara County, California. Included with them are the standard cast of characters dramatized by Chávez in the grape picker strikes: the company owner, Turner, the stooge overseer, Morales, and the exploited Chicano brothers and sisters.

870   BRIGHT, ROBERT. The Life and Death of Little Jo. Garden City, New York: Doubleday and Company, 1944. 216p.
       The scene is the Taos, New Mexico area and the story is about the community life in an isolated little village.

871   BRYANT, EDWIN. Rocky Mountain Adventures, Bristling With Animated Details of Fearful Fights of American Hunters With Savage Indians, Mexican Rancheros, and Beasts of Prey.... New York: Hurst and Company, n.d., 425p.
       A handy journal written in diary form and full of action, real or imagined. Worth reading for the flavor of those times and for the attitudes displayed. Originally published in 1848 under the title: What I Saw in California.

CAMARILLO, ALBERT. See 874.

872   CARDONA-HINE, ALVARO. Agapito. New York: Charles Scribner's Sons, 1967.
       Poetry by one of the leading West Coast writers.

873   CARRILLO, LEO. The California I Love. Englewood Cliffs, New Jersey: Prentice-Hall, 1961. 280p.
       Autobiography of a famous Californian, a film star and the member of a pioneer family. Full of lore, romantic tales of the past, and picturesque details.

MINORITY STUDIES: AN ANNOTATED BIBLIOGRAPHY

SPANISH AMERICANS

874   CASTILLO, PEDRO and ALBERT CAMARILLO. Furia Y Muerte: Los Bandidos Chicanos. Los Angeles: Aztlán Publications, 1973. 171p.
> The stories of five bandits: Vásques, Murieta, Baca, Cortina, and Gregorio Cortez presented here as part of the Chicano resistance to Anglo control, hence culture heros.

875   CATHER, WILLA. Death Comes For the Archbishop. New York: Alfred A. Knopf, 1927. 303p.
> New Mexico and Arizona as fictionalized by a leading American novelist. Father Latour, a French Archbishop, comes to Santa Fe in 1851 to live among the Indians and Spanish Americans in that region.

CHÁVEZ, CÉSAR. See 916.

876   CHÁVEZ, FRAY ANGELICO. New Mexico Triptych. New Jersey: St. Anthony Guild Press, 1949. 76p.
> A collection of poetry from The Angel's New Wings, The Penitente Thief, and Hunchback Madonna. Fray Chávez has also written Clothed with the Sun (1939) and other books. Reprint of 1940 edition.

877   CHICANO POETRY ANTHOLOGY 1968-1973. Los Angeles: Aztlán Publications, 1974.
> A representative collection of Chicano poets from all over the United States.

878   COLES, ROBERT. The Old Ones of New Mexico. Albuquerque: University of New Mexico Press, 1973. 74p.
> Interviews and portraits of some of the old Spanish Americans who have lived their lives in simple but eloquent style.

879   COOLIDGE, DANE. Gringo Gold. New York: E. P. Dutton and Company, 1939. 249p.
> A historical novel based upon the life of the Mexican bandit Joaquin Murieta. Takes in the California Gold Rush as added excitement. Presents a sympathetic attitude towards Mexicans in California.

880   CORLE, EDWIN. Burro Alley. New York: Random House, 1938. 279p.
> Story of the incidents of one night in Sante Fe during the tourist season. Though there is little plot, the book has great character interaction.

881 CORTES, ELIAS HRUSKAY. This Side and Other Things. San
Francisco: Ediciones Pocho-Che, 1971. 46p.
The other side of a book of poetry shared with Roberto
Vargas. Well-illustrated.

882 COX, WILLIAM. Chicano Cruz. New York: Bantam Books, 1972.
216p.
Mando Cruz, barrio son of a wetback, sets out to make it
up the ladder of success via baseball. After learning how
to use his Chicano strength in the Pennjersey league, he
returns to California and, before the entire Cruz family,
hits a homer on his first time up at bat in the big
leagues. Girl friend, family, and his new Gold Sox team
are ecstatic with pride.

883 CRICHTON, KYLE SAMUEL. Law and Order, Ltd.; The Rousing Life
of Elfego Baca of New Mexico. Santa Fe: New Mexican Publishing Corporation, 1928. 219p.
A romantic version of the life and adventures of the
bandit, seen in terms of the Wild Old West.

884 _____. The Proud People, A Novel. New York: Charles Scrib-
ner's Sons, 1944. 368p.
A novel about a once powerful and wealthy family of
Spanish descent living in Albuquerque in the 1940s.

885 DANA, RICHARD HENRY. Two Years Before the Mast. New York:
Globe Books, 1954. 275p.
The classic story of a New Englander who sailed around
to the West Coast and wrote about his adventures. Good
descriptions of ranchero life in Spanish California. Reprint of 1840 edition.

886 DAVIS, JAMES F. The Road to San Jacinto. Indianapolis:
Bobbs-Merrill, 1936. 334p.
A historical novel set during the Texan struggle for
independence. Depicts in detail the massacre of San
Jacinto.

887 DAY, DONALD and HARRY HERBERT ULLOM, eds. The Autobiography
of Sam Houston. Norman: University of Oklahoma Press,
1954. 298p. Bibliography.

888 DE VILLAGRA, GASPAR. History of New Mexico. Los Angeles:
The Quivira Society, 1933.
Translated by Gilberto Espinos. A long epic poem, the
first written in what is now the United States. Reprint
of 1610 edition.

SPANISH AMERICANS

889   ELIZONDO, SERGIO and GUSTAVO SEGADO, trans. Perros Y Anti-
        perros: Una Epica Chicana. Berkeley: Quinto Sol Pub-
        lications, 1972. 76p.
          A collection of poems about the Chicano experience in
        the Southwest.

      ESPINOS, GILBERTO. See 888.
      FADERMAN, LILLIAN. See 935.

890   FERBER, EDNA. Giant. Garden City, New York: Doubleday, 1952.
        447p.
          A novel about Texas bigness, a biased treatment of Mexi-
        can Americans, and lots of cattle.

891   FERGUSSEN, HARVEY. The Blood of the Conquerors. New York:
        Alfred A. Knopf, 1921. 265p.
          This book details the effects of land dispossession on
        an angry Chicano heir cheated by big businessmen. Part of
        Followers of the Sun, A Trilogy of the Santa Fe Trail
        (1929). Fergussen is an underrated Southwestern writer.

892   _____. The Conquest of Don Pedro. New York: Morrow, 1954.
        250p.
          Story of a New Yorker who comes to a frontier New
        Mexico town just after the Civil War, to start a business.
        Good on landscape but clumsy with dialogue and ethnic por-
        trayal. Fergusson is interested in inter-racial conflicts
        and his novels are good for his attempts to show what
        happens between people and environment.

893   FOREMAN, LEONARD LONDON. The Road to San Jacinto. New York:
        Dutton 1943. 285p.
          A historical novel of the Texas War for Independence.

894   FOSTER, JOSEPH O'KANE. In the Night Did I Sing. New York:
        Charles Scribner's Sons, 1942. 324p.
          The lives of Mexican Americans in the Taos valley told
        with humor and understanding.

895   GALARZA, ERNESTO. Barrio Boy. Notre Dame: University of
        Notre Dame Press, 1971. 275p.
          One of the best-written autobiographies about migration
        from Mexico and life in the United States. Galarza starts
        his narrative in the mountain village where he was born and
        succinctly relates his experiences in becoming a Mexican-
        American. A Glossary of Spanish words at the end.

896   ____. Rimas Tontas. San Francisco: Coleccion Mini-Libros, 1971.
      Poems by a West Coast Chicano poet.

897 GALLEN, A. A. The Wetback. Boston: Bruce Humphries, 1961. 243p.
      Novel highlights the social stereotypes of the wetback in Texas.

898 GAMIO, MANUEL, coll. The Life Story of the Mexican Immigrant: Autographic Documents. New York: Dover Publications, 1971. 288p.
      Seventy-six Mexican immigrants to the United States are interviewed for this sociological record. The interviews tell why they left Mexico and what they found in the States. Reprint of 1931 edition.

899 ____, ed. The Mexican Immigrant, His Life Story: A Community Study. New York: Arno and The New York Times Press, 1969. 288p.
      A collection of autobiographical documents from 57 immigrants who came to the United States from Mexico in the 1930s. A strong love of Mexico and mixed emotions about the United States are shown in these interviews. Reprint of 1931 edition. See also 748.

900 GARNER, CLAUDE. Wetback, A Novel. New York: Coward-McCann, 1947. 215p.
      The attempt of a young Mexican to become an American citizen.

901 GEROULD, KATHERINE F. Conquistador. New York: Charles Scribner' and Sons, 1923. 205p.
      A young railroad engineer inherits an ancestral estate in Mexico and goes there during the time of Pancho Villa's raids. He is part-Mexican and part-Creole.

902 GONZALES, RODOLFO. I Am Joaquin. Oakland: La Causa Distribution Center, 1967. 20p.
      An epic poem, also made into an excellent film, depicting the feelings of a Chicano about his life and his history. A "must" for basic readings in Chicano literature.

903 GORMAN, HERBERT SHERMAN. The Wine of San Lorenzo. New York: Farrar and Rinehart, Incorporated, 1945. 472p.
      Novel of the time of the Mexican war. Opens with the battle of the Alamo. An American boy is adopted by Santa Ana and raised within the Mexican culture.

SPANISH AMERICANS

904   GUZMAN, MARTIN LOUIS. The Eagle and the Serpent. Austin:
      University of Texas Press, 1965.
          A thinly fictionalized account of the author's experi-
      ence in the Mexican Revolution of 1910.

      HERNANDEZ, JUDITH ELENA. See 949.

905   HRUSKAY CORTES, ELIAS. This Side and Other Things. San Fran-
      cisco: Ediciones Pocho-Che, 1971.
          In this small volume of poetry, Hruskay Cortes and
      Roberto Vargas are published back to back.

906   JACKSON, HELEN HUNT. Ramona. New York: Grosset and Dunlap,
      1912. 490p.
          One of many editions of this famous novel about the
      beautiful Mexican-Indian girl who tries to reconcile love
      of a simple man with the facts of Spanish oppression dur-
      ing the ranchero era. Reprint of 1884 edition.

907   JESSEY, CORNELIA. Teach the Angry Spirit. New York: Crown
      Publishers, 1949. 249p.
          A novel about the Los Angeles barrio, shown as a place
      of racial and cultural conflict during World War II. A
      brother and a sister try to span the White and Brown
      cultures.

908   KIRKLAND, ELITHE. Divine Average. Boston: Little, Brown
      and Company, 1952. 378p.
          A cowboy's hatred for Mexicans and Indians undergoes
      great changes as he learns racial tolerance in this novel
      about Texas from 1838-58.

909   LAURITZEN, JONREED. The Cross and the Sword. Garden City,
      New York: Doubleday and Company, 1965. 275p.
          Fictional portrayal of Padre Junipero Serra and Juan
      Bautista de Anza.

910   LAWRENCE, D. H. The Plumed Serpent. New York: Alfred A.
      Knopf, 1951. 445p.
          Quetzalcoatl and Lawrence's theory of the power of the
      "blood" come together in a story about the experiences of
      an Irish woman who falls in love with a Mexican leader.
      Interesting anthropologically because Lawrence uses more
      Hopi Indian mythology than Mexican. Reprint of 1926
      edition.

911   LEA, TOM. <u>The Hands of Cantu</u>. Boston: Little Brown, 1964.
       244p.
       A historical fiction of the Southwest.

912   _____. <u>The Wonderful Country</u>. Boston: Little Brown and
       Company, 1952. 387p.
       A novel about the many people who built the town of
       Puerto, Texas in the 1880s.

913   LUDWIG, ED and JAMES SANTIBAÑEZ, eds. <u>The Chicanos: Mexican
       American Voices.</u> Baltimore: Penguin, 1971. 268p.
       Selections from fiction, poetry, and historical doc-
       uments. The Chicano's relationship with himself and the
       struggle for survival in the fields, in the barrios, and
       the White and Brown worlds of his America. A good cross
       section of Mexican-American writers. Biographies and a
       brief bibliography.

914   LUMMIS, CHARLES FLETCHER. <u>The Land of Poco Tiempo</u>. Albuquer-
       que: University of New Mexico Press, 1966. 210p.
       Reissued a number of times, this work is typical of the
       picturesque school of regional writing in which history
       and lore and travelogue are mixed together in a series of
       personalized essays. A period piece worth reading for its
       attitudes. Reprint of 1893 edition.

915   MAC LEISH, ARCHIBALD. <u>Conquistador</u>. Boston: Houghton,
       Mifflin, 1932. 113p.
       A heroic poem that retells Cortez conquest of the Plains.

916   MATTHIESSEN, PETER. <u>Sal Si Puedes: César Chávez and the
       New American Revolution.</u> New York: Dell, 1969. 372p.
       A well-written and sympathetic biography of the famous
       Chicano leader and his activities during the California
       grape strike.

917   MOODY, ALAN B. <u>Sleep in the Sun.</u> Boston: Houghton, Mif-
       flin Company, 1945. 137p.
       Episodes in the lives of poor Mexicans in California.

918   MORIN, RAUL. <u>Among the Valiant; Mexican-Americans in World
       War II and Korea.</u> Los Angeles: Borden Publishing
       Company, 1963. 290p.
       Mexican American military heroes.

       MURIETA, JOAQUIN. <u>See</u> **879, 927.**
       NASON, THELMA CAMPBELL. <u>See</u> 948.

SPANISH AMERICANS

919 NAVARRO, J. L.   Blue Day on Main Street; and Other Short
     Stories. Berkeley: Quinto Sol Publications, 1973. 127p.
        Short stories of Los Angeles city life as seen by Chi-
     canos who reflect on it and reject it.

920 NELSON, EUGENE. The Bracero. Berkeley: Thorp Springs Press,
     1972. 309p.
        A novel about Nacho, his migration from Mexico and his
     life as a bracero in California.

921 NERUDA, PABLO. Splendor and Death of Joaquin Murieta. New
     York: Noonday Press, 1972. 182p.
        A bilingual edition of the Chilean Nobel Prize winner's
     peom-play about Murieta who became a bandit after the rape
     and death of his young wife during the California gold rush.

922 NEWLON, CLARKE. Famous Mexican-Americans. New York: Dodd
     Mead, 1972. 187p.
        Brief biographies of twenty Mexican Americans in the
     fields of government, sports, entertainment, education,
     etc. Bibliography.

923 ORTEGO, PHILIP D., ed. We Are Chicanos: An Anthology of
     Mexican-American Literature. New York: Pocket Books,
     1973. 330p.
        Selections from history, folklore, fiction, drama, and
     poetry, all written by Mexican-Americans. Each section is
     introduced by commentary. Brief glossary and a few sug-
     gestions for further reading.

924 PALOU, FRANCISCO. Life of Fray Junipero Serra, translated
     and annotated by Maynard J. Geiger. Washington, D. C.:
     Academy of American Franciscan History, 1955. 547p.
        The life of the famous California priest. Bibliography.

925 PAREDES, AMÉRICO and RAYMOND PAREDES. Mexican-American
     Authors. Boston: Houghton Mifflin Company, 1972.
     152p.
        A collection of short stories making heavy use of folk
     material, one play, a corrido (border ballad), some dichos
     (sayings), and peotry by Mexican American writers. Dis-
     cussion questions after each selection and a brief vocab-
     ulary of Spanish words and phrases at the end.

PAREDES, RAYMOND. See 925.

926 PEREZ, RAYMUNDO, (TIGRE). Free, Free at Last. Corpus Christi:
     El Tercer Sol Book Store Incorporated, 1970. 28p.

(PEREZ, RAYMUNDO.) (TIGRE)
A Chicano poet who writes both bitter social protest and hopeful social plans for a new age. Excellent short book of lively, intense verse.

927 RIDGE, JOHN ROLLIN. The Life and Adventures of Joaquin Murieta, The Celebrated California Bandit. Norman: University of Oklahoma Press, 1965. 159p.
A narrative which borders on the bizarre as it goes through robbery, kidnapping, cattle and horse stealing, slaughter of innocent people, and so on. A classic of Western Americana popular literature. Reprint of 1955 edition.

928 RIVERA, TOMÁS. And the Earth Did Not Part: Y No Se Lo Tragó La Tierra. Berkeley: Quinto Sol Publications, 1971. 199p.
Dr. Rivera is a Chicano writer of short stories with an international reputation. He has been compared with Juan Rulfo and Octavio Paz in his ability to capture the philosophy of a people.

929 ROBERTS, MARTA. Tumbleweeds. New York: G. P. Putnam's Sons, 1940. 294p.
A poverty-stricken Mexican American family of mother, father, and six kids finally returns to Mexico.

930 ROBINSON, CECIL. With the Ears of Strangers: The Mexican in American Literature. Tucson: University of Arizona Press, 1969. 338p.
A descriptive survey of American literature dealing with Mexican characters and stereotypes. Discusses writings of such writers as: Washington Irving, Mary Austin, Hart Crane, Bret Harte, John Steinbeck, Irving Shulman, and William Carlos Williams. Bibliography. Reprint of 1963 edition.

931 RODRÍGUEZ, ARMANDO RAFAEL, comp. The Gypsy Wagon - Un Sancocho de Cuentos Sobre La Experiencia Chicano. Los Angeles: Aztlán Publications, 1974. 90p.
Short stories by a variety of Chicano authors such as Yolanda A. Garcia, Mario Suarez, and Francisco Martínez.

932 ROMANO-V, OCTAVIO IGNACIO, comp. El Espejo - The Mirror: Selected Mexican-American Literature. Berkeley: Quinto Sol, 1969. 241p.
The first big anthology of poetry and prose by Chicano authors. Frequently used as a textbook, for the selections appear both in Spanish and English.

SPANISH AMERICANS

933 ROMANO-V, OCTAVIO IGNACIO, ed. Voices: Readings from El
     Grito, 1967-1973. 210p.
        The second edition of Voices, enlarged from the 1971
     issue. It is divided into five sections, with articles
     from El Grito that created the most response from readers.
     Section One deals with sociology; Two, with Bibliography;
     Three, Four, and Five contain essays on history, education,
     and Chicanos in the modern state, respectively.

934 SALINAS, LUIS OMAR. Crazy Gypsy. Santa Barbara, California:
     Origines Publication, 1970. 87p.
        Omar is the Crazy Gypsy, whistler of tunes. These are
     his poems about his experiences as a Chicano. Included is
     the much anthologized poem "Aztec Angel." Beautifully
     illustrated.

935 SALINAS, LUIS OMAR and LILLIAN FADERMAN. From the Barrio: A
     Chicano Anthology. San Francisco: Canfield Press, 1973.
     154p.
        "My Revolution" and "My House" are the titles of the
     two sections of poetry, essays, fiction, and drama, fram-
     ing the two attitudes emphasized in this good collection:
     political stance and life style.

936 SÁNCHEZ, RICARDO. Canto Y Grito Mi Liberación (The Liberation
     of a Chicano Mind). Garden City, New York: Doubleday,
     1973. 159p.
        A re-publication of the first Mictla Publications
     edition, a press dedicated to Aztlán. Poems of Chicano
     liberation, short prose pieces, and essays. Well-illus-
     trated by Manuel G. Acosta.

     SANTIBANEZ, JAMES. See 913.
     SEGADO, GUSTAVO. See 889.
     SERRA, FRAY JUNIPERO. See 924.

937 SHULAR, ANTONIA CASTENEDA, TOMAS YBARRA-FRAUSTO and JOSEPH
     SOMMERS. Literatura Chicano; Texto Y Contexto: Chicano
     Literature; Text and Context. Englewood Cliffs, New Jer-
     sey: Prentice-Hall, 1972. 368p.
        An anthology of Chicano literature from the United
     States, Mexico, and Latin America. Most selections are in
     Spanish and English. The Chicano experience is shown in
     three main categories: social protest, culture, and mi-
     gration. Brief introductions.

938 SHULMAN, IRVING. The Square Trap. Boston: Little, Brown and Company, 1953. 374p.
A Chicano from Los Angeles becomes a boxer in order to escape the barrio.

939 SIMMEN, EDWARD, comp. The Chicano: From Caricature to Self Portrait. New York: New American Library, 1971. 318p.
Short stories, mainly by non-Chicanos, illustrating the evolution of the Chicano stereotype in American literature. Includes Steinbeck, Horgan, Jack London, Bret Harte. A few Mexican Americans are included in the final section.

SOMMERS, JOSEPH. See 937.

940 SORENSEN, VIRGINIA. The Proper Gods. New York: Harcourt Brace and Company, 1951. 309p.
A Yaqui Indian, who has grown up in Arizona, rejoins his family in Mexico after serving in World War II.

941 STEINBECK, JOHN. The Pearl. New York: Viking Press, 1947. 122p.
The finding of a miraculous gem has disastrous results for a poor Mexican pearl-fisherman. Steinbeck is important because he is supposed to have given such a free and liberal portrayal of Mexican and Chicano characters. Today his books seem sentimental and biased.

942 _____. Tortilla Flat. New York: Viking Press, 1969. 179p.
A famous book about a group of paisanos who live in Monterrey, California and display, as Steinbeck sees them, ignorance, laziness, drunkeness, lawlessness and other un-desirable characteristics. Sentimentalized as typical of the loving and simple folk who form a Chicano King Arthur's Court. Reprint of 1935 edition.

943 STEINER, STAN and LUIS VALDEZ. Aztlan: An Anthology of Mexi-can American Literature. New York: Random House, 1972. 410p.
Excerpts ranging from Aztec and Mayan legends to the Chicano Liberation Youth Movement. Includes short stories, poems, drama, and social and political writings.

944 STILWELL, HART. Border City. Garden City, New York: Double-day and Company, 1945. 276p.
A tragic story of racial intolerance and political cor-ruption in an American border city. Heroine is a Mexican girl; hero is a newspaper man.

SPANISH AMERICANS

945 SUMMERS, RICHARD A. Dark Madonna. Caldwell, Idaho: Caxton
Printers, 1937. 294p.
Superstition and realism in a Tucson, Arizona barrio in
a moving novel about a young Mexican girl living there.

946 _____. The Devil's Highway. Nashville, Tennessee: Thomas
Nelson, Inc., 1938. 299p.
A historical romance about a young soldier who accompa-
nied Padre Kino across the deserts of the southwest to Baja,
California.

947 TERÁN, HERIBERTO. Vida De Ilusiones. Corpus Christi, Texas:
El Tercer Sol Book Store, Inc., 1971.
Poems in Spanish and English with illustrations by
Teran's brother, Leonardo.

TIGRE. See 926.

948 ULIBARRI, SABINE R., translated from Spanish by Thelma Camp-
bell Nason. Tierra Amarilla: Stories of New Mexico/
Cuentos De Nuevo. Albuquerque: University of New Mexico
Press, 1971. 167p.
Stories about Tierra Amarilla, a small Spanish-American
village in northern New Mexico. The stories are auto-
biographical in tone and reflect the author's childhood.
Spanish and English facing pages.

ULLOM, HARRY HERBERT. See 887.

949 URISTA HEREDIA, ALBERTO BALTAZAR (ALURISTA). Floricanto En
Aztlán. Los Angeles: Chicano Cultural Center, University
of California, Los Angeles, 1971. 100p.
One hundred cantos in pochismos, a mixture of English
and Spanish now being used by Chicanos. The poems range
from political propaganda to barrio scenes to personal
lyrics. Alurista is an important Chicano poet and leader.
Illustrated with 16 linoleum cuts by Judith Elena
Hernandez.

950 _____. Nationchild Plumaroja. San Diego: Centro de Estudios
Chicanos Publications, 1972.
Poems in the mixture of Spanish and English that is
characteristic of Alurista's verse.

951 VALDEZ, LUIS. Actos. Fresno: Cucatacha Press, 1971.
Valdez, prime organizer, writer-director, etc., of El
Teatro Campesino, presents some of the plays put on by the
group.

VALDEZ, LUIS. See 943.

952   VARGAS, ROBERTO. Primeros Cantos. San Francisco: Ediciones
Pocho-Ché, 1971. 42p.
    Half of a double book of poetry, shared with Elias
Hruskay Cortes concerning Chicano response and liberation.
Admirably illustrated by the poet.

953   VASQUEZ, RICHARD. Chicano. Garden City, New York: Doubleday
and Company, 1970. 350p.
    The story of the migration of the Sandoval family from
New Mexico to east Los Angeles and the resulting breakup
of the family as their dreams fall apart. El Grito con-
siders the novel a misinterpretation and stereotyping of
Mexican-Americans.

954   VILLAREAL, JOSÉ ANTONIO. Pocho. Garden City, New York:
Doubleday, 1970. 186p.
    The book was published before the present Chicano move-
ment but deals with the problems that created it. The story
is about the migration of the Rubio family from Mexico to
the Santa Clara valley and the development of Richard, the
pocho, or second generation Mexican American, trying to
balance between the Mexican traditions of his family and
the Anglo pressures outside of it. Ramon Ruhiz, who writes
the introduction, calls Pocho the first novel by a Mexican
American contemporary writer. Reprint of 1959 edition.

955   VILLASEÑOR, EDMUND. Macho! New York: Bantam Books, 1973.
245p.
    Roberto García leaves home in Jalisco at seventeen and
migrates North to become a bracero in the 1950s. This
novel takes him through the 1960s, Chavez and the fight with
the growers in California, and a brief return to Mexico to
shoot it out in a family feud with the Reyes brothers. In
the violent finale, Roberto tries to come to terms with his
new Chicano concept of macho, different from his father's.

956   WATERS, FRANK. People of The Valley. New York: Farrar and
Rinehart, 1941. 309p.
    Maria del Valle is a goat girl and a curandera. She
lives for ninety years in a small valley in New Mexico.
Through her, Waters tells about the changes that come to
the land and to the people on that land when the government
decides to build a dam.

SPANISH AMERICANS

957   WHITE, STUART EDWARD. Ranchero. Garden City, New York:
      Doubleday and Company, 1933. 302p.
          A mountain man finds friends and a wife among the
      Spanish settlers in California during the 1830s.

958   WILDER, ROBERT. The Wine of Youth. New York: G. P. Putnam's
      Sons, 1955. 377p.
          Life in a Texas oil town in 1929 as lived by a Mexican
      American boss. This book touches on the themes of big
      business, labor exploitation, and political racketeering
      in Texas just before and during World War II.

      YBARRA-FRAUSTO, TOMAS. See 937.

                    C. Puerto Rican Americans

               1. Bibliographical and Reference Works

959   BAYITCH, S. A. Latin America and the Caribbean: A Biblio-
      graphical Guide to Works in English. Coral Gables: Uni-
      versity of Miami Press, 1967. 943p.
          A seven-section comprehensive bibliography divided by
      subjects as well as by areas and countries.

960   BRAVO, ENRIQUE R., comp. An Annotated Selected Puerto Rican
      Bibliography: Bibliografía Puertorriqueña Selecta Y
      Anotada, translated by Marcial Cuevas. New York: Urban
      Center of Columbia University, 1972. 114p.
          A selection of 338 basic works in both Spanish and
      English listings.

      BUCCHIONI, EUGENE. See 963.

961   COMMONWEALTH OF PUERTO RICO. The People of Puerto Rico: A
      Bibliography. New York: Commonwealth of Puerto Rico,
      Department of Labor, Migration Division. 75p.
          Everything about the Puerto Rican in the United States.

962   CONSTITUTIONAL CONVENTION, 1952. Notes and Comments on the
      Constitution of the Commonwealth of Puerto Rico. Washing-
      ton, D. C., 1952. 123p.
          The English text of the Puerto Rican Constitution plus
      the historical background and history of its adoption.

963   CORDASCO, FRANCESCO and EUGENE BUCCHIONI, comps. The Puerto
      Ricans 1493-1973: A Chronology and Fact Book. Dobbs Ferry,
      New York: Oceana Publications, 1973. 137p.
          Documents of the United States/Puerto Rico Commission on

Puerto Rican Americans

(CORDASCO, FRANCESCO and EUGENE BUCCHIONI, comps.)
the status of Puerto Rico. Also includes a history of immigration to the United States.

964   DOSSICK, JESSE JOHN. Doctoral Research on Puerto Rico and Puerto Ricans. New York: New York University Press, 1967. 34p.
    340 doctoral dissertations covered. Half of the reports,
written at mainland universities, were by Puerto Ricans
during the period 1898-1966.

965   HILL, MARNESBA A. and HAROLD B. SCHLEIFER. Puerto Rican
Authors: A Bibliographic Handbook. Metuchen, New Jersey:
Scarecrow Press, Inc., 1974. 277p.
    A bilingual, partially annotated bibliography of the
history of literature of Puerto Rico from 1493 to the present. Bibliographical information also included as well as
three indexes: topical, chronological, and title.

SCHLEIFER, HAROLD B. See 965.

966   VIVO, PAQUITA, ed. The Puerto Ricans: An Annotated Bibliography. New Jersey: Scarecrow Press, 1974. 267p.
    An up-to-date and informative bibliography divided
topically.

2. General Culture and Community Life
(Economics, Education, Immigration, Literature, Sociology, etc.)

967   ABRAMSON, MICHAEL. Palante. New York: McGraw-Hill, 1971.
159p.
    Essays by the Young Lords and Abramson's photographs of
them make up this handsome volume. The Young Lords are an
offshoot of a Chicago Puerto Rican street gang. Their
history, their program, several poems, and articles pertaining to the group. The Young Lords are now called the
Puerto Rican Revolutionary Workers Organization.

968   BERLE, BEATRICE. 80 Puerto Rican Families in New York City;
Health and Disease Studied in Context. New York: Co-
lumbia University Press, 1958. 331p.
    An in-depth study of public health practices.
Bibliography.

969   BRAND, HORST. Poverty Area Profiles: The New York Puerto
Rican: Patterns of Work Experience. New York. U. S.
Bureau of Labor Statistics, Middle Atlantic Regional Office,
(Regional Reports No. 19), 1971. 62p.
    Findings of the Urban Employment Survey show that Puerto
Ricans are the most deprived of all New York's poor.

BUCCHIONI, EUGENE. See 974.

161

SPANISH AMERICANS

BUCKINGHAM, JAMIE. <u>See</u> 976.

970   CHENAULT, LAWRENCE R. <u>The Puerto Rican Migrant in New York City</u>. New York: Russell and Russell, 1970. 190p.
     An early study of both Puerto Rico as a migration source and the Puerto Rican worker and his family in New York City. The bibliography is annotated and gives a survey of the publications at the time of first printing. Reprint of 1938 edition.

971   COLE, MARY. <u>Summer In The City</u>. New York: P. J. Kenedy & Sons, 1968. 221p.
     Puerto Rican participants in a Catholic Summer in the City Program and their peace processions during the East Harlem riots of 1967.

972   COLON, JESUS. <u>A Puerto Rican in New York and Other Sketches</u>. New York: Mainstream Publishers, 1961. 202p.
     Essays on Colón's childhood, New York life, and other writers. Revised as <u>Puerto Ricans In New York</u> (1970). An important book to read for background.

973   COOPER, PAULETTE. <u>Growing Up Puerto Rican</u>. New York. Arbor House Publishing Company, 1972. 131p.
     Contains seventeen character sketches of Puerto Ricans, including: Fernanda, who was told she was too stupid to go to school, and now has a master's degree; Carmelita, a beautiful girl who resisted "the life"; Juan, an addict and a pimp before he was eighteen; Ricky the hustler; Mario, the Young Lord. All speak for themselves of the sordidness of the ghettos of Spanish Harlem and San Juan. Foreword by Jose Torres.

974   CORDASCO, FRANCESCO and EUGENE BUCCHIONI. <u>The Puerto Rican Community and Its Children on the Mainland: A Source Book For Teachers, Social Workers and Other Professionals</u>. Metuchen, New Jersey: Scarecrow Press, 1972. 465p.
     A thorough study of Puerto Rican culture and family life as experienced on the mainland.

975   COVELLO, LEONARD. <u>The Heart Is the Teacher</u>. New York: McGraw-Hill, 1958. 275p.
     The principal of Benjamin Franklin high school in East Harlem writes an interesting autobiography about his school experiences.

976   CRUZ, NICKY and JAMIE BUCKINGHAM. <u>Run Baby Run</u>. Plainfield, New Jersey: Logos International 1968. 240p.

(CRUZ, NICKY and JAMIE BUCKINGHAM)
Nicky Cruz came to New York from Puerto Rico at the age of 15. Tells about his life of crime, his reform, and his subsequent profession as a Pentecostal Preacher in California.

977 CRUZ, VICTOR HERNANDEZ. Mainland. New York: Random House, 1973. 83p.
Travels across the United States as seen by a Puerto Rican poet. There was a Puerto Rican man who came to New York. He came with a whole shopping bag full of seeds strange to the big city....(76)

978 _____. Snaps; Poems. New York: Random House, 1969. 135p.
Poems about New York City and being Puerto Rican.

979 DOOLEY, ELIZA BELLOWS. Puerto Rican Cookbook. Richmond: Dietz Press, 1948. 175p.
Adapted for American use in the States. Contains many West Indian recipes also.

980 EHLE, JOHN. Shepherd of the Streets: The Story of the Reverend James A. Gusweller and His Crusade on the New York West Side. New York: William Sloane Associates, 1960. 239p.
An Episcopal minister takes over a Puerto Rican church in New York City.

981 FENTON, JERRY. Understanding The Religious Background of The Puerto Rican. Cuernavaca, Mexico: Centro Intercultural de Documentación, 1969. 72p.
A discussion of the Puerto Rican on the island and in New York and his religions: Catholic, Protestant, Pentecostal, and Spiritist.

982 FISHMAN, JOSHUA and others, eds. Bilingualism In the Barrio. Bloomington: Indiana University, 1971. 696p. (Indiana University Publications, Language Science Monographs, v. 7)
A two-year study of Puerto Rican bilingualism in New York City.

983 FITZPATRICK, JOSEPH P. Puerto Rican Americans: The Meaning of Migration To The Mainland. Englewood Cliffs, New Jersey: Prentice-Hall, Inc., 1971. 192p.
A good overall survey of the migration and adjustment of Puerto Ricans to New York City. Includes a discussion of identity, community, family, color, religion, education, welfare, mental illness, and drug abuse. Statistical tables and a bibliography in the footnotes.

MINORITY STUDIES: AN ANNOTATED BIBLIOGRAPHY

SPANISH AMERICANS

GOLDSEN, ROSE KOHN. See 993.

984   HEMOS TRABAJADO BIEN. A Report on the First National Confer-
        ence of Puerto Ricans, Mexican Americans and Educators on
        the Special Educational Needs of Puerto Rican Youth.
        New York: Aspira Press, 1968. 74p.
           Summarizes discussions of issues affecting Puerto Rican
        students in the United States, such as bilingualism,
        teacher-student attitudes, curriculum, textbooks, and
        community involvement.

985   HERNANDEZ ALVAREZ, JOSÉ. Return Migration To Puerto Rico.
        Berkeley: University Of California Press, 1967. 153p.
           Immigration, and the struggle for jobs that forced return
        migration for many after 1918.

986   KLEIN, WOODY. Let In The Sun. New York: The Macmillan Co.,
        1964. 297p.
           A newspaperman describes the New York barrio.

987   LAGUERRE, ENRIQUE A. The Labyrinth, translated by William
        Rose. New York: Las Americas Publishing Company, 1960.
        275p.
           The victims of the symbolic labyrinth monster are Puerto
        Ricans fighting in the Revolution. This novel starts in
        New York City as Porfirio Uribe finishes law school, and
        ends with his death in Puerto Rican revolutionary fighting
        and betrayal.

988   LEWIS, OSCAR. A Study of Slum Culture: Backgrounds for La
        Vida. New York: Random House, 1968. 240p.
           The culture of poverty as studied by a sociology expert.
        Puerto Ricans in New York.

989   LEWIS OSCAR. La Vida: A Puerto Rican Family In The Culture
        of Poverty-San Juan and New York. New York: Random House,
        1965. 667p.
           The story of one family as told by its members, rela-
        tives, and friends. San Juan and Spanish Harlem described.
        A seminal and very famous work, now coming under criticism
        for ethnic distortion.

990   LOPEZ, ALFREDO. The Puerto Rican Papers; Notes on the Re-
        Emergence of a Nation. Indianapolis: Bobbs-Merrill compa-
        ny, 1973. 383p.
           An important collection of essays on the Puerto Rican,
        his historic background on the island, and his development
        in New York City. Written by a strong anti-colonialist and

(LOPEZ, ALFREDO)
Puerto Rican nationalist, highly personalized by the author's own experiences. Discusses the barrio and the development of political movements in it.

991 MATILLA, ALFREDO and IVÁN SILÉN, eds. The Puerto Rican Poets: Los Poetas Puertorriqueños. New York: Bantam Books, 1972. 231p.
A bilingual anthology of poets from the Mainland and the Island. The first section includes important poets pre-1955 such as Luis Torres. The second section is called: "The Major Poets" and has the works of Luis Matos, Julia de Burgos, and Hugo Margenat. The third section contains post-1955 poetry which includes much experimentation.

992 MAYCROON, CHARLOTTE LEON, ed. Two Blocks Apart: Juan Gonzales and Peter Quinn. New York: Holt, Rinehard and Wright, 1965. 125p.
Interviews with two 17-year-olds: a poor Puerto Rican and a White.

993 MILLS, C. WRIGHT, CLARENCE SENIOR, and ROSE KOHN GOLDSEN. The Puerto Rican Journey: New York's Newest Immigrants. New York: Russell and Russell, 1967. 238p.
A sociological field study of two geographical areas of New York City. Statistics gathered include those on family, age, jobs, income, education, etc. Reprint of 1950 edition.

994 MORRISON, JOHN CAYCE, DIRECTOR. The Puerto Rican Study: 1953-1957: A Report on the Education and Adjustment of Puerto Rican Pupils in the Public Schools of the City of New York. New York: New York City Board of Education, 1972. 265p.
The most complete study of Puerto Ricans in the New York public shcools, their impact on the school system, and its impact on them. This study led to many other publications and twenty-three recommendations for changes in curriculum, program development, methods of teaching, classroom materials, etc. Reprint of 1958 edition.

995 NEW YORK MAGAZINE Volume 5, Number 32 (August 7, 1972).
A special issue on the Latin settlements in Nueva York.

996 PADILLA, ELENA. Up From Puerto Rico. New York: Columbia University Press, 1958. 317p.
An anthropologist looks at a small sampling of the Puerto Ricans in New York City and tells about their culture.

SPANISH AMERICANS

997   PUERTO RICAN FORUM. <u>A Study of Poverty Conditions In The New York Puerto Rican Community</u>, 3rd edition. New York: Puerto Rican Forum, 1970. 86p.
       A survey of jobs, housing, health conditions, politics, and other aspects of Puerto Rican life in New York City during the mid 1960s. This third edition is updated with a short essay that shows that conditions have deteriorated for Puerto Ricans compared to Blacks and Whites in the city.

998   RAND, CHRISTOPHER. <u>The Puerto Ricans</u>. New York: Oxford Press, 1970. 178p.
       Reprint of a 1958 series of <u>New Yorker</u> magazine articles about Nueva York in the 1950s.

999   RIBES TOVAR, FEDERICO. <u>Handbook of the Puerto Rican Community</u>. New York: Plus Ultra Educational Publishers, 1970.
       Life in Spanish Harlem plus a listing of some of the better-known community Puerto Ricans. Reprint of 1968 edition.

1000   ROGLER, LLOYD HENRY. <u>Migrant In The City; The Life of a Puerto Rican Action Group</u>. New York: Basic Books, 1972. 251p.
       A four year history of the Hispanic Confederation of Maplewood, New Jersey and how it functioned as an action group. Bibliography.

SENIOR, CLARENCE. <u>See</u> 993.

1001   SEXTON, PATRICIA CAYO. <u>Spanish Harlem: An Anatomy of Poverty</u>. New York: Harper and Row, 1965. 208p.
       The standard sociological description of the New York Puerto Rican ghetto.

SILÉN, IVÁN. <u>See</u> 991.

1002   SPECIAL ISSUE - PUERTO RICO INTERNATIONAL MIGRATION REVIEW Vol. 2, No. 2 (Spring, 1968). New York: Center for Migration Studies.
       Devoted to migrants on the United States mainland and their experiences.

1003   THOMAS, PIRI. <u>Down These Mean Streets</u>. New York: Alfred A. Knopf, 1967. 333p.
       An autobiographical account of an East Harlem childhood. Thomas is a Black Puerto Rican who grows up angry, but experiences a religious conversion.

1004   THOMAS, PIRI. Savior, Savior, Hold My Hand. Garden City,
        New York: Doubleday and Company, 1972. 372p.
            Sequel to Down These Mean Streets. Piri Thomas returns
        home to the East Harlem ghetto after seven years in jail
        and shows the life there as a non-beautiful experience.
        Essays and some poetry.

1005   U. S. DEPARTMENT OF COMMERCE. Bureau of the Census. Puerto
        Ricans in the United States. Final Report PC (2) I. D.
        U. S. Census of Population: 1960. Washington, D. C.:
        U. S. Government Printing Office. U. S. Census of Popula-
        tion: 1960, July 1963 III-XIV. 140p.
            Statistics compiled in 1959-1960 which cover the United
        States as a whole plus selected areas, and are concerned
        with population and sociological and economic tables.

1006   WAKEFIELD, DAN. Island in the City: The World of Spanish
        Harlem. Boston: Houghton Mifflin and Company, 1959.
        278p.
            A look at the ghetto by a fine reporter who lived for
        six months in Spanish Harlem.

IV. AFRO-AMERICANS

A. Bibliographical Works

1007 ARNO PRESS/New York Times Reprints. Included are: The
      American Negro: His History and Literature, Series, I, II,
      III. 140 books. The Anti Slavery Crusade in America, 69
      books. The Crisis, A Record of the Darker Races, 1910-
      1960, 50 books.

1008 BIBLIOGRAPHIC SURVEY: The Negro in Print. Washington, D. C.:
      The Negro Bibliographic and Research Center. 1965-1968.
      Vols. I-III.
          Bimonthly listings of reports and reviews from both
      foreign and American publications by and about Blacks. In-
      cludes adult and youth fiction and nonfiction, current and
      historical books. Annotated.

1009 BROOKS, ALEXANDER C. Civil Rights and Liberties in the
      United States: An Annotated Bibliography, with a Selected
      List of Fiction and Audio-Visual Materials. New York:
      Civil Liberties Educational Foundation, 1962. 151p.
          Selective bibliography of books published after 1940.
      Among topics: prejudice, psychology, intergroup
      relationships.

      BROWN, ROSCOE C. See 1021.

1010 BROWN, WARREN H. Check List of Negro Newspapers in the
      United States, 1827-1946. Jefferson City, Missouri:
      Lincoln University Press, 1946. 37p.
          Listing of Black newspapers.

1011 CENTRAL STATE University, Hallie Q. Brown Memorial Library.
      Index to Periodical Articles by and About Negroes. Boston:
      G. K. Hall and Company, 1950.
          An annual index. Ten-year cumulations: 1950-1959, and
      1960-1970.

169

AFRO-AMERICANS

1012   DAVIS, JOHN PRESTON, ed. The American Negro Reference Book,
       Vols. 1 and 2. Yonkers, New York: Educational Heritage,
       Inc., 1966. 886p.
       Part of the Negro Heritage Library. Contains historical
       documents, statistics, reference materials prepared by
       various experts. Vol 1: tables, statistics, etc. Vol 2:
       protest movement, Negro women, Negro scholars, jazz, art.

1013   EBONY. The Negro Handbook. Chicago: Johnson Publishing
       Company, 1966. 535p.
       Practical, factual information. Tables and charts.

       FISHER, MARY L. See 1016

1014   HAYWOOD, CHARLES. A Bibliography of North American Folklore
       and Folksong. 2nd rev. ed., Vol. 1. 748p. New York:
       Dover Publications, 1961.
       The Negro section includes folktales, spirituals, work
       songs, and blues.

1015   INTERNATIONAL Library of Negro Life and History. New York:
       Publishers Company, 1967, 1968.
       Ten volumes put out by the Association for the study of
       Negro Life and History. Titles include theater, biographies,
       medicine, the Civil War, art, sports, and literature.

1016   MILLER, ELIZABETH W. The Negro in America; A Bibliography,
       2nd ed., revised and enlarged, compiled by Mary L. Fisher.
       1970. 351p.
       Excellent bibliography arranged by categories with
       emphasis on contemporary publications. The last section
       contains other bibliographies. Annotated.

1017   NATIONAL Education Association. The Negro American in
       Paperback. Washington, D. C.: National Education
       Association, 1968.
       For thirty-five cents you can order by writing to the
       above at 1201 Sixteenth Street N. W., Washington,
       D. C. 20036.

1018   NEGRO American Literature Forum. School of Education,
       Indiana State University, Terre Haute, Indiana 47809.
       For school and university teachers. Articles and
       bibliographies on special topics, such as children's
       literature.

1019   NEW YORK Public Library. Dictionary Catalog of the Schomburg
        Collection of Negro Literature and History. Boston:
        G. K. Hall & Co., 1962. 9 Vols. Supplement I, 2 Vols,
        1967. Supplement II, 4 Vols, 1972.
            Catalog of one of the great collections of
        Afro-Americana.

1020   NEW YORK Public Library. No Crystal Stair: A Bibliography
        of Black Literature. New York: The New York Public
        Library, 1971. 63p.
            Committee selection of the significant books on black
        culture published since 1965 with selected classic titles
        added. Annotated. Includes general reference, history and
        documentary history, politics and government, and contempor-
        ary literature and the arts.

1021   PLOSKI, HARRY A. and ROSCOE C. BROWN, comp. The Negro Almanac
        New York: Bellweather Publishing Company, 1967. 1012p.
            Wide coverage of information with good arrangement of
        facts and chronology. Maps and bibliography.

1022   PORTER, DOROTHY B., ed. The Negro in the United States: A
        Selected Bibliography. Washington, D. C.: Library of
        Congress, 1970. 313p.
            Topical bibliography with author-subject index. Includes
        publications by both Whites and Blacks.

1023   PORTER, DOROTHY B. North American Negro Poets: A Biblio-
        graphical Checklist of Their Writings, 1760-1944. New
        York: Burt Franklin, 1963. 90p.
            Also lists the libraries where the poetry can be found.
        Reprint of 1945 edition.

1024   SZABO, ANDREW. Afro-American Bibliography: List of the Books,
        Documents and Periodicals on Black-American Culture
        Located in San Diego State College Library. San Diego:
        Library, San Diego State College, 1970. 327p.
            Excellent, easy-to-handle bibliography of over 2000
        titles listed by topics with an index. Includes Armed
        Forces, Films, Intermarriage, Labor Unions, Race Relations,
        Sports, and Youth among others. Not annotated.

THOMPSON, ALMA M. See 1025.

Minority Studies: An Annotated Bibliography

AFRO-AMERICANS

1025 THOMPSON, EDGAR TRISTRAM and ALMA M. THOMPSON. Race and Region, A Descriptive Bibliography Compiled with Special Reference to the Relations between Whites and Negroes in the United States. Chapel Hill: University of North Carolina Press, 1949. 194p.
Sections on the Negro family, religion, and language. Dated but useful.

1026 No Entry.

1027 WELSCH, EDWIN K. The Negro in the United States; A Research Guide. Bloomington: Indiana University Press, 1965. 142p.
462 annotated entries of books and periodical articles on black literature. References are historical and non-technical. Appendices with bibliographies, periodical lists, and publishing houses. Reprint of 1964 edition.

1028 WEST, EARLE H., comp. A Bibliography of Doctoral Research on the Negro, 1933-1966. n. p.: University Microfilms, 1969.

1029 WHITEMAN, MAXWELL. A Century of Fiction by American Negroes; A Descriptive Bibliography, 1853-1952. Philadelphia: Saifer, 1955. 64p.
Not up-to-date, but good for nineteenth century.

B. Periodicals

1030 BIBLIOGRAPHIC Survey: Negro in Print. Negro Bibliographic and Research Center, Inc., 117 R Street, N. E., Washington, D. C. 20002

1031 BLACK Information Index. P. O. Box 332, Herndon, Virginia 22070
Published by a consortium of Black libraries. Focuses on bibliographies, book reviews, and source materials. Tries to keep as up-to-date as possible.

1032   THE BLACK SCHOLAR: Journal of Black Studies and Research.
P. O. Box 908, Sausaliot, California 94965
Various monthly issues feature special topics such as
Black politics, athletes, Pan-Africanism, and Black
prisoners.

1033   EBONY. 1820 South Michigan Avenue, Chicago, Illinois 60616.
A pictorial monthly of wide general circulation. Contains Black news and cultural events.

1034   FREEDOMWAYS: A Quarterly Review of the Negro Freedom Movement.
799 Broadway, New York, New York 10003.
Very good for new materials on current cultural movements. Contains bibliographical articles.

1035   THE JOURNAL of Afro-American Issues. 1629 K Street, N. W.,
Suite 520, Washington, D. C., 20006.
A quarterly magazine which also puts out special issues
such as Blacks and the U. S. Criminal Justice System, and
Black Women in America.

1036   JOURNAL OF BLACK STUDIES. 275 South Beverly Drive, Beverly
Hills, California 90212.
Articles on economics, politics, sociology, history,
literature, and philosophy.

1037   THE JOURNAL of Negro Education. Howard University, Washington,
D. C. 20001.
Of interest to teachers, White or Black.

1038   THE JOURNAL of Negro History. The Association for the Study
of Negro Life and History. 1538 Ninth Street, N. W.,
Washington, D. C. 20001.
Covers the field of history and Black culture.

1039   PHYLON: Review of Race and Culture. Atlanta University,
223 Chestnut Street, S. W., Atlanta, Georgia 30314.
Published quarterly, issues are devoted to special
topics such as literature.

AFRO-AMERICANS

C. History and Politics
(The Fact and Effect of Slavery, Racism and Civil Rights)

1040   ADOFF, ARNOLD, ed.   Black on Black; Commentaries by Negro
          Americans.   New York: The Macmillan Company, 1968.   236p.
             A collection of articles, letters, and excerpts from
          famous Black leaders.   Emphasis is on history and sociology,
          but there is a commentary section on Black authors.
          History.

ANTHONY, EARL.   See   1108.

1041   APTHEKER, HERBERT.   Afro-American History: The Modern Era.
          Secaucus, New Jersey: The Citadel Press, 1971.   324p.
             The author addresses recent Afro-American history in
          the context of what he sees as necessary for black studies
          programs: a reexamination of certain historical theories.
          History.

1042   _____.   American Negro Slave Revolts.   New York: Inter-
          national Publishers, 1969.   409p.
             A well-documented study with emphasis on the colonial
          period.   Bibliography.   Reprint of 1943 edition.

1043   _____, ed.   A Documentary History of the Negro People in the
          United States.   New York: The Citadel Press, 1968-1969.
          2 Vols.   942p.
             A very complete historical record of Negro life in
          America from colonial times to 1910.   Reprint of 1951
          edition.

1044   AUSTIN, LETTIE J., LEWIS H. FENDERSON, and SOPHIA P. NELSON,
          eds.   The Black Man and the Promise of America.   Glenview,
          Illinois: Scott, Foresman and Company, 1970.   523p.
             A big textbook that provides history, sociology, and
          literature.   One interesting section concerns itself with
          the psychological effects of racism and contains a chapter
          of excerpts from literature on the white personality.

1045   BAKER, RAY STANNARD.   Following the Color Line: American
          Negro Citizenship in the Progressive Era.   New York:
          Harper and Row, Publishers, 1964.   311p.
             A study of race relations at a time of racial ferment.
          The three sections take up the Negro in the north, south,
          and in the nation.

BALDWIN, JAMES.   See   1122.

1046   BELL, INGE POWELL. CORE and the Strategy of Non-Violence.
       New York: Random House, 1968. 214p.
           A sociological study of the Congress of Racial Equality
       (CORE) showing the group's change from direct action to
       community organization. The relationship between CORE,
       SNCC, and the Black Muslims is also shown.

1047   BENNETT, LERONE. Before the Mayflower: A History of the
       Negro in America, 1619-1964. Baltimore: Penguin Books,
       1966. 435p.
           A good, detailed history, including an extensive
       bibliography. Revised version of 1962 edition.

1048   BLACK STUDIES: How it Works at Ten Universities. New York:
       Management Division, Academy for Educational Development,
       March, 1971.
           The survey focuses on: program organization, staffing,
       director's responsibilities, financial support, anticipated
       major problems, and projected growth. It was conducted at:
       Atlanta; Duke; Howard; Lincoln; New York; Princeton;
       Rutgers; Stanford; Vanderbilt; and Yale universities.

1049   BLAUSTEIN, ALBERT P. and ROBERT L. ZANGRANDO, eds. Civil
       Rights and the Black American: A Documentary History.
       New York: Simon and Schuster, 1970. 663p.
           A fine reference book. Examines documents relating to
       Civil Rights and the Blacks in America. Reprint of 1968
       edition.

1050   BOGGS, JAMES, The American Revolution: Pages from a Negro
       Worker's Notebook. New York: Monthly Review Press, 1963.
       93p.
           Thoughts of a Black factory worker on capitalism,
       racism, technology, society, and revolution in America.

1051   BONTEMPS, ARNA & JACK CONROY. Anyplace But Here. New York:
       Hill and Wang, 1966. 372p.
           A revised version of They Seek A City, a study of Black
       migration in the U. S.

1052   BONTEMPS, ARNA W. 100 Years of Negro Freedom. New York:
       Dodd, Mead and Company, 1961. 276p.
           History--from Frederick Douglass to date of publication.
       Good for background reading, especially for biographical
       materials.

AFRO-AMERICANS

1053   BOULWARE, MARCUS. The Oratory of Negro Leaders: 1900–1968.
        Westport, Connecticut: Negro Universities Press, 1969.
        312p.
            Black orators and their place in Black history.

1054   BRAZIER, ARTHUR M. Black Self-Determination: The Story of
        the Woodlawn Organization. Grand Rapids, Michigan:
        William B. Eerdmans Publishing Company, 1969. 148p.
            The way one Black community organized for self-deter-
        mination in Chicago.

1055   BREITMAN, GEORGE. The Last Year of Malcolm X; The Evolution
        of a Revolutionary. New York: Schocken Books, 1968.
        169p.
            Analysis of the ideas and philosophy of Malcolm X a
        year before his assassination. Bibliography. Reprint of
        1967 edition.

        BREITMAN, GEORGE. See 1117, 1118, 1150.

1056   BRINK, WILLIAM and LOUIS HARRIS. Black and White; A Study of
        U. S. Racial Attitudes Today. New York: Simon and
        Schuster, 1967. 285p.
            An expansion of the August 22, 1966 issue of Newsweek
        which investigated attitudes about civil rights, Black
        power, Negro progress in America and White reactions to
        all of this. Representative statements from both sides.
        Questionnaires and statistics.

1057   BRODERICK, FRANCIS L. and AUGUST MEIER, eds. Negro Protest
        Thought in the Twentieth Century. Indianapolis: Bobbs-
        Merrill Company, 1966. 443p.
            Survey of the materials in the field with short intro-
        ductions. Pamphlets and periodical materials difficult
        to find are included. Reprint of 1965 edition.

1058   BRONTZ, HOWARD. The Black Jews of Harlem: Negro Nationalism
        and the Dilemmas of Negro Leadership. New York: The
        Free Press, 1964. 144p.
            Deals with a small group of "Black" Jews but more
        widely with the whole Black power movement.

1059   BROWN, TURNER, Jr., Black Is. New York: Grove Press, 1969. 95p.
            Sharp and pithy little book of definition. Illustrated by
        Ann Weisman.

CLARK, KENNETH B. See 1132.

1060   CARMICHAEL, STOKELY and CHARLES V. HAMILTON. Black Power;
        The Politics of Liberation in America. New York: Random
        House, 1967. 198p.
            History of the Black power movement and what it could
        be. Bibliography.

1061   CLEAVER, ELDRIDGE. Post-Prison Writings and Speeches. New
        York: Vintage Books, 1969. 211p.
            Collection of political essays and speeches.

1062   CONOT, ROBERT. Rivers of Blood, Years of Darkness. New York:
        Bantam Books, 1967. 497p.
            Conot was a special consultant to the National Advisory
        Commission on Civil Disorders, thus in a good position to
        obtain materials and evaluate the riots in Watts (Los
        Angeles) during August, 1965. Sections include: The Two
        Americas, The Fires of Discontent, The Legacy, and The
        Black Print of the Negro. Appendices give methodology,
        sources and references and a bibliography.

CONROY, JACK. See 1051.
COWLEY, MALCOLM. See 1121.

1063   COX, ARCHIBALD, MARK DE WOLFE HOWE, and JAMES R. WIGGINS.
        Civil Rights, The Constitution, and the Courts. Cambridge,
        Massachusetts: Harvard University Press, 1967. 76p.
            Three lectures by Harvard Law School professors about
        the cause and effects of the civil rights movement and the
        power of the courts.

1064   CROSS, THEODORE L. Black Capitalism: Strategy for Business in
        the Ghetto. New York: Atheneum, 1969. 274p.
            A banking authority gives the motives and possibilities
        for business action in the ghetto and offers correctives to
        the economic dislocation of that area. Appendices and
        further reading sources.

1065   CROWE, CHARLES, ed. The Age of Civil War and Reconstruction,
        1830-1900. Homewood, Illinois: Dorsey, 1966. 479p.
            A fine collection of articles by leading experts in
        nineteenth-century American history. Each section of
        essays has a bibliography and introduction.

1066   CRUSE, HAROLD. Rebellion or Revolution? New York: William
        Morrow and Company, 1968. 272p.
            Collection of articles written from a Marxist critical
        position about the Black power movement as a middle-class
        democratic nationalist movement.

Minority Studies: An Annotated Bibliography

AFRO-AMERICANS

1067 CURTIN, PHILIP D. The Atlantic Slave Trade: A Census. Madison: University of Wisconsin Press, 1969. 338p.
A very extensive history of the slave trade in North and South America with emphasis on the trader countries. Includes a good bibliography and Koelle's Linguistic Inventory of slaves held in Sierra Leone.

1068 DAVIS, ANGELA Y. and OTHER POLITICAL PRISONERS. If They Come in the Morning: Voices of Resistance. New York: The Third Press, 1971. 281p.
The prison system, the realities of repression, and the Angela Davis trial are among the sections.

1069 DIXON, THOMAS, JR. The Clansman: An Historical Romance of the Ku Klux Klan. Lexington: The University Press of Kentucky, 1970. 374p.
Reprint of the famous 1905 racist novel.

1070 DIXON, THOMAS, JR. The Leopard's Spots: A Romance of the White Man's Burden 1865-1900. Ridgewood, New Jersey: Gregg Press, 1967.
A classic of Southern racism. Reprint of 1902 edition.

1071 DRIMMER, MELVIN, comp. Black History: A Reappraisal. Garden City, New York: Doubleday and Company, 1968. 553p.
A comprehensive series of essays in chronological arrangement with an introduction to each section. Bibliography.

1072 DUBOIS, WILLIAM E. B. Black Reconstruction in America: An Essay Toward a History of the Part which Black Folk Played in the Attempt to Reconstruct Democracy in America, 1860-1880. New York: Atheneum Publishers, 1969. 746p.
The history of the Blacks during the Civil War and after. Bibliography. Reprint of 1935 edition.

1073 _____. Dusk of Dawn: An Essay Toward an Autobiography of a Race Concept. New York: Schocken Books, Inc., 1968. 334p.
Reprint of 1940 edition.

178

1074   _____, ed. The Negro in Business; Report of a Social Study
Made Under the Direction of Atlanta University, Together
with the Proceedings of the Fourth Conference for the
Study of Negro Problems, Held at Atlanta University,
May 30-31, 1899. New York: AMS Press, 1971. 77p.
Reprint of 1899 edition.

DUBOIS, WILLIAM E. B. See also 1154.

1075 DURHAM, PHILIP and EVERETT L. JONES. The Negro Cowboys.
New York: Dodd, Mead, 1965. 278p.
A documentary history of the part played by Blacks in
the opening up of the West. Bibliography.

1076 ELKINS, STANLEY M. Slavery: A Problem in American Institutional and Intellectual Life, 2nd edition. Chicago:
University of Chicago Press, 1968. 264p.
An important discussion of various concepts about
slavery. A look at various viewpoints and stereotypes,
arguments and approaches, personality responses to slavery,
slavery in capitalistic and non-capitalistic countries,
sin and reform. Appendices, one on materials and methods
used. Bibliographic footnotes. A very fascinating book
that raises many questions about human behavior. Reprint
of 1959 edition.

1077 ESSIEN-UDOM, E. U. Black Nationalism: A Search for an
Identity in America. Chicago: University of Chicago
Press, 1967. 367p.
In-depth study of the Black Nationalist movement with
some interpretation of its strength and meaning. Reprint
of 1962 edition.

1078 FAGER, CHARLES E. White Reflections on Black Power. Grand
Rapids, Michigan: William B. Eerdmans, 1967. 118p.
White middle-class, college-educated, northern city man
looks at Black power. Good bibliography.

FENDERSON, LEWIS H. See 1044.

1079 FONER, PHILIP S., ed. The Black Panthers Speak. Philadelphia:
J. B. Lippincott Company, 1970. 274p.
Documentary record of the Panthers' program and articles
by leaders such as Newton, Seale, and Cleaver.

AFRO-AMERICAN

FOX, DANIEL M. See 1095

1080 FRANKLIN, JOHN HOPE. From Slavery to Freedom: A History of
Negro Americans, 3rd ed. revised and enlarged. New
York: Alfred A. Knopf, 1967. 686p.
A history of the Negro in America from his origins in
Africa through the post-World War II period. Also includes
the West Indies, Latin America, and Canada. An extensive
bibliography. Reprint of 1947 edition.

1081 FRAZIER, EDWARD FRANKLIN, ed. On Race Relations: Selected
Writings. Chicago: University of Chicago Press, 1968.
331p.
A collection of addresses, essays, and lectures about
race. Bibliography of Frazier's writings.

1082 FRAZIER, E. FRANKLIN. Race and Culture Contacts in the
Modern World. New York: Knopf, 1957. 338p.
European expansion brought about racial frontiers and
racial confrontations. Discusses the ecological,
economic, political and social organization, and the
racism that resulted.

1083 FREDRICKSON, GEORGE M. The Black Image in the White Mind:
The Debate on Afro-American Character and Destiny,
1817-1914. New York: Harper and Row, 1971. 343p.
Survey of the development of Black racial steroetypes
in America. Chapters on "Uncle Tom," White nationalism,
the Negro as beast, and accommodationist racism. No
bibliography, which is a bad oversight in this book, but
bibliographic footnotes.

GARVEY, MARCUS. See 1099

1084 GENOVESE, EUGENE D. Roll Jordan Roll: The World The
Slaves Made. New York: Pantheon Books, 1974. 823p.
This new study is highly praised by The New York Review
of Books (XXI: 15) for its unparochial and rounded view,
which is not to describe a peculiar institution but to un-
fold the historical impress of slavery upon an entire
society, so as to show a way of life that developed because
of it.

GOODMAN, BENJAMIN. See 1116

1085   GRANT, JOANNE, comp. Black Protest; History, Documents and
       Analyses, from 1619 to the Present. New York: St. Martin's
       Press, 1970. 505p.
           Collection of documents with interpretive materials.
       Emphasis on current material and civil rights. Bibliog-
       raphy. Reprint of 1968 edition.

1086   GRANT, MADISON. The Conquest of a Continent; or, the Expansion
       of Races in America. New York: Charles Scribner's Sons,
       1933. 393p.
           Includes an introduction by Henry Fairfield Osborn.
       Bibliography and maps. Reprints of 1865 edition.

1087   GRIGGS, SUTTON ELBERT. The Hindered Hand; or, the Reign of
       the Repressionist. New York: AMS Press, 1969. 333p.
           A counterattack upon Thomas Dixon's The Leopard's Spots
       and books like it which were designed to rouse anti-Black
       feelings especially about the fear of miscegenation or
       Black/White sex. Reprint of 1905 edition.

       HAMILTON, CHARLES V. See 1060.
       HARRIS, LOUIS. See 1056.

1088   HAWKINS, HUGH, ed. Booker T. Washington and His Critics; The
       Problem of Negro Leadership. Boston: D. C. Heath and
       Company, 1962. 113p.
           Includes a number of articles by both Black and White
       writers about Washington. Part of the "Problems in
       American Civilization" series.

1089   HENTOFF, NAT. The New Equality. New York: Viking, 1964.
       243p.
           Black power movement discussed from the viewpoint of a
       heavy sympathizer.

1090   HERNTON, CALVIN C. Sex and Racism in America. New York:
       Grove Press, 1966. 180p.
           Sexual myths and bugaboos, its connection with racism,
       and the use made of both by the American politico-economic
       system are analyzed in a mixture of personal experience
       and acute sociological understanding. Reprint of 1965
       edition.

AFRO-AMERICANS

1091   HERNTON, CALVIN. White Papers for White Americans.
       Garden City, New York: Doubleday and Company, 1966. 155p.
       Blacks, Whites, racism, and psychology.

1092   HERSEY, JOHN. The Algiers Motel Incident. New York:
       Alfred A. Knopf, Inc., 1968. 397p.
          By means of interviews and the examination of police
       and court records, Hersey has reconstructed the events
       leading to the deaths of three Blacks at the hands of
       police during the Detroit Riots of 1967. Does not include
       a follow-through about the trials and acquittals of the
       policemen.

       HERSKOVITS, FRANCES S. See 1094.

1093   HERSKOVITS, MELVILLE J. The Myth of the Negro Past. Boston:
       Beacon Press, 1958. 368p.
          An excellent study of the American Negro and his
       African cultural antecedents by a world-wide expert.
       References and bibliography. Reprint of 1941 edition.

1094   _____. The New World Negro; Selected Papers in Afro-American
       Studies, edited by Frances S. Herskovits. Bloomington:
       Indiana University Press, 1966. 370p.
          Essays by a leading expert. Bibliography of ethno-
       history.

       HOWE, MARK DE WOLFE. See 1063.

1095   HUGGINS, NATHAN I., MARTIN KILSON, and DANIEL M. FOX, eds.
       Key Issues in the Afro-American Experience, I & II.
       New York: Harcourt, Brace, Jovanovich, 1971.
          A collection of writings surveying political, social,
       and cultural developments in Afro-American history. Head-
       ings such as: "The Urban Setting," and "Toward a New
       Identity."

1096   HUGHES, LANGSTON, Fight for Freedom; The Story of the NAACP.
       New York: W. W. Norton, 1962. 224p.
          A history of the NAACP movement. Bibliography.

1097   JACKSON, GEORGE. Blood in my Eye. New York: Random House,
       1972. 197p.
          Jackson's call for Revolution with an Afterword by
       Huey Newton.

1098   JACKSON, GEORGE. Soledad Brother: The Prison Letters of
       George Jackson. New York: Coward McCann, 1970. 330p.
          Descriptions and personal essays taken from letters

182

(JACKSON, GEORGE)
> written in prison, as Jackson waited his trial. Shows the development of a man's personality from bitterness to love and acceptance.

1099   JACQUES-GARVEY, AMY, ed. Philosophy and Opinions of Marcus Garvey, Vols. I & II. New York: Atheneum, 1971. 412p.
> Brings together speeches, articles, letters, and statements by Marcus Garvey, the exponent of pan-African nationalism in the 1920s. Another in the series, Studies in American Negro Life. Reprint of 1923 edition.

JONES, EVERETT L. See 1075.

1100   JORDAN, WINTHROP. White Over Black: American Attitudes Toward the Negro, 1550-1812. Baltimore, Maryland: Penguin Books, 1969. 651p.
> A book that has received, and rightly, wide attention for its scholarship and topic treatment. The origins and development of racism in this country are traced and documented in a convincing manner. Bibliography. Reprint of 1968 edition.

1101   KATZ, WILLIAM LOREN. The Black West. Garden City, New York: Doubleday and Company, 1971. 336p.
> A history of the Black men who helped settle the West. Includes explorers, trappers, the military, and outlaws as well as such famous characters as Deadwood Dick and Cherokee Bill. Bibliographic notes.

1102   _____, ed. Five Slave Narratives. New York: Arno Press and The New York Times, 1969. 400+p.
> Reprints, using actual plates and illustrations, from five nineteenth-century accounts taken down or written out by escaped slaves. The narratives offer an in-depth look at the South's "peculiar institution."

1103   _____. Teacher's Guide to American Negro History. Chicago: Quadrangle Books, 1971. 192p.
> A practical teacher's aide with chapters organized around an integrated curriculum. Includes annotated topical bibliographies as well as listings of inexpensive or free teaching materials. Also lists museums of Negro history.

1104   KELLOGG, CHARLES F. NAACP: A History of the National Association for the Advancement of Colored People, Vol. I, 1909-1920. Baltimore: Johns Hopkins Press, 1967. 332p.
> The first years of the NAACP. Bibliography.

AFRO-AMERICANS

1105   KILLIAN, LEWIS MARTIN. The Impossible Revolution? Black
        Power and the American Dream. New York: Random House,
        1968. 198p.
            Black freedom movement from 1954 to the present with
        emphasis upon the increased revolutionary stance of Blacks
        and their connection with the "Third World" movement. As
        a sociologist, Professor Killian is pessimistic about a
        good solution to current racial problems. Bibliography.

        KILSON, MARTIN. See   1095

1106   KING, MARTIN LUTHER. The Trumpet of Conscience. New York:
        Harper and Row, 1968. 78p.
            The Massey Lectures of 1967 concerning civil rights and
        social emancipation.

1107   KING, MARTIN LUTHER, Jr., Where Do We Go From Here: Chaos or
        Community? New York: Bantam Books, 1968. 242p.
            Contemporary Black history and the civil rights move-
        ment. Black power and White backlash are also discussed.
        Bibliography. Reprint of 1967 edition.

1108   KING, WOODIE and EARL ANTHONY, eds. Black Poets and Prophets:
        The Theory, Practice, and Esthetics of the Pan-Africanist
        Revolution. New York: New American Library, 1972. 188p.
            Important collection of essays that combines politics,
        history, Black magic and Black art. Statements by Fanon,
        Carmichael, Cleaver, and Karenga.

1109   KNOWLES, LOUIS L. and KENNETH PREWITT, eds. Institutional
        Racism in America. Englewood-Cliffs, New Jersey: Prentice-
        Hall, 1970.
            How American institutions, such as schools, banks, and
        law courts, keep racism established and maintain the
        ghettos. Reprint of 1969 edition.

1110   LECKIE, WILLIAM H. The Buffalo Soldiers: A Narrative of the
        Negro Cavalry in the West. Norman: University of
        Oklahoma Press, 1967. 290p.
            The 9th and 10th Cavalry Regiments were Black troops led
        by White officers. They shipped out West after the Civil
        War and fought American Indians. Bibliography.

1111   LESTER, JULIUS. Look Out Whitey! Black Power's Gon' Get
        Your Mama. New York: Grove Press, 1969. 150p.
            The Establishment criticized in terms of its stereotyping,
        by an influential SNCC official, folksinger, and essayist.
        Humor and pride and a selected bibliography.

1112　LESTER, JULIUS. Revolutionary Notes. New York: R. W. Baron, 1969. 209p.
　　　　Another series of original, witty, and perceptive essays.

1113　LIGHTFOOT, CLAUDE M. Ghetto Rebellion to Black Liberation. New York: International Book Publishers, 1968. 192p.
　　　　Communist interpretation of the Black power movement.

1114　LINCOLN, CHARLES ERIC. The Black Muslims in America. Boston: Beacon Press, 1973. 302p.
　　　　The first in-depth study of the Black Muslim movement. Reprint of 1961 edition.

1115　_____. My Face is Black. Boston: Beacon Press, 1964. 137p.
　　　　An analysis of the race question and the Black Muslims in terms of "mood ebony." Beacon - 1973.

1116　LITTLE, MALCOLM. The End of White World Supremacy: Four Speeches. Benjamin Goodman, ed. New York: Merlin House, Inc., 1971. 148p.
　　　　Speeches made during Malcolm X's last year of affiliation with the Black Muslims.

1117　_____. Malcolm X on Afro-American History. New York: Pathfinder Press, 1970. 74p.

1118　_____. Malcolm X Speaks: Selected Speeches and Statements, ed. by George Breitman. New York: Grove Press, 1965.
　　　　Speeches and statements by the great Black leader made during the last year of his life. See also 1399 and 1435.

　　　　LITWACK, LEON F. See 1145.

1119　LOMAX, LOUIS E. The Negro Revolt. New York: Harper and Row, 1971. 377p. Revised edition.
　　　　History of Black attitudes and strategies for gaining freedom, focusing on recent developments as part of a historical progression.

1120　McKITRICK, E. L., ed. Slavery Defended: The Views of the Old South. Englewood Cliffs, New Jersey: Prentice-Hall, 1963. 180p.
　　　　A collection of articles representing a southern viewpoint on slavery.

Minority Studies: An Annotated Bibliography

AFRO-AMERICANS

MALCOLM X. See 1055, 1116, 1117, 1118, 1200.

1121   MANNIX, DANIEL PRATT and MALCOLM COWLEY. Black Cargoes: A History of the Atlantic Slave Trade. New York: Viking Press, 1962. 306p.
       A history of the slave trade.

1122   MEAD, MARGARET and JAMES BALDWIN. A Rap on Race. New York: Dell Publishing Company, 1971. 256p.
       A transcript of a tape-recorded conversation between Mead and Baldwin in 1970. Informal and vernacular, and all over the place, from virgin birth to slavery to Spiro Agnew.

1123   MEIER, AUGUST and ELLIOTT M. RUDWICK, eds. Black Protest in the Sixties. Chicago: Quadrangle Books, 1970. 355p.
       Compendium of articles on the Black Power movement.

1124   MEIER, AUGUST. Negro Thought in America 1880-1915: Racial Ideologies in the Age of Booker T. Washington. Ann Arbor: The University of Michigan Press, 1963. 336p.
       Examines the Black response to social and economic conditions and the careers of Dubois and Washington.

MEIER, AUGUST. See also 1057.

1125   MELTZER, MILTON, ed. In Their Own Words: A History of the American Negro. New York: Thomas Y. Crowell Company, 1964, 1965, 1967. 195p; 180p; 213p.
       A three-volume set of documents from Black history. Volume I includes the years from 1619 to 1865; volume 2, 1865-1916; and volume 3, 1916-1966. Includes a handy calendar of Black history and an annotated selected bibliography.

1126   MILLER, LOREN. The Petitioners: The Story of the Supreme Court of the United States and the Negro. New York: Pantheon Books, 1966. 461p.
       The history of the Supreme Court and its actions on cases involving black problems from the eighteenth century to date of publication.

1127   No Entry.

1128   MUSE, BENJAMIN. The American Negro Revolution; from Non-
violence to Black Power, 1963-1967. Bloomington: Indiana
University Press, 1968. 345p.
The history of the change from civil rights sit-downs
to violence in the 1960s.

1129   MYRDAL, GUNNAR. An American Dilemma: The Negro Problem and
Modern Democracy. New York: Harper and Row, 1969.
1483p.
Every aspect of slavery and the problem of racism in the
United States is explored in this mammoth and important
work, the result of much research and study. Some of the
topics covered include: American idealism, race, economics,
migration, justice, leadership and Black protest, religion,
and community. 10 appendices go into further details.
Reprint of 1944 edition.

NELSON, SOPHIA P. See 1044

1130   NEWBY, IDUS. Jim Crow's Defense: Anti-Negro Thought in
America, 1900-1930. Baton Rouge: Louisiana State University Press, 1965. 230p.
The development of racism in the first part of the
twentieth century. Bibliography.

1131   OFARI, EARL. The Myth of Black Capitalism. New York:
Monthly Review Press, 1970. 126p.
A discussion of the functional character of American
capitalism, the weakness of Black capitalism, and its
effect on the ghettoes. Bibliography.

1132   PARSONS, TALCOTT and KENNETH B. CLARK, eds. The Negro
American. Boston: Houghton, Mifflin and Company, 1966.
781p.
Thirty articles on the race crisis in America.

PREWITT, KENNETH. See 1109

1133   QUARLES, BENJAMIN. The Negro in the Civil War. Boston:
Little, Brown, 1969. 379p.
A history of the part played by Blacks during the Civil
War. Bibliography. Reprint of 1953 edition.

1134   _____. The Negro in the Making of America. New York: Collier
Books, 1969. 288p. Revised edition.
The Civil Rights struggle is described in a popular
history which follows a chronological pattern from the
beginnings of slavery in Africa through the 1950s. Selected
bibliography.

Minority Studies: An Annotated Bibliography

AFRO-AMERICANS

1135   REDDING, SAUNDERS. They Came in Chains: Americans from Africa.
        Philadelphia: J. B. Lippincott, 1950. 320p.
        Greed and blood. Bibliography.

1136   ROGERS, JOEL AUGUSTUS. From "Superman" to Man. New York:
        J. A. Rogers, 1957. 123p.
        A train trip which involves a continuous dialogue
        between two people about race relationships in the United
        States. Reprint of 1917 edition.

1137   ROSE, ARNOLD. The Negro in America. New York: Harper and
        Row, 1964. 324p.
        A condensed version of An American Dilemma, one of the
        most comprehensive studies out on the Black-White racial
        problem.

1138   ROWAN, CARL T. South of Freedom. New York: Alfred A. Knopf,
        1952. 270p.
        The race problem and the lives of those who must live
        heavily under it in the South.

        RUDWICK, ELLIOTT M. See   1123

1139   SALK, ERWIN A. A Layman's Guide to Negro History, new
        enlarged ed. New York: McGraw Hill, 1967. 196p.
        Part I is a historical fact book. Part II contains
        bibliographies of history books by period. Other listings
        include children's books, phonograph records, and visual
        materials.

1140   SEALE, BOBBY. Seize the Time: The Story of the Black Panther
        Party and Huey P. Newton. New York: Random House, 1970.
        429p.
        Tapes and articles from Ramparts magazine edited in
        sequence.

1141   SEWALL, SAMUEL. The Selling of Joseph; A Memorial Colophon.
        Boston; Bartholomew Green, and John Allen, June 24, 1700.
        Amherst: University of Massachusetts Press, 1970.
        The earliest writing in America dealing with the slavery
        question. Sewall was a noted Quaker. Reprint of 1936
        edition.

1142   SILBERMAN, CHARLES E. Crisis in Black and White. New York:
        Vintage Books, 1964. 370p.
        A thorough and probing book about Black-White relation-
        ships in the United States. Discussions of the basis and
        meaning of racism and prejudice. Excellent for classroom
        use.

1143   STALVEY, LOIS MARK. The Education of a WASP. New York:
       Morrow Publishing, 1970. 327p.
          The education of a White woman to the American facts of
       racism. Introduction by Shirley Chisholm.

1144   STAMPP, KENNETH M. The Peculiar Institution: Slavery in the
       Ante-Bellum South. New York: Alfred A. Knopf, 1965. 436p.
          The setting, the people, and the profit and loss of
       slavery. A classic. Reprint of 1956 edition.

1145   STAMPP, KENNETH M. and LEON F. LITWACK, eds. Reconstruction:
       An Anthology of Revisionist Writings. Baton Rouge:
       Louisiana State University Press, 1969. 531p.
          Reconstruction seen from a viewpoint sympathetic to
       Black experience.

1146   STANTON, WILLIAM. The Leopard's Spots: Scientific Attitudes
       Towards Race in America 1815-59. Chicago: University of
       Chicago Press, 1960. 244p.
          A well documented and fascinating study of racism.
       Bibliographic notes.

1147   STONE, CHUCK. Black-Political Power in America. New York:
       Dell Publishing Co., 1970. Revised edition. 303p.
          The history of Blacks in American politics.

1148   STORING, HERBERT J., ed. What Country Have I? Political
       Writings by Black Americans. New York: St. Martin's
       Press, 1970. 235p.
          Compendium of the best political writings of the past
       two centuries. Includes Frederick Douglass, James Weldon
       Johnson, Eldridge Cleaver, and James Baldwin. Selective
       bibliography.

1149   TABB, WILLIAM K. The Political Economy of the Black Ghetto.
       New York: W. W. Norton and Company, 1970. 152p.
          Topics discussed include the concept of the Black ghetto
       as an example of American internal colonialism, urban
       poverty, public policy, and the labor market.

1150   TROTSKY, LEON. Leon Trotsky on Black Nationalism and Self
       Determination. George Breitman, ed. New York: Merit
       Publishers, 1967. 66p.
          Compilation of Trotsky's views, especially as they apply
       to the Black Power movement in this country.

Minority Studies: An Annotated Bibliography

AFRO-AMERICANS

1151   UNITED STATES National Advisory Commission on Civil Disorders.
        <u>Report of the United States National Advisory Commission
        on Civil Disorders</u>. New York: Bantam Books, 1968. 425p.
            The famous and controversial Kerner report. Documents
        the need for reform.

1152   WALTON, HANES, Jr. <u>Black Political Parties: An Historical
        and Political Analysis</u>. New York: The Free Press, 1972.
        276p.
            Tries to cover everything in one volume. A bit sketchy.

1153   WARREN, ROBERT PENN. <u>Segregation: The Inner Conflict in the
        South</u>. New York: Random House, 1956. 66p.
            Warren's impressions and interviews from travels in
        the South in the early 1950s during early days of the
        civil rights movement.

1154   WASHINGTON, BOOKER T. and WILLIAM E. B. DUBOIS. <u>The Negro
        in the South, His Economic Progress in Relation to His
        Moral and Religious Development</u>. Philadelphia: G. W.
        Jacobs, 1907. 222p.
            The William Levi Bull Lectures for 1907. Bibliography.

        WIGGINS, JAMES R. <u>See</u>   1063

1155   WISH, HARVEY, ed. <u>Slavery in the South</u>. New York: Farrar,
        Straus and Giroux, 1968. 290p.
            A collection of contemporary accounts documenting the
        plantation system of slavery in the eighteenth and nine-
        teenth centuries. This book takes on three different points
        of view: the Blacks, that of the northern visitor, and
        the southern White plantation owner. Reprint of 1964
        edition.

1156   WISTER, OWEN. <u>Lady Baltimore</u>. New York: Macmillan Company,
        1906. 406p.
            Since this was so widely read, it deserves mention here.
        Wister demonstrates in this novel about the deep South,
        that the Negro must be racially inferior because, among
        other reasons, he has a smaller brain than his White masters.

1157   WOODWARD, COMER VANN. <u>The Strange Career of Jim Crow</u>, 2nd
        rev. ed. New York: Oxford University Press, 1966. 205p.
            A classic on racism, the development of stereotyping and
        segregation.

1158 WRIGHT, NATHAN, Jr. Black Power and Urban Unrest; Creative
Possibilities. New York: Hawthorn Books, 1967. 200p.
A clear description of Black Power and its philosophy
written by the chairman of the 1967 National Conference
on Black Power. The relationship of the church to the
movement is outlined.

1159 WYNES, CHARLES E., ed. The Negro in the South since 1865;
Selected Essays in American Negro History. Birmingham:
University of Alabama Press, 1965. 253p.
Covers history, politics, education, religion, and
other cultural subjects. Southern historical publications
no. 10. Bibliography.

1160 YOUNG, RICHARD P., ed. Roots of Rebellion: The Evolution of
Black Politics & Protest Since WW II. New York: Harper
and Row, 1970. 482p.
Collection of social science writings on recent
developments in Black politics and ideology.

ZANGRANDO, ROBERT L. See 1049

1161 ZINN, HOWARD. SNCC: The New Abolitionists. Boston: Beacon
Press, 1969. 286p.
History of the Student Nonviolent Coordinating Committee
with emphasis on its work in the early '60s. Reprint of
1965 edition.

D. Education

1162 BANKS, JAMES A. and JEAN DRESDEN GRAMBS. Black Self-Concept;
Implications for Education and Social Science. New York:
McGraw-Hill, 1972. 234p.

1163 BANKS, JAMES A. Teaching the Black Experience: Methods and
Materials. Belmont, California: Fearon Publishers, 1970.
90p.
A practical and down-to-earth book on how to organize
and teach historical materials, especially for intergroup
relevance. Resources section includes annotated background books.

1164 BARATZ, JOAN and ROGER SHUY, eds. Teaching Black Children
to Read. Center for Applied Linguistics, 1969.

MINORITY STUDIES: AN ANNOTATED BIBLIOGRAPHY

AFRO-AMERICANS

1165   BLACK STUDIES: How it Works at Ten Universities. New York:
       Management Division, Academy for Educational Development,
       March, 1971.
          The survey focuses on: program organization, staffing,
       director's responsibilities, financial support, anticipated
       major problems, and projected growth. It was conducted at:
       Atlanta; Duke; Howard; Lincoln; New York; Princeton; Rut-
       gers; Stanford; Vanderbilt; and Yale universities.

1166   DILLARD, J. L. Black English: Its History and Usage in the
       United States. New York: Random House, 1972. 361p.
          A fascinating and thorough book on Black English, its
       structure, use and its relationship to the educational
       system in the United States. Also included is a chapter
       on Pidgin English-Black, Red, and Yellow. Bibliography.

GRAMBS, JEAN DRESDEN. See 1162.

1167   HENTOFF, NAT. Our Children are Dying. New York: Viking
       Press, 1966. 141p.
          An examination of New York City's public school segre-
       gation problems and a study of P.S. No. 119 and Principal
       Elliott Shapiro's attempts to increase the learning chances
       of ghetto children.

1168   KOHL, HERBERT. 36 Children. New York: New American Library,
       1967. 227p.
          36 Black ghetto children, ages 11-14, encounter a
       Harvard-trained White teacher. A detailed account of what
       to do when Dick and Jane readers don't work because they
       are meaningless.

1169   KOZOL, JONATHAN. Death at an Early Age: The Destruction of
       the Hearts and Minds of Negro Children in the Boston Public
       Schools. New York: Bantam Books, 1968. 242p.
          The experience of a teacher in an overcrowded Boston
       ghetto school. Kozol changes names and identities to pro-
       tect the people he is writing about, but their acts and
       attitudes are presented as truths.

SHUY, ROGER. See 1164.

1170   WRIGHT, NATHAN, JR., ed. What Black Educators are Saying.
       New York: Hawthorn Publishers, 1970. 286p.
          Sections include: The Black Educator, The White Estab-
       lishment, The University Scene, Educational Redefinition,
       and Community Involvement and Action. Dedicated to the
       "need for humanizing the schools."

E. General Culture and Community Life
(Archaeology, Folk Tales, Linguistics, Medicine, Music: Blues and
Jazz, Mythology, Philosophy, Psychology, Religion and Sociology)

1171   BARBOUR, FLOYD B., ed. The Black Seventies. Boston: Porter
Sargent Publisher, 1970. 335p.
Onward, inward, and forward read the sections of this
book of essays on Black consciousness, religion, the arts,
and Black nationalism. The book ends with postscripts
including a finale letter from H. Rap Brown.
Bibliography.

1172   CASH, W. J. The Mind of the South. London: Thames and
Hudson, 1971. 445p.
The philosophical outlook and social customs of the
South, the temperament and life style are analyzed and
interpreted. The author tries to explain how and why the
Southern ethos developed, and predicts the future. Reprint
of 1941 edition.

1173   CHARTERS, SAMUEL B. The Country Blues. New York: Rinehart
and Company, Inc., 1959. 288p.
The development of rural blues music and its influence
on American and world music.

1174   CLARK, KENNETH B. Dark Ghetto: Dilemmas of Social Power.
New York: Harper and Row, 1965. 251p.
Harlem described in terms of its power structures and
the interrelationships of politics, religion, economics,
and intellectual leadership.

COBBS, PRICE M. See 1188

1175   CONE, JAMES H. Black Theology & Black Power. New York:
The Seabury Press, 1969.
An examination of Black and White religion, religious
teachings, and Black power in historical and contemporary
context.

1176   _____. The Spirituals & The Blues. New York: The Seabury
Press, 1972. 152p.
An interpretation of the religious and cultural com-
ponents of spirituals and the rise of blues as a "secular
spiritual."

1177   COURLANDER, HAROLD. Negro Folk Music, U. S. A. New York:
Columbia University Press, 1963. 324p.
A good collection which includes both music and lyrics.
Bibliography and discography.

MINORITY STUDIES: AN ANNOTATED BIBLIOGRAPHY

AFRO-AMERICANS

1178   CRUSE, HAROLD. The Crisis of the Negro Intellectual. New
       York: William Morrow and Company, 1967. 594p.
          A provocative book by Cruse who is a Marxist critic.
       A thorough discussion of American intellectual life in
       terms of the Black culture. Bibliography.

1179   DECARAVA, ROY and LANGSTON HUGHES. The Sweet Flypaper of Life.
       New York: Hill and Wang, 1967. 96p.
          A picture story book of life in Harlem.

1180   DOVER, CEDRIC. American Negro Art, 3rd ed. Greenwich,
       Connecticut: New York Graphic Society, 1965. 186p.
          Chronological history of Black art in America.
       Bibliography. Reprint of 1960 edition.

1181   DUBOIS, WILLIAM E. B., ed. The College-Bred Negro; Report of
       a Social Study made Under the Direction of Atlanta Univer-
       sity; together with the Proceedings of the Fifth Conference
       for the Study of Negro Problems, held at Atlanta University,
       May 29-30, 1900. Atlanta: Atlanta University, 1900. 115p.

1182   FACTOR, ROBERT L. The Black Response to America: Men, Ideals,
       and Organization from Frederick Douglass to the NAACP.
       Reading, Massachusetts: Addison-Wesley Publishing Co.
       1970. 385p.
          A social and political history of Black strategies
       for meeting White oppression.

1183   FEATHER, LEONARD. The New Edition of the Encyclopedia of Jazz.
       New York: Bonanza Books, 1960. 537p.
          A chronological historical survey plus biographies is
       included in this compendium. Discography and bibliography.
       Criticized by Kofsky (Journal of Black Studies 1:4) for
       White bias.

1184   FRAZIER, EDWARD FRANKLIN. Black Bourgeoisie; The Rise of a
       New Middle Class in the United States. New York:
       MacMillan, 1962. 222p.
          The behavior, values and culture of a group isolated
       between White middle class America and the Black ghetto
       poor. Frazier is justly famous for this book. Bibliography.

1185   _____. The Free Negro Family. New York: Arno Press and The
       New York Times, 1968. 75p.
          Black history, literature, and sociology. Bibliography.
       Reprint of 1932 edition.

194

1186   (FRAZIER, EDWARD FRANKLIN)
        The Negro Church in America. New York: Schocken Books,
        1964. 92p.
            A history of the development of the Black church. The
        footnotes contain bibliography. Reprint of 1963 edition.

1187   _____. The Negro Family in the United States, revised and
        abridged. Chicago: University of Chicago Press, 1966.
        372p.
            A valuable contribution to the literature about the
        Black family in the United States, focusing on the Negro
        family as a natural human association and a social institu-
        tion subjected to all the stresses of American social
        change.

        FRIEDBERG, BERNARD. See 1201

1188   GRIER, WILLIAM H. and PRICE M. COBBS. Black Rage. New York:
        Basic Books, 1968. 213p.
            Two Black psychiatrists look at the conflicts and anger
        of the Black man in America today.

        HARWOOD, EDWIN. See: 1201

1189   HOUGH, JOSEPH C., Jr. Black Power and White Protestants; A
        Christian Response to the Negro Pluralism. New York:
        Oxford University Press, 1968. 228p.
            The Chairman of the Religious faculty at Claremont
        Graduate School examines the Church, the new Black power
        role in society, and the traditionalist White American who
        is afraid of change.

        HOWARD, JOHN. See 1201
        HUGHES, LANGSTON. See 1179
        JOHNSON, J. ROSAMOND. See 1190

1190   JOHNSON, JAMES WELDON and J. ROSAMOND JOHNSON. The Book of
        American Negro Spirituals. New York: Viking Press, 1940.
        189p.
            A collection of poetry and music, songs played and sung
        in a folk tradition for over a hundred years. The authors
        discuss the origin, artistic quality, and historic signifi-
        cance of the material. Reprint of 1925 edition.

1191   JONES, LEROI. Black Music. New York: William Morrow and
        Company, 1967. 221p.
            Essays, reviews, interviews, record-liner notes, musical

AFRO-AMERICANS

(JONES, LEROI)
analysis and personal impression of the jazz musicians of
today. Includes such great ones as John Coltraine, Onnette
Coleman, Sonny Murray and others. A brief discography of
new music.

1192 _____. Blues People: Negro Music in White America. New
York: William Morrow and Company, 1963. 224p.
Traces the development of Black music and its effects
on White America. This book also gives a chronological
history of Black music from Africa to the modern scene and
places jazz and blues in context. Bibliographical
footnotes.

1193 KEIL, CHARLES. Urban Blues. Chicago: University of Chicago
Press, 1966. 231p.
The introduction to this survey is one of the best on
Black culture in general. Highly recommended.

1194 KOFSKY, FRANK. Black Nationalism and the Revolution in Music.
New York: Pathfinder Press, 1970. 280p.
Examines the history and settings of recent developments
in jazz in the context of Black nationalism. Included are
an examination of Leroi Jones' Blues People, a closely
detailed study, including interviews with the John Coltrane
Quartet, and a short discussion of Malcom X.

1195 KRONUS, SIDNEY. The Black Middle Class. Columbus, Ohio:
Charles E. Merrill Publishing Company, 1971. 182p.
A study of the changing patterns within the Black middle
class. Includes field questionnaire and bibliography.

1196 LERNER, GERDA. Black Women in White America: A Documentary
History. New York: Pantheon Books, 1972. 630p.
A collection of writings by and about Black women from
slavery to Shirley Chisholm. A number of items are taken
from slave documents and historical documents of Black
women's clubs. Bibliographical references.

1197 LEWIS, SAMELLA S. & RUTH G. WADDY, eds. Black Artists on Art.
(Vols. I & II). Los Angeles: Contemporary crafts, 1969.
Contains examples of works and comments by many con-
temporary Black artists in various media.

1198 LIEBOW, ELLIOT. Tally's Corner; A Study of Negro Streetcorner
Men. Boston: Little Brown and Company, 1967. 260p.
The blighted section of Washington's Inner City during
the early 1960s is the setting and source for this fine
study of what happens at a streetcorner. Bibliography.

MINORITY STUDIES: AN ANNOTATED BIBLIOGRAPHY

Culture

1199   LOCKE, ALAIN LEROY, ed. The Negro in Art: A Pictorial Record
       of the Negro Artist and of the Negro Theme in Art. Washing-
       ton, D.C., Associates in Negro Folk Education, 1940. 224p.

1200   LOMAX, LOUIS. When the Word is Given: A Report on Elijah
       Muhammad, Malcolm X and the Black Muslim World. Cleveland:
       World Publishing Company, 1963. 223p.
            An easy-to-read study of the Muslims based on newspaper
       articles and personal interviews. Muslim texts included
       plus an interview with Malcolm X.

1201   McCORD, WILLIAM and JOHN HOWARD, BERNARD FRIEDBERG, and EDWIN
       HARWOOD. Life Styles in the Black Ghetto. New York:
       W. W. Norton and Company, Inc., 1969. 334p.
            A study of Black urban life developed from interviews
       and direct observation of riots in Watts, Oakland, and
       Detroit, among others. Bibliography.

1202   MAJOR, CLARENCE. Dictionary of Afro-American Slang. New York:
       International Publishers, 1970. 127p.
            From "Absofuckinglutely" to "Zoot suit action."
       Bibliography.

1203   MORAIS, HERBERT M. The History of the Negro in Medicine.
       New York: Publishers Company, Inc., under the auspices of
       the Association for the Study of Negro Life and History,
       1969. 322p.
            Chapters on self-taught healers, the Freedman's
       hospital, health care in the ghettos, and the history of
       the National Medical Association. One of the volumes in
       the International Library of Negro Life and History.
       Appendix and an extensive bibliography.

1204   OLIVER, PAUL. The Meaning of the Blues. New York: Collier
       Books, 1962. 378p.
            A study of the background, imagery, themes, and motiva-
       tion of the blues. Includes a foreword by Richard Wright.
       Discography of the blues and a selected bibliography.

1205   PINKNEY, ALPHONSO. Black Americans. Englewood Cliffs, New
       Jersey: Prentice-Hall, Inc., 1969. 226p.
            Sociological study which includes chapters on popula-
       tion, status, social deviance, and assimilation. One of
       the Ethnic Groups in American Life series. Bibliography.

1206   PLEASANTS, HENRY, Serious Music and all that Jazz. New York:
       Simon and Schuster, 1969. 256p.
            Examines styles of Black music as "an idiomatic pheno-
       menon within...the evolution of Western music." Sees Black

197

AFRO-AMERICANS

    (PLEASANTS, HENRY)
       music as a way of breaking out of the limits of the
       European tradition.

1207   PUGH, RODERICK W., ed. Psychology and the Black Experience.
       Belmont, California: Brooks/Cole Publishing Company,
       1972. 118p.
         A collection of writings on the psychological contexts
       of Black power, psychotherapy, and psychohistories.

1208   REIMERS, DAVID. White Protestantism and the Negro. New York:
       Oxford University Press, 1965. 236p.
         Traces the historical development of White attitudes.
       Bibliography.

1209   SCHUCHTER, ARNOLD. White Power, Black Freedom; Planning for
       the Future of Urban America. Boston: Beacon Press, 1968.
       650p.
         A review of sociological studies concerned with the
       problems of Black and White power. Comprehensive and
       thoughtful. Bibliography.

1210   SOUTHERN, EILEEN. The Music of Black Americans; A History.
       New York: W. W. Norton & Co., 1971.
         A history of almost every aspect of Black music from
       1619 to the 1960s. Very complete, containing excellent
       references and an extensive bibliography and discography.

1211   STEARNS, MARSHALL. The Story of Jazz. New York: New Ameri-
       can Library, 1958. 272p.
         Fifteen lectures on the history of jazz. Describes the
       contributions of Louis Armstrong, Dizzy Gillespie, Charlie
       Parker, and others. Bibliography.

       SZWED, JOHN F. See 1212
       WADDY, RUTH G. See 1197

1212   WHITTEN, NORMAN E., Jr. and JOHN F. SZWED. eds. Afro-American
       Anthropology: Contemporary Perspectives. New York: The
       Free Press, 1970. 468p.
         Twenty-two essays on the Black experience in both North
       and South America. Includes both village and ghetto ethnog-
       raphy. A large bibliography.

          F. Literature by and about Afro-Americans
    (Anthologies, Autobiography, Biography, Drama, Literary
        Criticism and History, Poetry and Prose)

1213   ADLER, BILL. Black Defiance: Black Profiles in Courage.
       New York: William Morrow and Company, 1972. 240p.

(ADLER, BILL)
Stories of Blacks who stood up to White oppression from
the days of slavery to the Black Panthers.

1214   ____, ed. Growing Up Black. New York: Pocket Books, 1968.
256p.
Autobiographical essays by 19 prominent Black Americans.

1215 ADLER, BILL and ELAINE CRANE, eds. Living Black in White
America. New York: William Morrow and Company, 1971.
317p.
Personal experiences of 25 Black writers in dealings
with White America.

1216 ADOFF, ARNOLD, comp. I am the Darker Brother; An Anthology of
Modern Poems by Negro Americans. New York: Macmillan Co.,
1968. 128p.
Includes all the well-known contemporary poets.

1217 ALHAMISI, AHMED and HARUN KOFI WANGARA, eds. Black Arts, an
Anthology of Black Creations. Detroit: Black Arts Publi-
cations, 1969. 158p.
Writings by Black brothers and sisters from the Black
Power and Black Cultural revolutionary movements. Includes
Ed Bullins, Don L. Lee, Nikki Giovanni, Larry Neal, and
many more. Poetry, drama, essays, prose, and pictures.

1218 ANDERSON, ALSTON. All God's Children. Indianapolis: Bobbs-
Merrill, 1965. 221p.
The story of a slave before the Civil War.

1219 ____. Lover Man. Garden City, New York: Doubleday and
Company, 1959. 312p.
Simple folk-type stories full of Black slang and humor.

1220 ANDERSON, MARIAN. My Lord What a Morning. New York: Viking
Press, 1956. 177p.
Autobiography of a great singer.

1221 ANGELOU, MAYA. I Know Why the Caged Bird Sings. New York:
Random House, 1971. 281p.
From Mississippi to California, this land was not made
for Maya Angelou. Being Black and talented, she had to
battle for her place in it. A moving autobiography, highly
recommended for personal reading or classroom use, especially along with her poetry. Reprint of 1970 edition.

1222

ARMSTRONG, LOUIS. Satchmo; My Life in New Orleans. New York:
Prentice-Hall, 1954. 240p.

199

MINORITY STUDIES: AN ANNOTATED BIBLIOGRAPHY

AFRO-AMERICANS

(ARMSTRONG, LOUIS)
Autobiography of the famous trumpet player.

1223　ATTAWAY, WILLIAM. Blood on the Forge, A Novel. Garden City,
New York: Doubleday, Doran and Company, 1941. 279p.
Three Kentucky sharecropping brothers migrate to the
steel mills and meet up with White and Slavic immigrants.

1224　_____. Let Me Breathe Thunder. Garden City, New York:
Doubleday, Doran and Company, Inc., 1939. 267p.
A novel about the Great Depression.

AUSBY, ELLSWORTH. See 1468.

1225　BAKER, HOUSTON, Jr. Black Literature in America. New York:
McGraw-Hill Company, 1971. 443p.
An anthology of Black literature from early folklore
and song through the Black Renaissance and the 1960s.
Brief biographies.

1226　BALDWIN, JAMES. Another Country. New York: The Dial Press,
1963. 366p.
Harlem and Greenwich Village seen as "another country,"
full of interracial strife. Deals also with homosexuality.

1227　_____. Blues for Mister Charlie. New York: Dial Press, 1964.
158p.
A drama based on the 1955 Mississippi murder of Emmitt
Till. The play takes place in Plagueville, U. S. A., the
plague being racism and perverted Christianity.

1228　_____. The Fire Next Time. New York: Dell Publishing, 1962.
120p.
Two essays on Black-White relationships, both in the
form of letters. The first, "My Dungeon Shook," is in
honor of the 100th anniversary of the Emancipation Procla-
mation; the second, "Down at the Cross," is subtitled
"Letter from the Region in my Mind."

1229　_____. Giovanni's Room. New York: Dial Press, 1956. 248p.
Paris and Southern France are the scene of this tri-
angle love story involving homosexuality.

1230　_____. Go Tell it on the Mountain. New York: Alfred A.
Knopf, 1953. 303p.
The narrator is a fourteen year old boy who converts to
a fundamentalist church on his birthday. The story is told
in flashbacks. Emphasizes is the emotional despair of
growing up in a ghetto like Harlem.

1231 (_____.) Going to Meet the Man. New York: Dial Press, 1965.
249.
A collection of short stories which deals with such
themes as violence, homosexuality, and miscegenation.

1232 _____. Nobody Knows My Name; More Notes of a Native Son.
New York: Dell Press, Inc., 1961.
Thirteen essays about Europe, Harlem, and the South,
and a variety of themes related to such geography.

1233 _____. Notes on a Native Son. Boston: Beacon Press, 1955.
175p.
Essays on a variety of topics such as "Everybody's
Protest Novel," "The Harlem Ghetto," and "A Question of
Identity."

1234 BARTON, REBECCA, ed. Witnesses for Freedom: Negro Americans
in Autobiography. New York: Harper & Brothers, 1948.
294p.

1235 BECKWOURTH, JAMES P. The Life and Adventures of James P.
Beckwourth, edited by T. D. Bonner. New York: Arno Press
and The New York Times, 1967. 537p.
Autobiography of a great Western explorer, hunter, and
trapper. Reprint of 1856 edition.

1236 BOLES, ROBERT. Curling. Boston: Houghton Mifflin Co., 1968.
259p.
Chelsea, a Black who is brought up by rich Anglos, has
a series of week-end adventures until he gets into a fatal
fight in New Bedford. Good psychological analysis of a
young Black man.

1237 _____. The People One Knows. Boston: Houghton Mifflin
Company, 1964. 177p.
Novel about a young Black soldier in France who attempts
suicide and is then sent to a recovery hospital.

1238 BONE, ROBERT, The Negro Novel in America, revised edition.
New Haven: Yale University Press, 1965. 289p.
The first, and considered by many the standard, history
of Black fiction. Commentaries, criticism and bibliography.
Reprint of 1958 edition.

BONNER, T. D. See 1235

Minority Studies: An Annotated Bibliography

AFRO-AMERICANS

1239   BONTEMPS, ARNA, ed. American Negro Poetry. New York: Hill
       and Wang, 1963. 197p.
             A collection of poetry spanning seventy years. Includes
       all the well-knowns. Brief biographies.

1240   _____. Black Thunder. Boston: Beacon Press, 1968.
       224p.
             Explores the theme of Black power in terms of a historic
       slave insurrection in Virginia in 1800 led by the slave
       Gabriel. Reprint of 1936 edition.

1241   _____. God Sends Sunday. New York: Harcourt Brace and
       Company, 1931. 199p.
             Of interest mainly because it is Bontemps' first novel.
       It tells the adventures of a Black jockey.

       BONTEMPS, ARNA. See   1328, 1352.
       BOYAR, BURT. See   1282
       BOYAR, JANE. See   1282

1242   BRAWLEY, BENJAMIN, ed. Early Negro American Writers; Selec-
       tions with Biographical and Critical Introductions.
       Chapel Hill, North Carolina: University of North Carolina
       Press, 1935. 305p.

1243   _____. The Negro in Literature and Art. New York: Duffield
       and Company. 1918. 176p.
             Essays by an important Black critic of this period.

1244   _____. Paul Laurence Dunbar, Poet of His People.
       Chapel Hill: University of North Carolina Press, 1936.
       159p.
             Biography of the well-known novelist, short story writer,
       and poet. Bibliography.

1245   BREWER, JAMES MASON, ed. American Negro Folklore. Chicago:
       Quadrangle Books, 1968. 386p.
             A hugh collection of tales, songs, riddles, personal
       experiences, and other folk materials.

1246   BROOKS, GWENDOLYN. Annie Allen. New York: Harper and Row,
       1949. 60p.
             Poetry.

1247   _____. Selected Poems. New York: Harper and Row, 1963.
       127p.
             Selections from earlier volumes such as A Street in
       Bronzeville.(1945) and The Beam Eaters (1959).

1248   BROWN, CECIL. <u>The Life and Loves of Mr. Jiveass Nigger</u>.
New York: Farrar, Strauss and Giroux, 1969. 213p.
A satiric novel about a young Black's adventures in
Europe. Reprint of 1969 edition.

1249   BROWN, CLAUDE. <u>Manchild in the Promised Land</u>. New York:
Macmillan Company, 1965. 415p.
The classic autobiography of a Negro who grew up in the
Harlem ghetto in the 1940s and 1950s. Boy meets family,
boy meets society, boy turns bad with drugs and goes to
jail.

1250   BROWN, FRANK LONDON. <u>Trumbull Park</u>. Chicago: Henry Regnery
Co., 1959. 432p.
A novel about the Martin family who lived on Chicago's
South Side.

1251   BROWN, STERLING A., ARTHUR P. DAVIS, and ULYSSES LEE, eds.
<u>The Negro Caravan</u>. New York: Arno Press and <u>The New
York Times</u>, 1969. 1082p.
A well-rounded anthology of the literature of the Negro
Renaissance. Reprint of 1941 edition.

1252   BROWN, STERLING. <u>Negro Poetry and Drama and the Negro in
American Fiction</u>. New York: Atheneum Press, 1969. 209p.
A new edition of Brown's commentaries, published in
one volume. A must for understanding the mid-century.
Reprint of 1937 edition.

1253   _____. <u>Southern Road</u>. New York: Harcourt, Brace, 1932. 135p.
Poems.

1254   BROWN, WILLIAM WELLS. <u>Clotel; or, the President's Daughter;
A Narrative of Slave Life in the United States</u>. New York:
Collier Books, 1970. 202p.
The earliest known novel by a Black American. Published
a year after Uncle Tom's Cabin in 1853, this book shows
slavery from a melodramatic point of view. It was reissued
from time to time with plot adaptations of historic interest. In the first version, Clotel and Althesa are daughters
of Thomas Jefferson. This was acceptable in England but
not in America, where another edition alters the father
and makes him a U. S. Senator. Clotel fulfills the stereotype of the tragic mulatto.

BROWN, WILLIAM WELLS. <u>See also</u>   1308

AFRO-AMERICANS

1255   BULLINS, ED. Five Plays: Goin'a Buffalo; In the Wine Time;
        A Son, Come Home; The Electronic Nigger; Clara's Old Man.
        Indianapolis: Bobbs-Merrill Company, 1968. 282p.
            Bullins' best five plays.

1256   _____, ed. New Plays from the Black Theatre. New York:
        Bantam Books, 1969. 304p.
            Includes plays by LeRoi Jones, Ed Bullins, Herb Stokes,
        Sonia Sanchez, Ben Caldwell, N. R. Davidson, Jr., Charles
        Fuller, Jr., Salimu, and Kingsley B. Bass, Jr., Angry
        writers, some of these.

        BURROUGHS, MARGARET G. See 1435

1257   BUTCHER, MARGARET. The Negro in American Culture, Based on
        Materials Left by Alain Locke. New York: Alfred A. Knopf,
        1972. 313p.
            A synthesis of Locke's lectures, articles, and notes
        with emphasis on the Black influence in literature and the
        arts. Reprint of 1956 edition.

1258   CARSON, JOSEPHINE. Silent Voices; The Southern Negro Woman
        Today. New York: Delacorte Press, 1969. 273p.
            Interviews with Black women from every cultural level
        who talk about their hopes, their lives, and their total
        reality.

1259   CARVER, GEORGE WASHINGTON. George Washington Carver: An
        American Biography. Garden City, New York: Doubleday and
        Company, 1943. 342p.
            Life story of the famous scientist and teacher at
        Tuskegee. Carver was famous for his work on soil conser-
        vation and crop diversification.

1260   CAYTON, HORACE R. Long Old Road. New York: Trident Press,
        1964. 402p.
            Autobiography of a Black sociologist and newspaperman.
        Reprint of 1963 edition.

1261   CHAPMAN, ABRAHAM. ed. Black Voices: An Anthology of Afro-
        American Literature. New York: New American Library, 1968.
        718p.
            Excerpts and articles showing the developments of Black
        literature. Good prose and poetry selections. Biographies
        of writers and a bibliography. One of the standard works.

1262   _____. New Black Voices: An Anthology of Contemporary Afro-
        American Literature. New York: New American Library, 1972.
        606p.
            A companion to Black Voices, this one follows the same
        format but adds writers of the late sixties and early
        seventies. A good bibliography.

1263   CHESNUTT, CHARLES WADELL. The Conjure Woman. Ann Arbor:
        University of Michigan Press. 1969. 229p.
            Seven famous folk tales about conjuring, magic, and
        superstition. Told in dialect with humor and style.
        Reprint of 1899 edition.

1264   _____. The House Behind the Cedars. New York: Collier, 1969.
        291p.
            This important historical novel in the development of
        black literature. Treats the post-Civil War South and the
        intraracial tensions of a heroine, Rena Walden, who "passes".
        Reprint of 1900 edition.

1265   CHISHOLM, SHIRLEY. Unbought and Unbossed. Boston: Houghton
        Mifflin and Company, 1970. 177p.
            Autobiography of the Congresswoman and 1972 presidential
        aspirant.

1266   CLARKE, JOHN HENRIK, ed. American Negro Short Stories. New
        York: Hill and Wang, 1966. 355p.
            Includes selections by DuBois, Wright, Sterling Brown,
        Jones, and others. Brief biographies of the writers.

1267   _____, comp. Harlem. New York: New American Library, 1970.
        222p.
            A collection of short stories by a wide range of Black
        authors such as Cullen, Hughes, and McKay.

1268   _____, ed. William Styron's Nat Turner: Ten Black Writers
        Respond. Boston: Beacon Press, 1968. 120p.
            The contributors to this series of essays state that
        Styron distorted the character of Nat Turner due to his
        White racial bias.

1269   CLEAVER, ELDRIDGE. Soul on Ice. New York: McGraw Hill,
        1968. 210p.
            The best-selling autobiographical collection of essays
        by the controversial Black leader. Cleaver's most famous
        essay on the stereotyping of the Black man and the White
        woman is included.

AFRO-AMERICANS

CLEMENS, SAMUEL. See 1460

1270 COLTER, CYRUS. The Beach Umbrella. Chicago: The Swallow
Press, 1970. 225p.
Collection of Colter's best short stories.

1271 COOK, MERCER & STEPHEN E. HENDERSON. The Militant Black
Writer in Africa and the United States. Madison:
University of Wisconsin Press, 1969. 136p.
Two essays entitled "African Voices of Protest" and
"Survival Motion: A Study of the Black Writer and the
Black Revolution in America."

CRANE, ELAINE. See 1215

1272 CRONON, EDMUND DAVID. Black Moses: The Story of Marcus
Garvey and the Universal Negro Improvement Association.
Madison: University of Wisconsin Press, 1968. 278p.
Biographical sketch of an important Black leader of
the 1920s and the history of his Universal Negro Improve-
ment Association.

1273 CULLEN, COUNTEE. Caroling Dusk: An Anthology of Verse by
Negro Poets. New York: Harper and Brothers, 1927. 237p.
The Harlem Renaissance poets.

1274 _____. Copper Sun. New York: Harper and Brothers, 1927.
89p.
One of the poet's collections of poetry.

1275 _____. On These I Stand. New York: Harper and Brothers,
1947. 197p.
The "poet laureate" of the Black Renaissance of the
1920s has included selections from all his poetry.

1276 _____. One Way to Heaven. New York: Harper and Brothers,
1932. 280p.
Cullen's only novel is about Harlem life in some of its
unromantic aspects.

1277 DALY, VICTOR. Not Only War, A Story of Two Great Conflicts.
Boston: Christopher Publishing House, 1932. 106p.
Novel about a Black soldier during World War I who falls
in love with a Black woman also loved by a White southerner.

1278   DAVIS, ARTHUR P. and SAUNDERS REDDING, eds. Cavalcade:
       Negro American Writing from 1760 to the Present. Boston:
       Houghton Mifflin Company, 1971. 905p.
           A big, well-edited anthology, with the following head-
       ings: Pioneer Writers, Freedom Fighters, Accommodation
       and Protest, The New Negro Renaissance and Beyond, and
       Integration Versus Black Nationalism. Selective
       bibliography.

       DAVIS, ARTHUR P. See also   1251

1279   DAVIS, BEN J. Communist Councilman from Harlem: Autobio-
       graphical Notes Written in a Federal Penitentiary. New
       York: International Publishers, 1969. 218p.
           Autobiography of a Black lawyer who became a key figure
       in New York politics.

1280   DAVIS, CHARLES T., & DANIEL WALDEN, eds. On Being Black:
       Writings by Afro-Americans from Frederick Douglas to the
       Present. Greenwich, Connecticut: Fawcett Publications,
       1970. 383p.
           Includes fiction, poetry, and rhetoric by 30 noted
       Black writers.

1281   DAVIS, OSSIE. Purlie Victorious. New York: Samuel French,
       1962. 90p.
           A three-act comedy that is fun to read as well as to
       act out.

1282   DAVIS, SAMMY, Jr. with JANE and BURT BOYAR. Yes I Can.
       New York: Farrar, Strauss and Giroux, 1965. 612p.
           Autobiography of Sammy Davis, Jr.

1283   DELANY, MARTIN R. Blake or the Huts of America. Boston:
       Beacon Press, 1970. 321p.
           An incomplete piecing together of what is reputed to be
       the third Black novel every published in America. It
       appeared in installments in The Anglo-African Magazine
       and The Weekly Anglo-African. Takes place throughout the
       South and Southwest. Also an account of Cuban society in
       the 1850s. Reprint of 1859 edition.

1284   DELGADO, MARTÍN MORÚS. Sofia. La Habana, Cuba: Edición de
       la Comisión del Centenario de M. Moruá Delgado, 1957.
           Delgado, Black Cuban leader has written an Abolitionist
       novel which involves colonial Cuba in the problems of
       slavery, miscegenation, and in this book, incest. Reprint
       of 1891 edition.

AFRO-AMERICANS

1285   DEMAREST, DAVID P. and LOIS S. LAMDIN. The Ghetto Reader.
       New York: Random House, Inc., 1970. 361p.
       Compendium of selections which includes such areas as:
       The Street, Parents and Children, Workers and Professionals,
       and Prophets and Politicians.

1286   DEMBY, WILLIAM. Beetlecreek, A Novel. New York: Rinehart
       and Company, 1950. 223p.
       A novel set in the South centering around a young Black
       boy, his family, and a White recluse named Bill Trapp.

1287   _____. The Catacombs. New York: Harper and Row, 1965. 244p.
       A contemporary novel about the Roman catacombs and film
       making as the hero searches for personal meaning to his
       life. Bob Bone in his introduction calls this a novel of
       reconciliation and return.

1288   DODSON, OWEN. Powerful Long Ladder. New York: Farrar, Straus
       and Young, 1946. 103p.
       A collection of lyrics, verse drama, sonnets, and songs.

1289   DORSON, RICHARD M., ed. American Negro Folktales. Greenwich,
       Connecticut: Fawcett Publications, 1967. 378p.
       A noted American folklorist's collection. Bibliography
       and index of motifs. Reprints of 1956 edition.

       DOUGLASS, FREDERICK. See   1433

1290   DROTNING, PHILLIP T. Black Heroes in our Nation's History:
       A Tribute to those Who Helped Shape America. New York:
       Cowles Book Co., 1969. 242p.
       Black profiles in courage; war heroes, trail blazers,
       and those who revolted against slavery. Bibliography.

1291   DUBOIS, WILLIAM E. B. An ABC of Color: Selections from over
       a Half Century of the Writings of W. E. B. DuBois. Berlin:
       Seven Seas Publishers, 1964. 211p.
       A compendium of the best of DuBois' extensive writings.

1292   _____. The Autobiography of W. E. B. DuBois; A Soliloquy on
       Viewing my Life from the Last Decade of its First Century.
       New York: International Publishers, 1968. 448p.
       Includes a bibliography of all of DuBois' writings in
       print.

1293   _____. The Black Flame Trilogy. New York: Mainstream Pub-
       lishers, 1957, 1959, 1961. 316p., 367p., 349p.
       A series about a Black hero: The Ordeal of Mansart,
       Mansart Builds a School, and Worlds of Color.

1294   ____. Darkwater; Voices from Within the Veil. New York: AMS Press, 1969. 276p.
DuBois' most famous novel. Reprint of 1920 edition.

1295   ____. The Souls of Black Folk. New York: New American Library, 1969. 280p.
Autobiographical series of essays considered one of the great Negro classics. Bibliography. Many editions. Reprint of 1903 edition.

DUBOIS, wILLIAM E. B. See also 1444
DUFTY, WILLIAM. See 1347

1296   DUNBAR, PAUL LAURENCE. The Complete Poems of Paul Laurence Dunbar. New York: Dodd, Mead and Co., 1968. 289p.
Includes introduction to "Lyrics of Lowly Life" by William Dean Howells. Reprint of 1913 edition.

1297   ____. Lyrics of Lowly Life. New York: Arno Press and The New York Times, 1969. 208p.
Reprint of Dunbar's best known volume of poetry, originally published in 1899.

1298   ____. The Sport of the Gods. New York: Arno Press and The New York Times, 1969. 255p.
The story of some Southern blacks who migrate to Harlem. Reprint of 1902 edition.

1299   ____. The Strength of Gideon and Other Stories. New York: Arno Press, 1969. 362p.
A collection of some of Dunbar's best short stories. Reprint of 1900 edition.

1300   ELDER, LONNE III. Ceremonies in Dark Old Men. New York: Farrar, Straus and Giroux, 1969. 179p.
Adele who is thirty and unmarried, is sick of supporting three men, which includes her father, and Theo and Bobby, her two brothers. Enter Blue into this drama. He offers money and a chance to live out fantasies, and the play goes into action until Bobby is killed in a robbery and the old man goes back to playing checkers. Reprint of 1965 edtion.

1301   ELLISON, RALPH. Invisible Man. New York: New American Library, 1964. 503p.
A Major American novel which **must** be read by anyone studying the American culture in general or Black culture

AFRO-AMERICANS

(ELLISON, RALPH)
in particular. The hero goes through a variety of phases which take him from the rural South to the urban North, in order to make himself into a visible being. National Book Award Winner for 1952. Reprint of 1947 edition.

1302 _____. Shadow and Act. New York: New American Library, 1966. 302p.
Excellent essays by an important American writer. Some are on American fiction, some on jazz, some on Harlem and elsewhere. Contains Ellison's theories of writing: "The Art of Fiction: An Interview." Reprint of 1953 edition.

1303 EMANUEL, JAMES A. and THEODORE GROSS. Dark Symphony: Negro Literature in America. New York: The Free Press, 1968. 604p.
Selections from thirty-four Black writers from Frederick Douglass to LeRoi Jones. Critical essays also and bibliography of the authors. A good, well-rounded anthology.

EQUIANO, OLUADAH. See 1462.

1304 EVANS, MARI. I am a Black Woman. New York: William Morrow and Company, 1970. 95p.
Poems on the Black experience, poignantly illustrated.

1305 FAIR, RONALD. Hog Butcher. New York, Harcourt Brace. 1966. 182p.
Chicago shown as a "butcher" of Blacks who live in the ghettos there. Two ten year olds start the story when they see two policemen accidently shoot their adult friend.

1306 _____. Many Thousand Gone: An American Fable. New York: Harcourt, Brace and World, 1965. 114p.
An old Black woman and her militant young friends bring down the Establishment who are holding their people in that Southern area in slavery and ignorance. Told with style and humor.

1307 FAIRBAIRN, ANN. Five Smooth Stones. New York: Crown Publishers, 1966. 256p.
A novel about David Champlin who lived in New Orleans during the Depression and falls in love with a White woman.

1308 FARRISON, WILLIAM EDWARD. William Wells Brown: Author and Reformer. Chicago: University of Chicago Press, 1969. 482p.

(FARRISON, WILLIAM EDWARD)
Tells about Brown's career, from his birth as a slave in 1814 to his devotion to anti-slavery causes and his writings. From the Negro American Biography and Autobiography.

1309   FAUSET, JESSIE REDMOND. The Chinaberry Tree. A Novel of American Life. New York: Frederick A. Stokes Company, 1931. 341p.

1310   _____. There is Confusion. New York: Boni and Liveright, 1924. 297p.
The first of four novels about the Black middle class in America.

1311   FERGUSON, BLANCHE E. Countee Cullen and the Negro Renaissance. New York: Dodd, Mead and Company, 1966. 213p.
Biography of the famous poet. Bibliography.

1312   FISHER, RUDOLPH. The Conjure Man Dies; A Mystery Tale of Dark Harlem. New York: Covici-Friede, 1932. 316p.
The first Black detective novel. The scene takes place in Harlem.

1313   FORD, NICK AARON, ed. Black Insights: Significant Literature by Black Americans 1760 to the Present. Waltham, Massachusetts: Ginn and Co., 1971. 373p.
This anthology is divided into four sections with an introduction for each one. The first, The Pathfinders, includes authors ranging from Wheatley to Chestnutt. The Torchbearers, The Alienated, and The Revolutionists continue from Johnson to Lee, covering a wide range of writers. Comments and questions plus a selective bibliography.

1314   GAINES, ERNEST J. The Autobiography of Miss Jane Pittman. New York: Dial Press, 1971. 245p.
The fictional autobiography of a 110-year-old Black woman, and of her remembrances of the Black struggle for freedom.

1315   _____. Bloodline. New York: Dial Press, 1968. 249p.
Five stories about life in Louisiana. The title story "Bloodline" concerns itself with a mulatto who returns to the old plantation. Another is about three men in a jail-cell. Reprint of the 1963 edition.

AFRO-AMERICANS

1316   GAINES, ERNEST J. Of Love and Dust. New York: Bantam Books,
          1968. 277p.
             A Louisiana plantation in the summer heat is the setting
          for this novel of love and murder. The story is told by
          a narrator, Jim Kelly, who sees the hero, Marcus, as a
          doomed but spirited man. Reprint of 1967 edition.

       GARVEY, MARCUS. See   1272

1317   GAYLE, ADDISON, ed. The Black Aesthetic. Garden City, New
          York: Doubleday and Company, 1971. 432p.
             A collection of writings on the elements and principles
          of Black culture and the role of the Black artist in
          America.

1318   GAYLE, ADDISON, Black Expression: Essays by and about Black
          Americans in the Creative Arts. New York: Weybright
          and Talley, 1969. 394p.
             Includes essays on Black folk culture, poetry, drama
          and fiction.

1319   GIOVANNI, NIKKI. Black Feeling Black Talk Black Judgement.
          New York: William Morrow and Company, 1970. 98p.
             "i am 25 years old/Black female poet" goes one of this
          collection of poems, lyric and protesting by one of the
          best of this generation of writers.

1320   _____. Gemini: An Extended Autobiographical Statement on my
          First Twenty-Five Years of being a Black Poet. Indianapo-
          lis: Bobbs-Merrill, 1971. 149p.
             Self definition by a remarkably talented poet who calls
          a honky a honky and herself--well, read it!

1321   GREENLEE, SAM. The Spook Who Sat by the Door. New York:
          Richard W. Baron, 1969. 248p.
             A gripping novel about Freeman, who trains with the CIA
          in order to learn the techniques to pass on to his organ-
          ization so that they can make war against the Whites in
          America.

1322   GREGORY, DICK, with ROBERT LIPSYTE. Nigger. New York:
          Pocket Books, 1964. 224p.
             Autobiography of a famous night club comedian, athlete,
          and Civil Rights marcher who tell it straight and bitter.

1323   GRIGGS, SUTTON ELBERT. Imperium in Imperio. New York: Arno
          Press, 1969. 265p.

(GRIGGS, SUTTON ELBERT)
Griggs first novel is about Black nationalism; unusual
and ahead of its times. The plan to capture Texas on the
part of the national organization, Imperium in Imperio,
does not succeed. Reprint of 1899 edition.

1324 _____. Overshadowed. Freeport, New York: Books For Libraries
Press, 1971. 217p.
Miscegenation and lynching in Virginia. The novel also
includes as characters some Black trade unionists. Reprint
of 1901 edition.

1325 _____. Pointing the Way. Nashville, Tennessee: The Orion
Publishing Company, 1908. 233p.
The life of Blacks in the South. Includes racism, mis-
cegenation, and conflict.

1326 GROSS, SEYMOUR L. and JOHN EDWARD HARDY. eds. Images of the
Negro in American Literature. Chicago: University of
Chicago Press, 1966. 321p.
The image of the Negro from Colonial times to the pre-
sent as shown in literature. Includes discussions of
Stowe, Faulkner, Baldwin, and Ellison, among others.
Bibliography.

GROSS, THEODORE. See 1303
HALEY, ALEX. See 1399

1327 HAMMON, BRITON. A Narrative of the Uncommon Sufferings, and
Surprizing Deliverance of Briton Hammon, a Negro Man....
First prose writing by a Black in America.

1328 HANDY, WILLIAM C. Father of the Blues: An Autobiography
of W. C. Handy. London: Sidewick and Jackson, 1957.
317p.
This autobiography, edited by Arna Bontemps tells of the
life of the great jazz musician. Includes a bibliography
of Handy's music.

1329 HANSBERRY, LORRAINE. A Raisin in the Sun; A Drama in three
Acts. New York: Random House, 1959. 142p.
One of the most famous plays in Black literature. Also
a motion picture script and a TV serial. Ghetto family
life.

1330 _____. The Sign in Sidney Brustein's Window; A Drama in
Three Acts. New York: Random House, 1965. 143p.
Another well-known drama about ghetto life.

AFRO-AMERICANS

1331   HANSBERRY, LORRAINE. <u>To Be Young, Gifted and Black</u>. Engle-
        wood Cliffs, New Jersey: Prentice-Hall, 1969.
        Autobiography of the playwright and author.

        HARDY, JOHN EDWARD. <u>See</u> 1326.
        HARRIS, CHARLES A. <u>See</u> 1470.

1332   HAYDEN, ROBERT E. <u>Selected Poems</u>. New York: October House,
        1966. 79p.
            A poet who likes to write about Black historical figures,
        such as Nat Turner, as well as about the whole American
        scene.

1333   HENDERSON, GEORGE WYLIE. <u>Jule</u>. New York: Creative Age
        Press, 1946. 234p.
            A Black sharecropper goes north to Harlem.

1334   HENDERSON, STEPHEN E. <u>Understanding the New Black Poetry:
        Black Speech and Black Music as Poetic References</u>. New
        York: William Morrow and Co., 1973. 394p.
            An anthology of poetry and blues lyrics with extensive
        historical and explanatory notes.

        HENDERSON, STEPHEN E. <u>See</u> 1271.

1335   HENSON, JOSIAH. <u>Father Henson's Story of his own Life,</u>
        originally published as <u>Truth Stranger than Fiction:
        Father Henson's Story of his own Life</u>. New York: Corinth
        Books, 1962. 212p.
            Story of the man supposed to be the original of Harriet
        Beecher Stowe's Uncle Tom. Reprint of 1858 edition.

1336   HENSON, MATTHEW A. <u>A Black Explorer at the North Pole</u>.
        New York: Arno Press and <u>The New York Times</u>, 1969. 190p.
            Black explorer who discovered the North Pole with
        Admiral Peary. Reprint of 1912 edition.

1337   HEYWARD, DUBOSE. <u>Porgy</u>. New York: George H. Doran Co.,
        1925. 196p.
            Collection of folk material drawn upon to create Porgy,
        the Begger. Adapted by George Gershwin for his opera,
        <u>Porgy and Bess</u>.

1338   HILL, HERBERT, ed. <u>Anger and Beyond: The Negro Writer in
        the United States</u>. New York: Harper and Row, 1968. 227p.
            Selected essays by Black and White critics, such as
        Arna Bontemps and Robert Bone, dealing with Black writing
        from poetry and blues to fiction.

1339   _____, ed. <u>Soon, One Morning; New Writings by American Negroes</u>, New York: Alfred A. Knopf, 1968. 617p.
A broad anthology of essays, fiction, and poetry. Introduction and biographical notes by the editor.

1340   HIMES, CHESTER. <u>Cast the First Stone</u>. New York: Coward-McCann, 1952. 346p.
The psychological study of a prisoner.

1341   HIMES, CHESTER B. <u>Cotton Comes to Harlem</u>. New York: G. P. Putnam's Sons, 1965. 223p.
Negro detectives, Grave Diggers Jones and Coffin Ed Johnson act as heroes in a swindle scheme.

1342   _____. <u>If He Hollers Let Him Go</u>. Garden City, New York: Doubleday and Company, 1945. 249p.
Racism at the shipyards during World War II.

1343   _____. <u>Pinktoes</u>. New York: G. P. Putnam's Sons, 1965. 256p.
Mamie Mason is the "heroine" of this interracial satire that takes place in Harlem.

1344   _____. <u>The Quality of Hurt: The Autobiography of Chester Himes</u>. Garden City, New York: Doubleday and Company, 1972. 351p.
Are the first forty-five years the hardest? The novelist answers.

1345   _____. <u>Run Man Run</u>. New York: Dell Publishing Company, 1969. 192p.
The novel starts out with Fat Sam and Luke shot by a drunken detective, a White blue-eyed detective who forgot where he had parked his car and claimed it had been stolen. The violence continues as Jimmy, fingered for the murders, and Sgt. Brock race to see who can catch Walker first. Reprint of 1966 edition.

1346   _____. <u>The Third Generation</u>. Cleveland: World Book Company, 1954. 350p.
The history of a family from slvery times to the present day; a portrayal of the rise and fall of the Taylors.

1347   HOLIDAY, BILLIE, with WILLIAM DUFTY. <u>Lady Sings The Blues</u>. Garden City, New York: Doubleday and Company, 1956. 250p.
Autobiography of one of the greatest blues singers of all time. Includes a discography of her works.

MINORITY STUDIES: AN ANNOTATED BIBLIOGRAPHY

AFRO-AMERICANS

1348 HUGGINS, NATHAN IRVIN, Harlem Renaissance. New York:
Oxford University Press, 1971. 343p.
A history of the Black cultural growth centered in
Harlem in the early 1900s, emphasizing both its interplay
with White culture and its own internal impetus. Includes
photographs of, and works by, artists from the period.

1349 HUGHES, JOHN MILTON CHARLES. The Negro Novelists: A Discussion of the Writings of American Negro Novelists,
1940-1950. Freeport, New York: Books for Libraries
Press, 1967. 288p.
A survey of the Black prose writers of the '40s decade.
A bibliography of the novels as well as pertinent
non-fiction. Reprint of 1953 edition.

1350 HUGHES, LANGSTON. The Best of Simple. New York: Hill and
Wang, 1968. 245p.
The author's own selection of his famous Simple stories.
Simple is a comic and satiric distortion of the White
stereotype of the stupid Negro. Reprint of 1961 edition.

1351 _____. The Big Sea: An Autobiography. New York: Hill and
Wang, 1963. 335p.
"Life is a big sea full of many fish. I let down my
nets and pull." Thus starts the autobiography of this
famous Black poet. Reprint of 1940 edition.

1352 HUGHES, LANGSTON and ARNA BONTEMPS, eds. The Book of Negro
Folklore. New York: Dodd, Mead and Company, 1958. 624p.
Animal tales, games, spirituals, blues, modern gospel
songs, jazz, early slave memories, and folk tales.

1353 HUGHES, LANGTON, ed. The Book of Negro Humor. New York:
Dodd, Mead and Company, 1966. 265p.
A compendium of rural, folk, and urban humor in dialect
and out of it.

1354 _____. I Wonder as I Wander; An Autobiographical Journey.
New York: Hill and Wang, 1964. 405p.
Hughes' own account of his life as a writer.

1355 _____. Not Without Laughter. New York: Collier Books,
1969. 304p.
The coming to manhood of Sandy in a small Kansas town
in the 1930s. Hughes' first novel written when he was an
accomplished poet and part of the Harlem Renaissance
movement. Reprint of 1930 edition.

216

1356   _____, ed. The Panther and the Lash: Poems of our Times.
New York: Alfred A. Knopf, 1967. 101p.
    Collection of Hughes' best Civil Rights poems; including
"Backlash Blues," "Black Panther," "Bombings in Dixie,"
and "Militant."

1357   _____. Selected Poems. New York: Alfred A. Knopf, 1967.
297p.
    The best of Hughes' poetry as selected by the author.

1358   _____. Something in Common, and Other Stories. New York:
Hill and Wang, 1963. 236p.
    Short stories.

1359   _____. The Ways of White Folks. New York: Alfred A. Knopf,
1963. 248p.
    Fourteen stories about prejudice. Reprint of 1934
edition.

1360 HUNTER, KRISTIN. God Bless the Child. New York: Bantam
Books, 1970. 279p.
    What makes Rosie Fleming run in Harlem? Life in Harlem
for a young woman. Reprint of 1964 edition.

1361   _____. The Landlord. New York: Avon Publishing, 1969. 272p.
    Black tenants and a White landlord work it out in this
novel about racial interrelationships.

1362 HURSTON, ZORA NEALE. Dust Tracks on a Road; An Autobiography.
Philadelphia: J. B. Lippincott Company, 1971. 286p.
    Black woman writer tells it like it is. Reprint of
1942 edition.

1363   _____. Jonah's Gourd Vine. Philadelphia: J. B. Lippincott
Company, 1971. 316p.
    A novel about the deep South that uses folklore and
dialect, humor and humanity. Reprint of 1934 edition.

1364   _____. Mules and Men. New York: Negroes University Press,
1969. 342p.
    Black folktales, some involving Hoodoo. Reprint of
1935 edition.

1365   _____. Seraph on the Suwanee: A Novel. New York: Charles
Scribner's Sons, 1948. 311p.
    Novel about river plantation life set on the Suwanee
River in Florida.

Minority Studies: An Annotated Bibliography

AFRO-AMERICANS

1366   HURSTON, ZORA NEALE. Their Eyes were Watching God.
        New York: Fawcett Publications, 1969. 159p.
        A classic novel from the Harlem Renaissance era, this
        one is about Janie, a forty-year-old Black woman who goes
        off for adventure with Tea Cake. Reprint of 1937 edition.

        HUTCHINSON, HELENE D. See 1450

1367   ISAACS, EDITH. The Negro in the American Theatre. College
        Park, Maryland: McGrath Publishing Company, 1968. 143p.
        Traces the early history and development of the role
        played by Blacks in the American theatre. Not up-to-date.
        Reprint of 1947 edition.

1368   JACKSON, BRUCE, comp. Wake up Dead Man: Afro-American Work-
        Songs from Texas Prisons. Cambridge, Massachusetts:
        Harvard University Press, 1972. 326p.
        An interesting anthology which contains music and lyrics.
        Bibliography.

1369   JAMES, CHARLES L., ed. From the Roots: Short Stories by
        Black Americans. New York: Dodd, Mead and Company, 1970.
        370p.
        An excellent collection of short stories, 1890-1969,
        arranged chronologically. Each section contains additional
        reading suggestions and historical information, plus, of
        course, an introduction.

1370   JOANS, TED. Black Pow Wow: Jazz Poems. New York: Hill and
        Wang, 1969. 130p.
        Jazz poems collected from Greenwich Village to the
        Sahara Desert.

1371   JOHNSON, EDWARD AUGUSTUS. Light Ahead for the Negro. New
        York: The Grafton Press, 1904. 132p.
        The first Utopian novel by a Black writer. Discusses
        racism in the year 2007.

1372   JOHNSON, JACK. Jack Johnson is a Dandy: An Autobiography.
        New York: Chelsea House, 1969. 262p.
        Life of the great prize fighter, originally completed
        as a manuscript in 1926.

1373   JOHNSON, JAMES WELDON. The Auto-Biography of an Ex-Colored
        Man. New York: Avon Books, 1965. 211p.
        A famous and popular fiction which originally appeared
        anonymously. Not the autobiography it purports to be.
        Reprint of 1912 edition.

Minority Studies: An Annotated Bibliography

Literature

1374 _____. Black Manhattan. New York: Atheneum Publishing Co., 1972. 284p.
A critical history of the Harlem Renaissance by one who participated actively in it. Reprint of 1930 edition.

1375 _____. God's Trombones; Seven Negro Sermons in Verse. New York: Viking Press, 1969. 56p.
Uses old-time folk-style preaching to create a genre of verse that helped make Johnson's reputation during the Harlem Renaissance. A reissue. Also on records. Reprint of 1927 edition.

1376 JONES, LEROI and LARRY NEAL, eds. Black Fire: An Anthology of Afro-American Writing. New York: William Morrow and Company, 1969. 670p.
Anthology of writings by seventy Black writers. Includes essays, short stories, plays, etc. Emphasis is on those writers involved in Black Power and the Black Consciousness movements. Brief biographies of the writers.

1377 JONES, LEROI. Black Magic Poetry. 1961-1967. Indianapolis: Bobbs-Merrill Company, 1969. 225p.
A compendium of three of Jones' books of poetry: Sabotage, Target Study, and Black Art (1961-1966).

1378 _____, The Dead Lecturer. New York: Grove Press, 1964. 79p.
Poems.

1379 _____. The Dutchman and the Slave. London: Faber and Faber Publishing, 1965. 88p.
Two of Jones' more famous and controversial plays, concerned with White/Black conflicts.

1380 _____. Home: Social Essays. New York: William Morrow and Company, 1966. 252p.
Discusses the assassination of Malcolm X, the Cuban Revolution, and the Birmingham and Harlem riots.

1381 _____. The System of Dante's Hell. New York: Grove Press, 1966. 154p.
Using Dante's structure, Jones writes about Black childhood and youth in a small Southern town and Newark, New Jersey. Rather a personalized tone-poem, or theme with variations on myself. Reprint of 1965 edition.

1382 _____. Tales. New York: Grove Press, 1967. 132p.
The Black hero in White America as depicted in sixteen short stories. Reprint of 1967 edition.

219

AFRO-AMERICANS

1383   KEARNS, FRANCIS E., ed. The Black Experience; An Anthology
        of American Literature for the 1970's. New York: The
        Viking Press, 1970. 650p.
            Includes examples of the different images of Blacks in
        the works of both Black and White authors, Black spirituals,
        poetry, and literary criticism, including an interview with
        Ralph Ellison.

1384   KECKLEY, ELIZABETH. Behind the Scenes; Thirty Years a Slave
        and Four Years in the White House. New York: Arno Press,
        1968. 371p.
            Most unusual autobiography from the nineteenth century.
        Reprint of 1868 edition.

1385   KELLEY, WILLIAM MELVIN. Dancers on the Shore. Garden City,
        New York: Doubleday and Company, 1964. 201p.
            Sixteen short stories about Blacks.

1386   _____. dem. New York: Collier Books, 1964. 141p.
            dem is White folks seen by Black folks. This satire
        tells how they live. When Ms. Mildred Pierce bears twins,
        one White and one Black, her husband goes to Harlem to
        track down her Black lover.

1387   _____. A Different Drummer. Garden City, New York: Double-
        day and Company, 1969. 200p.
            Answers the problem question of what would happen if
        all Blacks left the South and migrated North.

1388   KILLENS, JOHN OLIVER. And Then we Heard the Thunder. New
        York: Alfred A. Knopf, 1963. 485p.
            An angry novel about Blacks in World War II. Reprint
        of 1962 edition.

1389   _____. Youngblood. New York: Dial Press, 1954. 566p.
            Novel of Georgia Negroes around the early twentieth
        century.

1390   KING, CORETTA SCOTT. My Life with Martin Luther King, Jr.
        New York: Holt, Rinehart and Winston, Inc., 1969. 372p.
            Wife's account of the great leader. Their participation
        in the civil rights movement.

1391   KING, WOODIE, ed. Black Short Story Anthology. New York:
        Columbia University Press, 1972. 381p.
            Protest, pride, and power are some of the themes of Black
        consciousness introduced in this anthology. Includes
        writings by Ellison, Gaines, Baldwin, Kelly, etc., 28 stories
        in all. A good selection.

1392   KITT, EARTHA. Thursday's Child. New York: Duell, Sloan and
Pearce, 1956. 250p.
Eartha's story from South to North, and from the
Katherine Dunham dancers to becoming a singer in Paris and
on to Broadway.

1393   KNIGHT, ETHERIDGE and other inmates of Indiana State Prison.
Black Voices from Prison. New York: Pathfinder Press,
1970. 189p.
Essays, stories and poems, autobiographical sketches,
and a one-act play.

LAMDIN, LOIS. See 1285.

1394   LARSEN, NELLA. Quicksand. New York: Alfred A. Knopf, 1928.
301p.
A good example of the tragic mulatto theme.

1395   LEE, DON L. Black Pride. Detroit: Broadside Press, 1968.
34p.
One of the best known of Lee's volumes of poetry which
includes: Think Black (1967), Don't Cry, Scream (1969) and
We Walk the Way of the New World (1970).

1396   _____. Don't Cry! Scream! Detroit: Broadside Press, 1969.
64p.
Poems.

LEE, ULYSSES G. See 1251.

1397   LESTER, JULIUS. Black Folktales. New York: Grove Press,
1969. 159p.
A retelling of several traditional Black folktales,
including both African and American origins. Afterword
gives a brief annotated bibliography on sources.

1398   LEVY, EUGENE. James Weldon Johnson: Black Leader, Black
Voice. Chicago: University of Chicago Press, 1973. 380p.
Biography spanning Johnson's long life that takes in
the post-Reconstruction period and the Harlem Renaissance.

LIPSYTE, ROBERT. See 1322.

1399   LITTLE, MALCOLM, with the assistance of ALEX HALEY. The
Autobiography of Malcolm X. New York: Grove Press, 1965.
455p.
One of the most extraordinary autobiographies ever
written in America. Must reading for any student of Black

AFRO-AMERICANS

(LITTLE, MALCOLM...)
literature, history, or philosophy--American history and
literature, for that matter. Traces the early childhood,
Harlem, prison years, the Black Muslim ministry, and the
final violent death of a great hero. See also 1116, 1117,
1118, 1435.

1400 LITTLEJOHN, DAVID. Black on White: A Critical Survey of
Writing by American Negroes. New York: The Viking Press,
1969. 180p.
An analysis of twentieth-century Black literature in
terms of its being protest literature and in terms of its
educational value for White readers.

1401 LOCKE, ALAIN, ed. The New Negro; An Interpretation.
New York: Arno Press, 1968. 446p.
A milestone book in Black literature, now reprinted as
part of the series, Studies in American Negro Life. There
is a new preface by Robert Hayden. Several articles on
the Black Renaissance in art and literature of the 1920s.
Selections include fiction, poetry, drama, folklore, and a
series of critical articles on tradition and the current
scene by various other writers. An important selective
bibliography of Negro Americana and Africana plus bibliographies of the Negro in literature, drama, music, folklore, and race problems. Reprint of 1925 edition.

LOCKE, ALAIN LEROY. See 1257.

1402 LOMAX, ALAN and RAOUL ABDUL, eds. 3000 Years of Black Poetry.
Greenwich, Connecticut: Fawcett Publications, 1970. 261p.
This is world poetry that focuses only on the blackness
of the poet; it ranges from primitive song to Egypt and on
to the United States chronologically and through all the
continents.

1403 MACEBUK, STANLEY (Nigeria). James Baldwin: A Critical Study.
New York: The Third Press, 1973. 116p.
First in a projected series of critical studies of
Third World literature. Baldwin is discussed in terms
of the effect of his life on his work. Selected
bibliography.

1404 McKAY, CLAUDE. Banana Bottom. New York: Harper and Brothers,
1933. 317p.
Novel set in Jamaica and England about a young woman
sent to England for her education. Picaresque novel.

1405 _____. Gingertown. Freeport, New York: Harper, 1972. 274p.
Twelve short stories, six about Harlem. Reprint of
1932 edition.

1406   _____. Home to Harlem. New York: Pocket Books, 1965. 180p.
        McKay's first novel gives a gaudy picture of Harlem.
        Reprint of 1928 edition.

1407   _____. A Long Way from Home. New York: Arno Press, 1969.
        354p.
        Autobiography of a poet famous during the Harlem Renais-
        sance. Reprint of 1937 edition.

1408   _____. Selected Poems. New York: Harcourt, Brace and World,
        1969. 110p.
        Reprint of 1953 edition.

1409   MAJOR, CLARENCE, comp. The New Black Poetry. New York:
        International Publishers, 1969. 156p.
        Poems by 76 young Black writers.

1410   MARSHALL, PAULE. Brown Girl; Brownstones. New York: Avon
        Publishing, 1970. 255p.
        Story of Blacks and Whites when a Negro family moves
        into a brownstone district in Brooklyn. Reprint of 1959
        edition.

1411   _____. Soul Clap Hands and Sing. Chatham, New Jersey:
        Chatham Booksellers, 1971. 177p.
        Four novellas which describe the human confrontation
        with age and death. Reprint of 1961 edition.

1412   MAYFIELD, JULIAN, ed. Ten Times Black; Stories from the Black
        Experience. New York: Bantam Books, 1972. 149p.
        Ten short stories by current writers in the Black cul-
        tural revolution: Evan K. Walkers, Nikki Giovanni, Maya
        Angelou, Sam Greenlee, and others.

1413   MAYS, BENJAMIN ELIJAH. The Negro's God, as Reflected in his
        Literature. New York: Russell and Russell, 1968. 269p.
        A survey of Black literature from 1760 to 1937 and the
        concepts of God discussed from a sociological, psychologi-
        cal, and theological viewpoint. Included are spirituals,
        sermons, prayers, and works by Langston Hughes, and James
        Weldon Johnson. Bibliography. Reprint of 1938 edition.

1414   MERIWETHER, LOUISE. Daddy was a Number Runner. Englewood
        Cliffs, New Jersey: Prentice-Hall, 1970. 208p.
        A novel set in Harlem about the experiences of a Black
        girl growing up.

1415   METCALF, GEORGE R. Black Profiles, 2nd edition. New York:
        McGraw-Hill, 1971. 229p.

AFRO-AMERICANS

(METCALF, GEORGE R.)
Biographies of Black leaders from the nineteenth and twentieth centuries. Reprint of 1970 edition.

1416   MILLER, DAVID, ed. Dices or Black Bones; Black Voices of the Seventies. New York: Houghton Mifflin, 1970.
An anthology of experimental verse and short stories.

1417   MITCHELL, LOFTEN. Black Drama: The Story of the American Negro in the Theatre. New York: Hawthorne Books, 1967. 248p.

1417a   MITCHELL, MARGARET. Gone with the Wind. New York: Macmillan, 1936. 1037p.
An American classic. But read the pages on the novel carefully for Ms. Mitchell's White Southern attitudes towards Blacks. She was depicting the era of the Civil War, but she does not have to wrestle with her attitudes towards the lowly slaves.

1418   MOODY, ANNE. Coming of Age in Mississippi. New York: Dial Press, 1968. 384p.
Autobiography of a young Black woman, which reads like the autobiography of the South, starting on a plantation and ending up with SNCC and NAACP and the Civil Rights Movement.

NEAL, LARRY. See 1376.

1419   NICHOLAS, A. X. The Poetry of Soul. New York: Bantam Books, 1969. 103p.
The lyrics from soul music as sung by Aretha Franklin, Otis Redding, Nina Simone and others. The Black world of passion, pain, protest, and celebration. Discography at the end.

1420   NORFOLK PRISON Brothers. Who Took the Weight? Black Voices from Norfolk Prison. Boston: Little, Brown and Company, 1972. 265p.
Poems, essays, stories and plays by ten Black inmates of Massachusetts Correctional Institute-Norfolk, prepared under the supervision of Elma Lewis.

1421   PANGER, DANIEL. Ol'Prophet Nat. Winston-Salem: J. E. Blair, 1967. 159p.
A novel about Nat Turner.

1422   PARKS, GORDON. A Choice of Weapons. New York: Berkley Publishing Corporation, 1969. 222p.
Autobiographical sketch of the author's fight against poverty and racism. Reprint of 1966 edition.

1423   _____. The Learning Tree. Greenwich, Connecticut: Fawcett
Crest Publications, 1968. 240p.
    Novel of interrelationships in Cherokee Flats, Kansas in
the 1920s. Reprint of 1963 edition.

1424   PATTERSON, LINDSAY. Black Theatre: A 20th Century Collection
of the Work of its Best Playwrights. New York: Dodd, Mead,
1971. 493p.
    Includes all the well-known dramatic writers, such as
Bontemps, Bullins, Hughes, Hansberry, Jones.

1425   _____. An Introduction to Black Literature in America; from
1746 to the Present. New York: Publishers Company, 1968. 302p.
    Chronological survey of Negro American literature. One
of the series in "International Library of Negro Life and
History." Bibliography.

1426   PAYNE, DANIEL ALEXANDER. Recollections of Seventy Years.
New York: Arno Press, 1968. 335p.
    Life story of the Bishop of the African Methodist Church
and his travels in both slave and free territory in the United
States. Includes his visit to the White House. Reprint of
1888 edition.

1427   PETERKIN, JULIA. Scarlet Sister Mary. New York: Pocket
Books, Inc., 1940. 218p.
    Sister Mary was a prostitute who supported her family
with her earnings. The scene is Louisiana. The writing won
the book a Pulitzer Prize. Reprint of 1928 edition.

1428   PETRY, ANN LANE. Country Place. Chatham, New Jersey: Chatham
Booksellers, 1971. 266p.
    A novel about a Black soldier when he returns to New Eng-
land after World War II. Reprint of 1947 edition.

1429   _____. Harriet Tubman: Conductor of the Underground Railroad.
New York: Crowell, 1955. 247p.
    A fictional account of this great Black woman who fought
for emancipation and freedom.

1430   _____. The Narrows. Boston: Houghton, Mifflin Company, 1953.
428p.
    Link Williams, a Black man, falls in love with a White
woman.

1431   _____. The Street. New York: Pyramid Books, 1961. 270p.
    Mr. Petry's most famous novel. It is the story of a young
Black woman in Harlem who struggles to retain her own integ-
rity against formidable odds. Winner of the Houghton-Mifflin
Literary Fellowship Award. Reprint of 1946 edition.

Minority Studies: An Annotated Bibliography

1432   POWELL, ADAM CLAYTON. Against the Tide. New York: R. R. Smith. 1938. 327p.
        Autobiography of the dapper politician from Harlem.

1433   QUARLES, BENJAMIN, ed. Narrative of the Life of Frederick Douglass an American Slave Written by Himself. Cambridge, Massachusetts: Harvard University Press, 1960. 163p.
        One of several reprints of the famous autobiography of Douglass, who was a runaway slave and then an advisor to President Lincoln.

1434   RANDALL, DUDLEY, ed.. Black Poetry: A Supplement to Anthologies which Exclude Black Poets. Detroit: Broadside Press, 1969. 48p.
        Collection of the best poems of 24 noted Black poets, from Claude McKay to Nikki Giovanni.

1435   RANDALL, DUDLEY & MARGARET G. BURROUGHS. For Malcolm: Poems on the Life and Death of Malcolm X. Detroit: Broadside Press, 1969. 127p.
        Collection of poetry inspired by the life and death of Malcolm X. Includes a preface and eulogy by Ossie Davis, biographical information about the poets, and an extensive bibliography of writings about Malcolm. Bibliography.

1436   REDDING, JAY SAUNDERS. The Lonesome Road. New York: Doubleday and Company, 1958. 355p.
        Biographies of 12 Blacks. Bibliography.

1437   _____. To Make a Poet Black. College Park, Maryland: McGrath Publishing Company, 1968. 142p.
        Criticism of Black literature. Bibliography. Reprint of 1939 edition.

REDDING, JAY SAUNDERS. See also 1278.

1438   REED, ISHMAEL. The Free-Lance Pallbearers. New York: Bantam Books, 1969. 116p.
        A surreal novel about Sam's Island and Black Bay wherein live Doopeyduk and Fannie Mae his bride, wherein rules, until he disappears down the John, the self-styled Harry Sam. "It's a cruel, cruel world and you gots to be swift." Reprint of 1967 novel.

1439   _____. Mumbo Jumbo. New York: Bantam Books, 1972. 256p.
        This is another of Reed's satiric recocco novels, also a history of America in terms of Jes Grew and Papa LaBas and his Mumbo Jumbo Kathedral. Of course, the history of America is the history of Moses, too. A most interesting "Partial Bibliography."

1440   _____. 19 Necromancers from Now. Garden City, New York:
        Doubleday and Company, 1970. 369p.
             One of the first Third World anthologies of American
        poetry, prose, drama, and essay. Includes Victor Hernandez
        Cruz (Puerto Rican) and Frank Chin (Chinese American) as
        well as some of the most experimental Black writers of
        today.

1441   _____. Yellow Back Radio Broke-Down. Garden City, New York:
        Doubleday and Company, 1969. 177p.
             The Loop Garoo Kid is Black and uninhibited about the
        American Dream in this satiric second novel by Reed.
        Indians and Whites abound in this parody of the Western.

1442   ROBINSON, WILHELMENA S. Historical Negro Biographies. New
        York: The Publishing Company. 1969. 291p.
             Black lives through the twentieth century. Bibliography.

1443   ROLLINS, BRYANT. Danger Song. Garden City, New York: Double-
        day and Company, 1967. 280p.
             What happens when two families in Boston, one White and
        one Black, have two children wanting to play Romeo and
        Juliet.

1444   RUDWICK, ELLIOTT M. W. E. B. DuBois, Propagandist of the Negro
        Protest. New York: Atheneum Publishers, 1968. 390p.
             One of several biographies of this famous man.
        Bibliography.

1445   SACKLER, HOWARD. The Great White Hope. New York: Bantam
        Books, 1969. 239p.
             Play about Jack Jefferson, and his rise and fall as the
        first Black heavyweight champion of the world. Reprint of
        1968 edition.

        SAMUELS, CHARLES. See 1467

1446   SANCHEZ, SONIA, ed. We be Word Sorcerers: 25 Stories by
        Black Americans. New York: Bantam Books, 1973. 284p.
             Alice Walker, Dudley Randall, Ed Bullins, Gwendolyn
        Brooks, and Imamu Amiri Baraka are among those writers
        chosen for this book in praise of Blackness.

1447   SCHECHNER, RICHARD, ed. Black Theatre. New York: New York
        University Press, 1968.
             Reviews of plays by Leroi Jones, Ed Bullins, and other.
        The reviews include criticism of the Black Revolutionary
        Theatre and the Theatre of Black Experience.

AFRO-AMERICANS

1448   SCHULBERG, BUDD. From the Ashes; Voices of Watts. New York:
        New American Library, 1967. 277p.
                A rather uneven collection of poems, short stories,
        essays, and plays by participants in the Watts Writers'
        Workshop.

1449   SCHUYLER, GEORGE SAMUEL. Black No More. Being an Account of
        the Strange and Wonderful Workings of Science in the Land
        of the Free, A. D. 1933-1940. New York: Collier Books,
        1971. 222p.
                A satire about Blacks and Whites describing what happens
        when a scientific method is developed to turn anybody
        "White." The patterns of Southern society are almost com-
        pletely destroyed.

1450   SIMMONS, GLORIA M. and HELENE D. HUTCHINSON. Black Culture:
        Reading and Writing Black. New York: Holt, Rinehart and
        Winston, 1972. 328p.
                An excellent collection of Black poetry, essays, humor,
        psychology and photography.

1451   STERLING, PHILIP, ed. Laughing on the Outside. New York:
        Grosset and Dunlap, 1965. 254p.
                An anthology of Black tales and humor, from slavery
        times to the present.

1452   STOWE, HARRIET BEECHER. A Key to Uncle Tom's Cabin: Present-
        ing the Facts and Documents Upon Which the Story is
        Founded. Boston: J. P. Prewett, 1853. 504p.
                Written in response to demands about the truth of Uncle
        Tom's Cabin.

1453   _____. Uncle Tom's Cabin. Garden City, New York: Doubleday
        and Company, 1965. 451p.
                One of the many editions of the famous 1852 story that
        created the stereotype of "Uncle Tom." This is one of the
        most famous American novels of all time and had a profound
        international influence when it appeared. It is credited
        with keeping Great Britain neutral during the Civil War.
        Reprint of 1852 edition.

1454   STYRON, WILLIAM. The Confessions of Nat Turner. New York:
        New American Library, 1966. 404p.
                Controversial Pulitzer Prize interpretation of Turner's
        insurrection and life, told in the first person.

1455   TOLSON, MELVIN B. <u>Harlem Gallery: Book I, The Curator</u>.
        London: Collier-Macmillan, Ltd., 1969. 155p.
            The first volume of a planned long work, this uses
        symbolic Harlem characters and sets them in the 1920s and
        then mixes poetry with wit. Reprint of 1965 edition.

1456   TOOMER, JEAN. <u>Cane</u>. New York: Harper and Row, 1969.
        239p.
            Reissue of the very famous 1923 book which is a collec-
        tion of stories, sketches and poems about rural Georgia
        and urban Washington in terms of the Black experience.

1457   TURNER, DARWIN T., comp. <u>Afro-American Writers</u>. New York:
        Appleton-Century-Crofts, 1970. 117p.
            Background materials, literary history and criticism,
        other bibliographies. Selected criticism in the appendix.

1458   _____., ed. <u>Black American Literature: Essays, Vols. 1-3</u>.
        Columbus, Ohio: Merrill Publishing Company, 1969. 142p.+
            Includes essays by W. E. B. DuBois, Ralph Ellison,
        Langston Hughes, James Weldon Johnson, James Baldwin, LeRoi
        Jones, and Eldridge Cleaver. Bibliography.

1459   _____. <u>Black Drama in America: An Anthology</u>. Greenwich,
        Connecticut: Fawcett Publications, 1971. 630p.
            Contains plays by 9 Black playwrights and an extensive
        bibliography.

1460   TWAIN, MARK (pseudo). <u>The Tragedy of Pudd'nhead Wilson, and
        the Comedy of those Extraordinary Twins</u>. Hartford,
        Connecticut: American Publishing Co., 1894. 133p.
            A problem novel which deals with what happens when a
        Black baby and a White baby are switched at birth.

1461   VAN DYKE, HENRY. <u>Ladies of the Rachmoninoff Eyes</u>. New York:
        Farrar, Straus and Giroux, 1965. 214p.
            This is a novel about two widows. The poor one is
        Black, and the rich one is White, but they become close to
        each other anyway.

1462   VASSA, GUSTAVUS (Olaudah Equiano). <u>The Interesting Narrative
        of the Life of Olaudah Equiano, or Gustavus Vassa, the
        African</u>. New York: Negro Universities Press, 1969. 294p.
            One of the first Black autobiographies. This tells
        the life story of the famous Haitian revolutionary.
        Reprint of 1789 edition.

WALDEN, DANIEL. <u>See</u>   1280

AFRO-AMERICANS

1463   WALKER, JOSEPH A. The River Niger. New York: Hill and Wang,
        1973. 177p.
            A drama about Harlem and the members of the Johnny
        Williams family as they confront their human rights winning
        dignity and death.

1464   WALKER, MARGARET. For My People. New York: Arno Press,
        1968. 58p.
            Collection of poetry. Won the Yale Younger Poets Award
        when it first appeared in 1942.

1465   ____. Jubilee. New York: Bantam Books, 1967. 416p.
            A Houghton Mifflin Literary Fellowship Award novel about
        Vyry, daughter of a slave and a master, who grows up on
        his plantation, finds freedom after the Civil War and be-
        comes a farmer's wife. A Gone With The Wind from the Black's
        viewpoint.

WANGARA, HARUN KOFI. See 1217.

1466   WASHINGTON, BOOKER TALIAFERRO. Up from Slavery: The Future
        of the American Negro. New York: Doubleday, Page and
        Company, 1901.
            A famous autobiographical classic of how Booker T. rose
        to fame. Washington was always pragmatic about helping the
        Blacks to help themselves. His works include: Character
        Building (1902), Working With The Hands (1904), and The
        Negro In Business (1907).

1467   WATERS, ETHEL, with CHARLES SAMUELS. His Eye is on the
        Sparrow. New York: Pyramid Books, 1967. 278p.
            From the Black ghetto to stardom.

1468   WATKINS, MEL, with drawings by ELLSWORTH AUSBY. Black Review
        No. 2. New York: William Morrow and Company, 1972. 158p.
            Criticism, poetry, short stories and art are intermixed
        Includes works by Larry Neal, Judy Simmons, and Julius
        Lester.

1469   WEBB, FRANK J. The Garies and Their Friends. New York:
        AMS Press, 1971. 392p.
            Prejudice, violence, and miscegenation in Philadelphia
        before the Civil War. Reprint of 1857 edition.

1470   WILLIAMS, JOHN A. and Charles F. Harris, ed. Amistad 2.
        New York: Vintage Books, 1971. 338p.
            Sequel to Amistad 1, this is another collection of fic-

(WILLIAMS, JOHN A. and CHARLES F. HARRIS, ed.)
tion, criticism, and photography. Includes Richard Wright's
"Blueprint for Negro Literature," Haywood Burns' "Racism and
American Law," and Paula Giddings' "From a Black Perspective:
The Poetry of Don L. Lee."

1471   WILLIAMS, JOHN A. Beyond the Angry Black. New York: Cooper
Square, 1966. 198p.
An anthology of stories, articles, and poems expressing
strong responses to the violence and prejudice of White/
Black America.

1472   _____. The Man Who Cried I Am. New York: New American
Library, 1968. 334p.
Cancer, spying, Black and White, men and women having
tense love relationships are some of the elements mixed up
together in this novel of death and violence in Europe,
shown here as the meeting place for Africa and America.
Max Reddick is the Black hero. Reprint of 1967 edition.

1473   _____. Sissie. Garden City, New York: Anchor Books, 1969.
228p.
Sissie lies dying. The novel is about her life and that
of her two children, told in flashbacks to give you the
struggle for affirmation of a non-stereotyped Black matri-
arch. Reprint of 1963 edition.

1474   WRIGHT, RICHARD. Black Boy. New York: Harper and Row, 1964.
285p.
Wright's memoir of his life in the South. Reprint of
1945 edition.

1475   _____. Eight Men. New York: Pyramid Books, 1969. 204p.
Eight excellent short stories about Black men and their
struggles to survive in an alien world, whether it be the
rural South or the urban North.

1476   _____. Native Son. London: Cape, 1969. 392p.
One of the most famous novels in America, this is
Wright's version of crime and punishment. Bigger Thomas
murders a White girl and suffers the consequences. Wright
has written other novels and short stories including Uncle
Tom's Children, Four Novellas (1938) and a series of essays
about racial conflict: White Man, Listen! (1957). Reprint
of 1940 edition.

1477   YERBY, FRANK. Floodtide. New York: Dell Publishing, 1967.
318p.
A historical romance about Natchez, Old Natchez.

V. ASIAN AMERICANS

A. General Asian Americans

1. Bibliographical Works and Directories

1478 BARNHART, EDWARD N. Japanese American Evacuation and Re-
        settlement. Berkeley: University of California, General
        Library, 1958. 178p.
            A bibliography of the holdings at U. C. Berkeley librar-
        ies. Includes books, diaries, photographs, reports, etc.

1479 COWAN, ROBERT ERNEST and ROBERT GRANNISS COWAN. A Bibliog-
        raphy Of California, 1510-1930, 4 vols. San Francisco:
        John Henry Nash, 1933-1964.
            Vol. 1 lists information about Chinese immigration. Vol.
        4 is by R. G. Cowan, Los Angeles: Torrez Press, 1964.

1480 COWAN, ROBERT ERNEST and BOURTWELL DUNLOP. Bibliography Of
        The Chinese Question In The United States. San Francisco:
        A. M. Robertson, 1909. 68p.
            Nineteenth century attitudes towards the Chinese.

      CUMMINGS, ORPHA. See 1483.
      DUNLOP, BOUTWELL. See 1480.

1481 FUJIMOTO, ISAO, MICHIYO YAMAGUCHI SWIFT, and ROSALIE ZUCKER,
        eds. Asians In America: A Selected Annotated Bibliography.
        Davis, California: Working Publication No. 5, Asian Ameri-
        can Research Project, Asian American Studies Division, De-
        partment of Applied Behavioural Sciences, University of
        California at Davis, June, 1971. 295p.
            Bibliography divided into sections: Chinese, Japanese,
        Pilipino, East Indian, Korean, and Thai. Author-subject
        Index with a list of magazines and newspapers. Especially
        useful chronological readings.

1482 HANSEN, GLADYS C., Selector, and WILLIAM F. HEINTZ, Annotator.
        The Chinese In California: A Brief Bibliographic History.
        Portland, Oregon: Richard Abel and Company, Inc., 1970. 140p.

ASIAN AMERICANS

(HANSEN, GLADYS C., Selector, and WILLIAM F. HEINTZ, Annotator)
All of the materials in the San Francisco Public Library's extensive "California Collection" are listed and annotated. An author-subject index.

HEINTZ, WILLIAM F. See 1482.

1483   HENEFRUND, HELEN E. and ORPHA CUMMINGS, comp. Bibliography of the Japanese in American Agriculture. Washington, D. C.: U. S. Government Printing Office, 1943. (U. S. Department of Agriculture, Bibliographical Bulletin No. 3)   61p.
A list of books, articles, and documents concerning Japanese Americans in American agriculture since the turn of the century. Many of the materials are annotated.

1484   ICHIOKA, YUJI. A Buried Past: An Annotated Bibliography of the Japanese American Research Project Collection. Berkeley: University of California Press, 1974.
A definitive book.

JUNG, E. See 1485.

1485   KITANO, HARRY H. L., with E. JUNG, C. TANAKA, and B. WONG. Asian Americans: An Annotated Bibliography. Los Angeles: Asian American Studies Center, UCLA, 1971. 76p.
300 annotations of general works concerning Chinese, Japanese, and Filipinos in the United States. Subject sections include: psychology, sociology, immigration, race relationships, economics, and Japanese relocation.

1486   LIU, KWANG-CHING. Americans and Chinese: A Historical Essay And Bibliography. Cambridge, Massachusetts: Harvard University Press, 1963. 210p.
An essay on the history of American and Chinese contacts and a 150-page bibliography.

1487   LO, SAMUEL E. Asian Who? In America. Roseland, New Jersey: East-West Who? Inc., 1971. 329p.
A Who's Who of Asian Americans giving brief biographies with heavy emphasis on the sciences.

1488   LUM, WILLIAM WONG. Asians In America: A Bibliography Of Master's Theses and Doctoral Dissertations. Davis, California: Asian American Research Project, Department of Applied Behavioural Science, University of California at Davis, 1970. 78p.
750 dissertations and master's theses about the Asian American experience in this country.

Minority Studies: An Annotated Bibliography

1489   ____, ed. <u>Asians In America: A Bibliography</u>. Davis, Cali-
     fornia: Asian American Studies Division, Department of
     Applied Behavioural Science, University of California at
     Davis, 1969. 48p.
       This bibliography, with two supplemental bibliographies,
     unannotated, lists all the Asian American materials in the
     U. C. Davis library.

1490 McCUTCHEON, JAMES M. <u>China and America: A Bibliography of
     Interactions, Foreign and Domestic</u>. Honolulu: University
     Press of Hawaii, 1972. (East-West Bibliographic Series)
     75p.
       Sections of this bibliography, which contains some anno-
     tated materials, include: China and American Foreign
     Policy and Public Opinion, The Chinese Community in the
     United States, China and American Literature, and China and
     the Arts. Author index.

     McCLELLAN, ROBERT. See 1551.

1491 MATSUDA, MITSUGU. <u>The Japanese In Hawaii, 1868-1967: A Bibli-
     ography Of The First Hundred Years</u>. Honolulu: Social
     Science Research Institute, University of Hawaii, 1968.
     (Hawaii Series, No. 1) 222p.
       There are a few items concerning the Chinese in this an-
     notated bibliography which is the first in a series being
     compiled by the University. Entries are in both English and
     Japanese although all titles are translated into English.

1492 NG, PEARL. <u>Writings On The Chinese In California</u>. San Fran-
     cisco: R. and E. Research Associates, 1972. 118p.
       A bibliography that includes a fifty-page history of
     Chinese immigration and its effect on California's develop-
     ment.

1493 NIMURA, TAKU F. <u>Japanese In The United States: A Bibliog-
     raphy</u>. Sacramento: Sacramento State College Library,
     1969. 26p.
       A short, annotated bibliography of items in the library.
     Excludes periodical and pamphlet materials.

1494 RATHMORE, CAROL S. <u>A Guide To Collections In American Museums</u>.
     New York: Asia Society, 1964.
       Lists and describes museum collections of Oriental art.

1495 RUBANO, JUDITH. <u>Culture and Behaviour in Hawaii</u>. Honolulu:
     Social Science Research Institute, University of Hawaii,
     1971. (Hawaii Series, No. 3) 147p.
       An annotated bibliographic survey that covers the multi-
     ethnic character of Hawaii.

Minority Studies: An Annotated Bibliography

ASIAN AMERICANS

SWIFT, MICHIYO YAMAGUCHI. See 1481.
TANAKA, C. See 1485.

1496   U. S. DEPARTMENT of Commerce. Social and Economic Statistics
Administration. Bureau of the Census. Japanese, Chinese,
and Filipinos in the United States 1970 Census of Population, July, 1973. Washington, D. C.: U. S. Government
Printing Office, 1973.

1497   U. S. LIBRARY OF Congress. General Reference and Bibliographical Division. Japanese In The United States: A Selected
List of References. Compiled by Helen D. Jones. Washington, D. C.: U. S. Government Printing Office, 1946. 36p.
    Especially good for materials between 1940 and 1946.
Items are arranged according to format: books and pamphlets, bibliographies, periodical articles, periodicals, and
unpublished materials. Some items are annotated.

WONG, B. See 1485.
WONG, BUCK. See 1533.
WONC, EDDIE. See 1553.

1498   WYNAR, LUBOMYR R. Encyclopedic Directory of Ethnic Newspapers
and Periodicals in the United States. Littleton, Colorado:
Libraries Unlimited, 1972. 260p.
    The first guide to the current ethnic press in the United
States, although it leaves out American Indians, Blacks, and
Chicanos. Included and annotated are such presses as the
Arabic, German, Jewish, etc., and for the purposes of this
bibliography, the Chinese and Japanese.

1499   YOUNG, NANCY FOON. The Chinese In Hawaii: An Annotated Bibliography. Honolulu: Social Science Research Institute,
University of Hawaii. (Hawaii Series, No. 4)
    A general, annotated bibliography using materials drawn
from the archives of the University of Hawaii as well as
their libraries, the Hawaiian State Library, the Hawaiian
Chinese Historical Center, the Hawaiian Historical Society,
and the Hawaiian Mission Children's Society Library.

ZUCKER, ROSALIE. See 1481.

2. Periodicals

1500   AION. 675 Thirty-Fifth Avenue, San Francisco, California
94121
    Features articles, poetry, and short stories.

Minority Studies: An Annotated Bibliography

1501 AMERASIA Journal. UCLA Asian American Studies Center, Campbell
Hall, Los Angeles, California 90024
The first national critical journal devoted to the Asian
American experience. Deals with the cultural problems
facing Third World groups.

1502 ASIAN Women's Journal. c/o Asian Women, 3405 Dwinelle Hall,
UC, Berkeley, Berkeley, California 94720
Devoted to the problems and expressions of Asian Women.
Well-written and always stimulating to read.

1503 BRIDGE. Basement Workshop, Inc., 54 Elizabeth Street, New
York, New York 10013
Lively and interesting magazine devoted to articles
about Asian American life, cartoons, book reviews, poetry,
and prose.

1504 BULLETIN of Concerned Asian Scholars. Bay Area Institute, 604
Mission Street, Room 1001, San Francisco, California 94105
Noteworthy is the entire issue devoted to Asian Americans: Volume 4, Number 3 (Fall 1972). This contains
poetry, several articles of sociological import, an autobiographical narrative by Frank Chin and an introduction to
Asian American writing which appears in Aiieeee!

1505 EAST/West. 758 Commercial Street, San Francisco, California
94108
A weekly community newspaper that appears half in English
and half in Chinese. Editorials, news, and feature articles.

1506 GETTING Together. 30 Market Street, New York City, New York
10002

1507 GIDRA. P. O. Box 18046, Los Angeles, California 90018
A monthly newspaper that started at UCLA's Asian American
Center and then went out on its own. Contains editorials,
articles, poetry and prose, as well as good photography.
Sometimes puts out special issues, such as a Women's issue.
Now out of production.

1508 HAWAII Pono Journal. 1176 University Avenue, West Hall 208,
University of Hawaii, Honolulu, Hawaii 96822
A quarterly devoted to Third World issues as they appear
on the Hawaiian scene. Occasionally puts out special issues.

1509 KOREA Focus. American Korean Friendship and Information Center,
160 Fifth Avenue, Suite 809, New York, New York 10010
Contains articles of general interest plus news of the
community.

ASIAN AMERICANS

1510   NEW China. U. S. - China Peoples Friendship Association, Room
       1228, 41 Union Square West, New York, New York 10003
           A national publication to promote people-to-people
       friendship between the U. S. and P. R. C.

1511   RAFU Shimpo. 242 South San Pedro Street, Los Angeles, Cali-
       fornia 90012
           The best known Japanese newspaper in the Southern
       California area.

1512   RODAN. 1808A Sutter Street, San Francisco, California 94115
           A monthly newspaper that focuses on Northern California
       Asian American communities.

1513   WEI Min. P. O. Box 6075, San Francisco, California 94101
           Wei Min bao means "newspaper for the people." Bilingual
       and monthly.

                    3.   General Culture and Community Life and
                              United States Relationships

1514   AUERBACH, F. L. Immigration Laws of the United States.
       Indianapolis: Bobbs-Merrill, 1961. 584p.
           A well researched compendium of immigration laws.
       Reprint of 1955 edition.

1515   BERTON, PETER and WEN-CHIN WU. Contemporary China: A Research
       Guide. Stanford: Hoover Institution on War, Revolution
       and Peace, Stanford University, 1967. 695p.
           A comprehensive annotated bibliography covering printed
       material from Eastern and Western sources pertaining to
       China studies, from pamphlets, texts, and documents to
       other bibliographies, theses, and indexes.

       CHAN, JEFFREY PAUL. See 1516.

1516   CHIN, FRANK, JEFFREY PAUL CHAN, LAWSON FUSAU INADA, and SHAWN
       HSU WONG, eds. AIEEEEE! Washington, D. C.: Howard Uni-
       versity Press, 1974.
           This anthology of Asian American writing is edited by
       Asian American writers themselves. Limited to Chinese and
       Japanese Americans. The Preface and Introduction contain
       a history and analysis of Asian American writing that makes
       the book an important one.

1517   CHRISTY, ARTHUR E. The Asian Legacy and American Life.
       New York: Greenwood Press, 1968. 276p.

(CHRISTY, ARTHUR E.)
Articles by experts on such varied topics as the Oriental influence on Western music by Curt Sachs; poetry, by W. Y. Tindall; Religion, by Pearl S. Buck. Studies also on art and agriculture. Reprint of 1945 edition.

1518 CHUNG, HENRY. The Oriental Policy of the United States. New York: Arno Press and The New York Times, 1970.
This is a history of American imperialism from 1898 to 1914. Bibliography. Reprint of 1919 edition.

1519 FARMER, GEORGE L. Education: The Dilemma Of The Oriental American. Los Angeles: School of Education, University of Southern California, 1969. 164p.
This study is divided into three parts: Japanese, Chinese, and Filipino. The achievements of each cultural group through education in the American pluralistic society is demonstrated. Charts and tables of statistics.

1520 FRIEDMAN, EDWARD and MARK SELDEN, eds. America's Asia: Dissenting Essays On Asian-American Relations. New York: Vintage Books, 1971. 458p.
This is the fourth in a series of anti-texts or revisionist political histories. It examines American distortions about Asia, specifically China, Japan, Vietnam, and Laos after World War II, and American attitudes towards revolution.

1521 HSU, KAI YU and HELEN PALUBINSKAS. Asian American Authors. Boston: Houghton-Mifflin and Company, 1972. 184p.
Selections of prose and poetry and a brief historical chronology for each group as well as a brief biography of each author. Contains works by Chinese, Japanese, and Filipino Americans.

INADA, LAWSON FUSAU. See 1516.

1522 IRIYE, AKIRA. Across The Pacific: An Inner History of American-East Asian Relations. New York: Harcourt, Brace and World, Inc., 1967. 361p.
Deals with East Asians in America, Asian responses to America and U. S. relations with China and Japan, contrasting these two countries in their dealings with America. Puts U. S. diplomacy and activities in the Pacific in context with the world-wide imperialism of the nineteenth century.

KITANO, HARRY H. L. See 1532.

MINORITY STUDIES: AN ANNOTATED BIBLIOGRAPHY

ASIAN AMERICANS

1523 KONVITZ, MILTON R. The Alien And The Asiatic In American Law.
Ithaca, New York: Cornell University Press, 1946. 298p.
An important book on immigration laws, citizenship,
exclusion, and other legal situations involving Chinese,
Japanese, Pilipinos, and Korean immigrants and American
residents.

1524 LIGHT, IVAN. Ethnic Enterprise in America, Business and Welfare Among Chinese, Japanese and Blacks. Berkeley: University of California Press, 1972. 200p.
A sociologist examines the differing business successes
of various Third World cultural groups. Amerasia Journal
declares this book an example of stereotyping overkill but
praises it for its research and intelligent synthesis of
economic factors.

1525 LYMAN, STANFORD M. The Asian In the West. Reno, Nevada:
Desert Research Institute, 1970. 168p.
A well-annotated sociological study of various aspects
of Chinese and Japanese life in the United States and
Canada. Includes a discussion of immigrant Chinese family
life from 1850 to 1960, and the social demography of
Chinese and Japanese in the United States. Identifies
economic competition as the main cause of anti-Chinese
prejudice.

1526 McWILLIAMS, CAREY. Factories In The Field: The Story of
Migratory Farm Labor in California. Santa Barbara:
Peregrine Publications, 1971. 335p.
This famous study of agricultural workers, now in a
paperback reprint, traces the history of the migratory farm
laborers in California from mid-nineteenth century to 1935.
An entire chapter is devoted to the Chinese. Japanese and
Pilipinos are also discussed. Reprint of 1939 edition.

1527 MAR, DAVID and JOYCE SAKAI, eds. Asians In America: Selected
Student Papers. Davis, California: Asian American Research
Project, University of California at Davis, Working Publication No. 3, 1970. 96p.
An anthology of sociological criticism and commentary
that ranges from a section of autobiography called "The
Personal Perspective" to articles on the use and mis-use
of information. Some of this material has been printed and
reprinted elsewhere.

1528 MAY, ERNEST R. and JAMES C. THOMSON, JR., eds. American-East
Asian Relations: A Survey. Cambridge, Massachusetts:
Harvard University Press, 1972. 425p.

MATSUDA, MITSUGU. See 1491.

(MAY, ERNEST R. and JAMES C. THOMSON, JR., eds.)
A review of the literature on American relationships
with East Asia. The series includes articles on immigration problems in the United States. Bibliographic references.

1529   MELENDY, H. BRETT. The Oriental Americans. New York:
Twayne Publishers, 1972. 235p.
The Eastward movement of the Chinese and Japanese to-
wards America and their cultural adjustment to immigration.
Extensive notes and bibliography as well as statistical
appendices on immigration.

ODO, FRANKLIN. See 1533.
PALUBINSKAS, HELEN. See 1521.
SAKAI, JOYCE. See 1527.
SELDON, MARK. See 1520.

1530   SOJOURNER II. Berkeley: Berkeley High School, Asian American
Studies, June, 1973.
An excellent reader put together by Korean, Chinese,
Japanese, and Pilipino students about their experiences.
Short stories, articles and poetry. One of a yearly series.

1531   SUE, STANLEY and NATHANIEL N. WAGNER, eds. Asian Americans:
Psychological Perspectives. Ben Lomond, California:
Science and Behaviour Books, 1973. 298p.
Anthology of articles about Chinese, Japanese, and Pilipino Americans. Divided into five sections: an introduction on racism, assimilation and sex roles, personality,
mental health, and contemporary issues. Bibliographies at
the end of each article.

1532   _____, and HARRY H. L. KITANO, eds. Asian Americans: A
Success Story? Ann Arbor, Michigan: The Journal of Social
Issues 29:2, 1973. 218p.
The entire issue of this publication of the Society for
the Psychological Study of Social Issues is devoted to
articles on the so-called "model" minorities. Adjustment
problems and minority acceptance in the United States are
discussed. Included also are articles on stereotypes and
mental illness.

1533   TACHIKI, AMY, EDDIE WONG and FRANKLIN ODO, with BUCK WONG.
Roots: An Asian American Reader. Los Angeles: Asian
American Studies Center, UCLA, 1971. 345p.
A variety of articles, interviews, book reviews, ex-
cerpts, and poetry give a cross section of current Asian

ASIAN AMERICANS

(TACHIKI, AMY...)
American attitudes and interests. A list of Movement
journals is given at the end.

WAGNER, NATHANIEL. See 1531.

1534   WAND, DAVID HSIN-FU. Asian-American Heritage. An Anthology
of Prose and Poetry. New York: Washington Square Press,
1974.
Writings by Asians and Overseas Asians (American-born)
as well as Pilipino and Korean writings are included in
this collection.

WONG, BUCK. See 1533.
WONG, SHAWN, HSU. See 1516.
WONG, EDDIE. See 1533.
WU, WEN-CHIN. See 1515.

1535   YELLOW Pearl. New York: Basment Workshop, 1972.
A community book in a box, large sheets of yellow paper
graphically illustrative of the Asian American experience
in poetry, prose, editorials, cartoons, and songs.

1536   YOUNG Asians for Action. The Asian American Poetry Book.
Seattle: Young Asians for Action, 1971.

B. Chinese Americans
1. History, Politics, Immigration, Racism,
U. S./China Relationships

1537   BANCROFT, HUBERT HOWE. Essays and Miscellany. New York:
McGraw-Hill Book Company, 1967.
Long chapter on Chinese culture in America which includes
art and architecture, clothing, theater, living conditions,
and employment as well as religion and philosophy. Reprint
of Works, Volume XXXVIII.

1538   _____. The Works of Hubert Howe Bancroft. 39 vols. San Francisco: A. L. Bancroft, 1883-1890.
See Vols. VII, and XVIII through XXIV for chapters about
the Chinese on the West Coast. Bancroft is a nineteenth
century Anglo historian and writes from a "superior race"
viewpoint, but he is meticulous in his research and his
details.

1539   BARTH, GUNTHER. Bitter Strength: A History of the Chinese in
the United States, 1850-1870. Cambridge, Massachusetts:

(BARTH, GUNTHER)
Harvard University Press, 1964. 305p.
Barth's thesis is that California represented the ideal state in the hierarchy of the American dream sequence of Manifest Destiny. The presence of Chinese labor working under near slave conditions tarnished this image causing hatred. Currently under strong criticism by Chinese American critics for offering a sophisticated apology for the anti-Chinese movement in this country. Excellent research and notes.

1540   CALIFORNIA Legislature. Chinese Immigration. The Social, Moral and Political Effect of Chinese Immigration. Testimony Taken Before A Committee of the Senate of the State of California Appointed April 3, 1876. Sacramento: Reported by Frank Shay and published under an order of the Senate by F. P. Thompson, 1876.
As a document of discrimination, this report is a liberal education. The hearings covered many topics including housing, employment and wages, cleanliness, prostitution and gambling, and includes the personal opinion of witnesses about the morality of Chinese immigrants.

1541   CHINN, THOMAS W., ed. A History of the Chinese in California: A Syllabus. San Francisco: Chinese Historical Society of America, 1969. 81p.
The 1850s to the 1960s are covered in this brief history. The usual topics: immigration, occupations, the development of Chinese communities and culture, and anti-Chinese repression. A basic and valuable handbook. Bibliography at the end of each chapter.

1542   CHIU, PING. Chinese Labor In California, 1850-1880; An Economic Study. Madison: University of Wisconsin Press, 1963. 299p.
A survey of California's economy in the nineteenth century and the role played in it by Chinese labor. Discusses such industries as mining, agriculture, textile and shoe, cigar, and clothing manufacturing.

CHOY, PHILIP O. See 1548.

1543   CHU, DANIEL and SAMUEL CHU. Passage to the Golden Gate: A History of the Chinese in America to 1910. Garden City, New York: Doubleday, 1967. 117p.
For young adults. Emphasizes the contributions of the Chinese to American commercial development. Little or no emphasis on political problems or anything of a controversial nature.

243

CHINESE AMERICANS

CHU, SAMUEL. See 1543.

1544 COOLIDGE, MARY ROBERTS. Chinese Immigration. New York: Arno
      Press and The New York Times, 1969. 516p.
         A study of the nineteenth-century immigration of the
      Chinese, their restricted lives, and the exclusion laws
      that resulted from their arrival. Bibliography. Reprint
      of 1909 edition.

1545 FAIRBANK, JOHN KING. The United States and China, 3rd edition,
      completely revised and enlarged. Cambridge, Massachusetts:
      Harvard University Press, 1971. 507p.
         The standard, definitive text on China and Chinese-
      American relations. The political and cultural history of
      China is discussed chronologically. There are chapters on
      Chinese society, Confucianism, and the Chinese language as
      well as analysis of political patterns including the dynas-
      ties and the People's Republic. Bibliography consists of
      an extensive list of readings, briefly annotated.

1546 KOEN, ROSS Y. The China Lobby In American Politics, edited by
      Richard C. Kagan. New York: Harper and Row, 1974. 279p.
         Reprint of a book first published here in 1960 and then
      suppressed by the efforts of the China Lobby, then repre-
      senting the government of Chiang Kai-shek. The book dis-
      cusses the workings of the Lobby on American and Chinese-
      American opinion and its powerful effect on United States
      governmental policies. A very important book.

1547 KUNG, SHIEN-WOO. Chinese In American Life; Some Aspects of
      Their History, Status, Problems, and Contributions.
      Seattle: University of Washington Press, 1962. 352p.
         Why are Chinese Americans and other Americans different
      from one another? This is the central concept of this his-
      tory of the Chinese immigrants and the special Chinese
      American culture which developed. A basic book. Extensive
      bibliography.

1548 LAI, H. MARK and PHILIP O. CHOY. Outline History of the
      Chinese In America. San Francisco: Chinese-American
      Studies Planning Group, San Francisco Chinatown, 1973. 163p.
         A very helpful outline of the historical role of the
      Chinese in America. Contents include: a history of Kwan-
      tung, China, early contacts between China and the West,
      Chinese Labor, Fisheries and Farming, the Anti-Chinese
      movement and exclusion, Chinese Associations, and popula-
      tion distribution of the Chinese in the U. S. mainland.
      Bibliographies with each section.

1549   LEE, ROSE HUM. The Chinese In the United States of America.
        Hong Kong: Hong Kong University Press, 1960. 465p.
            This book is a detailed and scholarly overall survey of
        the acculturation, assimilation, and integration of the
        Chinese after they came to the United States. Criticized
        by young Chinese American scholars who feel that she places
        on the Chinese immigrants themselves some of the blame for
        the prejudice they encountered in America. Excellent docu-
        mentation and bibliography.

1550   LOEWEN, JAMES W. The Mississippi Chinese, Between Black and
        White. Cambridge, Massachusetts: Harvard University
        Press, 1971. 237p.
            A detailed case study of the Chinese living in the Delta
        region of Mississippi. Gives their social position, his-
        tory, and shows them to be an example of ethnic integration
        as well as non-integration in the South. Loewen's study
        explains discrimination, in part, as the result of Chinese
        behavior patterns, such as clannishness.

1551   McCLELLAN, ROBERT. The Heathen Chinese, A Study of American
        Attitudes Toward China, 1890-1905. Columbus: Ohio State
        University Press, 1971. 272p.
            The relationship of American foreign policy to the anti-
        Chinese movement are traced. Concerned with the evolution
        of stereotypes and their use to mold attitudes. The por-
        trayal of the Chinese in American literature is discussed
        as well as the concept of China itself.

1552   MILLER, STUART C. The Unwelcome Immigrant: The American
        Image of the Chinese, 1785-1882. Berkeley: University of
        California Press, 1969. 259p.
            A history of Chinese immigration with emphasis upon the
        prejudice encountered. The book's thesis is that this bias
        was national, not regional, and that it preceded the big
        migration to America. Extensive notes and a brief descrip-
        tive bibliography.

1553   PEOPLE V. HALL. 4 California, p. 399.
            This case is included here because it is one of the most
        famous of all the cases, acts, and legislations aimed at
        controlling or excluding Asian Americans. The argument
        made is that a Chinese man is not enough of a human being
        to have his testimony accepted under oath in a murder trial.
        The judge ruled his evidence was not valid and the White
        man charged with the murder was freed.

CHINESE AMERICANS

1554   RIGGS, FRED W. Pressures On Congress; A Study of the Repeal
        of Chinese Exclusion. New York: King's Crown Press, 1950.
        260p.
            Details the background and development of Chinese exclu-
        sion policies and the fight to repeal the laws that resulted.
        There is also a good discussion of the various forces at
        work in the American society that produced first the ex-
        clusion acts and then the repeal of them.

1555   SANDMEYER, ELMER CLARENCE. The Anti-Chinese Movement In
        California. Urbana: University of Illinois Press, 1939.
        127p.
            Devoted solely to the topic of the whys and wherefores
        of the anti-Chinese movement. Well-researched and with an
        extensive bibliography.

        SCHELL, ORVILLE. See 1556.

1556   SCHURMANN, FRANZ and ORVILLE SCHELL. The China Reader in 4
        volumes: Imperial China: The Decline of the Last Dynasty
        and The Origins of Modern China. The Eighteenth and Nine-
        teenth Centuries. 322p. Republican China: Nationalism,
        War, and The Rise of Communism. 1911-1949. 394p. Com-
        munist China: Revolutionary Reconstruction and Internal
        Confrontation. 1949 To Present. 667p. The China Reader
        IV: Social Experimentation, Politics, Entry Onto the
        World Scene, 1966-1972. New York: Vintage Books, 1967-
        1974.
            A documentary history of China in four volumes, this
        valuable series is well edited and annotated with introduc-
        tions for each section.

1557   SUNG, BETTY LEE. Mountain of Gold: The Story of the Chinese
        in America. New York: Macmillan, 1967. 341p. Reissued
        in paperback as: The Chinese In America. New York:
        Collier, 1971.
            Examines the Chinese experience in America which stresses
        the goal for Chinese Americans of assimilation and accept-
        ance. Thorough detailing and documenting of immigration and
        resettlement experiences of Chinese immigrants from the Gold
        Rush to the present. Bibliography. Ms. Sung's book is
        coming under heavy criticism from revisionist scholars.

1558   UNITED STATES Congress, Joint Special Committee to Investigate
        Chinese Immigration. Report of the Joint Special Committee
        to Investigate Chinese Immigration. February 27, 1877.
        Washington, D. C.: U. S. Government Printing Office, 1877.
            A sample of the kinds of materials available for re-
        searchers, a 1,100 page testimony on the subject of the

(UNITED STATES Congress)
Chinese in California. Very detailed and very biased, it
still contains reams of accurate and statistical material
as well as the atmosphere of the times.

1559 U. S. STATE Department, Immigration Series No. 3, Publication
No. 910. Admission of Chinese Into the United States.
Washington, D. C.: U. S. Government Printing Office, 1936.
43p.
The government interpretation of the Chinese exclusion
laws and Immigration Act of 1924.

1560 WU, CHENG-TSU. "Chink." New York: World Publishing Company,
1972. 288p.
Documents pertaining to the origin and development of
anti-Chinese racism in the United States are run off one
after the other. This is a pertinent but difficult book
to use as there is no table of contents nor index for the
selections. They are presented in narrative form. Short
bibliography.

2. General Culture and Community Life
(Art, Chinatowns, Health Education, Music,
Philosophy, Psychology and Sociology)

1561 ADAMS, BEN. San Francisco: An Informal Guide. New York:
Hill and Wang, 1961. 238p.
A guide book to San Francisco, includes sections on
Chinese American history, as well as Chinatown.

1562 CATTELL, STUART H. Health, Welfare and Social Organization in
Chinatown, New York City. New York: Department of Public
Affairs, Community Service Society of New York, 1970. 142p.
A study originated to discover Chinese American attitudes
towards health and illness. Goes into the setting and his-
tory of New York Chinatown, the demography, social struc-
ture, and health situations. Appendices and bibliography.
Reprint of 1962 edition.

1563 CHINESE-AMERICAN School and Community Problems. Chicago:
Integrated Education Associates, 1972. 76p.
Essays by Asian Americans and others on Chinese communi-
ties in San Francisco, New York City, Boston, and Hawaii.
Selected references for reading by M. Weinberg. Bibliog-
raphy.

CHINESE AMERICANS

1564   COLMAN, ELIZABETH. Chinatown, USA. New York: The John Day
       Company, 1946. 88p.
             The first century of Chinese life in the United States
       is viewed through a combination of text and photographs of
       Chinatowns in several large American cities.

1565   DILLON, RICHARD H. The Hatchet Men: The Story of the Tong
       Wars in San Francisco's Chinatown. New York: Howard-
       McCann, 1962. 375p.
             Gambling, opium selling, and prostitution are described
       in this behind-the-scenes book about the money-making pro-
       fessions in San Francisco's Chinatown. Chapters also on
       the social life of immigrants and the influence of the Tong
       wars on Chinatown and San Francisco. The book ends with
       the 1906 earthquake which the author feels marked the be-
       ginning of a new cultural era for Chinese residents, in
       which they began feeling like Americans and not like so-
       journers.

1566   GLIDE Urban Center. Ting: The Cauldron--Chinese Art and
       Identity In San Francisco. San Francisco: Glide Urban
       Center Publications, 1970. 112p.
             Ting is a symbolic hexagram which represents artistic
       and spiritual sustenance. This book is an interesting
       compendium of writings and art presentations. Included is
       a biography of "Dr. Mah" the Chinese herbalist as well as
       poems by non-Chinese writers such as Gary Snyder and
       Kenneth Rexroth.

1567   GRUSKIN, ALAN D. The Water Colors Of Dong Kingman, and How
       the Artist Works. New York: Studio Publications, 1958.
       138p.
             The achievements of a Chinese American artist are de-
       scribed with many reproductions of his landscape and urban
       paintings of America. Includes an Introduction by William
       Saroyan.

1568   HOY, WILLIAM. The Chinese Six Companies. San Francisco: The
       Chinese Consolidated Benevolent Association, 1942. 33p.
             A descriptive and historical account of the origin,
       function, and influence of the Chinese Six Companies in
       California.

1569   HSU, FRANCIS L. K. Americans and Chinese: Reflections on Two
       Cultures and Their People. Garden City, New York:
       Doubleday, 1970. 493p.
             Dr. Hsu embarks on a psychological-sociological-anthro-
       pological interpretation of Chinese immigrant adjustment to
       the United States. He develops a theory of the Chinese as

(HSU, FRANCIS L. K.)
    situation-centered and White Americans as individual-centered. Other broad contrasts include Chinese worship of the past traditions versus Anglo worship of the future and familial dependencies versus social self-reliance. Bibliography. Dr. Hsu's theories are being challenged today by some young Chinese American scholars. Reprint of 1953 edition.

1570   _____. The Challenge of the American Dream: The Chinese in the United States. Belmont, California: Wadsworth Publishing Company, 1971. 160p.
    One of a series called Minorities in American Life, this book is a popularized account of the Chinese American culture as seen by a sociologist. Chapters deal with such topics as Chinese language, family and kinship ties, religion, adolescence, and Americanization. Several pages of annotated recommended reading.

1571 JACKSON, HELEN HUNT. Bits of Travel at Home. Boston: Roberts Bros., 1895. 304p.
    A little-known book by the famous author of Ramona in which she describes Chinatown (San Francisco) in the 1870s. Reprint of 1872 edition.

1572 JACOBS, A. GERTRUDE, comp. The Chinese-American Song and Game Book. New York: A. S. Barnes and Company, Inc., 1944. 96p.
    Chinese folk songs, Chinese children's song and games set to music.

1573 LEE, CALVIN. Chinatown U. S. A. Garden City, New York: Doubleday, 1965. 154p.
    The history and culture of the Chinese ghetto as seen by one who grew up in New York's Chinatown. Chapters on Chinese social structure, religion and customs written from the viewpoint of breaking down negative stereotypes.

1574 LEONG, GOR YUN. Chinatown Inside Out. New York: Barrows Mussey, 1936. 256p.
    A description of the old Chinatowns with excellent prints and photographs.

1575 LIN, YUTANG. The Importance of Living. New York: Reynal and Hitchcock, c. 1937. 459p.
    Lin's most popular book - a collection of philosophical essays that mix Chinese thought with American mode.

CHINESE AMERICANS

1576 _____. On the Wisdom of America. New York: The John Day
       Company, 1950. 462p.
          Collected essays. See also 1605.

1577 McLEOD, ALEXANDER. Pigtails and Goldust: A Panorama of
       Chinese Life in Early California. Caldwell, Ohio: Caxton
       Printers, Ltd., 1947. 325p.
          San Francisco's Chinatown in the nineteenth century.
       Also chapters on the Sierra Nevada mines.

NEE, BRETT DE BARY. See 1578.

1578 NEE, VICTOR G. and BRETT DE BARY NEE. Longtime Californ':
       a Documentary Study of an American Chinatown. New York:
       Pantheon Books, 1972. 410p.
          One of the first revisionist studies to be made about
       Chinese American life. Highly recommended as a key book.
       Narratives and interviews in the style of Oscar Lewis which
       show the development of San Francisco's Chinatown in terms
       of its residents. The field work is thorough. In five
       parts: the Bachelor Society, the Family Society, the Re-
       fugees, the Emergence of a New Working Class, and Radicals
       and the New Vision. Commentary and historical background
       given with each set of interviews.

1579 SAN FRANCISCO Chinese Community Citizens' Survey and Fact
       Finding Committee Report (abridged edition). San Francisco:
       H. L. Carle and Sons, 1969. 227p.
          This report, heavy with statistics and well-indexed, in-
       vestigates every area of community life. Reports include
       immigration, impact, housing, employment, social services
       and health, senior citizen problems, education, culture,
       and police relations.

WEINBERG, M. See 1563.

1580 YEE, CHIANG. The Silent Traveller in San Francisco. New York:
       W. W. Norton & Company, Inc., 1964. 366p.
          One of a whole series of elegant books by a Chinese
       American artist and writer who has a philosophical overview
       of life which he presents as he travels around and describes
       what he sees and with whom he speaks. Other books include:
       The Silent Traveller in New York, Boston, London, etc.
       Beautifully illustrated. Poems in Chinese and in transla-
       tion included when appropriate.

YUTANG, LIN. See 1575, 1576.

3. Literature by and about Chinese Americans
(Anthologies, Autobiography, Biography, Poetry and Prose)

1581 AI, LI LING. Life is for a Long Time: A Chinese Hawaiian
      Memoir. New York: Hastings House, 1972. 343p.
         An interesting and informative autobiography by the
      daughter of two Cantonese doctors who migrated to Hawaii.

1582 ATHERTON, GERTRUDE. My San Francisco, A Wayward Biography.
      Indianapolis: The Bobbs-Merrill Co., 1946. 334p.
         Information about authors who have written about China-
      town or used Chinese subjects in their stories are included
      in this readable account of the early decades.

      CHAN, CANDICE CYNDA. See 1583.

1583 CHAN, MARCIA JEAN and CANDICE CYNDA CHAN. Going Back. n. p.:
      n. p., 1973. 133p.
         This is another in the important series of student
      writings and publications currently appearing. This group
      went to Hong Kong during the summer of 1972 to learn Can-
      tonese as the first step of their return to the China of
      their grandparents. The writings include excerpts from
      diaries kept of the trip, poems, stories, and analysis,
      such as reflections on the art of China, and the women of
      China.

1584 CHANG, DIANA. Frontiers of Love. New York: Random House,
      1956. 246p.
         Diana Chang was born in America but raised in Shanghai
      by a German father and a Chinese mother. This novel, her
      first, was written about the identity crisis of an Eurasian
      woman, Sylvia Chen, who has a romance with a Chinese na-
      tional, Feng Huang, during the Chinese-Japanese war. She
      cannot choose which culture, Asian or European, best repre-
      sents her inner self. There is no clear resolution of
      this problem in the novel.

1585 CHENNAULT, ANNA. A Thousand Springs; The Biography of a
      Marriage. New York: Paul S. Eriksson, Inc., 1962. 318p.
         The Chinese wife of a famous general of World War II
      describes the events of her life and his.

1586 CHOU, CYNTHIA L. My Life in the United States. North Quincy,
      Massachusetts: The Christopher Publishing House, 1970. 274p.
         Life experiences in the United States from an inquisitive
      immigrant who arrived in 1955.

Minority Studies: An Annotated Bibliography

CHINESE AMERICANS

1587 CHU, LOUIS. Eat a Bowl of Tea. New York: Lyle Stuart, 1961. 250p.
> The first Chinese American novelist to set his story in Chinese America, Louis Chu writes about the drabness, un-exotic life of New York Chinatown.

1588 DOYLE, DR. C. W. The Shadow of Quong Lung. Philadelphia: J. B. Lippincott Company, 1900. 267p.
> This is a collection of short tales about Chinatown, San Francisco. A good example of the type of anti-Chinese propaganda literature available to American readers at the turn of the century. Dedicated to Ambrose Bierce.

1589 FENN, WILLIAM PURMANCE. Ah Sin and his Brethren in American Literature. Peiping: College of Chinese Studies, 1933. 131p.
> The Chinese as portrayed in American literature during the last half of the nineteenth century.

1590 GLICK, CARL. Shake Hands with the Dragon. New York and London: Whittlesey House, 1941. 327p.
> The story of how an Anglo from Iowa in charge of a Methodist youth recreational program in New York Chinatown during the Depression came to learn and understand the Chinese people he met there.

1591 GRIGGS, VETA. Chinaman's Chance: The Life Story of Elmer Wok Wai. New York: Exposition Press, 1969.
> The as-told-to story of a Chinese American who lived with his family in San Francisco's Chinatown. The family lost everything in the earthquake and fire; Elmer became a gunman, among other occupations, ended up in San Quentin, and was released to become a houseboy.

HARTE, BRET. See 1610.

1592 HUIE, KIN. Reminiscences. Peiping: San Yu Press, 1932. 116p.
> The autobiography of a man who was born and finally buried in China, but who spent forty years as pastor of the First Chinese Church in New York.

1593 KUO, CHING CH'IU (HELENA KUO). I've Come a Long Way. New York: D. Appleton-Century Co., Inc., 1942. 369p.
> The autobiography of a Chinese essayist and novelist. Has also written Westward to Chungking (1944) and Peach Path, a collection of her personal essays for women.

KUO, HELENA. See 1593.

1594   LEE, CHIN-YANG. <u>Flower Drum Song</u>. New York: Farrar, Strauss, and Cudahy, 1957. 244p.

This has been a film and stage play. It is about San Francisco, romanticized with charming stereotypes. The most famous story by this prolific author.

1595   _____. <u>Lover's Point</u>. New York: Stratford Press, 1958. 249p.

The novel recounts the love of a Chinese exile from Communist China for a local Japanese waitress he meets when he is teaching at the Monterey Army Language School.

1596   LEE, JON, comp. <u>Chinese Tales Told in California</u>, revised by Paul Radin. San Francisco: California State Library, 1940, mimeograph. 123p.

Most of these stories came from the Province of Canton, but they were taken down in Oakland, California in the 1930s and translated into English. As far as I know, this is the only collection of this kind made in the United States.

1597   LEE, VIRGINIA CHIN-LAN. <u>The House That Tai-Ming Built</u>. New York: Macmillan, 1963. 246p.

A historical novel about life in San Francisco's famous Chinatown from the 1850s until World War II as it is lived by one Chinese family. This book has been criticized by Frank Chin in the <u>Bulletin of Concerned Asian Scholars</u> (IV:3, Fall, 1972), because it presents a stereotype of Chinese intellectual culture that is superior, hence not realistic of the bulk of Chinese immigration.

1598   LIN, ADET and ANOR. <u>Our Family</u>. New York: The John Day Company, 1939. 256p.

Collected autobiographical essays about Lin Yutang's family (his name is properly listed as Yutang Lin), as written by several of his daughters.

1599   LIN FAMILY: Lin, Adet, Anor, and Tai-yi Lin, daughters of Yutang Lin, all have revised names. Adet is listed also as Ju-ssu Lin and Anor and Tai-yi both go under the name of Wu-shuang Lin.

1600   LIN, ANOR. <u>The Lilacs Overgrow</u>. New York: World, 1960.

Tells of the lives of two young Chinese women who live in Shanghai in the period between the end of the Japanese occupation and the coming of the Chinese Communists.

LIN, ANOR. <u>See</u> 1598.

CHINESE AMERICANS

1601   LIN, TAIYI. The Golden Coin. New York: The John Day
        Company, 1946. 306p.
           A prolific novelist. This is a sample of the writings
        of one of Yutang Lin's daughters.

1602   LIN, YUTANG. Chinatown Family. New York: The John Day
        Company, 1948. 307p.
           A popular writer and editor of many books, Yutang Lin
        (usually incorrectly listed as Lin Yutang) in this novel
        tells the story of a brother and sister who migrate to the
        United States to live with their father.

1603   LOWE, PARDEE. Father and Glorious Descendent. Boston:
        Little, Brown and Company, 1943. 322p.
           An autobiographical account of the Lowe family from the
        late 1870s to the 1930s. Setting is San Francisco's China-
        town. Includes the crisis of the San Francisco earthquake.
        This is one of the best known and liked autobiographies and
        is written with humor and warmth.

        McCLELLAN, ROBERT. See 1551.

1604   MAY, WONG. Reports. New York: Harcourt, Brace, Javanovic,
        Inc., 1972. 140p.
           Various impressions and responses to love, religion, and
        the human condition are included in these free-form poems.

1605   OAKES, VANYA. Footprints of the Dragon. A Story of the
        Chinese and the Pacific Railways. Philadelphia, Toronto:
        John C. Winston Co., 1951. 240p.
           A historical novel featuring the Chinese railroad
        workers who helped build the Central Pacific Railroad in
        the 1860s. Soft-pedals the hardships of those who survived
        on the job. Reprint of 1949 edition.

1606   PARK, NO-YONG. Chinaman's Chance: An Autobiography. Boston:
        Meador Publishing Company, 1940. 198p.
           The life of a Chinese immigrant and how he became an
        American success.

        RADIN, PAUL. See 1596.

1607   ROHMER, SAX. The Book of Fu-Manchu, being a Complete and De-
        tailed Account of the amazing Career in Crime of the Sinis-
        ter Chinaman. New York: R. M. McBride and Company, 1929.
           Consists of four volumes in the Fu-Manchu saga: The In-
        sidious Dr. Fu-Manchu (383p.), The Return of Dr. Fu-Manchu
        (332p.), The Hand of Fu-Manchu (308p.), and The Golden
        Scorpion (308p.). Fu-Manchu and his dragon lady consorts

(ROHMER, SAX)
created the stereotype of the Oriental criminal, sinister, slinky, and evil, with opium pipe in hand (long nails, of course).

1608   SHEPHERD, CHARLES R. The Ways of Ah Sin: A Composite Narrative of Things as They are. New York: Fleming H. Revell, 1923. 223p.
A popular anti-Chinese propaganda novel that characterized the Chinese American world as one of Tong wars for the men and prostitution for the women. Ah Sin is a stereotyped character once as popular as Charlie Chan. Shepherd was director of the Chung Mei Orphanage for Boys which operated in the San Francisco Bay region. He also wrote: Lim Yik Choy, The Story of a Chinese Orphan (1932), another work of fiction, about an orphan who grows up in a Christian orphanage, becomes a big football star, and eventually returns to China as a missionary.

1609   SPARKS, THERESA. China Gold. Fresno: Academy Library Guild, 1954. 191p.
The story of Suey Chung, a Chinese immigrant, who becomes a miner in northern California during the Gold Rush. A true biography of his survival, his marriage, and the problems of raising a family that rejected the old family traditions for the new. 1880s to 1948.

1610   TWAIN, MARK and BRET HARTE. "Ah Sin" A Dramatic Work, edited by Frederick Anderson. San Francisco: Book Club of San Francisco, 1961. 90p.
These two famous writers took Harte's character "Ah Sin" and co-authored a play which was produced in New York in 1877. It was not a success, but the new edition is worth looking at to see how both these men felt about mining camps and the Chinese working there.

WAI, ELMER WOK. See 1591.

1611   WING, YUNG. My Life in China and America. New York: Henry Holt, 1909. 286p.
Yung Wing was the first Chinese student to study in America. His attempts to live in his two worlds are detailed in his autobiography. After graduating from Yale, he returned to China, but then came again to the United States as head of a Chinese education mission. The book is of historical interest to see what White Americans enjoyed reading by Chinese American writers.

Minority Studies: An Annotated Bibliography

CHINESE AMERICANS

1612 WONG, JADE SNOW. *Fifth Chinese Daughter*. New York: Harper and Row, 1950. 246p.

Considered to be the most popular Asian American autobiography. It tells, in the third person, of a second generation Chinese girl growing up in San Francisco's Chinatown and going off to college. Jade Snow Wong had the usual teen identity crises, especially concerning her desire to be independent and go to school, rather than conform to dominance by her family and get married. Currently criticized as part of the "old" school of Chinese American writing. Reprint of 1945 edition.

YUTANG, LIN. See 1602.

C. Japanese Americans

1. History, Immigration, Racism, Relocation and United States/Japanese Relationships

ADAMS, ANSEL. See 1640.

1613 BAILEY, PAUL. *Concentration Camp U. S. A.* New York: Tower Publications, 1972. 223p.

A readable version of Japanese American experience in the 1940s at the Japanese Relocation Camp in Poston, Arizona. This book is also in hardcover under the title *City in the Sun* (Los Angeles: Westernlore Press, 1971).

BARNHART, EDWARD N. See 1636.

1614 BOSWORTH, ALLAN R. *America's Concentration Camps: The Story of 110,000 Americans Behind Barbed Wire in the United States during World War II.* New York: W. W. Norton and Company, 1967. 283p.

A newspaperman's detailed account of the Japanese American internment during World War II. He discusses all the concentration camps located in western states. Bibliography.

1615 CONROY, HILARY and T. SCOTT MIYAKAWA, eds. *East Across the Pacific: Historical and Sociological Studies of Japanese Immigration and Assimilation.* Santa Barbara: American Bibliographical Center, Clio Press, 1972. 322p.

Covers Hawaii and the Pacific Islands as well as the Mainland from California to New York in a series of scholarly essays on historical and sociological topics. *Bridge* magazine feels that this book reflects an Anglo viewpoint.

256

CONRAT, MAISIE and RICHARD CONRAT. See 1642.

1616   CURTIS, GERALD L., ed. Japanese-American Relations in the
        1970s. Washington, D. C.: Columbia Books, Inc., 1970.
        204p.
            This paperback is put out by the American Assembly at
        Columbia University and consists of papers from the second
        Japanese-American Assembly held in Japan in 1969. Seventy
        scholars, government officials, and businessmen from Japan
        and America heard these papers discussing the various as-
        pects of the relationship between the two countries.

1617   DANIELS, ROGER. Concentration Camps, U. S. A., Japanese
        Americans and World War II. New York: Holt, Rinehart &
        Winston, 1971. 188p.
            A tightly written, solidly documented history of the
        Japanese American experience in the period of the last war.
        Includes a short, useful, descriptive bibliography, es-
        pecially good for the legal aspects of internment.

1618   _____. The Politics of Prejudice: The Anti-Japanese Movement
        in California and the Struggle for Japanese Exclusion.
        New York: Atheneum, 1968. 165p.
            The development of sentiment and action against the
        "Yellow Peril" from the arrival of the first immigrants in
        the nineteenth century to the passing of exclusion legisla-
        tion. A University of California Publication in History.
        Extensive notes and a select bibliography.

EATON, ALLEN HENDERSHOTT. See 1643.

1619   FISHER, ANNE REEPLOEG. Exile of a Race. Seattle: F. & T.
        Publishers, 1965. 245p.
            A history of the evacuation and imprisonment of Japanese
        Americans during World War II. Also a descriptive history
        of the Japanese settlement on the West Coast. Brief
        bibliography.

1620   GIRDNER, AUDRIE and ANNE LOFTIS. The Great Betrayal: The
        Evacuation of the Japanese Americans During World War II.
        New York: MacMillan, 1969. 562p.
            A well-documented and well-written history about the WRA
        concentration camps during World War II. The aftermath is
        also described. Appendices of pertinent historical docu-
        ments and a bibliography.

1621   GRODZINS, MORTON. Americans Betrayed. Chicago: University
        of Chicago Press, 1949. 445p.
            An important legal and constitutional study of the

JAPANESE AMERICANS

(GRODZINS, MORTON)
Japanese American evacuation and internment during World War II. Grodzins names individuals and organizations who promoted the anti-Japanese situation in California.

1622   GULICK, SIDNEY L. The American Japanese Problem: A Study of Racial Relations of the East and the West. New York: Charles Scribner's Sons, 1914.
Gulick is one of the few White writers before World War II who wrote against the concept of Anglo superiority. Here, he gives the prejudicial reasoning used to create anti-Japanese legislation and exclusion acts. He contrasts this propaganda with the actual living conditions of Japanese immigrants.

1623   HANSEN, ARTHUR A. and BETTY E. MITSON, eds. Voices Long Silent: An Oral History Inquiry into the Japanese American Evacuation. Fullerton, California: Japanese American Project, Oral History Program, California State University, Fullerton, 1974. 214p.
An Oral History of the Japanese American evacuation of World War II consisting of essays, transcripts of four oral history documents, and an annotated bibliography of one hundred interviews and lectures contained in the California State University, Fullerton, Oral History Collection.

HANSEN, ASAEL T. See 1635.

1624   IRIYE, AKIRA. Across the Pacific: An Inner History of American-East Asian Relations. New York: Harcourt, Brace and World, Inc., 1967. 361p.
A three-fold history book, it deals with East Asians in America, Asian responses to America, and U. S. relations with China and Japan, contrasting these two countries in their dealings with America. Puts U. S. diplomacy and activities in the Pacific in context with the world-wide imperialism of the nineteenth century.

1625   _____, ed. Mutual Images of Japan and America. Cambridge: Harvard University Press, 1973.

1626   _____. Pacific Estrangement: Japanese and American Expansion, 1897-1911. Cambridge, Massachusetts: Harvard University Press, 1972. 290p.
A study of American and Japanese imperialism in the Pacific.

ISHIGO, ESTELLE. See 1646.

1627   KAWAKAMI, KIYOSHI KARL. The Real Japanese Question. New York: MacMillan, 1921. 269p.

A Japanese writer argues against exclusion of Orientals from the United States and tries to answer charges, prevalent at the time, that the Japanese were non-assimilable and bad economic competition.

1628   KITAGAWA, DAISUKE. Issei and Nisei; The Internment Years. New York: The Seabury Press, 1967. 174p.

A socio-history of the barbed-wire experience lived by Japanese Americans during World War II. Kitagawa, a Japanese-born minister, visited all the concentration camps and writes a strongly autobiographical book about his own experiences. Brief descriptive bibliography.

1629   LANCESTER, CLAY. Japanese Influence in America. New York: Walton H. Rawls, 1963. 292p.

Historical relationships between Japan and the United States given as a background to a discussion of influences on American architecture and the arts.

1630   LANHAM, C. The Japanese in America. London: Longmans, Green, Reader and Dyer, 1872.

A nineteenth-century history of the Japanese immigration to the United States, including an overall description of Japan during that period.

1631   LEIGHTON, ALEXANDER H. The Governing of Men: General Principles and Recommendations Based on Experience at a Japanese Relocation Camp. Princeton: Princeton University Press, 1968. 404p.

A sociological and psychological study of the Japanese interned at Poston, Arizona during World War II. Life in the camp was studied including self-government, social organization, and the strike which took place at the relocation center. Part II analyzes the behavior of people under stress. An appendix details work methods and criteria. Reprint of 1945 edition.

LOFTIS, ANNE. See 1620.
LUOMALA, KATHERINE. See 1635.

1632   McWILLIAMS, CAREY. Prejudice: Japanese Americans - Symbols of Racial Intolerance. Hamden, Connecticut: The Shoestring Press, 1971. 337p.

In order to understand the evacuations of Japanese Americans to internment camps after Pearl Harbor, McWilliams feels it is necessary to trace the origin of racial antagonism from the arrival of the first immigrants. Reprint of 1941 edition.

JAPANESE AMERICANS

MITSON, BETTY E. See 1623.
MIYAKAWA, T. SCOTT. See 1615.

1633   MYER, DILLON S. Uprooted Americans: The Japanese Americans
        and the War Relocation Authority During World War II.
        Tucson: University of Arizona Press, 1971. 360p.
            Dillon's experiences as a War Relocation Director pro-
        vide a needed viewpoint in the history of the Japanese
        American in encampment and in the Armed Forces during World
        War II. Appendices of government documents and a bibliog-
        raphy.

NISHIMOTO, RICHARD S. See 1638.

1634   OGAWA, DENNIS M. From Japs to Japanese: An Evolution of
        Japanese-American Stereotypes. Berkeley: McCutcheon Pub-
        lishing Corporation, 1971. 67p.
            The author's thesis is that the Japanese immigrant
        started out with a bad image which has since become a good
        one. He briefly relates the evolution of this image, em-
        phasizing the "Jap" of World War II who has now become a
        good and successful quiet American. A discussion is also
        made about the function and dimensions of stereotypes.
        This short book tends to make many conclusive statements
        unsubstantiated by evidence other than newsclips for the
        earlier history.

OKOBO, MINÉ. See 1650.
OPLER, MARVIN K. See 1635.

1635   SPICER, EDWARD H., ASAEL T. HANSEN, KATHERINE LUOMALA, and
        MARVIN K. OPLER. Impounded People: Japanese-Americans in
        the Relocation Centers. Tucson: University of Arizona
        Press, 1969. 342p.
            The official War Relocation Authority Report written for
        the federal government by four anthropologists. An anno-
        tated bibliography of the community analysis section is
        included as well as an extensive bibliography of war relo-
        cation centers.

1636   TENBROEK, JACOBUS, EDWARD N. BARNHART, and FLOYD W. WATSON.
        Prejudice, War and the Constitution: Japanese American
        Evacuations and Resettlement. Berkeley: University of
        California Press, 1968. 408p.
            Emphasis is on the legal problems of the Japanese evacua-
        tion of World War II. Historical origins, political charac-
        teristics of Japanese Americans, and political responsibil-
        ity in America also studied. A very comprehensive book with

(TENBROEK, JACOBUS...)
    extensive notes. Volume Three of a series edited by
    Dorothy S. Thomas and put out by the University of Cali-
    fornia. Reprint of 1954 edition.

1637 THOMAS, DOROTHY SWAINE. The Salvage: Japanese-American
      Evacuation and Resettlement. Berkeley: University of
      California Press, 1952. 637p.
        Divided into two parts: the first talks about social
      patterns and sets up a historical background for the second
      section, which contains fifteen personal stories about what
      happened to the Japanese Americans after they left their
      relocation camps and resettled in the East and Mid-West.
      Volume Two in a series edited by Dorothy Swaine Thomas and
      published by the University of California.

1638 THOMAS, DOROTHY SWAINE and RICHARD S. NISHIMOTO. The Spoilage:
      Japanese-American Evacuation and Resettlement. Berkeley:
      University of California Press, 1946. 408p.
        The first volume in a series about the Japanese American
      concentration camps of World War II. (Others are listed
      here under Dorothy S. Thomas and Jacobus tenBroek.) Ana-
      lyzes the actuality of internment from a sociological view-
      point detailing the conflicts between the Japanese Americans
      and their guards, the accommodations required, and the re-
      volts and suppressions that occurred. Volume One in a
      series edited by Dorothy S. Thomas and published by the
      University of California. Both of the Thomas books are
      being challenged today for questionable perspective and
      methodology.

1639 UNITED STATES ARMY Western Defense Command and Fourth Army.
      Final Report: Japanese Evacuation from the West Coast,
      1942. Washington, D. C.: United States Government Printing
      Office, 1943. 618p.
        General DeWitt's justification for Japanese American
      evacuation by the Army in the interests of national security.
      Detailed maps and statistics as well as many pictures.

WATSON, FLOYD. See 1636.

    2. General Culture and Community Life
    (Art, Photography and Sociology)

1640 ADAMS, ANSEL. Born Free and Equal: The Story of Loyal
      Japanese Americans at Manzanar Relocation Center, Inyo
      County, California. New York: United States Camera, 1944.
      112p.

JAPANESE AMERICANS

(ADAMS, ANSEL)
A photographic record of Manzanar War Relocation Center as taken by a famous American cameraman.

BARNHART, EDWARD N. See 1636

1641   BENEDICT, RUTH. The Chrysanthemum and the Sword: Patterns of Japanese Culture. Cleveland: Word Publishing Company, 1967.
A study of the ideologies behind the Japanese culture and character written by an outstanding American anthropologist. Study was begun in 1944 during World War II so the author could not do field work in Japan. However, she relied on literature and interviews with Japanese in America. Reprint of 1946 edition.

1642   CONRAT, MAISIE and RICHARD CONRAT. Executive Order 9066. San Francisco: Scrimshaw Press, 1972. 120p.
A collection of photographs of the Japanese American relocation in concentration camps during World War II.

CONRAT, RICHARD. See 1642.

1643   EATON, ALLEN HENDERSHOTT. Beauty Behind Barbed Wire: The Arts of the Japanese in our War Relocation Camps. New York: Harper and Row, 1952. 208p.
Photographs mostly with captions and legends showcasing the arts created in the WRA camps. Includes wood-carving projects, flower-arrangements and miniature landscapes. Foreword by Eleanor Roosevelt.

HANSEN, ASAEL T. See 1635.

1644   HOSOKAWA, BILL. Nisei: The Quiet Americans. New York: William Morrow and Company, 1969. 522p.
A history commissioned by the Japanese American Citizens League. The historical period is before, during, and after World War II with emphasis on the role of the Nisei, or second generation Japanese Americans.

1645   ICHIHASHI, YAMATO. Japanese in the United States: A Critical Study of the Problems of the Japanese Immigrants and Their Children. New York: Arno Press and The New York Times, 1969. 426p.
Describes the character and causes of Japanese immigration, as well as acculturation problems, occupation, and exclusion. Also deals with international aspects of American internal policies towards Japanese Americans. Covers

262

(ICHIHASHI, YAMATO)
the late 1800s thru 1930. Still accepted as the standard
work on Japanese immigration. Bibliography. Reprint of
the 1932 edition in the American Immigration series.

1646 ISHIGO, ESTELLE. Lone Heart Mountain. Los Angeles: Anderson,
Ritchie and Simon, 1972. 104p.
Sketches and commentary by a White artist who accompanied
her Japanese husband to Lone Heart Mountain Internment Camp
in Wyoming during World War II.

1647 KITANO, HARRY. Japanese-Americans: The Evolution of a Sub-
Culture. Englewood Cliffs, New Jersey: Prentice-Hall,
1969. 186p.
Kitano is one of the leading sociologists on ethnic
topics in the United States. Here, he traces the history
of Japanese immigrants and their families, and outlines
their strategies for survival. Family and cultural patterns
are discussed. Bibliography and statistical appendix.

1648 MAYKOVICH, MINAKO K. Japanese American Identity Dilemma.
Tokyo: Wasedo University Press, 1972. 151p.
Part One of this cultural study deals with the background of the "Quiet American." Part Two discusses the
generation gap between the contemporary Sansei generation
and parents and grandparents, and the Sansei identity
crisis. Intended as a textbook in sociology or ethnic
studies.

1649 OKUBO, MINÉ. An American Experience. Oakland: The Oakland
Museum, July, 1972. 56p.
This delightful book, with commentary by Shirley Sun,
is the catalogue of the Museum's retrospective exhibit of
the first Japanese American woman artist.

1650 _____. Citizen 13660. New York: Columbia University Press,
1946. 209p. New York: AMS Press, Inc., 1968.
A Japanese American artist sketches in words and pictures her day-to-day life in a World War II evacuation
camp.

1651 PETERSON, WILLIAM. Japanese Americans: Oppression and
Success. New York: Random House, 1971. 268p.
A historical and sociological analysis of Japanese
Americans. Chapters on prison camps, religion, the family,
and the concept of what a subnation involves. Part of Ran-
dom House's Ethnic Group in Comparative Perspective Series.
Bibliography. Amerasia Journal Vol. 2 (Fall 1973) is

JAPANESE AMERICANS

(PETERSON, WILLIAM)
critical of Peterson's success criteria, his lack of establishing a causal link between success and identity, and the
racist implications of his subnation theory.

SAMUELS, FREDERICK. See 1710.

1652   SHIREY, ORVILLE C. Americans: The Story of the 442nd Combat
Team. Washington, D. C.: Infantry Journal Press, 1946.
151p.
The history of the most famous and most decorated Nisei
fighting group in World War II. Many pictures and an appendix which lists the Team's roster.

1653   UNITED STATES Department of the Interior, War Relocation
Authority. Community Analysis Reports 1-19. (October 1942-
June 1946).
A collection of nineteen reports analyzing Japanese cul-
ture in America, Buddhism in America, relocation problems
such as unrest and resistance, and problems encountered by
the Japanese when released from the evacuation camps.
Bibliography of Community Analysis newsletters.

1654   _____. People in Motion, The Post War Adjustment of the
Evacuated Japanese Americans. Washington, D. C.: United
States Government Printing Office, 1947. 270p.
A follow-up report on Japanese Americans in Chicago,
Denver, Los Angeles, and Seattle.

3. Literature by and about Japanese Americans
(Anthologies, Autobiography, Biography, Drama, Poetry and Prose)

ALLEN, REIKO HATSUMI. See 1666.

1655   BANCROFT, GRIFFING. The Interlopers: A Novel. New York:
The Bancroft Company, 1917. 397p.
A fictional account of Japanese farmers in California.
Interesting to read along with writings about the Exclusion
Act and the violence and racism that led up to it.

1656   BUCK, PEARL S. The Hidden Flower. New York: John Day
Company, 1962. 308p.
A novel about a Japanese war bride brought by her husband to live in Virginia, where she encounters not only
miscegenation laws but social prejudice.

1657   CHARYN, JEROME. American Scrapbook. New York: Viking Press,
       1969. 177p.
           The effects of the internment of Japanese Americans
       during World War II is effectively handled in this fic-
       tional account of the Tanaka family.

1658   ECKSTEIN, GUSTAV. Noguchi. New York: Harper and Row, 1936.
       419p.
           The biography of an Issei scientist. Reprint of 1931
       edition.

1659   EDMISTON, JAMES. Home Again. Garden City, New York:
       Doubleday and Company, Inc., 1955. 316p.
           A novel about a Japanese American family, particularly
       the experience of internment and their return to California
       after World War II.

ELLIOTT, LAWRENCE. See 1670, 1705.

1660   EMBREY, SUE KUNITOMI, ed. for the Manzinar Committee. The
       Lost Years, 1942-1946. Los Angeles: Moonlight Publica-
       tions, Gidra, Inc., 1972. 57p.
           A collection of poetry and essays concerning the Manzanar
       Relocation Camp and its meaning to the Japanese American
       people. Bibliography and chronology.

1661   FUJITA, JUN. Tanka: Poems in Exile. Chicago: Covic-McGee
       Co., 1923. 61p.
           Using short and traditional Japanese forms, this poet
       writes poignantly of loneliness and the problems of adjust-
       ment to living in the United States.

1662   FUKUZAWA, YUKICHI. The Autobiography of Yukichi Fukuzawa,
       revised translation by Eiichi Kiyooka. New York: Columbia
       University Press, 1966. 407p.
           The life of a samurai in the nineteenth century. Des-
       cribes his participation in the first Japanese mission to
       America in 1860 and his return trip for warships and rifles
       in 1867. Reprint of 1934 edition.

1663   HARTMANN, SADAKICHI. Buddha, Confucius, Christ: Three
       Prophetic Plays, Harry Lawton and George Knox, eds.
       New York: Herder and Herder, 1971. 167p.
           Hartmann is described by his editors as one of the Bo-
       hemians of the Mauve Decade. His Japanese mother died soon
       after his birth, and his German father brought him home to
       Germany where he lived until he was thirteen. At that
       point, a fight with his stepmother, who did not want a

Minority Studies: An Annotated Bibliography

JAPANESE AMERICANS

(HARTMANN, SADAKICHI)
half-breed around, caused him to emigrate alone to America. Hartmann is being rediscovered and republished now both as an art critic and a writer. These three symbolist plays were written between 1889-1897 and caused great interest at the time they were published.

1664   . White Chrysanthemums, Literary Fragments and Pronouncements. George Knowland and Harry M. Lawton, eds. New York: Herder and Herder, 1971. 163p.
A collection of Hartmann's poems, many of them using traditional Japanese forms.

HATANO, ICHIRO. See 1665.

1665 HATANO, ISOKO and ICHIRO HATANO. Mother and Son. Boston: Houghton Mifflin and Company, 1962.
Letters and autobiographical materials.

1666 HATSUMI, REIKO (Reiko Hatsumi Allen). Rain and the Feast of Stars. Boston: Houghton Mifflin and Company, 1959. 215p.
An autobiography about Japanese life by a Japanese woman now living in the United States.

HOSOKAWA, BILL. See 1698.
HOUSTON, JAMES D. See 1667.

1667 HOUSTON, JEANNE WAKATSUKI and JAMES D. HOUSTON. Farewell to Manzanar. Boston: Houghton, Mifflin and Company, 1973. 177p.
An autobiographical account of the Japanese internment experience and what it meant to the Wakatsuki family of Long Beach, California.

1668 HULL, ELEANOR. Suddenly the Sun. New York: Friendship Press, 1957. 130p.
The biography of an Issei, Shizuko Takahashi.

1669 INADA, LAWSON FUSAO. Before the War. New York: William Morrow and Company, 1971. 124p.
The first collection of poems by a Japanese American ever published in the United States. The poems are both biting and lyric. One section is a comment on Inada's family experience in an Evacuation Camp during World War II. Strongly recommended for excellence of style and relevance of content.

266

1670 INOUYE, DANIEL K. Journey to Washington, with Lawrence
Elliott. Englewood Cliffs, New Jersey: Prentice-Hall,
1967. 297p.
 The autobiography of the United States Senator from
Hawaii.

ISHIGAKI, AYAKO. See 1679.

1671 IRWIN, WALLACE. Letters of a Japanese Schoolboy. New York:
Doubleday, Page and Co., 1909. 370p.
 An Anglo writer imagines himself a Japanese visiting
this country. Irwin is noted for his disparaging burlesque
of Chinese immigrants.

1672 ISHIMOTO, BARONESS SHIDZUE. Facing Two Ways (The Story of my
Life). New York: Farrar and Rinehart, Inc., 1935. 373p.
 Autobiography.

IWAMATSU, JUN. See 1705.

1673 KANEKO, HIZAKAZU. Manjiro, The Man Who Discovered America.
Boston: Houghton Mifflin Company, 1956. 149p.
 Manjiro Nakahama (1827-1898) was shipwrecked in the
Pacific and rescued by a New England whaling ship in 1841.
He became the first Japanese to be educated in the United
States.

1674 KAWAKAMI, KIYOSHI KARL. Jokichi Takamine: A Record of His
American Achievement. New York: W. E. Rudge, 1928. 73p.
 The biography of an Issei scientist.

1675 KEHOE, KARON. City in the Sun. New York: Dodd, Mead and
Company, 1946. 269p.
 Ironically, this first novel to come out about Japanese
American internment during World War II was written by a
White American. Won the Intercollegiate Literary Fellow-
ship Prize.

1676 KIKUCHI, CHARLES. The Kikuchi Diary: Chronicle from an American Concentration Camp, edited and with an introduction by
John Modell. Urbana: University of Illinois Press, 1973.
258p.
 The day book of an inmate of a retention camp during
World War II, Charles Kikuchi was twenty-six years old in
1941, when he began his diary. Like many Japanese Americans, his camp experiences marked a psychological turning
point in his life. He never returned to the West Coast,
but moved to New York City.

JAPANESE AMERICANS

KIYOOKA, EIICHI. See 1662.

1677   KOIZUMI, KAZUO. Father and I. Memories of Lafcadio Hearn.
        Boston: Houghton Mifflin, 1935. 208p.
            The autobiography of Lafcadio Hearn's oldest son.

        KNOX, GEORGE. See 1663.
        LAWTON, HARRY M. See 1663.
        LERRIGO, MARION O. See 1680.

1678   MARTIN, RALPH G. Boy from Nebraska: The Story of Ben Kuroki.
        New York: Harper and Row, 1946. 208p.
            The biography of a Nisei who fought with a B-29 bomber
        outfit in Europe during World War II. His bravery and the
        prejudice he encountered are described in one of the few
        documents about any of the Japanese Americans who fought
        on the American side.

1679   MATSUI, HARU (Ayako Ishigaki). Restless Wave. New York:
        Modern Age Books, 1940. 251p.
            Autobiography.

1680   MATSUMOTO, TORU and MARION O. LERRIGO. A Brother is a
        Stranger. New York: John Day, 1946. 318p.
            Life in Japan and the United States between 1913 and
        1946 as told in this biography of a Japanese who married
        an American girl in this country.

1681   MATSUOKA, YOKO. Daughter of the Pacific. New York: Harper
        and Row, 1952. 245p.
            Autobiography.

1682   MEANS, FLORENCE CRANNELL. The Moved Outers. Boston:
        Houghton, Mifflin, 1945. 154p.
            A novel about Sue Ohara and her brother Kim and their
        mother and father and what they endure in a Japanese in-
        ternment camp during World War II. Despite all hardships,
        Sue has a romance with Jiro Ito before she is allowed to
        leave for college.

1683   MISHINA, SUMIE SEO. My Narrow Isle. New York: John Day
        Company, 1941. 280p.
            An autobiography about a woman who grew up in Japan,
        moved to the United States, and then returned to Japan.
        Details of the problems encountered from moving around in
        two cultures.

1684   MORI, TOSHIO. Yokahama, California. Caldwell, Idaho: The
        Caxton Printers, Ltd., 1949. 166p.

(MORI, TOSHIO)
Twenty-two short stories about life as a Japanese American in the San Francisco area before Pearl Harbor. Introduction by William Saroyan who comments patronizingly on Mori's use of English.

1685   NOGUCHI, YONE. The American Diary of a Japanese Girl (Miss Morning Glory). New York: Frederick A. Stokes Company, 1902. 261p.
A very popular writer at the turn of the century whose books are now being reconsidered for reprinting. Noguchi was a Japanese immigrant who wrote poetry, autobiography and non-fiction.

1686   _____. From the Eastern Sea. New York: M. Kennerley; Kamakura, Japan: The Valley Press, 1910. 67p.
A first book of poetry by a protege of Joaquin Miller. Other books of poetry include: Summer Clouds (1906).

1687   _____. The Story of Yone Noguchi Told by Himself. London: Chatto and Windus, 1914. 254p.
Autobiography. Includes his relationship with Joaquin Miller.

1688   OKADA, JOHN. No-No Boy. Rutland, Vermont: Charles E. Tuttle, 1957. 308p.
The first Japanese American novel about a Nisei hero who rejects being a dual personality, or merely Japanese or just American and insists upon being his own person. Refusing to be drafted, Ichiro returns to Seattle after two years in prison. He is on a search for himself but is full of self-hatred and despair; at the same time, he wants to be accepted and to accept himself.

1689   OKIMOTO, DANIEL. American in Disguise. New York and Tokyo: Walker/Weatherhill, Inc., 1971. 206p.
The autobiography of a Nisei born during World War II, at the Santa Anita Racetrack relocation center. The book details his growing up and trying to feel both American and Japanese. Foreword by James A. Michener. One reviewer accuses Okimoto of trying to outwhite the Whites.

1690   OTA, SHELLEY AYAME NISHIMURA. Upon Their Shoulders, A Novel. New York: Exposition Press, 1951. 262p.
The story of a Hawaiian Japanese family.

SHIROTA, JON. See 1711.

JAPANESE AMERICANS

1691   SONE, MONICA. Nisei Daughter. Boston: Little, Brown and
        Company, 1953. 238p.
            The autobiography of a Seattle girl and her family, es-
        pecially their experiences during World War II, when they
        were interned at a relocation center in Idaho. Well worth
        reading, if only for a comparison of the American public
        school system and Nihon Gakko, Japanese afternoon school.

1692   SUGIMOTO, ETSU (Inagaki). A Daughter of the Samurai: How the
        Daughter of Feudal Japan, Living Hundreds of Years in One
        Generation, Became a Modern American. Rutland, Vermont:
        Charles E. Tuttle, 1968. 314p.
            A famous autobiography, much read, and often quoted.
        The title explains the book. Period written about covers
        1850 to 1930. Reprint of 1925 edition.

        SUN, SHIRLEY. See 1649.

1693   TAMAGAWA, KATHLEEN. Holy Prayers in a Horse's Ear. New York:
        Ray Long and Richard R. Smith, 1932. 264p.
            Autobiography.

1694   TERASAKI, GWEN. Bridge to the Sun. Chapel Hill: University
        of North Carolina Press, 1957. 260p.
            The autobiography of an American woman who married a
        Japanese diplomat in the 1930s. Tells about the author's
        experiences during the war, both in the United States and
        Japan and her feelings upon returning to America after the
        war.

1695   UCHIDA, YOSKIKO. Journey to Topaz: A Story of the Japanese
        American Evacuation. New York: Charles Scribner's Sons,
        1971. 149p.
            A short novel for older children about a Japanese family
        and their experiences during World War II internment. Well-
        illustrated and historically accurate.

1696   YASHIMA, TARO (pseudo. Jun Iwamatsu). Horizon is Calling.
        New York: Henry Holt and Company, 1943. 276p.
            A companion book to The New Sun, this beautifully illus-
        trated story continues Yashima's life after he leaves
        prison and before he migrates to the United States. Short
        text is in English and Japanese.

1697   _____. The New Sun. New York: Henry Holt and Company, 1943.
        310p.
            Autobiographical story tells about Tashima's imprison-
        ment when he was still living in Japan in the 1930s. Worth
        a trip to the library for the illustrations which occupy
        every page of short text.

1698   YOSHIDA, JIM, with BILL HOSOKAWA. The Two Worlds of Jim
        Yoshida. New York: William Morrow and Company, Inc., 1972.
        256p.
            The true story of a Japanese American born in Seattle
        but trapped in Japan during World War II and forced to
        serve in the Japanese Army when it went to fight in China.
        Yoshida lost his American citizenship as a result of this.
        He regained it by serving in the Korean War.

                    D. Hawaiian Americans

                    1. General History and Culture

1699   AI, LI LING. Life is for a Long Time: A Chinese Hawaiian
        Memoir. New York: Hastings House, 1972. 343p.
            An interesting and informative autobiography by the
        daughter of two Cantonese doctors who migrated to Hawaii.

1700   BURROWS, EDWIN G. Hawaiian Americans: The Mingling of
        Japanese, Chinese, Polynesian and American Cultures.
        n.p.: Archon Books, 1970. 228p.
            Investigates the acculturation and value systems of the
        various ethnic groups in Hawaii. Emphasis on interrelation-
        ships between the native born, the Asian, and other immi-
        grants to the Haoles (Europeans and White Americans). Re-
        print of a 1947 Yale University Press study. Bibliography.

1701   DAWS, GAVAN. Shoal of Time; A History of the Hawaiian Islands.
        New York: Macmillan, 1968. 494p.
            Extensive bibliography.

1702   FUCHS, LAWRENCE. Hawaii Pono: A Social History. New York:
        Harcourt, Brace and World, 1961. 501p.
            "Pono", meaning "right" or "excellence", is the author's
        purpose in this book. His viewpoint is to tell the history
        of Hawaii to show it as the world's best example of "dy-
        namic social democracy." After a prologue on early history,
        the book emphasizes the twentieth century up to 1960.
        Bibliography.

1703   GRAY, FRANCINE DU PLESSIT. Hawaii: The Sugar Coated Fortress.
        New York: Random House, 1972. 145p.
            Originally published in the "New Yorker" magazine, a
        long profile essay on the fiftieth state.

MINORITY STUDIES: AN ANNOTATED BIBLIOGRAPHY

HAWAIIAN AMERICANS

1704   HOLT, JOHN DOMINIS. <u>Monarchy in Hawaii</u>, revised edition.
        Honolulu: Hogarth Press, 1971. 68p.
           A short history of the Hawaiian royal dynasties, espe-
        cially their development and downfall in the nineteenth
        century. Includes 22 portraits of royalty. Written from
        the viewpoint of a Hawaiian.

1705   INOUYE, DANIEL K. <u>Journey to Washington</u>, with Lawrence
        Elliott. Englewood Cliffs, New Jersey: Prentice-Hall,
        1967. 297p.
           The autobiography of the United States Senator from
        Hawaii.

1706   KUYKENDALL, RALPH SIMPSON. <u>The Hawaiian Kingdom</u>. Honolulu:
        The University of Hawaii Press, 3 vols. 1938-1967.
           The most thorough history available of the early Hawaiian
        period.

1707   LIND, ANDREW. <u>Hawaii's People</u>. Honolulu: University of
        Hawaii Press, 1967.
           A sociological description of the Hawaiians--who they
        are, how they live, and what their culture consists of.
        Lind is a prolific writer about Hawaii.

1708   MICHENER, JAMES. <u>Hawaii</u>. New York: Random House, 1959.
           A best selling novel about Hawaii by a popular writer.
        Traces the history of Hawaii and shows the interrelation-
        ships of Hawaiians, Chinese, Japanese, and Caucasians.

1709   MIYAMOTO, KANO. <u>Hawaii: The End of the Rainbow</u>. Rutland,
        Vermont: Charles E. Tuttle, 1964. 509p.
           An autobiographical novel about immigration to Hawaii
        and the life of the Miyamotos there. Ends with World War
        II.

        NORBECK. E. <u>See</u> 1751.
        OTA, SHELLEY. <u>See</u> 1690.

1710   SAMUELS, FREDERICK. <u>The Japanese and the Haoles of Honolulu:</u>
        <u>Durable Group Interaction</u>. New Haven: College and Uni-
        versity Press, 1970. 206p.
           The relationship between Caucasians (Haoles) and
        Japanese examined with theories advanced for group inter-
        action improvements. Appendices and notes.

1711   SHIROTA, JON. <u>Pineapple White</u>. Los Angeles: Ohara Publica-
        tions, 1972. Illus. Mark Komuro. 165p.
           A novel about a Japanese Hawaiian family. Focuses on
        the adjustment of the father, Kiro Saki, when he has to go

(SHIROTA, JON)
    to Los Angeles to live with his son, Mitsuo, who married a
    haole (White) girl. Story compounded by the fact that
    Carole's brother had been killed by the Japanese during
    World War II.

WENTWORTH, EDNA C. See 1752.

1712   WRIGHT, THEON. The Disenchanted Isles: The Story of the
        Second Revolution in Hawaii. New York: The Dial Press,
        1972. 304p.
            A history of Hawaii with emphasis on the period from
        1893 to the year 2000 (a consideration of Hawaii's Thirty
        Year Plan). The life story of Dan Inouye, the Nisei war
        hero and present Senator, used as a symbol of the Hawaiian
        Japanese.

1713   YOUNG, NANCY FOON. The Chinese in Hawaii: An Annotated Bibli-
        ography. Honolulu: Social Science Research Institute,
        University of Hawaii (Hawaii Series, No. 4), n. d.
            A general annotated bibliography using materials drawn
        from the archives of the University of Hawaii as well as
        their libraries, the Hawaiian State Library, the Hawaiian
        Chinese Historical Center, the Hawaiian Historical Society,
        and the Hawaiian Mission Children's Society Library.

                    E. Pilipino Americans

                    1. Bibliographical Works

1714   SAITO, SHIRO. Philippine Ethnography: A Critically Annotated
        and Selected Bibliography. Honolulu: University of Hawaii,
        East West Center, 1972. 512p.
            Saito is the social science bibliographer for the Uni-
        versity of Hawaii Library.

1715   . The Philippines: A Review of Bibliographies.
        Honolulu: University of Hawaii, East West Center, 1966.
        80p. (University of Hawaii East West Center, Occasional
        Paper No. 5)
            A bibliography of bibliographies which annotates general
        bibliographies on the Philippines as well as subject bibli-
        ographies and those on published and unpublished academic
        materials. Author and title index.

PILIPINO AMERICANS

1716   U. S. DEPARTMENT of Commerce, Social and Economic Statistics
        Administration, Bureau of the Census. Japanese, Chinese,
        and Pilipinos in the United States 1970 Census of Popula-
        tion, July, 1973. Washington, D. C.: U. S. Government
        Printing Office, 1973.

1717   WHITNEY, PHILIP B. "Forgotten Minority: Filipinos in the
        United States." Bulletin of Bibliography, XXIX: 3 (July-
        September, 1972), 73-83.
            The only bibliography to date on Filipinos in America,
        although one is now being prepared at the Filipino Center,
        UCLA. Gives books, monographs, periodical articles, docu-
        ments, newspapers and periodicals, and theses.

                    2. Periodicals

1718   ANG KATIPUNAN, bi-monthly. Oakland.

1719   FILIPINO-AMERICAN Herald. San Francisco.

1720   FILIPINO-AMERICAN Herald. San Francisco.

1721   PHILIPPINE NEWS. San Francisco.

                3. History, Politics and Revolution

1722   ABAYA, HERNANDO J. Betrayal in the Philippines. Quezon City:
        Malaya Books, 1970. 327p.
            Politics and government, 1946 to present.

1723   _____. The Untold Philippine Story. Quezon City: Malaya
        Books, 1969. 383p.
            The nationalist cause is outlined in this book which
        comes to a general conclusion that United States foreign
        policy since President McKinley has been interventionist.
        This book is banned in the Philippines for its anti-govern-
        mental perspective about President Marcos and his ruling
        group. Reprint of 1967 edition.

1724   AGONCILLO, TEODORO A. The Fateful Years, vols. I and II.
        Manila: R. P. Garcia, 1965. 1075p.
            History of the Japanese occupation of the Philippines,
        1942-1945.

1725   _____. The Political Development of the Philippines.
        Malacanang, Manila: Public Information Office. Back-
        grounder, 1970.
            Addresses, essays, and lectures.

1726   ____. A Short History of the Philippines. New York: Mentor, 1969. 319p.
    A shortened form of History of the Filipino People. Bibliography.

1727   ALFONSO, OSCAR M. Theodore Roosevelt and the Philippines, 1897-1909. Quezon City: University of the Philippines Press, 1970. 227p.
    Politics and government. Bibliography.

1728   CONSTANTINO, RENATO. The Making of a Filipino (A Story of Philippine Colonial Politics). Quezon City: Malaya Books, 1969. 342p.
    Contains also a selected bibliography on Claro M. Recto compiled by Hilda L. Beltrau, Zenalda Decena, and Elvira Cruz.

1729   GONZALES, NEPTALI A. Philippine Political Law. Manila: Rex Book Store, 1962. 405p.
    Bibliography and footnotes. Gonzales also wrote: Philippine Constitutional Law, 1962. 405p.

1730   GRAFF, HENRY FRANKLIN, ed. American Imperialism and the Philippine Insurrection; Testimony Taken from Hearings on Affairs in the Philippine Islands Before the Senate Committee on the Philippines, 1902. Boston: Little, Brown and Company, 1969. 172p.
    Selection from inquiries about the 1899-1901 revolution.

1731   GUERRERO, AMADO. Philippine Society and Revolution. Hong Kong: Ta Kung Pao, 1971. 296p.
    Deals with the history of the U. S.-Philippine relation in terms of the imperialism, the colonial attitudes on both sides, and the continuous exploitation of the Philippines' natural resources; how these relate to the condition of the Philippines as they have been; the corruption of the government by the monies of outside investors, the constant poverty, the devaluation of the currency, etc. In addition, explains a way of dealing with the problems. Guerrero is currently head of the Communist party in the Philippines.

1732   MANLAPIT, PABLO. Filipinos Fight for Justice: Case of the Filipino Laborers in the Big Strike of 1924, Territory of Hawaii. Honolulu: Kumalae Publications, 1933. 112p.

1733   MORALES, ROYAL. Makibaka, A Filipino Struggle. Los Angeles: Mountainview Press, Inc., 1974. 149p.
    Historical account of the Pilipino-American struggle from 1900 to the present. Emphasis on contemporary problems.

PILIPINO AMERICANS

1734   NELSON, EUGENE. Huelga! The First Hundred Days of the Great
        Delano Grape Strike. Delano: Farmworkers Press, 1966.
        The role of the Pilipinos depicted.

1735   POMEROY, WILLIAM. American Neo Colonialism: Its Emergence
        in the Philippines and Asia. New York: International
        Publishers, 1970. 255p.

1736   RIZAL, JOSE. Reminiscences and Travels. New York: Norton
        Publishing Co., 1961.
        Rizal was a national hero who was executed at the start
        of the Pilipino Rebellion against the Spanish. This book
        deals with his development from a member of the Philippine
        elite schooled in Europe to a leader in the fight for
        Pilipino liberties.

1737   ROMULO, CARLOS P. Mother America? A Living Story of Democ-
        racy. Garden City, New York: Doubleday and Company, 1943.
        234p.
        History of the Pilipino People from the Spanish-American
        war to the occupation of the islands by the Japanese during
        World War II. Overpraise of American-Colonial policies.
        Strong American sympathizer-distorted perspective of
        Pilipino-American relationship.

1738   SALAMACANCA, BONIFACIO S. The Pilipino Reaction to American
        Rule, 1901-1913. Hamden, Connecticut: Shoe-String Press,
        1968. 310p.
        Inquiry into the impact of American Civilization on
        Pilipino Institutions. Viewed from the standpoint of
        Pilipino reception of, or reaction to, American policies
        and institutions during that period.

1739   SANIEL, GOSEFA M. Filipino Exclusion Movement, 1927-1935.
        Quezon City: Institute of Asian Studies, University of
        Philippines, 1967. 51p.
        A collection of articles dealing with the Anti-Pilipino
        sentiment at that time. The struggle of the Pilipinos on
        the farms and in the cities on the west coast. Also deals
        with the laws affecting Pinoys at that time (Tydings-Mc-
        Duffy, Welch Bill, etc.).

1740   SCHIRMER, DANIEL. Republic or Empire: American Resistance to
        the Philippine War. Schenkman, 1972. 260p.
        Story of the U. S. struggle in the Philippines and the
        struggle of the Anti-Imperialist forces based on the East
        Coast (Boston, New York, etc.) who were ultimately defeated.

Minority Studies: An Annotated Bibliography

1741   WOLFF, LEON. <u>Little Brown Brother</u>. Makati, Erewhon, 1900.
364p.
Deals with the U. S. takeover of the Philippines from
the Spanish and the struggle with the Filipino guerrillas
led by Aguinaldo. Good in its objective approach; develops
well the whys and wherefores and other factors that led to
the takeover of the Philippines by the U. S.

1742   ZAIDE, GREGORIO F. <u>Great Filipinos in History, an Epic of
Filipino Greatness in War and Peace</u>. Manila: Verde Book
Store, 1970. 675p.

4. General Culture and Community Life

1743   AGONCILLO, TEODORO A. and GUERRERO, MILAGROS C. <u>History of
the Pilipino People</u>, 3rd edition. Quezon City: Malaya
Books, 1970. 724p.
Traces the development of the Pilipino people and its
culture from the early Moslem, Indian, Indonesian, Hindu,
and Chinese cultural influences through the Spanish and
finally the American influences. Very good in its detail.

1744   CLEMENTE II, WILFREDO ALEJANDRO. <u>Between Two Worlds - The
Other View</u>. n.p.: n.p., 1971. 169p.
Essays divided into two sections: Personal and autobi-
ographical accounts of life in the Philippines, and
"Amerika," detailing the need for a new social conscious-
ness.

1745   CONSTANTINO, RENATO. <u>Dissent and Counter-Consciousness</u>.
Quezon City: Malaya Books, 1970. 190p.
Social conditions in the Philippines, culture and national identity discussed book along with the various
strata of people. Bibliography.

1746   _____. <u>The Filipinos in the Philippines</u>. Quezon City:
Filipino Signatures, 1966. 152p.
Social life and customs, politics and government presented in a journalistic fashion in essays originally
published in local Sunday magazines.

GUERRERO, MILAGROS C. <u>See</u> 1743.

1747   JOCANO, RANDA F. <u>Growing up in a Philippine Barrio</u>. New York:
Holt, Rinehart, and Winston. Case Studies in Education and
Culture, 1969. 121p.
Social conditions on Panay Island.

PILIPINO AMERICANS

1748   LASKER, BRUNO. Pilipino Immigration to Continental United
        States and to Hawaii. New York: Arno Press and The New
        York Times, 1969.
            Gives a detailed history of Pilipino migration in terms
        of economic necessity, governmental policies, and programs.
        An American Immigration Collection reprint of the 1931 edi-
        tion. Appendices and bibliography.

1749   MUNOZ, ALFREDO N. The Filipinos in America. Los Angeles:
        Mountainview Publishers, 1971. 181p.
            The history of Pilipino migration and adjustment written
        in a surface newspaper style. One section names a lot of
        Pilipino-Americans who made it "up the ladder."

1750   NAVARRO, JOVINA. Diwang Filipino: Filipino Consciousness.
        Davis, California: Asian American Studies, UC at Davis,
        1974. 120p.
            A collection of articles and poems dealing with Pilipino
        Consciousness and the struggles of developing that con-
        sciousness. There is an emphasis on contemporary issues
        and on the farmworkers.

1751   NORBECK, EDWARD. Pineapple Town: Hawaii. Berkeley:
        University of California Press, 1959. 159p.
            The Pilipinos and other workers are part of this study
        of pineapple plantations on Mauna Loa. A sociological sur-
        vey of the cultures involved in a plantation community is
        the main focus.

1752   WENTWORTH, EDNA CLARK. Filipino Plantation Workers in Hawaii.
        American Council of Pacific Relations: Studies No. 7,
        1941. 245p.
            A study of incomes, expenditures, and living standards
        of Pilipino families on a Hawaiian sugar plantation.

1753   YABES, LEOPOLDO. The Filipino Struggle for Intellectual
        Freedom. Quezon City: n.p., 1959. 140p.
            Essays on Philippine life and thought.

                    5. Literature by and about Pilipinos
        (Anthologies, Autobiography, Biography, Drama, Folk-Tales,
             Literary Criticism and History, Poetry and Prose)

1754   AGCAOILI, TEO D., ed. Philippine Writing; An Anthology.
        Westport, Connecticut: Greenwood Publishing Company, 1971.
        351p.
            A reprint of book published in 1953 with an introduction
        by Edith L. and Edilberto K. Tiempo. Works are all in
        English. Reprint of 1953 edition.

ANTLER, JOYCE. See 1769.
BRAYMER, NAN. See 1775.

1755   BUAKEN, MANUEL. I Have Lived With the American People.
        Caldwell, Idaho: Caxton Printers, 1948. 358p.
            The autobiography of a Pilipino who immigrated to the
        U. S. at the age of fourteen. Tells about his experiences
        in the United States from 1927 to 1948. He describes his
        family life, and the problems he encountered in California
        with anti-Pilipino riots, discriminatory housing regula-
        tions, and restrictive jobs.

1756   BULOSAN, CARLOS. America is in the Heart: A Personal History.
        New York: Harcourt, Brace and Company, 1946. 326p.
        Reprinted by the University of Washington Press, 1974.
            The autobiography of a well-known Pilipino poet and his
        life in America from the 1920s to the end of World War II.
        Tells also of his childhood on the Islands. Bulosan worked
        in the fields and describes well the plight of the agricul-
        tural worker, the Pilipino culture, and his own thoughts
        about racial intolerance.

1757   _____. Chorus for America, Six Philippine Poets. Los Angeles:
        Wagon and Star Publishers, 1942. 39p.
            Contains writings by Jose Garcia-Villa, R. Zulueta Da
        Castra, R. T. Feria, C. B. Rigo, Cecilio Baroga, and Carlos
        Bulosan.

1758   _____. The Laughter of My Father. New York: Harcourt Brace
        and Co., 1944. 193p.
            A story developed from Pilipino folk tales and myths.
        He uses his "father" as the vehicle to give these tales and
        myths a continuity.

1759   _____. Letter from America. Prairie City, Illinois: The
        Press of J. A. Decker, 1942. 68p.
            Collected poetry.

1760   _____. Sound of Falling Light: Letters in Exile. Dolores
        Feria, ed. Quezon City: n.p., 1960. 91p.
            A collection of correspondence from the noted Pilipino
        writer and poet. It provided insight of his life after
        America is in the Heart (his autobiography).

1761   _____. The Voice of Bataan. New York: Coward-McCann, Inc.,
        1943. 28p.
            A series of poems dealing with the struggles of the war
        in the Philippines. It is broken down into the components
        of the war: the Japanese soldier, the American soldier,

PILIPINO AMERICANS

(BULOSAN, CARLOS)
the Pilipino Guerrilla. A patriotic glorification of the war. Published under the auspices of the Amer-Phil Foundation, Inc.

1762   CAIGOY, FAUSTINO. Collected Poems. Sue Houghins and Penny Choy, eds. Los Angeles: Inner City Press, 1974.

1763   CARUNUNGAN, CELSO AL. Like a Big Brave Man; a novel. New York: Farrar, Straus and Cudahy, Inc., 1960. 275p.
    Light story of a Pilipino immigrant and the culture shock he faces in New York. Throughout are glimpses of Pilipino social structure and their effects on the lives of Pinoys.

1764   CASPER, LEONARD. New Writing from the Philippines: A Critique and an Anthology. Syracuse: Syracuse University Press, 1966. 411p.
    Contains a bibliography and also a checklist of Philippine literary publications in the United States from 1930 to 1965. Selections from one writings of Gonzalez, Sautos, Moreno, Torres, and Joaquin, among others.

1765   _____. The Wounded Diamond: Studies in Modern Philippine Literature. Manila: Bookmark, 1964. 152p.
    History and criticism of Philippine literature. Bibliography.

CHOY, PENNY. See 1762.

1766   DELACRUZ, RAI PHILOMATHES M. Out of Me. San Juan, Rizal: Liz publishers, 1965. 142p.
    Short stories, poems, essays, dance, drama, and letters.

1767   FANSLER, DEAN SPRUILL. Filipino Popular Tales. Hatboro, Philadelphia: Folklore Association, 1965. 473p.
    Originally published in 1921 as one of the Memoirs of the American Folklore Society. Bibliography.

1768   FERIA, BENNY. Filipino Son. Boston: Meador Publications, 1954. 234p.
    An autobiographical account.

FERIA, DOLORES S. See 1760.

1769   FUCHS, ELEANOR and JOYCE ANTLER. Year One of the Empire. Boston: Houghton Mifflin, 1973. 233p.
    A play dealing with the American-Pilipino struggle at the turn of the century. Draws parallels with the Viet Nam

(FUCHS, ELEANOR and JOYCE ANTLER)
war in terms of the type of fighting in the Philippines, the type of treatment of the Pilipinos, the anti-imperialist struggles in the U. S., and the general atmosphere in the U. S. at the time.

1770 GALDON, JOSEPH A., ed. Philippine Fiction; Essays from Philippine Studies, 1953-1972. Quezon City: Ateneo de Manila at the University Press, 1972. 242p.
Essays by leading literati about such notables as Nixk Joaquin, Gregoria Brillantes, and Bienvenido Santos.

1771 GARCIA-VILLA, JOSÉ, ed. A Doveglion Book of Philippine Poetry. Manila: Lyd Arguilla Salas, 1962. 59p.
Contains poems by Bulosan, Dato, Gonzalez, and Virginia Moreno, among others.

1772 _____. Footnote to Youth. Tales of the Philippines and Others. New York: Charles Scribner's Sons, 1933. 323p.
Short stories.

1773 _____. Have Come, Am Here. New York: The Viking Press, 1941. 152p.
Poems published about some of his American experiences.

1774 _____. Poems 55 (The Best Poems of J. G. V. as Chosen by Himself). Manila: Alberto S. Florentino, 1962. 60p.

1775 HERNANDEZ, AMADO V. Rice Grains: Selected Poems, selected and translated by E. San Juan, Jr., ed. by Nan Braymer. New York: International Publi., 1966. 64p.
Hernandez is a Pilipino hero, the poet laureate of his country. Most of these poems were written during his six years of imprisonment. Accused of being a rebel, he was subsequently acquitted by the Supreme Court of the Philippine Republic. The first poem in this book begins: "I was betrayed by an underhand agent...."

HOUCHINS, SUE. See 1762.

1776 MANUUD, ANTONIO G., ed. Brown Heritage: Essays on Philippine Cultural Tradition and Literature. Quezon City: Ateneo de Manila University Press, 1967. 885p.
A collection of essays dealing with the cultural heritage and historical roots of Philippine life: the family structure, the dances, the arts, and the folklore.

1777 PEDROCKE, CONRADO V. The Ginger Girl and Other Stories; A Book of Philippine Folk Tales. Quezon City: Phoenix Publishing House, 1966. 133p.

1778 PILIPINO American Anthology Project. A Filipino American Anthology. Los Angeles: Asian American Study Center, U. C. L. A., Fall, 1974.
An anthology, now in preparation, that will contain poetry, short stories, and interviews with Filipinos, as well as essays on the Pilipino experience in this country.

1779 RAMOS MAXIMO and FLORENTINO B. VALEROS. Philippine Harvest. Quezon City: Phoenix Publishing, 1964. 327p.
Anthology of Pilipino writings in English. The textbook used in Pilipino schools for "young" readers (aids--brief headnotes, study questions, biography of authors after each section). Writings from 1941 on.

1780 RIZAL, JOSE. The Lost Eden (Noli Me Tangere). New York: Norton, 1961. 407p.
On the surface, a romantic-type novel. But on other levels gives insight to the Spanish-Pilipino relationship and also the relation of the Catholic church in maintaining the status quo. Scathing denouncement of the church, and attacks the Spanish through the use of caricatures.

1781 _____. The Subversive: A Novel. New York: Norton, 1962. 299p.
The sequel to Noli Me Tangere (The Lost Eden).

1782 SAN JUAN, EPIFANO, JR. Carlos Bulosan and the Imagination of the Class Struggle. Quezon City: University of the Philippines Press, 1972.
Biography of Carlos Bulosan, Revolutionary expatriate; from birth on the farmland to development as Pilipino writer and poet. Examination of Bulosan's short stories, poetry, and essays.

1783 SANTOS, ALFONSO. Luvinia. Quezon City: Balfon House, 1965. 56p.
A collection of patriotic poems.

1784 SANTOS, BIENVENIDO N. Brother, My Brother. Manila: Benipayo Publishers, 1960. 244p.
Short stories reprinted from Pilipino periodicals. One of the Benipayo series on Philippine contemporary writing.

1785   SANTOS, BIENVENIDO. The Day The Dancers Came. Manila:
Bookmark, 1967. 195p.
Collected short stories. Also a one-act play and auto-
biographical essays.

1786   _____. The Volcano. Quezon City: Phoenix Publishing House,
1965. 375p.
A novel about a White doctor who goes to the Philippines
to start a hospital. Through his experiences of interac-
tion with the Pilipinos, he starts to develop an understanding of Pilipino culture and how to best deal with
that culture in his efforts to help.

1787   _____. The Wounded Stag. Manila: Capitol Publishing House,
1956. 71p.
Collected poems.

1788   _____. You Lovely People. Manila: The Benipayo Press, 1955.
155p.
A loosely connected series of short stories similar to
Tortilla Flat.

VALEROS, FLORENTINO B. See 1779.
VILLA, JOSÉ GARCIA. See 1771-1774.

1789   YABES, LEOPOLDO. Philippine Literature in English: 1898-
1957; A Bibliographical Survey. Quezon City: University
of Philippines, 1958. 343-434p.

F.   Korean Americans

1790   CHAE-YON, NO. Chae My Hanin Saryak (A Short History of
Koreans in America). Los Angeles: n.p., 1951.

1791   KANG, YOUNGHILL. East Goes West: The Making of an Oriental
Yankee. Chicago: Follett Publishing Co., 1965. 401p.
An autobiography. Reprint of 1937 edition.

1792   _____. The Grass Roof. Chicago: Follett Publishing Co.,
1966. 377p.
Reprint of 1931 edition.

1793   KIM, C. I. EUGENE and HAN-KYU KIM. Korea and the Politics of
Imperialism, 1876-1910. Berkeley: University of California
Press, 1967.

KIM, HAN-KYU. See 1793.

283

KOREAN AMERICANS

1794   KIM, RICHARD. The Innocent. Boston: Houghton Mifflin Co.,
            1968. 384p.
            Told in the first person by a Korean patriot, Major
            Lee, this is a novel about a military coup d'etat in Korea.

1795   ____. Lost Names, Scenes from a Korean Boyhood. New York:
            Praeger, 1970. 195p.
            Autobiography.

1796   ____. The Martyred. New York: George Braziller, 1964.
            316p.
            A novel which describes the deaths of twelve Christian
            ministers captured by the North Koreans.

1797   KIM, WARREN Y. (Kim Won-yong). Chaemi Hanin Osip-Nyon Sa
            (Fifty Year History of Koreans in America). Reedley,
            California: Privately published, 1959.
            This book is about Korean immigration to Hawaii and
            America primarily, although it also mentions Korean groups
            in Mexico and Cuba. It tells about refugee students, pic-
            ture brides, and workers and their religious, educational,
            organizational, and other cultural activities.

1798   KIM, YONG IK. The Shoes From Yong Son Valley. Garden City,
            New York: Doubleday and Company, Inc., 1970. 61p.
            A novel by one of the most popular novelists in Asia
            who writes in English.

1799   KOH, TAIWON. The Bitter Fruit of Kim-Pown. Philadelphia:
            The John C. Winston Co., 1959. 148p.

1800   LEE, CHONG-SIK. The Politics of Korean Nationalism.
            Berkeley: University of California Press, 1963. 342p.
            The history of the Korean nationalist movement in the
            United States as well as in China, Korea, and Japan is
            presented in this detailed book.

        WON-YONG, KIM. See 1797.

Author/Title Index

A

Abaya, H., 1722, 1723
Aberle, S., 209
Abraham, H., 61
Abramson, M., 967
Acosta, A., 861
Acosta, O., 862, 863
Adair, J., 611, 663
Adams, A., 1640
Adams, B., 1561
Adams, G., 262
Adler, B., 1213, 1214, 1215
Adoff, A., 1216
Adorno, T. W., 62
ABC: Americans Before Columbus, 172
Agcaoli, T., 1754
Agoncillo, T., 1724, 1725, 1726, 1743
Ai, L., 1581, 1699
Aion, 1500
Akwesasne Notes, 173
Alcheringa, 174
Alexander, H., 303, 304
Alfonso, O., 1727
Alford, H., 666
Alhamisi, A., 1217
Allen, A., 121
Allen, Henry, 497
Allen, Hervey, 438
Allen, R., 1666
Allen, S., 706
Allen, T., 305, 547
Allen, Terry, 439
Allport, G., 63
Altman, R., 798
Altus, 671

Alurista. See 949, 950
Alworth, E., 440
Amerasia Journal, 1501
American Council on Education, 799
American Friends Service Committee, 197
American Indian, The, 175
American Indian Education, 132
American Indian Historical Society, 133, 292, 306, 441
American Indian Law Review, 176
American Indian Media Directory, 135
American Indians, 134
American Negro. See 1007
Amerindian, 177
Amsden, C., 612
Anaya, R., 864
Anderson, A., 1218, 1219
Anderson, D., 64
Anderson, J., 365
Anderson, Marian, 1220
Anderson, Maxwell, 865
Anderson, T., 800
Anderson-Imbert, E., 866
Andrew, M., 867
Andrews, R., 613, 442
Andrist, R., 198
Ang Katipunan, 1718
Angelou, M., 1221
Anthony, E., 1108
Antler, J., 1769
Applegate, F., 307
Appleton, L., 614
Aptheker, H., 1041, 1042, 1043
Arciniega, T., 669
Armer, L., 443

Armstrong, L., 1222
Armstrong, V., 444
Arnold, E., 445, 868
Art in America, 615
Asian Woman's Journal, 1502
Astrov, M., 446
Athearn, R., 199
Atherton, G., 1582
Atisbos: Journal of Chicano
  Research, 700
Attaway, W., 1223, 1224
Auerbach, F., 17, 1514
Ausby, E., 1468
Austin, L., 1044
Austin, M., 447, 448
Aztlan: Chicano Journal of the
  Social Sciences and the Arts,
  701

B

Babcock, C., 449
Baca, E., 883
Bad Heart Bull, A., 616
Baerreis, D., 293
Bahnimptewa, C., 664
Bahr, H., 308
Bailey, L., 200
Bailey, P., 1613
Baird, W., 450
Baker, B., 707
Baker, H., 1225
Baker, R., 65, 1045
Baldwin, J., 1122, 1226, 1227,
  1228, 1229, 1230, 1231, 1232,
  1233
Ballard, L., 309
Ballis, G., 708
Bancroft, G., 1655
Bancroft, H., 201, 709, 1538
Bandelier, A., 310, 710
Banks, C., 29
Banks, J., 18, 1162, 1163
Bannon, J., 711
Baratz, J., 1164
Barbour, F., 1171
Barker, G., 814
Barnes, N., 451
Barnhart, E., 1478, 1636
Barrett, S., 501
Barrios, E., 672
Barrios, R., 869

Barron, M., 19
Barrow, M., 136
Barrows, W., 202
Barth, G., 1539
Bartlett, J., 712
Barton, R., 1234
Barzun, J., 66
Bass, A., 590
Bayitch, S., 713, 959
Bayley, D., 20
Beadle, J., 203
Beal, M., 204
Beals, R., 801
Beck, W., 714
Beck, W., 715
Beckworth, J., 1235
Bedford, D., 452
Bedinger, M., 617
Belous, R., 618
Belting, N., 453, 454
Benedict, R., 311, 1641
Bengelsdorf, W., 1
Bennett, K., 455
Bennett, L., 1047
Bercow, L., 137
Berg, I., 21
Berger, T., 456
Berle, B., 968
Berrigan, P., 457
Berry, B., 67, 294, 312
Berton, P., 1515
Bettelheim, B., 68
Bibliographic Survey: The Negro
  in Print, 1008, 1030
Bierhorst, J., 458, 459
Binstock, R., 69
Black Elk, 317, 553
Black Hawk, 460
Black Information Index, 1031
Black Scholar, The: Journal of
  Black Studies and Research, 1032
Black Studies. See 1048, 1165
Blalock, H. M., Jr., 70
Blauner, R., 22, 71
Blaustein, A., 1049
Blawis, 716
Blish, H., 616
Boas, F., 72, 73, 313, 314, 315
Boatright, M., 815, 825
Bogardus, E., 717
Boggs, J., 1050
Boles, R., 1236, 1237

Bolling, P., 146
Bolton, H., 718, 719, 720
Bone, R., 1238
Bonner, T., 1235
Bonnerjea, B., 138
Bontemps, A., 1051, 1052, 1239, 1240, 1241, 1328, 1352
Borland, H., 461
Bosworth, A., 1614
Boulware, M., 1053
Bourke, J., 205
Boyar, B., 1282
Boyar, J., 1282
Boyce, G., 206
Boyd, W., 74
Boyer, M., 800
Bradshaw, B., 25
Brand, H., 969
Brandon, W., 207, 208, 462
Brant, C., 606
Bravo, E., 960
Brawley, B., 1242, 1243, 1244
Braymer, N., 1775
Brazier, A., 1054
Breitman, G., 1055, 1117, 1118, 1150
Brewer, J., 1245
Bridge, 1503
Briedberg, B., 1201
Brigham Young University, 139
Bright, R., 870
Brink, W., 1056
Brinton, D., 316, 463
Broderick, F., 1057
Brody, J., 619
Brooks, A., 1009
Brooks, G., 1246, 1247
Brophy, W., 209
Brotz, H., 1058
Brown, Cecil, 1248
Brown, Claude, 1249
Brown, D., 210
Brown, E., 148
Brown, F., 75, 1250
Brown, H., 1011
Brown, J., 317
Brown, R., 1021
Brown, S., 1251, 1252, 1253
Brown, T., 1059
Brown, V., 318
Brown, Warren W., 1010
Brown, William, 1254, 1308

Bruggs, D., 142
Brussell, C., 802
Bryant, E., 871
Bryde, J., 319
Buaken, M., 1755
Bucchioni, E., 963, 974
Buck, P., 1656
Buckingham, J., 976
Buffalo Bill. See 560
Bulletin of the Bureau of American Ethnology, 178
Bulletin of Concerned Asian Scholars, 1504
Bullins, E., 1255, 1256
Bulosan, C., 1756, 1757, 1758, 1759, 1760, 1761
Bunzel, R., 320
Burger, H., 673
Burma, J., 667, 816
Burnette, R., 211
Burroughs, M., 1435
Burrows, D., 97
Burrows, E., 1700
Burt, J., 212
Busch, N., 464
Bustamente, C., 721
Bustamente, P., 721
Butcher, M., 1257

C

Cabello, 677
Cahn, E., 213
Caigoy, F., 1762
California Legislature, 1540
California State College Sacramento, 674
California State Library Quarterly, 2
Californians of Spanish Surname, 668
Calloway, S., 321, 517
Camarillo, A., 874
Campa, A., 817, 818
Campbell, D., 98
Campbell, J., 322
Campbell, M., 465
Capote, T., 466
Capps, B., 467
Cardona-Hine, A., 872
Carlson, V., 468
Carmichael, S., 1060

Carpenter, E., 624
Carranza, E., 722
Carrillo, L., 873
Carson, J., 1258
Carter, T., 803
Carunungan, C., 1763
Carver, G., 1259
Casas, B., 214, 237, 723
Caselli, R., 3
Cash, J., 469
Cash, W., 1172
Caskey, O., 804
Casper, L., 1764, 1765
Castaneda, C., 724, 819, 820, 821
Castillo, G., 675
Castillo, P., 874
Caswell, H., 323
Cather, W., 470, 875
Catlin, G., 620, 621
Cattell, S., 1562
Cayton, H., 1260
Ceremonial Indian Book Service
   Order Catalog, 140
Chae-yon, N., 1789
Chalmers, H., 551
Chan, C., 1583
Chan, J., 1516
Chan, M., 1583
Chang, D., 1584
Chanimun, 349
Chapman, A., 1261, 1262
Charters, 1173
Charyn, J., 1657
Chavez, C., 916
Chavez, F., 876
Chee, H., 324
Chenault, L., 970
Chennault, A., 1585
Cherokee Executive Committee,
   215
Chesnutt, C., 1263, 1264
Chicano, The, 725
Chicano Coordinating Council on
   Higher Education, 805
Chicano Law Review, 702
Chicano Poetry Anthology, 877
Chief Joseph, 204, 514
Chin, F., 1516
Chinese-American School and
   Community Problems, 1563
Chinn, T., 1541
Chisholm, S., 1265

Chiu, P., 1542
Chona, M., 471
Chou, C., 1586
Choy, Penny, 1762
Choy, Philip, 1548
Christy, A., 1517
Chu, D., 1543
Chu, L., 1577
Chu, S., 1543
Chung, H., 1518
Clark, A., 472
Clark, E., 325
Clarke, J., 1266, 1267, 1268
Clark, K., 1132, 1174
Clark, L., 326
Clark, M., 822
Clark y Moreno, J., 676
Cleaver, E., 1061, 1269
Clemens, S., 1460
Clemente, II, W., 1744
Cline, H., 726
Clissold, S., 727
Cobbs, P., 1188
Cochise, 468
Coffin, T., 327
Cohen, F., 216, 217
Cohen, Leonard, 473
Cohen, Lucy, 217
Cohoe, W., 622
Coleman, J., 23
Cole, M., 971
Coles, R., 878, 728
Colón, J., 972
Collard, A., 214
Collier, D., 623
Collier, J., 218, 219
Collins, H., 624
Colman, E., 1564
Colter, C., 1270
Colton, H., 625
Commonwealth of Puerto Rico, 961
Cone, J., 1175, 1176
Conference on California Indian
   Education, 295
Conot, R., 1062
Conrat, M., 1642
Conrat, R., 1642
Conroy, H., 1615
Conroy, J., 1051
Con Safos, 703
Constantino, R., 1745, 1746, 1728

Constitutional Convention, 962, 1952
Cook, M., 1271
Coolidge, D., 879
Coolidge, M., 1544
Cooper, J., 474
Cooper, P., 973
Copeland, A., 239
Cordasco, F., 963, 974
Corle, E., 475, 880
Cornplanter, J., 328
Correll, J., 141, 142
Cortes, E., 881
Costo, R., 329
Council on Interracial Books for Children, 220
Courlander, H., 1177
Coustoki, V., 478
Covarrubias, M., 626
Covello, L., 975
Cowan, R. E., 1479, 1480
Cowan, R. G., 1479
Cox, A., 76, 1063
Cox, O., 77
Cox, W., 882
Craig, R., 729
Crane, E., 1215
Crashing Thunder, 476
Crazy Horse. See 581
Crichton, K., 883, 884
Cronon, E., 1272
Cronyn, G., 477
Crook, G., 221, 479
Cross, T., 1064
Crowe, C., 1065
Crow-Wing, 480
Cruse, H., 1066, 1178
Cruz, N., 976
Cruz, V., 977, 978
Cuellar, A., 730
Cuero, D., 481
Cullen, C., 1273, 1274, 1275, 1276
Curtin, P., 1067
Curtis, E., 613, 627
Curtis, G., 1616
Curtis, N., 330
Cushman, D., 482
Custer, E., 483
Custer, G., 483, 484

D

Daly, V., 1277
Dana, R., 885
Daniels, R., 78, 1617, 1618
Daves, F., 485
David, J., 486
Davis, Angela, 1068
Davis, Arthur, 1251, 1278
Davis, B., 1279
Davis, B., 487
Davis, C., 1280
Davis, D., 143
Davis, James, 886
Davis, John, 1012
Davis, O., 1281
Davis, S., 1282
Dawdy, D., 144
Daws, G., 1701
Day, A., 488
Day, D., 887
Day, M., 731
De Angulo, J., 489
Debo, A., 222, 223
De Bry, T., 644
DeCarava, R., 1179
Deetz, J., 395
Delacruz, R., 1766
De la Garza, R., 669
De Laguna, F., 624
Delany, M., 1283
Delgado, A., 732, 733
Delgado, M., 1284
Deloria, E., 331
Deloria, V., 224, 225, 226, 227, 332
Demarest, D., 1285
Demby, W., 1286, 1287
Denetsosie, 517
De Tocqueville, A., 79
De Villagra, G., 888
De Voto, B., 734
Dezba, 572
D'Harnoncourt, R., 629
Dickey, R., 823
Dickson, L., 490
Dillard, J., 1166
Dillon, R., 1565
Diné Baa-Hani, 179
Dinnerstein, L., 80
Disch, R., 119
Dixon, J., 491

Dixon, T., 1069, 1070
Dobie, J., 333, 824, 825, 826, 827
Dockstader, F., 334, 628
Dodge, R., 538
Dodson, O., 1288
Dooley, E., 979
Dorson, R., 1289
Dossick, J., 964
Douglas, F., 629, 1433
Dover, C., 1180
Doyle, C., 1588
Dozier, E., 335
Drimmer, M., 1071
Drinnon, R., 515
Driver, H., 336
Drothing, P., 1290
Dubois, W. E. B., 1072, 1073, 1074, 1154, 1181, 1291, 1292, 1293, 1294, 1295, 1444
Dufty, W., 1347
Dunbar, P., 1296, 1297, 1298, 1299
Dunlop, B., 1480
Dunn, D., 630
Dunne, J., 735
Duran, P., 677
Durham, P., 1075
Duster, T., 71
Dutton, B., 337
Dyk, W., 529

E

Early American, 180
Eastlake, W., 492
Eastman, C., 338, 493
East/West, 1505
Eaton, A., 1643
Ebony, 1013, 1033
Eckstein, G., 1658
Edmiston, J., 1659
Eggan, F., 339
Ehle, J., 980
Elder, L., 1300
Elder, P., 736
El Grito, 704
Elizondo, S., 889
Elkins, S., 1076
Elliott, L., 1670
Ellis, R., 228
Ellis, W., 110

Ellison, R., 1301, 1302
Ely, K., 69
Emanuel, J., 1303
Embree, E., 229
Embrey, S., 1660
Enloe, C., 24
Equiano, O., 1462
Erdoes, R., 230, 528
Erikson, E., 340
Espinel, L., 828
Espinos, G., 888
Espinosa, J., 829
Essien-Udom, E., 1077
Evans, M., 1304
Ewers, J., 631

F

Factor, R., 1182
Faderman, L., 25, 935
Fager, C., 1078
Fair, R., 1305, 1306
Fairbairn, A., 1307
Fairbank, J., 1545
Fairchild, H., 494
Fansler, D., 1767
Farb, P., 341
Farmer, G., 296, 1519
Farrison, W., 1308
Faulk, O., 737
Fauset, J., 1309, 1310
Feather, L., 1183
Federal Field Committee, 231
Feikema, F., 540
Feldman, S., 342
Feldstein, S., 81
Feltskog, E., 263
Fenderson, L., 1044
Fenn, W., 1589
Fenton, J., 981
Fenton, W., 343
Ferber, E., 890
Feder, N., 632
Ferguson, B., 1311
Ferguson, R., 212
Fergusson, E., 344, 738, 830
Fergusson, H., 495, 739, 891, 892
Feria, B., 1768
Feria, D., 1760
Fernandez-Florea, D., 740
Fey, H., 232
Fiedler, L., 496

Filipino-American Herald, 1719, 1720
Finerty, J., 233
Fischer, A., 395
Fisher, A., 1619
Fisher, C., 497
Fisher, M., 1016
Fisher, R., 1312
Fisher, V., 498
Fishman, J., 982
Fitzpatrick, J., 983
Fletcher, A., 345
Fogel, W., 741
Folsom, F., 633
Foner, P., 1079
Forbes, H., 831
Forbes, J., 26, 234, 235, 346, 742, 806
Ford, C., 559
Ford, N., 1313
Foreman, G., 236, 499, 893
Fortuine, R., 136
Foster, J., 894
Fourth World, 27
Fox, D., 1095
Franklin, J., 82, 1080
Frazier, E., 1081, 1082, 1184, 1185, 1186, 1187
Frazier, T., 28
Frederick, C., 347
Frederickson, G., 1083
Freedman, M., 29
Freedman, J., 145
Freedomways, 1034
Frenkel-Brunswik, E., 62
Fresno State Library, 678
Friar, N., 500
Friar, R., 500
Friede, J., 237
Friedman, E., 1520
Frink, M., 634
Fuchs, E., 297, 1769
Fuchs, L., 1702
Fujimoto, I., 71, 1481
Fujita, J., 1661
Fukuzawa, Y., 1662
Fusco, P., 743

G

Gaines, E., 1314, 1315, 1316
Galantière, L., 569

Galarza, E., 744, 745, 746, 747, 895, 896
Galdon, J., 1770
Gallen, A., 897
Gallegnos, H., 745
Gamio, M., 748, 898, 899
Garcia, G., 832
Garcia-Villa, J., 1771, 1772, 1773, 1774
Gardner, R., 749
Garner, C., 900
Garvey, M., 1099, 1272
Gayle, A., 1317, 1318
Gearing, F., 348
Genovese, E., 1084
Geronimo, Sol. See also 487.
Gerould, K., 901
Getting Together, 1506
Gidra, 1507
Gilbreath, K., 238
Gildner, G., 502
Gillham, C., 349
Gillmor, F., 503
Gilpin, L., 635, 750
Giovanni, N., 1319, 1320
Girdner, A., 1620
Glick, C., 1590
Glide Urban Center, 1566
Glasrud, B., 30
Glass, P., 350
Glazer, N., 83
Glock, C., 84
Goldsen, R., 993
Gomez, D., 751
Gomez-Q., J., 679
Gonzales, N., 1729
Gonzales, R., 902
Gonzalez, N., 752
Goodman, B., 1116
Gordon, M., 85
Gordon, S., 239
Gorman, H., 903
Gossett, T., 86
Graff, H., 1730
Grant, J., 1085
Grant, M., 87, 1086
Gray, F., 1703
Grebler, L., 753, 754
Greene, A., 504
Greenlee, S., 1321
Gregg, E., 505
Gregory, D., 1322

Grey Owl, 490
Gridley, M., 506, 507, 508
Grier, W., 1188
Griffis, J., 351, 509
Griffith, B., 833
Griggs, S., 1097, 1323, 1324, 1325
Griggs, V., 1591
Grinnell, G., 240, 352
Grodzins, M., 1621
Gropp, A., 680
Gross, S., 1326
Gross, T., 1303
Gruskin, A., 1566
Guerrero, A., 1731
Guerrero, M., 1743
Guie, H., 387
Gulick, S., 1622
Gutierrez, J., 755
Guzman, M., 904
Guzman, R., 681, 753

H

Haddox, J., 756
Hagan, W., 241, 242
Haines, F., 353
Hale, H., 354
Haley, A., 1399
Hall, E., 31
Hallenbeck, C., 834
Halsell, G., 510
Hamberg, J., 32
Hamilton, C., 1060
Hammon, B., 1327
Hammond, G., 757
Handlin, O., 33, 88
Handy, W., 1328
Hanke, L., 355, 758
Hannay, A., 137
Hannum, A., 511, 512
Hansberry, L., 1329, 1330, 1331
Hansen, Arthur, 1623
Hansen, Asael, 1635
Hansen, G., 1482
Harding, A., 146
Hardy, J., 1326
Hargrett, L., 147
Harkins, A., 148, 149
Harris, C., 1470
Harris, L., 1056
Harsha, J., 513

Harte, B., 1610
Hartmann, S., 1663, 1664
Harvard University, 356
Harvey, B., 636
Harwood, E., 1201
Haslam, G., 34
Hatano, Ichiro, 1665
Hatano, Isoki, 1665
Hatsumi, R., 1666
Haug, M., 860
Havinghurst, R., 297
Hawaii Pono Journal, 1508
Hawkins, H., 1088
Hayden, R., 1332
Haywood, C., 150, 1014
Heath, G., 35
Heathman, J., 682
Heins, M., 759
Heintz, W., 1482
Heizer, R., 36, 357, 642
Heller, C., 835, 836
Helm, J., 837
Hemos Trabajado Bien, 670, 984
Henderson, A., 838
Henderson, G., 1333
Henderson, S., 1271, 1334
Henefrund, H., 1483
Henry, J., 298
Henson, J., 1335
Henson, M., 1336
Hentoff, N., 1089, 1167
Hernandez, A., 1775
Hernandez, D., 121, 839
Hernandez, J., 949
Hernandez, L., 840
Hernandez, W., 808
Hernandez-Alvarez, J., 985
Hernton, C., 1090, 1091
Hersey, J., 1092
Herskovits, M., 1093, 1094
Hertzberg, H., 243
Heyward, D., 1337
Herzog, S., 37
Higham, J., 89
Hill, H., 1338, 1339
Hill, M., 965
Hilton, R., 683
Himes, C., 1340, 1341, 1342, 1343, 1344, 1345, 1346
Hirschfelder, A., 151
Hispanic Society of America, 684
Hodge, F., 358

Hoebel, E., 622
Holder, P., 313, 402
Holiday, B., 1347
Holt, J., 1704
Hoover, H., 469
Horgan, P., 38, 760, 761, 762
Horka-Follick, 841
Horner, V., 41, 807
Horsman, R., 244
Horwitz, G., 743
Hosokawa, B., 1644, 1698
Houchins, S., 1762
Hough, J., 1189
Houston, James, 1667
Houston, Jeanne, 1667
Howard, J., 1201
Howard, H., 514
Howard, J., 39
Howe, M., 76, 1063
Howling Wolf , 637, 665
Hoy, W., 1568
Hoyt, O., 245
Hruskay Cortes, E., 905
Hsu, F., 1569, 1570
Hsu, K., 1521
Huebner, J., 152
Huerta, J., 685
Huggins, N., 1095, 1348
Hughes, J., 1349
Hughes, L., 1096, 1179, 1350,
    1351, 1352, 1353, 1354, 1355,
    1356, 1357, 1358, 1359
Huie, K., 1592
Hull, E., 1668
Humphrey, N., 801
Hunt, W., 638
Hunt, Wolf, 359
Hunter, J., 515
Hunter, K., 1360, 1361
Hurston, Z., 1362, 1363, 1364,
    1365, 1366
Hutchinson, H., 1450
Hyde, P., 639

I

Ichihashi, Y., 1645
Ichioka, Y., 1484
Icolari, D., 155
Igauer, E., 360
Inada, L., 1516, 1669

Indian Affairs, 181
Indian Education, 182
Indian Historian, 183
Indian Law Reporter, 184
Indigena, 185
Inouye, D., 1670, 1705
International Library of Negro
    Life and History, 1015
International Migration Review, 14
Inverarity, R., 640
Iriye, A., 1522, 1624, 1625, 1626
Irvine, K., 153
Irving, W., 516
Irwin, W., 1671
Isaacs, E., 1367
Ishi, 524
Ishigaki, A., 1679
Ishigo, E., 1646
Ishimoto, S., 1672
Iwamatsu, J., 1696

J

Jackson, Bruce, 1368
Jackson, Donald, 460
Jackson, George, 1097
Jackson, George, 1098
Jackson, Helen Hunt, 246, 906,
    1571
Jacobs, A. Gertrude, 1572
Jacobs, Paul, 90
Jacobs, Paul, 40
Jacques-Gravey, Amy, 1099
Jaher, Frederic Cople, 80
Jalee, Pieree, 91
James, Charles L., 1369
Janowitz, Morris, 68
Jenkinson, Michael, 763
Jessey, Cornelia, 907
Jett, Stephen C., 639
Joans, Ted, 1370
Jacano, Brenda F., 1747
John, Vera P., 41, 807
Johnson, Broderick H., 517
Johnson, Edward Augustus, 1371
Johnson, Henry Sioux, 808
Johnson, Jack, 1372
Johnson, James Weldon, 1190, 1373,
    1374, 1375
Johnson, John J., 686
Johnson, J. Rosamond, 1190

Jones, Helen D., 1497
Jones, Helsie, 518
Jones, James M., 92
Jones, LeRoi, 1191, 1192, 1376, 1377, 1378, 1379, 1380, 1381, 1382
Jones, Louis Thomas, 519
Jordan, Lois B., 687
Jordan, Winthrop, 1100
Jorgensen, Joseph G., 361
Josephy, Alvin M., Jr., 247, 362, 520
Journal of American Folklore, 154
Journal of American Indian Education, 186
Journal of Afro-American Issues, The, 1035
Journal of Black Studies, 1036
Journal of Negro Education, The, 1037
Journal of Ethnic Studies, The, 15
Journal of Negro History, The, 1038
Jung, E., 1485

K

Kagan, Richard C., 1545
Kahn, Si, 93
Kane, Michael B., 42, 94
Kaneko, Hizakazu, 1673
Kang, Younghill, 1790, 1791
Kappler, Charles J., 248
Katz, William Loren, 1101, 1102, 1103
Kawakami, K., 74, 1627
Kearns, Francis E., 1383
Keating, C., 4
Keckley, E., 1384
Keen, Benjamin, 237
Keesing's Research Report, 111
Kehoe, K., 75
Keil, C., 1193
Keiser, A., 521
Kelley, W. M., 1358, 1386, 1387
Kellogg, C. F., 1104
Kelly, L. C., 249
Kiev, Ari, 842
Kikuch, C., 76

Killens, J. O., 1388, 1389
Killian, L. M., 1105
Kilpatrick, A. G., 363, 522
Kilpatrick, Jack Frederick, 363, 364, 522
Kilson, M., 1095
Kim, C. I. Eugene, 1792
Kim, Han-kyu, 1792
Kim, R., 1793, 1794, 1795
Kim, Warren Y., 1796
Kim, Yong Ik., 1797
Kimball, Y., 365
King, Charles B., 641
King, C., 1390
King, M. L., 1106, 1107
King, W., 1108, 1391
Kirkland, E., 908
Kitagawa, Kaisuke, 1628
Kitano, H., 78, 1485, 1532, 1647
Kitt, E., 1392
Kiyooka, E., 1662
Klah, Hosteen, 556
Klein, B., 155
Klein, W., 986
Kluckhohn, Clyde, 366, 367
Kluckhohn, C., 368
Kluckhohn, L. W., 36
KNBC, 764
Knight, E., 1393
Knowles, L. L., 95, 1109
Knor, Russell L., 152
Knox, G., 1663
Koen, R. Y., 1545
Kofsky, F., 1194
Koh, T., 1798
Kohl, H., 1168
Koisumi, K., 77
Konvitz, M. R., 1523
Kopit, A., 523
Korea Focus, 1509
Koster, John, 211
Kovel, J., 96
Kozol, J., 1169
Kroeber, A. L., 369
Kroeber, T., 370, 524
Kroeber, Theodore, 642
Kronus, S., 1195
Kruszewski, Z. A., 669
Kung, S., 1547
Kunitz, Stephen J., 377
Kuo, C., 1593
Kuo, H., 1593

Kuykendall, R., 1706

L

LaBarre, W., 371
Labov, W., 43
La Farge, O., 250, 525
Lafferty, R. A., 526
La Flesche, F., 527
La Flesche, S., 608
Laguerre, E., 987
Lai, H. M., 1548
Lamb, F. W., 643
Lamdin, L., 1285
Lame Deer, 528
Lancester, C., 1629
Landau, S., 40, 90
Lange, D. and P. T., 765
Lanham, C., 1630
Lapides, F. R., 97
Larsen, Nella, 1394
Larson, Nellie G., 137
Lasker, B., 1748
Laski, Vera, 372
Lauritzen, J., 909
Lavine, S. S., 373
Lawrence, D. H., 910
Lawton, H. M., 1663
Lea, Tom, 911, 912
Leacock, E. B., 374
Leckie, W. H., 1110
Lee, C., 1573
Lee, Ch., 1594, 1595
Lee, Chong, 1799
Lee, D. L., 1395, 1396
Lee, J., 1596
Lee, R. H., 1549
Lee, U. C., 1251
Lee, V. Ch., 1597
Left Handed, 529
Lehmann, Herman, 504
Leighton, A. H., 1631
Leighton, Alexander H., 375
Leighton, Dorothea, 366, 367, 375
Le Moyne, Jacques, 644
Leonard, I. A., 786
Leong, Cor. Y., 1574
Lerner, Gerde, 1196
Lerrigo, Marion O., 1680
Lester, J., 1111, 1112, 1397
Levine, R. A., 98

Levine, S., 376
Levinson, D. J., 62
Levi-Strauss, C., 99
Levy, Eugene, 1398
Levy, J. E., 377
Lewis, A., 530
Lewis, M., 251
Lewis, O., 988, 989
Lewis, Richard, 531
Lewis, S., 1197
Liberty, M., 589
Liberty, M., 532
Liebow, E., 1198
Light, I., 1524
Lightfoot, C. M., 1113
Lighthall, J. I., 378
Limbaugh, R. H., 533
Lin, A., 1598
Lin, Anor, 1598, 1600
Lin Family, 1599
Lin, T., 1601
Lin, Y., 1575, 1576, 1602
Lincoln, C. E., 1114, 1115
Lind, A., 1707
Linderman, F. B., 567
Link, M. S., 379
Lipsyte, R., 1322
Little, M., 1399
Little, M., 1055, 1116, 1117, 1118
Littlejohn, D., 1400
Litwack, L. F., 1145
Liu, K., 1986
Lloyd, H. M., 258
Locke, A. L., 1199, 1257
Locke, Alain, 1401
Loewen, J. W., 1550
Loftis, A., 1620
Lomax, A., 1402
Lomax, L. E., 1119, 1200
Lone-Dog, L., 534
Longfellow, H. W., 535
Lopez, A., 990
Lo, S. E., 1487
Lorant, S., 644
Los Angeles Superintendent of Schools Office, 5
Lott, M., 536
Lowe, P., 1603
Lowenfels, W., 44, 45
Lowie, R. H., 380

Lowry, A., 537
Ludwig, E., 913
Lum, W. W., 1488, 1489
Lummis, C. F., 914
Luomale, K., 1635
Lurie, N. O., 374, 376, 552
Lyman, S. M., 1525
Lynas, L., 156

M

Macebuk, S., 1403
Mack, R., 101
MacLeish, A., 915
Madsen, W., 844
Magusson, M., 253
Mahood, R. I., 660
Major, C., 1202, 1409
Major, M., 47
Malcolm X., 1055, 1116, 1117, 1118
Mallery, G., 647
Manfred, F., 540
Manlapit, P., 1732
Mannix, D. P., 1121
Manuel, H. T., 809
Manuud, A., 1776
Many Smokes, 187
Mar, K., 1527
Marden, C., 102
Maria, 542
Marquis, A., 158
Marquis, T., 541
Marriott, A., 381
Marriott, A., 382, 542
Marshall, G., 770
Marshall, P., 1410, 1411
Martin, R. G., 1678
Martinez, Cecilia J., 682
Martinez, J., 768
Marx, H. L., 254
Masson, M., 422
Matthews, J., 255, 383, 543
Matilla, A., 991
Matsuda, M., 1491
Matsui, H., 1679
Matsuoka, Y., 1671
Matthews, W., 384
Matsumoto, T., 1680
Matthiessen, P., 916

May, E., 1528
May, W., 1604
Maycroon, C., 992
Mayfield, J., 1412
Maykovich, M., 1648
Mayokuk, R., 323
Mays, B., 1413
McClellan, R., 1551
McCracken, H., 645
McCutcheon, J. M., 1690
McKay, C., 1404, 1405, 1406, 1407, 1408
McCord, W., 1201
McKitrick, E. L., 1120
McLeod, A., 1577
McCullough, J. B., 538
McGinnis, D., 558
McLean, R., 46
McLean, R. E., 414
McLuhan, T. C., 646
McMaster, J. B., 251
McNickle, D., 232, 252
McNichols, C. L., 539
McWilliams, C., 100, 766, 767, 843, 1526, 1632
Mead, M., 385
Mead, M., 1122
Means, F. C., 1682
Meier, A., 1057, 1124
Meier, A., 1123
Meier, M. S., 688
Meier, M. S., 689, 769
Meinig, D. W., 256
Melendy, H. B., 1529
Meltzer, N., 1125
Memmi, A., 103
Mendelsohn, H., 20
Mendes, Richard H. P., 6
Meriwether, L., 1414
Metcalf, G. R., 1415
Meyer, G., 102
Meyer, William, 257
Michener, J., 1708
Miller, D., 1416
Miller, A., 652
Miller, E. K., 845
Miller, E. W., 1016
Miller, L., 1126
Miller, M., 648
Miller, S., 1552

Mills, C. W. S., 993
Milton, J., 544
Milton, J. R., 545, 546
Minor, M., 649
Mishina, S., 1683
Mitchell, E. B., 647
Mitchell, M., 1417a
Mitchell, L., 1417
Mitson, B. E., 1623
Mittelbach, F., 770
Mottelbach, F., 771
Miyakawa, T. S., 1615
Miyamoto, K., 1709
Momaday, N. S., 548, 549, 550
Montagu, A., 104, 105, 106, 107
Monture, E. B., 551
Moody, A., 1418
Mody, A. B., 917
Mooney, J., 386
Moore, J., 730, 753
Moore, Joan W., 771
Moore, T. E., 772
Moquin, W., 773
Morais, H. M., 1203
Morales, A., 774
Morales, R., 1733
Mori, Toshio, 1684
Morgan, L., 258
Morin, R., 918
Morrison, J. C., 994
Mountain, W. W., 552
Mouring, D., 387
Moustafa, A. T., 846
Moynihan, D. P., 3
Munoz, A. N., 1740
Murdock, G. P., 159
Murieta, J., 927
Murokawa, M., 108
Murphey, E. V. A., 388
Murphy, J. M., 775
Muse, B., 1128
Myer, Dillon S., 1633
Myrdal, G., 1129

N

Nabakov, Peter, 597, 776
Nammack, G. C., 259
Nash, G. B., 109
Nash, C., 260
Nason, T. C., 948

National Advisory Committee on
    Farm Labor, 777
National Advisory Council on
    Indian Education, 299
National Conference on Educational
    Opportunities for Mexican Ameri-
    cans, 810
National Council for the Social
    Studies, 49
National Directory of Spanish
    Surname Elected Officials, 778
National Education Association of
    the United States, 811
National Education Association,
    1017
National Educational Task Force
    della Raza, 812
Navajo Times, The, 188
National Urban Coalition, 48
Nava, J., 779, 780, 781
Navajo Treaty, 261
Navarro, E., 690
Navarro, J. L., 919
Navarro Jovina, 1750
NCAI Sentinel, The, 189
Nee, B., 1578
Nee, Victor G., 1578
Negro American Literature Forum,
    1018
Neihardt, J. G., 553, 554, 555
Nelson, Eugene, 782, 920, 1734
Nelson, Sophia P., 1044
Nequatewa, E., 389
Nettl, B., 390, 921
Newberry Library, 160
Newby, Tidus, 1130
New China, 1510
Newcomb, F. J., 324, 556
Newland, S., 557
Newlon, C., 922
Newman, K. D., 50, 51
Newman, P., 783
New York Magazine, 995
New York Public Library, 1019,
    1020
Ng, Pearl, 1492
Nicholas, A. X, 1419
Nichols, R. L., 262
Niethamer, C., 391
Nimura, T. F., 1493
Nishimoto, R. S., 1638

Niswalder, J., 136
Neal, Larry, 1376
Nogales, L. G., 691
Noguchi, Y., 1685, 1686, 1687
Norbeck, E., 1751
Norfolk, P. B., 1420
North, D. S., 784
Nowell, C. J., 559

O

Oakes, M., 322
Oakes, Vanya, 1605
O'Connor, R., 560
Odo, Franklin, 1533
Ofari, E., 1131
Ogawa, D. M., 1634
Ohiyesa, 493
Okada, J., 1688
Okimoto, D., 1689
Okubo, M., 1649, 1650
Old Mexican, 561
Oliver, P., 1204
Opler, M. K., 1635
Orleans, P., 110
Ortego, P. D., 923
Ortiz, Alfonso, 392, 393
Osborn, L. R., 161
Oskison, J. M., 562
Oswalt, Wendell II, 394
Ota, S. A. N., 1690
Owen, Guy, 563
Owen, Robert C., 395
Owl, Ms. Samson, 396

P

Padilla, E., 996
Palou, F., 924
Palsson, H., 253
Palubinskas, H., 1521
Panger, D., 1421
Paredes, A., 847, 848, 859
Paredes, A., 925
Peredes, R., 925
Park, No-Yong, 1606
Parker, A. C., 397, 398, 564
Parkman, F., 263
Parks, Gordon, 1422, 1423
Parsons, E. C., 309
Parsons, T., 1132
Patterson, Lindsay, 1424, 1425

Payne, J. A., 1426
Pearce, T. M., 47
Paytiamo, J., 565
Paz, Octavio, 849
Pearce, Roy H., 566
Pedrocke, C. V., 1777
Peek, W., 580
Pell, Eva, 40
Pendleton, M., 650
People v. Hall, 1553
Perez, Raymundo, 926
Perrigo, Lynn, 785
Peterkin, J., 1427
Peterson, K. D., 622, 637
Peterson, W., 1651
Petry, Ann, 1428
Petry, A. L., 1429, 1430, 1431
Philippine News, 1721
Phinney, A., 400
Phylon: Review of Race and
  Culture, 1039
Picon-Sakas, M., 786
Pietroforte, A., 401
Pilipino A. A. P., 1778
Pinkney, A., 1205
Pitchlyn, Peter, 450
Pitt, Leonard, 850
Pleasants, H., 1206
Plenty-Coups, 567
Ploski, H. C., 1021
Pokagon, S., 568
Pomeroy, William, 1735
Poncins, G. de., 569
Porter, D. B., 1022, 1023
Potts, A. M., 7
Powell, A. C., 1432
Powell, J. W., 402
Pratson, F. J., 651
Pratt, T., 570
Prewitt, K., 95, 1109
Price, J. A., 162
Price, M. E., 264
Priest, Loring B., 265
Proctor, E., 403
Prucha, F. P., 266
Puerto Rican Forum, 997
Pugh, R. C., 1207
Pushmataha, Chief, 530
Putnam, H., 693

Q

Quaife, M. M., 484
Quarles, B., 1133, 1134, 1433
Qoyawayme, P., 571

R

Race Relations in the USA, 111
Race Relations Reporter, The, 16
Rachlin, C., 381
Radin, Paul, 404, 476, 1596
Rafu, Shimpo, 1511
Ramos, M., 1779
Rand, C., 998
Randall, D., 1434, 1435
Ranson, Harry, 825
Rathmore, C. S., 1494
Red, J., 564
Redding, S., 1135, 1437, 1278, 1436
Reed, Ishmael, 52, 1438, 1439, 1440, 1441
Reghaby, H., 53
Reichard, Gladys A., 572, 573
Reimers, D., 1208
Remington, F., 645
Rendon, Armando B., 787
Report of the National Advisory Commission on Civil Disorders, 112
Reports on Indian Legislation, 190
Ribes, T. F., 999
Richardson, Ken, 113
Richter, C., 574
Ridge, J. R., 927
Riggs, F. W., 1554
Rios, H., 675
Rivera, F., 692, 769
Rivera, Tomas, 928
Rizal, J., 1736, 1780, 1781
Robbins, Maurice, 405
Robe, S. L., 851
Roberts, M., 929
Robinson, C., 930
Robinson, W. S., 1440
Rodan, 1512
Rodriguez, A. R., 931
Roe, F. G., 406
Roessel, R. A., Jr., 407
Roessel, Ruth, 300, 408, 575

Rogers, J. A., 1136
Rogers, J., 576
Rogers, W., 440
Rogler, L. H., 1000
Rohmer, S., 1607
Rollins, B., 1443
Romano, O., 71
Romano-V, O. I., 932, 933
Romulo, C. P., 1737
Roosevelt, Th., 267
Rose, A. M., 114
Rose, A., 1137
Rose, C., 114
Rose, Kenneth, 577
Rose, P. I., 115
Rosebud, S. H., 191
Ross, M. C., 652
Rothenberg, J., 578
Rousseau, J. J., 116
Rowan, C. T., 1138
Rowen, H., 852
Rubano, J., 1495
Rubel, A. J., 853
Ruchames, L., 117
Rudwick, E., 1123, 1444
Ruiz, R. E., 788

S

Sackler, H., 1445
Sah-Gan-De-Oh, 609
Saito, S., 1714, 1715
Sakai, J., 1527
Salamanca, B., 1738
Salinas, L. O., 934
Salinas, L. O., 935
Salk, E. A., 1139
Samora, J., 745, 789, 854
Samuels, C., 1467
Samuels, E., 1710
Sanchez, G. I., 790
Sanchez, G., 693
Sanchez, R., 936
Sanchez, S., 1446
Sanchez, T., 579
Sanders, T. E., 580
Sandmeyer, E. C., 1555
Sandoz, N., 268, 269, 409 581,
Sanford, R. N., 62
San Francisco, 1579
Saniel, G. M., 1739
San Juan, E., Jr., 1775, 1782

Santa Barbara County Board of
  Education, 8
Santibanez, J., 913
Santos, A., 1782
Santos, B. N., 1783, 1784, 1785,
  1786, 1787
Sauer, C. O., 270
Saum, L. O., 271
Saunders, L., 855
Schechner, R., 1447
Schell, O., 1556
Schermerhorn, R. A., 9, 118
Schirmer, D., 1740
Schleifer, H. B., 965
Schmitt, M. F., 479
Scholder, F., 653
Schoolcraft, H. R., 410
Schramko, L. F., 694
Schuchter, A., 1209
Schulberg, B., 1448
Schultz, J. W., 582, 583
Schurmann, F., 1556
Schusky, E., 272
Schuyler, G. S., 1449
Schwartz, B. N., 119
Scott, J., 403
Scott, L., 537
Seale, B., 1140
Segado, G., 889
Sekaquaptewa, H., 584
Selden, M., 1520
Senior, C., 993
Senungetuk, J. E., 273
Sequoyah. See 499
Serra, F. J., 924
Servin, H. P., 791
Seton, E. T., 411
Seton, J. M., 411
Sewall, S., 1141
Seward, G., 54
Sewid, J., 585
Sexton, P. C., 1001
Shaw, A. M., 586
Shalkop, R. L., 856
Sheehan, B. W., 274
Shepherd, C. R., 1608
Sherarts, I. K., 148
Sherman, W. T., 199
Shipek, F. C., 481
Shirey, O. C., 1652
Shirota, J., 1711
Shular, A. C., 937

Shulman, I., 938
Shuy, R., 1164
Siegelman, E., 84
Silberman, C. E., 1142
Silen, I., 991
Silliman, E. L., 583
Simmen, E., 857, 939
Simmons, G. M., 1450
Simmons, L. W., 591
Simpson, G. E., 120, 412
Siqueiros, J. L., 713
Sitting Bull. See 599
Smith, A. M., 30
Smith, A. L., 121
Smith, R. W., 47
Smith, S., 301
Smithsonian Institute, 163, 413
Smoke, S., 192
Snodgrass, J. O., 654
Snodgrass, M. P., 164
Snyder, L. L., 122
Snyder, P., 798
Sorkin, A. L., 275
Soule, Will, 618
Spears, D., 113
Special Issue - Puerto Rican In-
  ternational Migration Review,
  1002
Speck, F. G., 396
Speck, G., 276
Specer, E., 55
Spicer, E. H., 277
Sojourner II, 1530
Sommers, J., 937
Sone, M., 1791
Sorenson, V., 940
Southern, E., 1210
Sparks, T., 1609
Spicer, E. H., 1635
Spradley, J. P., 585
Squires, J. L., 414
Stalvey, L. M., 1143
Stampp, K. M., 1144
Stampp, K. M., 1145
Standing, B. L., 587, 588
Stands in Timber, J., 532, 589
Stanford University Center for
  Latin American Studies, 695
Stanton, W., 1146
Starkloff, C. F., 415
Stearns, M., 1211
Steiger, B., 416
Steinbeck, J., 941, 942

Steiner, S., 610, 792, 978
Steiner, Stan, 943
Steinfield, M., 123
Sterling, P., 1451
Steward, J. H., 557
Stewart, J., 557
Stilwell, H., 944
Stocking, G. W., Jr., 124
Stoddard, E. R., 858
Stoddard, L., 125, 126
Stone, C., 1147
Stone, E., 417
Stone, P., 624
Stonequist, E. V., 127
Storing, H. J., 1148
Storm, H., 418
Stoutenburgh, J. L., Jr., 165
Stowe, H. B., 1452, 1453
Styron, W., 1454
Sue, S., 1531, 1532
Sugimoto, E., 1692
Summers, R. A., 945, 946
Sun, Shirley, 49
Sung, B. L., 1557
Swanton, J. R., 419
Sweezy, C., 590
Swift, M. Y., 1481
Szwed, J. F., 1212
Szabo, A., 1024

T

Tabb, W., 1149
Tachiki, A., 1533
Taft, R., 655
Tahan, 351, 509
Talayesva, D., 591
Tamagawa, K., 1693
Tanaka, C., 1485
Tanner, C., 656, 657
Taylor, P., 765
Taylor, P. S., 793, 794
Tebbel, J., 279
Tecumseh. See 562
Tedlock, D., 592
TenBroek, J., 1636
Terán, H., 947
Terasaki, G., 1694
Terrell, J., 420
Thatcher, B., 593
Thomas, D., 1637, 1638
Thomas, P., 1003, 1004

Thompson, A., 1025
Thompson, F., 1025
Thompson, H., 302
Thompson, R., 55
Thompson, S., 421
Thomson, J., 1528
Thrapp, D., 594
Tibbles, T., 595
Tigre. See 926
Tinker, E., 859
Todd, E., 516
Tolson, M., 1455
Toomer, J., 1456
Toward Equality Education for
    Mexican Americans, 813
Towendolly, G., 422
Traveller Bird, 423
Tribal News, 194
Trotsky, L., 1150
Tsali, 452
Turner, D., 1457, 1458, 1459
Turner, F., 596
Turner, K., 281
Turner, M., 56
Twain, N., 1460, 1610
Two Leggings, 597
Tyler, S., 282

U

Uchida, Y., 1695
Udall, L., 584
Ulibarri, S., 948
Ullom, H., 887
Ullom, J., 166
Underhill, R., 283, 424, 471
University of Nebraska Press, 168
University of Oklahoma Press, 169
Urista, H., 949, 950
Utley, R., 285, 589
U. S. Army Western Defense Command
    and Fourth Army, 1639
U. S. Arts and Crafts Board, 658
U. S. Bureau of the Census, 56a
U. S. Bureau of Indian Affairs,
    167, 284
U. S. Cabinet Committee on Oppor-
    tunity for the Spanish Speaking,
    10, 696
U. S. Commission on Civil Rights,
    128
U. S. Congress, 1558

U. S. Department of Commerce, 697, 1005, 1496, 1716
U. S. Department of the Interior, 1653, 1656
U. S. Department of Justice, 11
U. S. Inter-Agency Committee on Mexican American Affairs, 698
U. S. Library of Congress, 1497
U. S. National Advisory Commission on Civil Disorders, 1151
U. S. National Institute of Mental Health, 12
U. S. State Department, 1559

V

Valdez, L., 943, 951
Valeros, F., 1779
Van Den Berghe, P., 129
Van Der Beets, R., 598
Van Der Zanden, J., 130
Van Doren, C., 773
Van Dyke, H., 1461
Van Every, D., 286
Vargas, R., 952
Vasquez, R., 953
Vassa, G., 1462
Vaudrin, B., 425
Velarde, P., 426
Vestal, S., 599
Victorio, 594
Villa, J., 1771, 1772, 1773, 1774
Villareal, J., 954
Villaseñor, D., 659
Villaseñor, E., 955
Vivo, P., 966
Vizenor, G., 427, 600
Vlahos, O., 57
Vogel, V., 287, 428
Vogt, E., 429
Vroman, A., 660

W

Waddell, J., 430
Waddy, R., 1197
Wagner, H., 170
Wagner, N., 860, 1531
Wakefield, D., 1006
Wai, E., 1591

Wallace, A., 288
Wald, R., 707
Walden, D., 1280
Walker, J., 1463
Walker, M., 301, 1464, 1465
Walton, H., 1152
Waltrip, L., 601
Waltrip, R., 601
Wand, D., 1534
Wangara, H., 1217
Warpath, The, 193
Warren, R., 1153
Washburn, W., 289, 290
Washington, B., 1154, 1466
Wa-Sho-Quon-Asin. See 490
Wassaja, 195
Waters, E., 1467
Waters, F., 431, 602, 603, 956
Watkins, M., 1468
Watson, E., 142
Watson, F., 1636
Watson, M., 430
Wayilatpu. See 400
Webb, F., 1469
Webb, G., 432
Webb, W., 795, 796
Weber, D., 797
Weed, P., 13
Weewish Tree, The, 196
Wei Min, 1513
Weinberg, A., 131
Weinstein, R., 618
Weisman, J., 58
Weiss, G., 846
Weiss, K., 59
Weiss, R., 109
Welch, J., 604
Wellman, P., 291
Welsch, E., 1027
Weltfish, G., 433
Wentworth, E., 1752
West, E., 1028
Wetherills, 503
Whipple, M., 357
White, E., 605
White, E. Q., 571
White, J., 644
White, M., 661
White, S., 957
Whiteford, A., 662
Whiteman, M., 1029
Whitewolf, J., 606

Whitney, P., 1717
Whitten, N., 1212
Wiggins, J., 76, 1063
Wilder, R., 607, 958
Williams, D., 714
Williams, J., 1470, 1471, 1472, 1473
Williams, J. H., 834
Williams, M., 410
Wilson, D., 608
Wilson, E., 434
Wing, Y., 1618
Winnie, L., 609
Wise, J., 435
Wish, H., 1155
Wissler, C., 436
Wister, O., 1156
Witt, S., 610
Wolff, 1741
Wong, B., 1485, 1533
Wong, E., 1533
Wong, J., 1612
Wong, S., 1516
Wooden Leg. See 541
Woods, R., 148
Woodward, C., 1157
Worth, S., 663
Wright, B., 664
Wright, K., 60a
Wright, N., 1158, 1170
Wright, R., 1474, 1475, 1476
Wright, R. L., 64
Wright, T., 1712
Wu, C., 1560
Wynes, C., 1159
Wynar, L., 1498

Y

Yabes, L., 1753, 1788
Yale University Press, 171
Yashima, T., 1696, 1697
Yazz, B., 512
Ybarra-Frausto, T., 937
Yee, C., 1580
Yellowhair, B., 510
Yellow Pearl, 1535
Yerby, F., 1477
Yinger, M., 120, 412
Yoshida, J., 1698
Young Asians for Action, 1536

Young, N., 1499, 1713
Young, R., 1160
Yutang, L., 1602

Z

Zaide, G., 1742
Zamora, R., 707
Zangrando, R., 1049
Zinn, H., 1161
Zo-Tim, 665
Zucker, R., 1481
Zuni People, 437